Social Competence
(PGPS — 91)

Social Competence

Interventions for Children and Adults

Edited by
Diana Pickett Rathjen
Rice University

John P. Foreyt
Baylor College of Medicine

Published in Cooperation with the
Houston Behavior Therapy Association

Pergamon Press
New York • Oxford • Toronto • Sydney • Frankfurt • Paris

Pergamon Press Offices:

U.S.A.	Pergamon Press Inc., Maxwell House, Fairview Park, Elmsford, New York 10523, U.S.A.
U.K.	Pergamon Press Ltd., Headington Hill Hall, Oxford OX3 0BW, England
CANADA	Pergamon of Canada, Ltd., Suite 104, 150 Consumers Road, Willowdale, Ontario M2J 1P9, Canada
AUSTRALIA	Pergamon Press (Aust.) Pty. Ltd., P.O. Box 544, Potts Point, NSW 2011, Australia
FRANCE	Pergamon Press SARL, 24 rue des Ecoles, 75240 Paris, Cedex 05, France
FEDERAL REPUBLIC OF GERMANY	Pergamon Press GmbH, Hammerweg 6, Postfach 1305, 6242 Kronberg/Taunus, Federal Republic of Germany

Library of Congress Cataloging in Publication Data
Main entry under title:

Social competence.

(Pergamon general psychology series)
Bibliography: p.
Includes index.
1. Interpersonal relations. 2. Social adjustment.
I. Rathjen, Diana P. II. Foreyt, John Paul.
HM131.S583 1980 302 80-118
ISBN 0-08-025965-0

Printed in the United States of America

Contents

Preface

The relationship between peoples' social abilities and interpersonal skills and their satisfaction and productivity has long been recognized by professionals and the general public. For example, teachers have often noted the correlation between children's poor academic performance and their aggressive or withdrawn social behavior in the classroom, and managers have reported cases of otherwise bright employees who cannot relate well to people and thus fail to advance in their careers. Despite the crucial role that social abilities play in the coping processes, these skills are rarely taught in a systematic fashion. Although parents convey certain norms and rules governing appropriate social behavior and teachers tend to reinforce quiet and obedient classroom behavior, children are rarely given specific instruction in the methodology of coping with interpersonal activities such as making friends, handling disagreements, and dealing with stress. Instead, most people are expected to "pick up" these skills vicariously from cultural models, and those who feel they are less skilled than their peers can enroll in charm school, Toastmasters' clubs, and Dale Carnegie workshops. The persistent popularity of such courses, despite their sometimes high fees and the lack of evidence supporting their effectiveness, suggests that many people feel the need for more education in these areas.

Unfortunately, the people whose interpersonal coping skills are the most deficient may be the least likely to seek help at an early stage because our culture tends to view social abilities as a function of "personality," an amorphous, general, mystically acquired quality that allows people to be dichotomized as either competent (read extrovert, a leader, charismatic, popular, effective, confident) or incompetent (read introvert, follower, unpopular, insecure). Any effort to seek help is a tacit admission that one belongs in the latter category, since society views failure on specific tasks, such as "making friends," as evidence of major personality deficits and labels a person as unfriendly, antisocial, or unpopular rather than unskilled.

Although many therapeutic programs would involve a skills approach to such problems, the point to be made is that, from the client's viewpoint, social difficulties are often indicative of major personality aberrations rather than skill deficits.

In order to emphasize the prevalence of the therapeutic rather than educational model of social competence, we have chosen skill in forming peer relationships as a prototypical social ability. However, our discussion is not limited to the origins of popularity; similar thinking prevails with respect to many other social abilities as well.

A common belief is that either through heredity, upbringing, or social class, certain persons are imbued with magnetic, dynamic, effective personalities that lead to social success. The amorphous qualities which set these people apart are stated in general terms which defy specification and would seem to preclude the possibility of being learned by others not as favorably equipped. Social abilities often conceptualized in this manner include problem solving, decision making, conflict resolution, leadership, social influence, stress management, sexual prowess, and parenting. The lack of systematic educational efforts directed at the teaching of interpersonal skills is particularly ironic in light of the tremendous amount of basic research in such areas as friendship, social influence, and attitude change. Unfortunately, the interface between basic research and applied problems necessary for curriculum development was hindered for many years by the "trait" viewpoint of social competence.

However, in the 1960s, an alternative to the elusive concept of trait was presented by Albert Bandura's social-learning theory, which views human interaction as a series of overt behaviors that can be reliably measured. The critical characteristic of his model is the assumption that both normal and abnormal behavior can be explained by the same laws and that the most important laws governing human behavior are those derived from learning.

In the original formulation of social-learning theory, it was assumed that all behavior, whether socially competent or incompetent, is developed and maintained through three regulatory systems that create a reciprocal interaction between the person and his environment. The three systems are: (1) classical conditioning processes that lead to patterns of behavior largely determined by external events; (2) the process of external reinforcement; and (3) the person's cognitive mediational processes that determine which aspects of the environment are attended to, how they are perceived, and how they will influence future behavior.

Social-learning theory provided the missing link between basic research on social processes and the development of clinical interventions. Characteristics of the socially competent individuals described earlier were reconceptualized as specific behaviors demonstrated by competent people rather than personality traits of such individuals. Once social competence was operationally defined as a collection of specific behaviors, it became theoretically possible to use the principles of learning to develop programs to teach people more effective behaviors. It would appear that a social competence curriculum could be developed by combining the information on socially successful behaviors identified in the social research literature with the techniques for effective learning from the work of Bandura and his colleagues. However, the idea of one set of socially competent behaviors applicable in all settings is as erroneous and misleading as the former notion of ideal personality traits. The social effectiveness of behavior is a function of both the individual's characteristics and of the environment in which the behavior is performed.

Thus, after the initial presentation of Bandura's theory, two major challenges to the development of a systematic social competence curriculum remained: (1) identification of behaviors which would actually be effective in a particular situation, and (2) development of the most effective way to teach those behaviors to specific individuals. These are still major questions in the area of social competence, and much further work remains to be done. The present book is an effort to provide a state-of-the-art review of efforts to answer these questions by presenting research and interventions on social competence organized according to stages in the life cycle.

The answer to the first question regarding assessment is provided by a situational definition of social competence in which parameters of effective behavior are determined for a specific context. The idea that behavior is a function of both person and environment was first presented in Lewin's early writings on field theory (B = P + E) and Barker and Wright's emphasis on behavior settings. This notion was given further empirical support by Mischel's review of personality research, in which he concluded that behaviors were more consistent across similar situations than across similar individuals. The idea was again emphasized in Bandura's notion of reciprocity between person and environment. However, it was only in later research that the general concept of reciprocity was applied to the assessment of social competence. Only recently have researchers attempted to assess competence in a situational fashion. At this point in time, it is particularly exciting to present the work of authors, who have attempted to use the situational approach for a series of important life situations ranging from childhood to retirement.

The second question, concerning the most efficient way to teach socially competent behaviors, has been hotly debated within psychology. The original emphasis of the behaviorists on overt and easily measured behavior as the target of intervention was quickly challenged by others in the field who felt that human behavior could not be adequately explained without reference to thoughts and feelings. Both behavioral and cognitive perspectives have been employed in the study of social competence. Early studies emphasized the easily measured overt components of social behavior, such as verbal content, eye contact, and latency. With the increasing trend towards "going cognitive," more attention has been paid to emotional reaction, including anxiety and anger, and to cognitive components such as expectations, self-statements, and rules or strategies. Although all three components of social competence, behavior, affect, and thought, were included in Bandura's original formulation, research has tended to focus on one or another of the components at different points in time. The programs presented in this volume represent an effort to integrate all three components in terms of both assessment and treatment. The relative importance of the three components of behavior continues to be an unresolved issue in the field. Current research suggests that cognitive factors do play a critical role in behavior change, but that behavioral performance may be the best way to induce such change. Thus, it is clear that the cognitive perspective, particularly as espoused by Bandura's recent articles on the development of self-efficacy, is assuming a more crucial role in the development of intervention programs, but that a strong behavioral emphasis is also apparent in those programs that have proved successful. This volume presents an overview of validated and innovative interventions designed to enhance social competence in a variety of target populations throughout the life cycle. These programs represent many different solutions to the basic challenge of enhancing individuals' cognitive, affective, and behavioral repertoire to enable them to cope effectively with interpersonal relationship throughout life.

At this point in time, the diversity and creativity in the types of intervention programs that have been developed make the presentation of the most promising and best-validated research efforts a truly exciting task. In addition to recognition of the need for interventions specifically tailored for the particular individual in a given situation, the chapters in the current volume reflect the current focus on prevention and education, as well as the more tertiary aspect of treatment. The timing of this volume is appropriate, not only because of the exciting rapprochement between the cognitive and behavioral perspectives it represents from a theoretical view, but also in terms of the new perspectives which are represented from an applied view. The emphasis on an educational as well as a remedial perspective on social competence suggests that it is no longer necessary to be born a Dale Carnegie to enjoy successful relationships.

The idea for this book originated at the Seventh Annual Symposium of the Houston Behavior Therapy Association (HBTA). We are deeply indebted to the authors for their outstanding contributions. For their continued support, we are also grateful to the co-sponsors of the symposium: Baylor College of Medicine, Rice University, University of Houston, Harris County Department of Education, South Texas Dietetic Association, and Spring Branch Academy. Our symposium is successful each year only because of the hard work of many HBTA members, including Phyllis Massie, Robert Mitchell, Pat Doyle, Ed Keuer, Ben Williams, Lynne Scott, Francisco Barrios, and Eric Rathjen. Thanks also to Wanda Mollins, Steven D. Keener, Terry A. Needham, Lewis Dratt, Doris Murray, and Susi LeBaron for their help with the manuscript.

Diana Pickett Rathjen
John P. Foreyt

1
An Overview of Social Competence

Diana Pickett Rathjen

The purpose of this chapter is to review areas of psychological research relevant to the development of interventions that enhance or develop social competence. The importance of social ability has long been recognized, but only recently has it become the focus of educational and therapeutic programs. For many years, social abilities were assumed to be intrinsic characteristics that determined a person's success or failure in social situations, and the characteristics were not considered amenable to change. Two important developments in psychological theory led to a new conceptualization of social abilities that allowed them to be incorporated in an educational model. The first development was social learning theory by Albert Bandura in the 1960s.

In his theory, social abilities, along with other aspects of human functioning, were considered to be behaviors that were developed and maintained according to principles of learning and, unlike traits, were amenable to change through processes of relearning. The shift in focus from traits to behaviors suggested by his theory allowed social abilities to be defined in terms of behaviors that could be easily and reliably measured. Once the components of social abilities could be measured and changed, it was logical to consider them as skills similar to physical and intellectual abilities for which systematic curricula could be developed.

However, the choice of which behaviors should be included in the repertoire of a socially competent person is not clear; basic research on social processes indicates that behavior judged to be interpersonally effective in one situation may not be perceived as effective in another. In fact, the search for a list of behaviors that characterize the socially competent person may be just as fruitless as the former search for the traits that characterize the socially successful individual.

A second major redirection in psychological theory bears directly on this problem. Recent research in social psychology suggests that the most accurate picture of social interaction may be a reciprocal one which takes into account both the target person and the factors in his environment. It may be more useful to conceptualize social competence as the product of an interaction between the person and the situation. Use of the interactionist perspective has clarified several types of social behavior, such as helping behavior and interpersonal attraction. Recent reviews by Ekehammar (1974), Bowers (1973), and Endler and Magnusson (1976) conclude that person-situation interaction is more important than either situational or individual differences in explaining behavioral differences.

Recent studies in the social skills literature, particularly in the areas of assertiveness and dating, also suggest that the effectiveness of certain behaviors depends on the sex, status, and physical attractiveness of the individuals displaying them. Early attempts at interventions in these areas tended to downplay individual differences. For example, assertiveness training was often used as a remedy for social anxiety in diverse types of clients. Recent studies have focused on the differential effectiveness that assertive behavior may have for males and females.

Although the interactionist viewpoint is a relatively recent development, it shows the most promise for integrating the diverse number of variables that influence social behavior into one theoretical model. Much of the research most relevant to applied problems, such as the development of a social skills curriculum, is now being conducted within one of the various versions of the interactionist perspective. However, there are also data to support two other conceptualizations of social competence: the view that focuses primarily on the individual, and the view that emphasizes the role of environmental factors, both physical and social.

Each of the three perspectives provides a unique view of the criteria that should be used to distinguish competence from incompetence. A prominent researcher in this area, Edward Zigler, recently noted that he himself had used the construct in four entirely different contexts in the past fifteen years of research. However, building on the conceptual work of Kohlberg and Mayer (1972) and of Anderson and Messick (1974), Zigler and Trickett derive a twofold approach in which measures of social competence should reflect one of two major criteria (Zigler and Trickett 1978). They suggest that social competence must first reflect the success of the human being in meeting social expectancies, and second, that the measures of social competence should reflect something about the self-actualization or personal development of the human being (p. 795). As Zigler and Trickett suggest, any definition is arbitrary, and the issue is not accuracy but usefulness. The purpose of this chapter is to integrate the data on competence in a way that will be applicable to specific problems encountered by parents, teachers, and therapists. For our purposes, the definition provided by Zigler and

Trickett is a useful one if it is noted that each of their suggested criteria could be judged by either society or by the individual involved, and that each criterion could be measured either in the immediate situation or on a long-term basis. These last considerations emphasize contradictions that are inherent in a definition which uses multiple criteria for success. Examples of coping judged to be competent on the basis of one criterion and not on another come readily to mind. A child may induce his playmates into submission through aggression on the playground; such children often feel successful in the short run, but complain later when they are rejected by their peers. Such behavior, although initially successful, is considered unacceptable by society. It is clear that even an individual might consider the same action as either competent or incompetent.

From an applied standpoint, it seems reasonable to deal with the diversity of criteria by recognizing that there is not one competent solution to a given dilemma, but many. As researchers, we can gather data on the different competent solutions which appear in the laboratory or in field studies and then, as practitioners, attempt to match one of the possible solutions with the individual resources or goals of the person involved.

In addition to the problem of selecting criteria for successful coping, there are three other frequently debated questions: (1) What factors make up social competence? (2) How are these factors taught, developed or elicited? (3) What factor, if any, provides continuity in the development of social competence? This last question is one of the most intriguing and controversial. Each of the perspectives above would suggest a different way of asking the question and different variables to consider in providing an answer. Those who take an individual perspective might ask the question in terms of what leads to social adjustment or maturity, or how an individual develops effectiveness or mastery. They would look for individual skills that might increase with age and be appropriate across a wide variety of situations. Those who take the environmental view would want to know what leads to the generalization of behavior across settings, what factors in the environment are necessary to elicit coping behavior, which social arrangement or structure would facilitate social interaction. They would look for the influence of different environments, both physical and cultural, on social behavior, possibly using animal and cross-cultural data. The adherents of the interactionist perspective are currently in disagreement over the exact way to define and measure interaction (see Buss, 1977, for a discussion), but would agree that behaviors that are competent for an individual in one situation might not be judged so in another setting, or if displayed in the same setting by another person.

The next paragraphs review illustrative research conducted within each of the frameworks discussed above. Our goal is to abstract from each area the variables which have been empirically determined to be influential in creating competence and which, therefore, should be included in our multidimensional model. It is imperative that we identify the shortcomings or unanswered questions within each perspective which must be researched before the findings can be used in the development of intervention programs.

After examining the literature related to each perspective, we should have a list of factors that any model of social competence must include. In addition, we shall have identified the unresolved issues which require further research. It is clear that social competence is a multidimensional concept and that no research program or intervention is likely to address all issues. However, those interested in teaching competence have had to develop interventions on the basis of available data. The last section of the chapter will explore the practical answers to the questions raised by the empirical testing of the educational and therapeutic interventions.

Individual Perspective

The bulk of research on the factors involved in social competence has been conducted using characteristics of the individual as a starting point. This emphasis probably resulted from two assumptions that are currently being challenged, but that guided research for many years: the notion that there is behavioral consistency across situations as a function of individual traits, and the idea that the individual is the most appropriate focus of intervention efforts. Our review will consider the different classes of personal variables that have been shown to facilitate or hinder social competence and will provide illustrative examples of each.

Physical Characteristics

Researchers have been reluctant to include physical health measures among the determinants of social competence, perhaps because health is usually considered outside the intervention province of those typically interested in social development, e.g., teachers or psychologists. However, it has been known for a long time that physical limitations and handicaps, even minor ones such as not being able to run as fast as peers, lead to rejection from other children (Lippit and Gold 1959). Zigler and Trickett recently suggested that physical health measures be recognized as major determinants of social competence and that the measures already used in the assessment of childhood intervention programs such as Head Start be consulted in developing a social competence index (Zigler and Trickett 1978).

Another variable often ignored for the same reasons is physical attractiveness. Attractive children are viewed more favorably both by peers and teachers; in addition, expectations for future behaviors are more positive for more physically attractive children. Bersheid and Walster (1974) review the literature on the effects of physical appearance for both children and adults. Contrary to popular belief, the components of physical attraction are amenable to change—a good example is overweight. Experimental studies have successfully manipulated the perceived physical attractiveness of both men and women with clothing changes and make-up (Rathjen and Hiniker, 1977).

Most of the research on physical appearance suggests that good looks enhance an individual's social relationships because people tend to attribute other positive qualities to attractive people. Dion, Bersheid and Walster (1972) showed that attractive individuals of both sexes were rated as being more sociable, poised, outgoing, sexually warm and responsive, and interesting than less attractive persons. In addition, predictions about their future were more favorable. Attractive people were assumed to be more likely to attain high occupational status, to be more competent as spouses, and to have happier marriages. Frequent replications of these basic findings indicate that such stereotyped thinking prevails whether the other person is viewed as a potential casual acquaintance or a marriage partner and that the role of attractiveness seems to be more important in the evaluations that males make of females than vice versa (Huston and Levinger 1978). Several recent studies in the dating skills literature, however, indicate that physical attractiveness as assessed by female raters is one characteristic which distinguishes high- and low-frequency male daters (Kupke, Hobbs and Cheney 1979).

Although most reviews of the attractiveness literature conclude that physically attractive individuals generally elicit more favorable treatment from others in their environment, there are several studies which indicate that the effect of physical appearance depends on the particular situation. For example, two studies on the reactions of a simulated jury to defendants of varying degrees of attractiveness showed that harsher penalties were advocated for an attractive woman whose beauty was related to her crime (Sigall and Ostrove 1975). If friendships and relationships are taken as indices of social competence, it appears that physical attraction facilitates competence in some situations and not others.

Much research has shown that affiliative behavior is usually a function of a low perceived probability of rejection and a positive impression of the other person. In several studies, males have chosen actually to affiliate with the woman who was their second- or third-ranked choice in attractiveness, if acceptance by the woman was not guaranteed. There is some indirect evidence that women who are more attractive feel more confident, possibly because they assume chances for rejection are less.

An intriguing study that demonstrates the importance of maintaining an interactional perspective even when measuring what would seem to be a clear-cut individual variable—appearance—is an experiment by Snyder, Tanke, and Bersheid (1978) in which males were given information about the attractiveness of the females with whom they were interacting over an intercom and then elicited patterns of behavior consistent with the stereotype. Much further research is needed to assess the role of physical attraction in social competence. However, implications for interventions such as dating skills programs are clear; some of the anxiety and anticipated rejection which low-frequency daters report may be grounded in experience, and for some college students, techniques to enhance attractiveness as well as cognitive strategies to reduce excessive anxiety may be appropriate.

Other individual differences affecting social competence are culture, class, and ethnic background. These factors are discussed in the section on environmental influences. Differences in social behavior between the sexes have received much research attention (see Maccoby and Jacklin 1974 for a review). Recent research has focused on factors such as sex role stereotyping and cultural expectations, which lead men and women to adopt different techniques to cope with social situations. Early research in the area of social power, for example, revealed that a woman's sex was likely to limit her resources and thus the kinds of strategies she could use to exert social influence. In the terminology French and Raven (1959) originally used in their classic studies on power, women tend to use reward power while men have at their disposal coercive, expert, and referential power as well. Current research suggests that girls are often perceived as more socially competent than boys. Girls are rated as more skilled by parents and teachers and are referred for aggressive problems much less frequently (Maccoby and Jacklin, 1974). Many measures of social competence in adulthood such as assertiveness or ability to influence others tend to favor men as more competent than women. The possible differential effectiveness of intervention programs for adults, such as assertiveness training, depending on the sex of the client remains to be tested.

Although they could perhaps be more accurately considered as situational variables, physiological differences are often considered as individual difference factors. Much research has documented the detrimental effect on social behavior of such affective states as anxiety and anger.

Impulsiveness, or the tendency to respond quickly, particularly to stressful situations, has been related to aggressiveness in children (see chapter two). At this point few studies have reported a clinically significant improvement in social behavior merely as a result of reduced anxiety. In general, such interventions combined with the addition of new behaviors or modification of thinking patterns which generate anxiety have been more effective. However, it is interesting to note how a simple technique to allow a child to delay his impulsive behavior in stressful situations may enhance competence by facilitating use of other more complex social skills (see chapter four).

Behavioral Repertoires

One of the most productive areas of research in terms of explaining social interaction has been the study of behaviors that result in effective interpersonal relationships. In order to use the data on behavioral differences, we need to keep in mind several points. First, we must be careful not to confuse a list of specific behaviors with competence per se. A second mistake to avoid is the tendency to assume that people who do not display particular behaviors in an assessment setting do not have them in their repertoire. For example, Schwartz and Gottman (1976) found that high-assertive and low-assertive subjects were not distinguished by knowledge of the best behavioral responses or deliveries in hypothetical settings, but did differ on actual role-played responses and patterns of self-statements. Thus it is often the case that cognitive or affective factors may inhibit behaviors that are in a person's repertoire. When discussing observed behavioral differences in populations previously labeled as skilled and unskilled, one must be careful to avoid what McFall (1976) refers to as the error of the assumed essence: the difference observed, although real, may not be the critical factor that distinguishes the two groups. One further limitation on behavioral measures taken in simulated settings, such as the role-play assessment devices that have been so frequently employed in the social skills literature, is the question of whether or not the results obtained are the same as would be found using a more naturalistic assessment technique (Hersen and Bellack 1976). With these restrictions in mind, we can review some illustrative examples of research which indicate that behavioral differences do influence social competence.

In children, the aspect of social competence that has been most widely researched is popularity or peer acceptance, as measured by some form of sociometric test. Correlational studies have indicated that the following characteristics have been consistently associated with peer acceptance from children of preschool age through adolescence: friendliness, outgoingness, and social participation. In addition to these general attributes, the behaviors that accepted children demonstrate to peers include: the frequency with which the child dispenses positive social reinforcers, the extent to which nurturance is given, the frequency with which kindness is expressed, willingness both to give and receive friendly overtures and to respond to dependent behaviors of peers, and sensitivity to the social overtures of other children (Combs and Slaby 1978). Interestingly, the relationship between peer acceptance and aggression is mixed. In a recent review, Combs and

Slaby suggest that the aggression that rejected children express tends to be immature, indirect, and unprovoked, while more popular children display more socially acceptable types of aggression. Lesser (1959) found a positive correlation between popularity and provoked aggression among grade school boys, while a negative correlation was indicated between popularity and indirect aggression. This finding indicates the role of contextual factors in the evaluation of any behavior. Many authors have noted that acceptance and rejection are not inverse concepts; however, measures of aggression have been consistently found to relate to peer rejection.

An excellent review of the behavioral correlates of social acceptance is provided in Combs and Slaby's chapter on social skills in children. It is clear from their review, and from other studies in the area, that most of the research on children has focused on behaviors defined in a very general way. Vaguely defined terms such as "friendliness" are not very useful to those developing interventions. One exception to this type of research is the study by Gottman, Gonso and Rasmussen, (1975), which attempts to identify differences between popular and unpopular children in the performance of smaller behavioral components of general skills. For example, the task of "making friends" was broken down into the behaviors of greeting, asking for information, extending inclusion, and giving information. The only tasks that revealed differences between the groups of children were making friends and a referential-communication task in which the child had to communicate meaning to a listener by giving clues in a word game.

Gottman et al. suggest that skills must be empirically shown to relate to other indicators of social effectiveness and that the mere existence of differences in the skill across age groups is not sufficient evidence to conclude that the skill is critical to the development of social competence. This point is similar to McFall's arguments presented earlier.

Few other studies have used the experimental approach to identify behaviors that distinguish socially effective children from those who are less so. Researchers interested in improving children's peer relationships have identified several behaviors that lead to greater acceptance. The identification of critical behaviors has usually been the outgrowth of long-term research projects on the correlates of two particularly common peer problems in children: social isolation and aggression. Intervention programs with social isolates have focused on approach behavior, with increased interaction as the goal. Although an increase in the overall amount of interaction sometimes results in an increase in aggression, there are several studies which report greater acceptance of children after they have increased their participation. It is not clear whether initiation represents a new behavior for isolated children, as O'Connor (1972) suggested in noting the greater effectiveness of modeling films over shaping techniques, or whether it is an already existing behavior which increases upon contingent reinforcement, as some of the shaping intervention programs would suggest. A variety of studies have attempted to teach isolate children behaviors that have been found to be socially reinforcing to other children; these behaviors include laughing, touching affectionately, and smiling. In one study, only smiling, a behavior that was already high in the child's hierarchy, increased; consequently, it was difficult to note its effect on acceptance (Keller and Carlson, 1974).

Working from the view that mere increase of amount of interaction may not be sufficient to increase popularity, Oden and Asher (1977) used adults to coach children in specific techniques to use in making friends, such as taking turns, talking, and showing support by giving attention and help. They allowed the children to practice their newly acquired skills with peers by playing games. Their data with third and fourth graders indicated that the coached children did increase on peer play sociometric ratings to a greater degree than the control group or a peer pairing control, although no behavioral differences were noted. Their results suggest that mere increase in participation, as found in the peer pairing control group, may not be as effective in increasing popularity as the addition of other specific behaviors, such as turn taking, to the child's repertoire.

Basing their research on data that suggest that there is a relationship between psychiatric disorders and a deficit of social skills in adults, Bornstein, Bellack, and Hersen (1977) attempted to teach assertive behaviors to four children referred by their teachers as being low in assertion. Arguing that there are no objective criteria to use in identifying low assertiveness, the authors used a role-playing assessment device to identify deficient behaviors (the Behavioral Assessment Test for Children), and chose eye contact, loudness of speech, and making requests as the skills to be taught. Their study showed that the training was effective in teaching the skills, but they did not investigate whether the newly acquired skills led to increased popularity or acceptance.

As noted earlier, the failure to investigate experimentally which behaviors are actually related to social effectiveness is a shortcoming in the research on both adults and children. A related shortcoming in the research was noted by Combs and Slaby. They suggest that criterion measures should reflect a broader definition of social effectiveness, including outcomes valuable to the individual child as well as outcomes valued by society, such as reduced aggression or greater interaction. If increased confidence or reduced anxiety on the part of the child is an important component of competence, greater focus on behaviors that are adaptive from the child's viewpoint may need to be incorporated in interventions.

If our search for behaviors related to social competence is expanded to include those which increase the child's ability to handle social situations, several other intervention programs are relevant. Programs to increase a child's self-control and self-management skills (see chapter two), and to teach social problem solving (see chapter three) are excellent examples. Another research program oriented to the child's perspective empirically determined which social situations children found difficult (teasing, rejection, talking about oneself), and developed a program which included training and practice in behaviors related to those problematical situations—expressing feelings, making requests, and so forth (Rathjen, Hiniker, and Rathjen 1976). The Rathjen et al. program and school-wide interventions described in the Rotheram chapter and the Cox and Gun chapter include behaviors to influence the child's own responses, such as relaxation skills as well as novel behaviors designed to facilitate a positive response from others.

A strong emphasis in the Rathjen et al. program is increasing the children's behavioral repertoire so that they have multiple options in socially stressful situations; they are encouraged to try their newly acquired behaviors in naturalistic settings and decide for themselves which are most appropriate and effective. This emphasis is similar to the evaluation of social consequences taught in the Spivack and Shure programs (1974).

The research reviewed above suggests several behaviors that might be used in intervention programs to increase social competence. Much greater emphasis is needed, however, on the reciprocal nature of positive social interaction. The excellent work of Patterson and his colleagues on aggressive behavior in children and the intervention programs they developed over a 10-year period provide solid empirical evidence for the dual role of parents and children in perpetuating aggressive solutions to social situations (Patterson, Reid, Jones and Conger, 1975). Future success in identifying positive social behaviors would seem to proceed most efficiently by using a reciprocal perspective; several recent authors have outlined ways this research might be done (Bandura 1977; Trower, Bryant, and Argyle 1978; Rathjen, Rathjen, and Hiniker 1978).

Our discussion has focused on the identification of competent behaviors in children; the research on adults follows the same general pattern. Some positive behaviors have been identified. For example, Hersen and Bellack's (1976) work with psychiatric patients indicated that lack of social skill corresponded to the specific behaviors of poor eye contact and low voice tone. Particular behaviors which enhance liking, such as showing interest in the other person, have been identified in the basic research on interpersonal attraction. Once again, however, both the applied and basic research must be qualified. Work such as that done by Hersen and Bellack is primarily relevant to the particular subgroup studied, in this case psychiatric patients. Other studies have been done with college students who date infrequently and with unassertive women. In addition, the response from others in the environment must be considered. Numerous studies in the attraction literature have demonstrated that the behaviors most strongly related to liking are reciprocal in nature. People are liked more if they are perceived to be similar in such matters as background, attitudes, and circumstances, and if they are seen to be the kinds of persons who provide social support, bolster esteem, give praise, and reduce anxiety (Huston 1974).

Much of the research on individual differences in social competence has centered on cognitive factors. The specific cognitive skills, such as perspective taking and impulse control, shown to be important in the social adjustment of children are reviewed in chapters two, three, four, and five in this book. Recent reviews of the cognitive processes important in adult social interaction can be found in several sources (Trower, Bryant, and Argyle 1978; Foreyt and Rathjen 1978; Meichenbaum 1977; Mahoney 1974). Cognitive theorists have identified certain irrational beliefs and distorted thinking processes such as arbitrary inference, magnification, overgeneralization, dichotomous reasoning, and catastrophizing common to many depressed clients. More adaptive ways for these individuals to interpret their social environments would include drawing conclusions from adequate evidence, putting events in perspective, attending to all relevant aspects of social situations, generalizing from multiple rather than single instances, and making attributions along a continuum rather than dichotomously.

Individuals lacking in social competence may also make errors involving attention and perception (Mahoney 1974). Examples include: (1) failure to attend to cues from environment, such as feedback, (2) misperception or mislabeling of environmental cues, through projection, egocentrism, or "mind reading," (3) maladaptive focusing on stimuli irrelevant or deleterious to performance such as inhibition of assertive behavior in the presence of high status others, and (4) maladaptive self-arousal from excessive attention to internal cues.

In addition to attention and perception, other specific cognitive processes that have been shown to influence social competence in adults include attribution, appraisals, use of feedback, expectancies, and memory (Rathjen, Rathjen, and Hiniker 1978). More general factors, often referred to as cognitive structures rather than processes, shown to influence social behavior include meaning systems, current concerns, and world views (Zigler and Trickett 1978; Meichenbaum 1977).

In summary, our review of individual difference factors suggests three conclusions: (1) the importance of certain individual difference variables such as sex, physical abilities, and appearance depends on the particular social setting in which competence is being measured, (2) individual differences that are functions of an individual's background or learning history, such as culture, class and ethnic characteristics, may limit the types of interventions which are feasible with a given target group, and (3) cognitive processes and structures may account for the occasional consistencies in behavior which are found across situations and thus may help promote generalization of newly acquired competent behaviors.

Environmental Perspective

A variety of means have been used to measure the impact of environmental factors on individual coping responses. One of the most longstanding and still current methods is to correlate demographic and socioeconomic variables with psychopathology (see Derogatis, Yevzeroff, and Wittelsberger 1975). A more practical approach for the practitioner is to study the relationship of social class factors with types of intervention; for example, the work of Goldstein and his colleagues on the inappropriateness of verbally oriented insight therapy with lower-class patients (Goldstein 1973) and the subsequent development of alternative approaches tailored for effectiveness with this target group (see chapter 6 in this volume).

A related approach has been the study of developmental antecedents of competent behavior, particularly child-rearing practices. In a recent article on the development of adaptiveness, flexibility, and other components of social competence in children, O'Malley (1977) points out that such reviews of antecedents in socialization research usually produce only modest consensus and that experimentation designed to produce competence might be a more useful strategy. His suggestion that "analyses should be conducted of changes in competent interactions or in personal-social constructs contingent on environmental manipulation, and of the susceptibility of requisites for competence to experimental control" (p. 42) has been carried out in the work of Spivack and Shure (Spivack, Platt and Shure 1976; Spivack and Shure 1974). Efforts to change the cognitive and behavioral components of aggressive and impulsive children from lower-class backgrounds through parental programs and school interventions are described in the chapters by Shure and Camp in this volume.

In contrast to assessment measures that focus on the past impact of the environment on competence, the study of behavior settings originated by Barker and Wright in the 1930s focuses on the present influences of environmental factors. In one of the classic studies in this area, it was found that an important component of social competence, participation in social activities, was influenced by the size of the high school attended. In small schools, each student was forced to fill many roles, such as athlete, debator, class officer, in order for the system to function. Other examples of this type of research in field settings can be found in Willems & Raush (1969).

The influence of setting variables on social behavior has long been studied in the laboratory, but the implications for interventions have received less attention. For example, interpersonal attraction research has identified many setting variables which influence liking in the laboratory and field situations, such as how hot and crowded the room is, whether participants expect to interact again, and mere proximity. Children's peer relationships have been shown to be influenced by their own visibility (Clifford 1967) and the opportunity to interact with other children (Hartup 1976). The data needed for environmental redesign to promote competence exist; teachers could alter classroom structure to promote liking among students. Typically, the focus has been on intervention with individuals (such as skills training for shy or isolated children), rather than on environmental redesign.

Another environmental dimension is change. The early work by Holmes and Rahe (1967) on scaling the stressful impact of commonly occurring life events has been followed up with greater attention to the impact of positive versus negative types of change and efforts to increase the reliability of the measures (see Sundberg, Snowden and Reynolds 1978) for a discussion of this research.

Numerous researchers have attempted to develop a meaningful taxonomy of situations. Moos and his colleagues developed climate scales to measure subjective perceptions of various environments such as hospital wards and college dorms (Moos 1974). He identified certain dimensions which could be used to characterize a variety of situations including relationship, personal development, and system maintenance and change. His work provides the basis for a potential match of persons with situations most likely to elicit maximum competence.

Magnusson and Ekehammar (1975) have conducted a series of studies on the dimensions of situations using both individual perceptions and responses as criteria for categorization. Their results indicate similar dimensions using either method and indicate that similarities in individual behavior across situations are greater when the situations are perceived as similar. Their work on the characteristics of stressful situations is particularly relevant for the development of coping strategies. Once again, the research points to the utility of an interactionist perspective to integrate data on environmental variables. However, a complete taxonomy of situations has not been developed. Such development may prove very difficult because of the number of possibly relevant dimensions.

The most sophisticated approach to a meaningful analysis of situations from the viewpoint of individual coping is that presented by behavioral assessment techniques such as functional analysis (Hersen and Bellack 1976). Through the use of a variety of specific assessment techniques, situational events related to the problematical behavior of the client are identified. Behavioral observation in home and classroom settings to determine influences on children's social behavior is probably the most researched area to date (Patterson et al. 1975); similar techniques have been recently refined in the area of marital relationships (Weiss, Hops and Patterson 1973). Findings from this research indicate the importance of monitoring short-term changes in the social environment. Because spouse interaction is reciprocal, the behavior of both husband and wife must be measured simultaneously. It is too simplistic to look only at one person's behavior and label it as the "social environment" of the other person; important data emerge from a study of the pattern of interaction. Gottman's research, for example, showed that distressed and happily married couples tended to use different patterns of positive behavior, while distressed couples reciprocated immediately with like behavior. Happier couples tended to use a "bank account model" and reciprocated positive behaviors across longer time spans (Gottman 1976).

In summary, the literature on the impact of environmental factors on social interaction suggests that: (1) broad environmental factors such as social class are likely to affect the type of educational or therapeutic intervention that will be most effective with a given individual; (2) aspects of the physical environment can alter the pattern of social interaction and have the potential of being used as interventions to promote greater social competence; and (3) any effort to measure the impact of the social environment must proceed from a reciprocal or interactionist perspective. The two most promising avenues for application appear to be the redesign of physical environments to enhance better social relationships, as recently outlined by both psychologists and architects (see Moos 1976) or further basic research on the interface between situational factors and individuals' perceptions of their environment. The study of situations is currently at a very primitive stage, and further research is needed to clarify the impact on social behavior.

As briefly discussed in this chapter and elaborated upon in the Sundberg et al. (1978) review, efforts to identify problematical situations indicate some general consensus, but there is no agreement on the specification of the aspects of those situations which cause the most stress. Individual differences in appraisal and perception are likely to account for much of this variance, which leads us rather directly to our next topic, person-situation interaction.

Interactional Perspective

The concept of person-environment interaction is a long-standing one in the area of social psychology, dating back to Lewin's classic dictum that behavior is a function of both the person and the environment: $B = (P + E)$ (Lewin, 1935). Research in most areas of social psychology was guided by the Lewin principle, particularly such areas as attitude change and interpersonal attraction. A renewed interest in the concept followed Mischel's critiques of the trait concept and his reviews, which suggested that there is little behavioral consistency across situations (Mischel 1973). The nature of the interaction between person factors and situational variables is currently quite controversial (see Endler and Magnusson 1976).

Until recently, the main impact of these concepts in the applied areas was the use by behavioral therapists of environmental information in the form of stimulus or antecedent conditions through the use of techniques such as self-report, behavioral observations, and self-monitoring. In individual treatment plans, therapists were able to employ information about the person's resources and the support or lack of it in the environment. However, even those working in the behavioral framework initially overlooked interactional concerns in designing intervention programs. A good example is the initial development of intervention programs designed to enhance assertiveness and dating skills. Although the specific teaching methods were often tailored to fit the target group (e.g. different strategies for psychiatric patients as opposed to college students), little concern was paid to the differential response that the newly assertive behavior might provoke in natural settings. Programs did include instruction about what to do if an initial assertive response failed, but rarely did they investigate whether assertiveness per se was actually interpersonally effective. Fiedler and Beach (1978) demonstrated that concern about the consequences of assertive behavior played a major role in the decision of adult women to display such behavior. After many programs were able to teach new behaviors but failed to find generalization across settings, researchers began to look more carefully at environmental factors, particularly examining the possible differential response to a person displaying assertive behavior on the basis of sex or role (Rathjen and Hiniker 1977; Woolfolk and Denver 1979; Hull and Schroeder 1979). Other possible limitations on the effectiveness of the programs for certain individuals, such as the widely publicized view that such training might lead women clients in particular to become aggressive, hostile, and angry and thus jeopardize interpersonal relationships, were also explored (Linehan, Goldfried, and Goldfried 1979). These studies all lead to positive evaluations of assertive behavior, but need to be replicated in diverse settings.

One method for the incorporation of the person-environment construct into the area of applied interventions was presented by Goldfried and D'Zurilla in their behavioral analytic model for assessing competence, first presented in 1969. They outlined the steps by which situation-specific components of competence could be assessed by deriving behavioral definitions of competence from various sources in the target person's environment (through critical incidents, interviews, and the like) and subjecting them to empirical test, that is, seeing which behavior comes closest to achieving the client's goal. Although their method is widely cited, attempts to use it have been infrequent; Goldsmith and McFall (1975) used it with psychiatric patients, as did Freedman (1974) with juvenile delinquents. A related approach to task analysis was used by Schwartz and Gottman (1976) to map out the topography of competent responding in assertion situations. Such an approach is useful in identifying the multiple components of a social behavior, but is somewhat limited by the "error of the assumed essence" (McFall 1976) inherent in the known-groups approach, of which this is a variant.

Another way to use the interactionist perspective in studying social competence is to proceed from the assumption that people actively create their own social environments. This idea was inherent in the early writings of Lewin (1935) and further elaborated by Mischel (1973) in his cognitive social learning reconceptualization of personality, and in Bandura's reciprocal determinism (1978). Empirical data on the kinds of person-environment reciprocity that facilitates and hinders social competence can be found in the work of the social-exchange theorists (Kelley and Thibaut 1978), the work on attribution and social perception (Harvey, Ickes, and Kidd 1976; Harvey, Ickes, and Kidd 1978), and cognitive behaviorism (Meichenbaum 1977; Foreyt and Rathjen 1978; Mahoney 1974).

Our review of the interactionist perspective can be summarized by noting that it has the greatest potential for providing data that can be used in the development of intervention programs; however, it has generated a relatively small amount of research thus far. Much promising work is currently underway, particularly efforts to classify situations along dimensions meaningful to the individuals involved and research on the reciprocal processes by which people "create" their own social environments.

The empirical data on the role of individual, environmental, and situational factors in determining social competence reviewed above can be well integrated by using an educational model such as the one recently tailored specifically to social performance (see Rathjen, Rathjen, and Hiniker 1978). The model suggests six questions that must be answered in developing an intervention to enhance competence:

1. What are the relevant tasks a competent person must be able to perform?
2. What behavior defines competent and incompetent solutions for the population in question?
3. What is the subject population and what are its relevant processing characteristics?
4. What knowledge or underlying rules lead to competent and incompetent performance?
5. How is individual knowledge assessed?
6. How is the necessary knowledge taught and learned?

These questions reflect the issue, "Which method works best with each particular client?" This issue has replaced the earlier, simpler question, "which treatment works best?" Our view is similar to the one outlined by Goldstein and Stein (1976) regarding the desirability of prescriptive psychotherapies, but is broader, as it includes preventive programs as well as remedial ones.

To conclude the introduction, we will overview the contents of the book by discussing the authors answers to the first question; their responses to the other five will be covered in their respective chapters.

This book surveys interventions designed to promote social competence at each stage of the life cycle from childhood through retirement. At each point it is necessary to know what tasks a person must be able to perform successfully in order to be socially competent. From society's perspective, the list of tasks must include those related to getting along with other people and becoming a productive member of society. In addition to love- and work-related tasks, society expects people to be able to cope with life stresses such as the death of a loved one, unemployment, and advancing age. From an individual perspective the list might be expanded to include more personal tasks such as achievement of autonomy or self-confidence.

The specific tasks that are highlighted by the research and interventions in this book represent both of the perspectives. In chapter two, Bonnie Camp addresses the task of self-control necessary for children to meet social and academic demands. Myrna Shure considers the means that can be used to enable parents to teach their children problem-solving skills. Her program focuses on specific skills, such as generation of alternatives and evaluation of consequences, that are a part of the more general task of social problem solving. In her program, parents are taught to resist the urge to teach the child a specific solution to a given problem but rather to encourage behaviors that allow children to resolve personal difficulties themselves.

Rotheram's schoolwide program to teach children social skills described in chapter four encompasses a variety of tasks including improving peer relationships, dealing with authority figures, controlling negative emotions and expressing feelings, and developing assertive belief systems. Special attention is paid to the tasks faced by children with learning disabilities. The section on teenagers discusses differences between ninth and twelfth graders in the kinds of tasks they themselves consider important. The program for ninth graders is more didactic and focuses on relations with parents and authority figures; the program for twelfth graders involves greater participation and focuses immediately on peer problems. A final section considers general issues involved in program implementation, particularly in a bureaucratic setting.

While Rotheram's program was directed at the entire classroom, the curriculum described by Cox and Gunn in chapter 5 was developed for boys already referred to a special school on the basis of behavior problems. The tasks they consider are initiation and conflict resolution. It is interesting to note that conflict resolution was the task which best discriminated between the delinquent boys in their program and normal controls. All of the boys were able to deal with the initial task of responding to a provocation, but only the normal boys were able to cope with repeated provocations. Thus the task of paramount importance became one of controlling one's own negative emotions and learning how to persist assertively.

Perhaps the most complete range of tasks is presented in chapter six, on structured-learning therapy, by Sprafkin, Gershaw, and Goldstein. Using a wide variety of clients, including mental patients, aggressive teenagers, child-abusing parents, and police officers, they have developed packages for meeting the specific environmental demands each group faces. For example, a module designed for a patient returning to the community would involve multiple skills related to relationships with employers, landlords, and friends.

In chapter seven, Robins considers a task viewed by many researchers as critical in adolescent development: the adolescent's achievement of autonomy from the parents without excessive conflict. He conceptualizes parent-adolescent conflict as a family skill deficit involving a variety of cognitive interpersonal problem-solving and communication skills. His model allows families to resolve problems through democratic means rather than by the authoritarian power-based systems often used in troubled families. A separate manual, including assessment measures and work sheets, follows his chapter.

A task only recently recognized as one accompanied by a great amount of stress even for well-adjusted couples, the birth of the first child, is discussed by Vincent, Harris, Cook and Brady in chapter eight. By reviewing the relevant literature in child development, marital relations, and communication theory, they were able to develop a preventive program designed for expectant parents. Assessment measures to identify couples likely to experience problems are an integral part of the intervention.

The array of tasks related to successful performance in job-related activities is considered by Doyle, Smith, Bishop, and Miller in chapter nine. An intervention using video recording and simulated interaction training has been used with a variety of clients including police officers in stressful confrontations.

Ways to teach the general task of negotiating successful interpersonal relationships for clients with affective and psychosomatic disorders are presented in chapters ten and eleven. In chapter ten, Emery notes that depression is often associated with failure at maintaining good interpersonal relationships; a depressed person may become either overly dependent on those in his environment or socially isolated. Emery outlines cognitive and behavioral strategies that can assist a person who has already adopted one of these maladaptive modes of relating to others.

Research suggests that some individuals may make use of pain and other aspects of illness as tactics to influence other people in their environment and maintain relationships. In chapter eleven, Barrios provides a rationale for the use of skill training as a treatment for those with psychosomatic disorders and presents research comparing the skills treatment with more conventional ones.

The unique environmental situation of the elderly presents them with tasks that may exceed their coping resources. Rotheram and Corby, in chapter twelve, review such factors as powerlessness, social isolation, and negative stereotyping, which make the basic social tasks of forming relationships and maintaining autonomy difficult for elderly persons. Their program of assertiveness training is tailored uniquely for this client population; often elderly people dispute the belief systems used in typical assertiveness programs.

As can be seen from this brief overview, the tasks most critical for social competence vary greatly over the life cycle. The same is true for the behavior defined as competent, the processing characteristics of the clients, and the knowledge required change at different points in time. Unique methods of assessment and teaching are required at each stage, as the following chapters indicate.

References

Anderson, S. and Messick, S. 1974. Social competency in young children. *Developmental Psychology, 10,* 282-93.

Averill, J. A 1979 selective review of cognitive and behavioral factors involved in the regulation of stress. In *The psychiobiology of the depressive disorders: Implications for the effects of stress,* ed. R. A. Depue. New York: Academic Press, 1979.

Bandura, A. 1969. *Principles of behavior modification.* New York: Holt, Rinehart and Winston.

Bandura, A. 1977. Self-efficacy: Toward a unifying theory of behavioral change. *Psychological Review, 84,* 191-215.

Bandura, A. 1978. The self-system in reciprocal determinism. *American Psychologist, 33,* 344-58.

Bersheid, E. and Walster, E. 1978. Physical attractiveness. In *Advances in experimental social psychology,* vol. 7, ed. L. Berkowitz. New York: Academic Press. 1974.

Bornstein, M. R., Bellack, A.S. and Hersen, M. 1977. Social skills training for unassertive children: A multiple baseline analysis. *Journal of Applied Behavior Analysis, 10,* 183-94.

Bowers, K. S. 1973. Situationism in psychology: An analysis and a critique. *Psychological Review, 80,* 307-36.

Buss, A. R. 1977. The trait situation controversy and the concept of interaction. *Personality and Social Psychology Bulletin, 3,* 196-201.

Clifford, E. 1967. Social visibility. *Child Development, 38,* 993-1002.

Coelho, G. V., Hamburg, D.A. and Adams, J. E. 1974. *Coping and adaptation,* New York: Basic Books.

Combs, M. L. and Slaby, D. A. 1977. Social skills training with children. In *Advances in clinical child psychology,* vol. 1, ed. B. Lahey and A. Kazdin. New York: Plenum Press.

Derogatis, L. R., Yevzeroff, H., and Wittelsberger, F. 1975. Social class, psychological disorder, and the nature of the psychopathologic indicator. *Journal of Consulting and Clinical Psychology, 43,* 181-83.

Ekehammar, B. 1974, Interactionism in personality from a historical perspective. *Psychological Bulletin, 81,* 1026-48.

Ekehammar, B., Schalling, D. and Magnusson. 1975. Dimensions of stressful situations: A comparison between a response analytical and a stimulus analytical approach. *Multivariate Behavioral Research, 10,* 155-64.

Endler, N. S. and Magnusson, D. 1976. Toward an interactional psychology of personality. *Psychological Bulletin, 89,* 956-74.

Fiedler, D. and Beach, L. R. 1978. On the decision to be assertive. *Journal of Consulting and Clinical Psychology, 46,* 537-46.

Foreyt, J. and Rathjen, D. P., eds. 1978. *Cognitive behavior therapy: Research and application.* New York: Plenum Press.

Freedman, M. P. 1974. An analysis of social-behavioral skill deficits in delinquent and nondelinquent adolescent boys. Unpublished doctoral dissertation, University of Wisconsin, Madison.

French, J. R. and Raven, B. 1959. The bases of social power. In *Studies in social power,* ed D. Cartwright. Ann Arbor: University of Michigan Press.

Goffman, E. 1972. *Relations in public.* London: Allen Lane, Penguin Books.

Goldfried, M. R. and D'Zurilla, T. J. 1969. A behavioral analytic model for assessing competence. In *Current topics in clinical and community psychology,* vol. 1, ed. C. D. Spielberger. New York: Academic Press.

Goldsmith, J. B. and McFall, R. M. 1975. Development and evaluation of an interpersonal skill-training program for psychiatric inpatients. *Journal of Abnormal Psychology, 84,* 51-58.

Goldstein, A. P. 1973. *Structured learning therapy: Toward a psychotherapy for the poor.* New York: Academic Press.

Goldstein, A. P. and Stein, N. 1976. *Prescriptive psychotherapies.* New York: Pergamon Press.

Gottman, J., Notarius, C., Gonso, J., and Markham, H. 1976. *A couples' guide to communication.* Champaign, Illinois: Research Press.

Gottman, J. M., Gonso, J. and Rasmussen, B. 1975. Social interaction, social competence and friendship in children. *Child Development, 46,* 709-18.

Harre, R. 1977. The ethogenic approach: Theory and practice. In *Advances in experimental social psychology,* vol. 10, ed. L. Berkowitz. New York: Academic Press.

Hartup, W. 1976. Peer interaction and behavioral development of the individual child. In *Child development, deviations and treatment,* ed. E. Schopler and R. J. Reichler. New York: Plenum.

Harvey, J. H., Ickes, W.J. and Kidd, R. F. 1976. *New direction in attribution research,* vol. 1, New York: John Wiley.

Harvey, J. H., Ickes, W., and Kidd, R. F. 1978. *New directions in attribution research,* vol. 2. New York: John Wiley.

Hersen, M. and Bellack, A. S., eds. 1976. *Behavioral assessment: A practical handbook.* Oxford: Pergamon Press.

Holmes, T. H. and Rahe, R. H. 1976. The social readjustment rating scale. *Journal of Psychosomatic Research, 11,* 213-18.

Hull, D. B. and Schroeder, H. E. 1979. Some interpersonal effects of assertion, nonassertion. *Behavior Therapy, 10,* 20-28.

Huston, T. L. and Levinger, G. 1978. Interpersonal attraction and relationships. In *Annual Review of Psychology,* ed. M. R. Rosenzweig and L. W. Porter. Palo Alto, Calif.: Annual Reviews, Inc.

Huston, T. L. 1974. *Foundations of interpersonal attraction.* New York: Academic Press.

Keller, M. and Carlson, P. 1974. The use of symbolic modeling to promote social skills in preschool children with low levels of social responsiveness. *Child development, 45,* 912-19.

Kelley, G. 1955. *The psychology of personal constructs.* New York: Norton & Company.

Kelley, H. H. and Thibaut, J. W. 1978. *Interpersonal relations: A theory of interdependence.* New York: John Wiley.

Klinger, E. 1977. *Meaning and void: Inner experience and the incentives in people's lives.* Minneapolis: University of Minnesota.

Kohlberg, L. and Mayer, R. 1972. Development as the aim of education. *Harvard Educational Review, 42,* 449-96.

Kupke, T. E., Hobbs, S.A., and Cheney, T. H. 1979. Selection of heterosocial skills. *Behavior Therapy, 10,* 327-35.

Lesser, G. S. 1959. The relationship between various forms of aggression and popularity among lower class children. *Journal of Educational Psychology, 50,* 20-25.

Lewin, K. 1935. *A dynamic theory of personality.* New York: McGraw-Hill.

Linehan, M. M., Goldfried, M. R. and Goldfried, A. P. 1979. Assertion therapy: Skill training or cognitive restructuring. *Behavior Therapy, 10,* 372-88.

Lippit, R. and Gold, M. 1959. Classroom social structures as a mental health problem. *Journal of Social Issues, 15,* 40-49.

Maccoby, E. E. & Jacklin, C. N. 1974. *The psychology of sex differences.* Stanford, California: Stanford University Press.

Magnusson, D. & Ekehammar, B. 1975. Perceptions of and reactions to stressful situations. *Journal of Personality and Social Psychology, 31,* 1147-54.

Mahoney, M. J. 1974. *Cognition and behavior modification.* Cambridge, Mass.: Ballinger Publishing Co.

McFall, R. M. 1976. *Behavioral training: A skill-acquisition approach to clinical problems.* Morristown, N.J.: General Learning Press.

Meichenbaum, D. 1977. *Cognitive-behavior modification: An integrative approach.* New York: Plenum Press.

Miller, G., Galanter, E. and Pribram, K. 1960. *Plans and the Structure of behavior.* New York: Holt, Rinehart & Winston.

Miller, I. W., Norman, W. H. 1979. Learned helplessness in humans: A review and attribution-theory model. *Psychological Bulletin, 86,* 93-118.

Mischel, W. 1968. *Personality and assessment.* New York: Wiley.

Mischel, W. 1973. Toward a cognitive social learning reconceptualization of personality. *Psychological Review, 80,* 252-83.

Moos, R. H. 1974. *The social climate scales.* Palo Alto, California: Consulting Psychologists Press.

Moos, R. 1976. *The human context: Environmental determinants of behavior.* New York: Wiley.

O'Connor, R. D. 1972. Relative efficacy of modeling, shaping, and the combined procedures for modification of social withdrawal. *Journal of Abnormal Psychology, 79,* 327-34.

Oden, S. and Asher, S. 1977. Coaching children in social skills for friendship making. *Child Development, 48,* 495-506.

O'Malley, J. 1977. Research perspectives on social competence. *Merrill-Palmer Quarterly, 23,* 29-44.

Patterson, G. R., Reid, J. B., Jones, R. R., and Conger, R. E. 1975. *A social learning approach to family intervention: Families with aggressive children,* vol. 1. Eugene, Oregon: Castalia Publishing Co.

Rathjen, D., Hiniker, A., and Rathjen, E. 1976. Incorporation of behavioral techniques in a game format to teach children social skills. Presented at the Association for Advancement of Behavior Therapy, New York City, December 1976.

Rathjen, D. and Hiniker, A. 1977. Interpersonal effectiveness: Stereotypes, myths and data. *Rice University Studies,* Winter, 1977.

Rathjen, D., Hiniker, A., and Rathjen, E. 1976. The effect of physical attractiveness of an assertive individual on peer ratings of social skills. Unpublished manuscript.

Rathjen, D., Rathjen, E., and Hiniker, A. 1978. A cognitive analysis of social performance: Implications for assessment and treatment. In *Cognitive behavior therapy: research and application,* ed. J. Foreyt and D. Rathjen. New York: Plenum Press.

Scandura, J. M. 1973a. *Structural learning I: Theory and research.* New York: Gordon and Breach.

Scandura, J. M. 1973b. Structural learning and the design of educational materials. *Educational Technology, 13,* 7-13.

Scandura, J. M. 1977. Structural approach to instructional problems. *American Psychologist, 32,* 33-53.

Schwartz, R. and Gottman, J. 1976. Toward a task analysis of assertive behavior. *Journal of Consulting and Clinical Psychology, 44,* 910-20.

Sigall, H. and Ostrove, N. 1975. Beautiful but dangerous: Effects of offender attractiveness and nature of the crime on juridic judgment. *Journal of Personality and Social Psychology, 31,* 410-14.

Snyder, M., Tanke, E. and Berscheid, E. 1977. Social perception and interpersonal behavior: On the self-fulfilling nature of social stereotypes. *Journal of Personality and Social Psychology, 35,* 656-66.

Spivack, G., Platt, J. J., and Shure, M. B. 1976. *The problem solving approach to adjustment: A guide to research and intervention.* San Francisco: Jossey-Bass.

Spivack, G., and Shure, M. B. 1974. *Social adjustment of young children: A cognitive approach to solving real-life problems.* San Francisco: Jossey-Bass.

Sundberg, N. D., Snowden, L. R. and Reynolds, W. M. 1978. Toward assessment of personal competence and incompetence in life situations. In *Annual Review of Psychology,* ed. M. R. Rosenzweig & L. W. Porter. Palo Alto: Annual Review, Inc.

Trower, P., Bryant, B. and Argyle, M. 1978. *Social skills and mental health.* Pittsburgh, Pa.: University of Pittsburgh Press.

Weiss, R. L., Hops, H. and Patterson, G. R. 1973. A framework for conceptualizing marital conflict, a technology for altering it, some data for evaluating it. In *Behavior change: Methodology, concepts, and practice,* ed. L. A. Hammerlynck, L.C. Handy, and E. J. Mash. Champaign, Ill: Research Press.

White, R. C. 1959. Motivation reconsidered: The concept of competence. *Psychological Review, 66,* 297-333.

Willems, E. P. and Raush, H. L., eds. 1969. *Naturalistic viewpoints in psychological research.* New York: Holt, Rinehart & Winston.

Woolfolk, R. L. and Dever, S. 1979. Perceptions of assertion: An empirical analysis. *Behavior Therapy, 10,* 404-11.

Zigler, E. and Trickett, P. K. 1978. I.Q., social competence, and evaluation of early childhood intervention programs. *American Psychologist, 33,* 789-96.

2

Developing Self-Control Through Training in Problem Solving: The "Think Aloud" Program

Bonnie Camp and Mary Ann Bash

Investigators generally agree that some type of modeling is necessary for developing self-control (Hetherington and McIntyre 1975). Others have suggested that internalized liguistic tools, loosely described as verbal mediation skills, may also be a prerequisite for establishing inhibition of impulsive reactions and maintaining control over behavior (Razran 1961; White 1972a,b). Other research suggests that these linguistic tools develop as language achieves a regulatory function in addition to the social and instrumental functions it serves from an early age (White 1970).

In adults, these regulatory functions of language usually function automatically below the level of conscious awareness and only become conscious or overt when problems become difficult (Jensen 1966). Children, however, are thought to go through several stages before arriving at the smoothly functioning automatic stage of adults. Vygotsky (1962) has described four stages in the development of verbal control (inhibition) over behavior. With modifications, these can be viewed as follows: (1) Initially, language may provoke feeling or stop behavior through startling or distracting effects, but commands have no semantic meaning; (2) Young children begin to learn to respond to overt commands from another person, but they are unable to stop or inhibit their own behavior with their own verbal command, for example, the two-year-old who reaches for the cookies saying "no, no, no"; (3) Overt self-commands begin to function effectively in regulating, stopping, and inhibiting the child's own behavior, but covert (even whispering) commands are ineffective or inconsistent; (4) Regulation-inhibition occurs under the influence of covert thoughts.

White (1965, 1972) summarized data indicating that use of language as a regulator is basically dependent upon maturation that usually occurs during the age range of five to seven years. He also related development of verbal mediation skills to development of ability to inhibit impulsive responding and to shift from associative to logical thought. Jensen (1966) suggests that verbal mediation skills become increasingly important as the child grows older and failure to use them spontaneously accounts for much underachievement in school. Achenbach (1975) has expounded a similar view in his studies relating associative thinking (the tendency to give associations rather than use logic in thinking), impulsivity, and IQ-achievement discrepancies in junior and senior high school students. Loevinger (1975) discusses ego development along similar dimensions.

Although the capacity for verbal mediation activity may depend upon maturation, the variety and complexity of situations which show up deficiencies in its use suggest that factors other than maturation probably determine how much a child will come to rely on this ability or to use it spontaneously. If experiential factors could account for individual differences in the regularity and depth of spontaneous use of verbal mediation skills in learning and behavior, it seems reasonable to suppose that training and practice in using language as a regulator could produce smoother and more automatic application of them in a greater variety of situations. Thus, massive amounts of practice in verbal mediation skills could presumably produce the same type of automaticity commonly achieved in reading, playing a musical instrument, or speaking a language.

Several early studies demonstrated that brief training in use of overt, verbal self-instruction can improve test performance in children (Meichenbaum and Goodman 1971; Palkes, Stewart, and Kahana 1968). What early studies had not shown was whether one could produce clinically significant long-term changes in either the cognitive or social behavior of children with clinically significant problems.

"Think Aloud" was designed as an attempt to confront this issue by studying the effects of verbal mediation training on cognitive and social behavior of young aggressive boys. This group was selected because our earlier research (Camp et al. 1977a, 1977b) indicated that the cognitive pattern of young aggressive boys could be characterized as showing a deficiency in use of verbal mediation skills unless ostensibly solicited by the task. Because of the long-term stability of cognitive and behavior problems in aggressive children (Camp 1976; Kohlberg, LaCrosse and Ricks, 1972: Prentice and Kelly, 1963) we expected aggressive children to pose the most stringent test of any program. If a program could alter behavior in this group, it should also have a good chance of being successful with children demonstrating milder degrees of deficiency in verbal mediation skills.

Developing the Program

Since features of the "Think Aloud" program were designed specifically to meet the problems encountered in young aggressive boys, some description of the group and its cognitive characteristics seems desirable. Initially, we studied first and second grade boys who were two or more standard deviations above the mean on the Aggressive Scale of Miller's (1972) School Behavior Checklist completed by the students' regular classroom teacher in late October or early November of the school year. This meant that they displayed a large number of behaviors such as the following: "starts fighting over nothing," "interrupts whomever is speaking," "hits and pushes other children," "does things to get others angry," "will put up an argument when told can't do something," "uses abusive language toward other children," "is infuriated by any form of discipline," "boasts about being tough," "tries to be the center of attention," "sulks when things go wrong," "resents even the most gentle criticism of own work," "tries to get other children into trouble," "has a chip on the shoulder."

Psychological testing also showed a characteristic pattern of behavior and test results which distinguish aggressive boys from normal boys (Camp et al. 1977; Camp 1977). Despite basically adequate verbal development, they tended to use these abilities only when specifically requested to do so and failed to use them in thinking through and planning solutions to other problems. They talked a lot, but the majority of their verbal output was immature, self-stimulating, and often irrelevant to the task at hand. They had more difficulty on tasks that did not explicitly call for verbal planning and reasoning (e.g. complex mazes) but which could not be solved without such reasoning. They had more difficulty inhibiting responses in a "Simon Says" game. When specifically instructed to remind themselves verbally to inhibit a reaction, they were able to do so even more readily than normals. However, when expected to perform the same inhibitions with covert (whispering) control they were inconsistent. They also had difficulty with sequential memory, and reading achievement was somewhat depressed.

Our first step in planning a training program was to construct procedures for counteracting these problems. Thus our initial objectives were to use language to slow down, to inhibit the first reaction, to decrease impulsiveness, and to internalize this process. Previous research suggested that these could be achieved by use of modeling and overt verbalization of thoughts and plans. These features were expected to achieve inhibition of impulsiveness through internalization of linguistic controls. Our analysis of skills needed to cope successfully with either cognitive or social situations suggested that inhibition of impulsiveness might be a necessary feature, but it was not the only skill which needed to be covered by a problem-solving program.

Clearly, one may delay one's reaction but have no organized approach to dealing with a problem, or no repertory of alternative reactions to substitute after the first reaction is blocked. Without a repertory of alternatives, inhibition may simply delay expression of the same poorly adaptive response.

Generalization was also a problem that needed to be addressed. In its simplest form, generalization needed to be assured to cover many different types of problems varying in degree of difficulty, type and mode of presentation (e.g. auditory or visual, verbal or kinesthetic response), and kind of activity (mazes, inductive reasoning, recognizing similarities). Generalization to "real-life" situations posed a different type of problem.

Transfer to real-life situations requiring cognitive problem-solving such as application to study of reading or math could be readily developed. Generalization of verbal mediation skills to social situations might not be expected so readily. In fact, achieving generalization to real life social situations seems to have been a problem for all cognitive behavior modification therapy programs. Thus, it seemed that generalization to social behavior outside the training program might be a chancy affair unless it was explicitly included in the program. On the other hand, Shure and Spivack's (1974) success in training preschool and kindergarten children in social problem-solving situations would occur more quickly, completely, and reliably if the program included specific training for such generalization.

Once we reviewed the Shure and Spivack scripts for their social training program, we realized that two additional features of problem-solving activity needed to be made explicit. These were an understanding of cause and effect and some repertory for evaluating outcomes. Both of these features tend to be implicit in dealing with cognitive problems. The question of cause and effect seldom arises in cognitive problems, and evaluation of outcomes is almost always a matter of determining what is "correct" against some standard of fact or solution that fits all the requirements of the problem (as in completing a puzzle). Even so, making evaluation explicit in cognitive problems could serve as a bridge for introducing evaluation strategies in the more ambiguous social situations.

Finally, initial trials with the program brought to our attention the possibility that a certain amount of immature, irrelevant speech and activity might actually inhibit or interfere with acquisition of verbal mediation skills. Consequently, revisions of the program included general dialogues that could be used to decrease silliness by introducing incompatible behavior.

By reorganizing and regrouping elements included in the "Think Aloud" program, we arrived at the following features:

1. Use of modeling, overt verbalization and self-guiding speech;
2. Developing an organized plan of approach to problems;
3. Decreasing interfering behaviors;
4. Increasing skill in following a plan, independence in applying the skill and fading to a covert level;
5. Increasing repertory of alternative responses;
6. Increasing generalization to different types of problems varying in difficulty, type of presentation, etc.;
7. Increasing generalization to real-life social situation;
8. Developing understanding of cause and effect;
9. Developing repertory of evaluation skills.

The following section will describe how we approached the construction of the program.

Modeling and Eliciting Self-guiding Speech

How do you get children to think aloud? How do you get them to attend to and imitate the important features of a model's behavior? Many young children do not understand what you want them to do when you say "think out loud." Even if the teacher says, "Watch what I do, now you do it," many young children will overlook crucial features of the model's behavior and copy superficial aspects. Meichenbaum prompted verbalization by creating a game in which the child had to perform some function such as that of an air traffic controller "talking a plane into landing." Shure and Spivack counted on imitation of peers and enough different responses in a group to provide many alternatives. In our program, we used the "copy cat" game as a means of insuring that the child attended to all aspects of the model's speech and behavior. The problem with this approach is that it arouses the specter of monotonous, meaningless repetitions of the model's speech with no internalization of the actions. Shure feels this approach may be counterproductive and prefers spontaneous imitation of peers' behavior. Meichenbaum (1975) has also warned against passive repetition.

Nevertheless, "copy cat" is an easily understood way to elicit a young child's attention to all aspects of speech and behavior in another person. Furthermore, with this mechanism one can proceed to build in a problem-solving procedure through modeling and self-instructions.

Later on, new tasks are introduced by having the child play "copy cat" while the teacher models ways of thinking through a problem and coping with mistakes.

Developing an Organized Approach to Problems

Meichenbaum and Goodman (1971) recognized that the first step in problem solving involves understanding of the problem. They introduced the use of four questions to organize the child's approach: (1) What is my problem? (2) What is my plan or How can I do it? (3) Am I following my plan? (4) How did I do? In the "Think Aloud" program, these four questions are introduced through the use of the four cue cards. A set of these four cards is given to each child for personal use and large sets are displayed in the room during training. Initially the teacher asks herself each of the questions and answers them with the child playing copy cat. This is illustrated in the following script used in the second lesson.

Day 2—20-25 minutes

Copy Cat

Teacher: Let's play copy cat again. Remember you have to say what I say and do what I do. If I point my finger, you point your finger.* *(Continue with Copy Cat, emphasizing* Do what I do *with gestures.)*

Children: ____________________

Teacher: Good. Today I'm going to show you a new way of doing a problem. I call it thinking out loud. What do I call it?

Children: ____________________

Teacher: We'll start with a real easy problem: You probably would not think of it as a problem. But we're going to pretend it is like a problem we have to solve. Later on we will do lots harder problems, and then this thinking out loud will really help. To teach you to think, we'll use our copy cat game. You will be the copy cats, and you must say and do just what I say and do.

Coloring Shapes

Teacher: *(Give children and yourself the paper of shapes to be colored. Select the circle with a fat border first.)* We each have a paper with some shapes on it. The problem *(insert classroom teacher's name)* gave us is to color this shape the best we can without going outside the lines. Pick a colored pencil and I'll pick one.

Children: ____________________

Teacher: Let's learn to think out loud to help us do this paper. Remember you must copy what I say and do. Let's try it.

Teacher: *(Without putting pencil to paper.)*

Q. OK. What is my problem?*

A. I am supposed to color this circle without going outside the lines.*

Q. How can I do it?*

*Indicates statement children should copy.

Each of the questions may be used for specific purposes depending upon the age of the child and the situation. With very young children, "What is my problem?" may only prompt them to restate the problem or verbalize the most obvious description of the task or problem. In this form, it is primarily attention directing. In programs for older children, this question may be utilized to develop lessons for finding different ways of stating or locating the problem as well. Similarly, "What is my plan?" is initially used to prompt simple statements of how to complete a task. Later, after the concept of alternative ideas has been introduced, children may be encouraged to develop many plans. Also in the early lessons, children are allowed to select the desired plan uncritically. After concepts of evaluating alternatives and consequences have been introduced, those concepts can be applied to evaluating plans.

"Am I following my plan?" was included primarily to introduce some concept of self-monitoring. In practice, it was perhaps the least effective question, except in situations where the response to this monitoring might be a change in plans. Initially, "How did I do?" elicited the almost universal answer, "Fine." Consequently, we began early in the program to encourage the child to determine whether he followed his plan, whether he thought out loud, whether he corrected his mistakes, and whether he achieved his goal. Later, as lessons in evaluation were introduced, answers to this question were also amplified.

Once children have become comfortable with the questions and the concept of developing answers appropriate to the task at hand, the teacher begins to guide the child to ask the questions for himself and develop his own answers. Later, she asks him to perform the whole sequence of solving a problem without prompting.

Decreasing Interfering Behavior

Several types of behavior interfere with skills sought by the program. These include clowning, profanity, silliness, shouting answers out of turn, name calling and belittling. Instructions for dealing with these behaviors or suggested dialogues are included in the program. One of the more difficult of these behaviors to discourage is silliness. We tried to deal with this through heightening the child's awareness of his silliness and use of a signal for incompatible activity. The following instructions to teachers illustrate this.

Children sometimes get into a habit of being silly and after time lose sight of instances of their silliness. "Think Aloud" attempts to help silly children recognize their silliness and then curb it. For example, if a child uses baby talk or a funny voice inappropriately, we might say, "That's one way you could talk. What's a different way to say it?" Or if a child says something irrelevant which pulls him or others off task, we inquire, "Does that help you solve your problem? What is something different you could say to help you with your work?"

Whenever a child begins to pull himself or others off task by verbal or nonverbal silliness, help guide his attention back to his problem and elicit on-task verbalizing.

To help the child achieve internal control of his silliness, we ask a child to put his hand to his mouth when he starts to be silly... to trap it inside. If it is too difficult for the child to recognize his own silliness, other children can use the gesture to signal the offender. [Camp and Bash 1978]

Increasing Independence

In early lessons and during introduction of totally new material, the teacher models all aspects of her cognitions in solving a problem and requests the child to play copy cat. During this period, the child is seated physically close to the teacher with undivided attention. As the child is able to drop the copy cat game and demonstrate his own organized approach to problems, the teacher may ask him to go ahead and work on a problem using "Think Aloud" while she busies herself with some other papers or with another child. When the child is able to handle this successfully, she may separate him physically from her. At the same time she begins to encourage whispering. And finally as success with more and more difficult problems is achieved, she encourages complete fading to a covert level. By then, one can usually watch a child's eyes and hands to monitor his thinking processes. This is illustrated in the following instructions to teachers on "Fading the 'Out-loud' of Thinking":

> Some children will be very verbal from the outset, suffering little frustration from thinking out loud while working. For these children, fading of *overt* verbalizations may begin early. Suggest to these children that they use their fingers to let you know what they are thinking about in their brains. They can touch their fingers to details they are examining or paths they are exploring. The ultimate goal is for all children to arrive at the covert level of performance. This process, however, cannot be rushed. [Camp and Bash 1978]

Increasing Repertory of Alternatives

In the Shure and Spivack programs, children are introduced very early to the concept of "think of as many different ideas as you can." A companion concept to be mastered by the teacher is the response, "That's one idea. What's a different idea?" In the "Think Aloud" program, the concept of seeking different ideas is introduced in the third lesson without specific attention to finding all possible ideas. The following portions of a puzzle sequence are illustrative:

Day 3

Teacher: Yesterday we learned the questions we ask ourselves when we mented extensively on the inhibiting effect of early evaluation for a variety of group problem-solving discussions.

Developing Skill with a Variety of Problems

To keep children interested, difficulty of the tasks needs to be maintained at a level which is challenging, neither *too* difficult to be frustrating nor *too* easy to be boring. Many children may actively resist systematic use of verbal mediation rather than merely having a high threshold for arousal. Overt verbalization requires one to perform tasks more slowly and often less smoothly, especially well-known tasks. If the program is not well tailored to the child's level of cognitive development, boredom and resistance will become evident. In addition to matching difficulty with the child's level, we use dramatic staging, game format, props such a listening ears, hats, and puppets to sustain attention and to improve motivations when performing is difficult. We also found that cognitive problems that do not touch on areas of emotional problems are often less threatening than problems dealing with interpersonal relations. Consequently, they may be experienced as easier than social problems. This is not true for all children. Occasionally, one finds a child who is uninterested in the cognitive problems but takes readily to social problem solving.

Another area of consideration was modality for presenting tasks. Most early studies used visual tasks almost exclusively (Palkes, Stewart, and Kahana 1968; Meichenbaum and Goodman 1971). And, indeed, visual tasks are often the easiest. They are usually more concrete, require less memory, and tend to be simpler than verbal problems. As demonstrated in the previous script, "Think Aloud" instruction begins with a simple visual task, coloring within lines, and a simple verbal task, following directions. These were followed by increasingly difficult problems such as complex matrices, stencil designs, and mazes.

We were particularly concerned, however, with developing problems that could be presented in the auditory-verbal modality with stress on development of inhibition. Our work with aggressive boys suggested they had significant problems with impulsive responses to problems presented in the auditory-verbal modality as well as with visually presented problems. Many of the auditory problems designed for this program were developed specifically to induce greater depth in verbal mediation activity. One of the complex games was based on the Simon Says game, with the added twist that children had to remember whether Simon said to do something similar to or something different from the performance cue.

Two of the complex auditory games were based on tasks reported by Razran (1961) to investigate semantic conditioning. In both of these games, auditory association and auditory inhibition, children were given a piece of cardboard with a fluorescent spot in the center. Their task was to "hit the spot whenever the stimulus conformed to a predetermined set of characteristics. In the simplest version of the association task, the child had to detect the occurrence of a key word, such as "look," embedded in a series that included random presentations of phonetically similar words (such as: lake, luck, lock) and semantically similar words (such as: see, stare, peek). Words were presented one at a time via tape recorder.

After practice with different lists of words, a more difficult version was introduced. In this version children were instructed, "Do not hit on the word 'look.' Do hit the spot on any other word that tells something we do with our eyes."

The most difficult task we named auditory inhibition. In this task, the child was instructed to listen to and remember four words. If "ball" was one of the words, he was to "hit the spot." Next, he was given practice with groups of four words with instructions to "hit the spot" if the list contained a color. And finally, he was asked to respond only if a set of four words contained both the word "ball" and a color name. The following script demonstrates how this task was incorporated into the "Think Aloud" format.

Auditory Inhibition

Whole task should be completed at one sitting; one child only.

Teacher: On other days we have listened to words that sound a little alike and you had to hit the spot when you heard one word. Remember?

Child: ______________________

Step One

Teacher: Today we'll listen to words again, but the game is a little different. This time I'll say four words, then I'll pause; I'll be quiet. If you hear the word *ball,* hit the spot when I pause. What are you supposed to do?

Child: ______________________

Teacher: Remember, listen to all four words first. When I stop talking, if you heard the word *ball,* hit the spot once. Are you going to hit the spot right when you hear the word *ball?*

Child: ______________________

Teacher: Let me hear you think out loud.

Child: ______________________

Teacher: Let's try some for practice. Rat come ball ask.

Child: ______________________

Teacher: *(Record child's performance on Auditory Inhibition Recording Form. Wait for self-evaluation.)*

Child: ______________________

Teacher: *(If child failed to hit spot during pause, say:)* I'll say the words again and you copy the words—you say the words after I do. *(Repeat words.)* Did we say the word *ball?* _________ If you hear the word *ball,* what are you supposed to do? _________ What do you need to remind yourself? ________

Teacher: Let's try another one. Hat roll plant saw. *(Continue in order through Step One items on Auditory Inhibition Recording Form.)*

Child: ______________________

Step Two

Teacher: Now we'll change the game a little. Again I'll say four words and then pause. This time you should listen for a color name. What kind of word should you listen for?

Child: ______________________

Teacher: If you heard a color name, hit the spot when I pause. Will you hit the spot right when you hear a color name?

Child: ______________________

Teacher: Let me hear you think out loud. *(Plan may include thinking of colors he might hear.)*

Child: ______________________

Teacher: *(Point to cue picture 2 to elicit plan.)* Are you thinking of some words you might hit on?

Child: ______________________

Teacher: *(Pause so perhaps child will flash color names through his mind.)* Here we go. Angel dot brown dry.

Child: ______________________

Teacher: *(Record responses under Step Two items on Recording Form. Continue through Step Two items. If child begins to err, point to cue picture 3 to elicit reminders to task. At conclusion of task, look to child for self-evaluation.)*

Step Three

Teacher: Now we'll change the game again. I will still say four words. If one of the words is ball alone, do not hit the spot. If one of the words is a color name alone, do not hit the spot. If I say the word ball and a color, do hit the spot. When will you hit the spot?

Child: ______________________

Teacher: I'll try a couple to see how it works.

Q. What's my problem?

A. I'm supposed to hit the spot if I hear both the word ball *and* a color name.

Teacher: *Q.* How can I do it?

A. I'll listen to all four words and I'll remind myself to listen for ball and a color—both.

Teacher: *(Play tape recorded watch cut brown beach. Modeling instruc-*

tions: shake head on each non-ball, non-color, reminding yourself with whispered cue words—BALL, COLOR. When hearing color, whisper:) OK, there's a color. After all four words, I'm not supposed to hit on only a color: I have to hear ball, too. I only heard brown, so I won't hit.

Teacher: Q. How did I do?

A. I really thought quietly so I wouldn't make a mistake. I listened carefully to all the words. I waited for ball, but I didn't hear ball, so I could not hit.

Teacher: *(Play Act ball bright purple. Follow some modeling procedures. When you hear ball say:)* OK. I heard ball: now a color. *(Shake head no on "bright," then repeat word "purple.")* Purple is a color. I heard ball and a color so what should I do? Yes, I should hit the spot.

Teacher: I thought really hard. My plan worked to remind myself quietly what to listen for. Is it a good idea to talk loudly when your problem is to listen?

Child: ______________________

Teacher: Your turn. Let me hear you think out loud on this new problem. Apple ball run black. *(Continue in order through Step Three items. If a child errs on "silver" or "white" items, repeat them at end of list. If he errs again, ask him to name all the colors he can. If he includes white, silver, and gold in list, repeat items. At end of task, look to child for self-evaluation.)*

Child: ______________________

(Note: If a child likes to take teacher's role, allow him to make up a sequence of items and you assume role of student.)

Increasing Generalization to Real-Life Social Situations

Two aspects of the program were directed specifically toward the goal of increasing generalization in real-life social situations. One aspect involved structuring the program to provoke behavior and reactions in the training sessions which commonly occur in the classroom and to try out new ways of coping with the situation. Such reactions were elicited by including two children in the training sessions to provide the natural stimulus of another child, by using provocative questions and situations, and by the teacher's dramatic enactment of an individual child's reaction pattern, especially his self-destructive reactions to frustration.

Use of more adaptive mechanisms was then encouraged through: (1) stressing cooperation between the children and use of self-verbalization to achieve this, (2) stimulating empathic responses, (3) providing cognitive strategies for coping with feelings as part of dramatic outbursts, and (4) simply discussing other situations in which "Think Aloud" strategies might be helpful. Later, teachers were trained to elicit "Think Aloud" behavior in the classroom. The following dialogue demonstrates a suggested procedure for encouraging listening, waiting for each person to make a contribution, and assuming a helpful attitude.

Suggested Social Dialogue

Suggested Dialogue for Cooperation Training
To be used upon first need: when one child helps other when assistance isn't requested.

Teacher: We have a new problem. Whose turn is it?
Children: ____________________
Teacher: So who should be thinking out loud on this problem?
Children: ____________________
Teacher: Was *(child's name)* stuck on his problem?
Children: ____________________
Teacher: Sometimes it is good to help someone work on his problems. When might it be a good idea to help each other?
Children: ____________________
Teacher: How could we tell if someone needs help? How could we find out?
Children: *(You can ask him. Look at his face.)*
Teacher: If someone doesn't ask for help and they don't look like they need help, is it a good idea to help them?
Children: ____________________
Teacher: What plan could we make for this new problem: We know the answer but it isn't our turn?
Children: ____________________
Teacher: *(Thinking out loud might take the following direction.)*
Q. What's my problem?
A. I know the answer, but it isn't my turn.
Q. How can I solve it?
A. I'll wait. And I'll keep reminding myself what the answer is.
Q. Am I using my plan?
A. Yes, I'm remembering my answer.
Q. How did I do?
A. I was good at waiting. I remembered the answer I thought was right.

Principles derived from the Shure and Spivack work were applied directly whenever conflict broke out between the two children, as in the following dialogue to discourage name calling and belittling.

Suggested Dialogue for Discouraging Name Calling or Belittling

To be used whenever need arises. At least to be introduced sometime following "Is Anybody Listening" lesson.

Teacher: Is it a good idea to laugh at people when they don't know an answer or to call people names?

Children: ____________________

Teacher: Was it a good idea for Melvin to make fun of Billy? *(From "Is Anybody Listening" story.)*

Children: ____________________

Teacher: What might happen next if you laugh at someone or if you call someone a name?

Children: ____________________

Teacher: What plan could we make to stop us from laughing when someone doesn't know the answer or calling someone a name?

Children: ____________________

Teacher: *(Thinking out loud might take the following direction.)*

Q. What is my problem?

A. I am not supposed to call people a name. But I feel like it now.

Q. How can I solve it?

A. I'll (yawn/swallow/clench my teeth) instead of saying names. *(Any behavior incompatible with talking will suffice.)*

Q. Am I using my plan?

A. Yes, I'm ____________.

Q. How did I do?

A. Good. I used my plan and I didn't call him a name.

The second approach to promoting generalization to real-life social situations incorporated the social problem-solving program of Shure and Spivack (1974). Where possible, we used their materials, sequence of lessons, structure, objectives and design. However, their materials had to be adapted for the cognitive level of the children in the present program. For example, Shure and Spivack used 18 lessons to build up a vocabulary for use in identifying emotions and for learning the use of words such as "different," "same," "and," "but"; concepts such as "if. . .then," and "why . . . because"; and answers to questions such as "what might happen next," and "is that a good idea or not a good idea." These lessons were condensed into approximately seven lessons for the children in the present program. For older children these lessons could probably be condensed even further to a set of ground rules.

In the Shure and Spivack program, children are first led to develop as many solutions to a problem as possible in a given conflict situation. For example, the following problem, adapted from their program, is posed in social lesson number 8.

Social 8 *(Use Social Development Picture 12—Helping Pets)*

Teacher: We have a new kind of problem today. *(Show picture and point to respective children.)* This boy wants the girl to let him feed the hamsters. What does he want her to do?

Children: ________________________

Teacher: My problem is to think of something he can do so he can get a chance to feed the hamsters. I'll write down all the things I think of for the boy to do so he gets a chance.

Children: ________________________

Teacher: Q. OK. What's my problem?
A. I am supposed to think of something this boy can do so he can get a chance to feed the hamsters.

Teacher: Q. What's my plan?
A. I can't think of a good plan. I'll just have to try hard to think of lots of different things he could do.

Teacher: OK. One thing for sure, he could ask her if he could feed them. That's one idea. *(List and number all doing responses.)* I need to think of lots of different ways this boy can get the girl to let him feed the hamsters. He could grab the food from her and feed them. That's another thing he could do. Now I have two different ideas *(show fingers)*. He could ask her or he could grab the food.

Teacher: Let's see. He could give something. He could give the girl some potato chips if she will let him feed the hamsters. Yeah, but maybe she doesn't like potato chips. How could he find out if she likes potato chips? He could ask her. If she would not like potato chips, what is something different he could do to get to feed the hamsters? Hum, are they at school? If they are, he could tell the teachers. That's another idea. Now I've got four different things the boy could do. I'm really doing good. *(Reviewing list of responses, say)* he could ask her, or he could grab the food from her, or he could give her something she likes, or he could tell somebody—the teacher.

Teacher: How did I do? I thought of lots of different things he could do. That made me tired.

Teacher: Now it's your turn to think of lots of different things the boy could say to get a chance to feed the hamsters. *(Elicit preliminary verbalizations. Then categorize each of children's re-*

sponses by type—ask, tell, give, trade, trick, hurt, share, wait—and present appropriate social-cue picture. List and number all responses. If children give few responses, you might contribute one or two, but do not show respective cue pictures for your ideas.)

Children: ________________________
Teacher: That's hard to think of lots of different ideas. How did we do?
Children: ________________________
Teacher: How does that make you feel?
Children: ________________________

Because we did not have the benefit of alternatives developed within a normal peer group, we prepared a group of cue cards covering most of the alternatives suggested by children. As a child thought of one alternative, it was written down and he was given the appropriate card. This was especially useful in dealing with two or more children at a time since each child could collect the cards representing the solutions which he had offered. It also helped to maintain a distinction between "different" answers and answers which were merely enumerations or variations of previous ones.

Understanding Cause and Effect

Developing an understanding of cause and effect is a principal thrust in the Shure and Spivack program, and the "Think Aloud" program follows their format and sequence closely. Essentially, this aspect of the program begins with preliminary games addressed to developing many answers to nonthreatening social questions such as, "Why do I like birthdays?" Answers are developed using the clause "because." Other preliminary games deal with answering, "What might happen next?" and, "Is it a good idea?"

After children have practiced thinking of many different solutions to social problems, they are introduced to lessons which focus on thinking of all the things which could "happen next." For example, children are given the problem to think of all the things which could happen next in the following situations: (1) "Mickey wants to play with Lucy and her friend so he pushes Lucy," and (2) "Your friend chases you in the halls, but running in the halls is against the rules."

Finally, social problems are posed and children are asked to evaluate each solution on the basis of the possible consequences. The following dialogue illustrates this type of lesson:

Social 16 —*In gym you get the old bean bag for the bean bag toss.*

Teacher: Let's pretend your class is having a bean bag toss in the gym.

The teacher passes out new bean bags. *(1st child's name)* gets a new one. But when she gets to *(2nd child's name)*, all she has left is an old bean bag. *(To 2nd child)* you get an old bean bag, but you want a new one. What is the problem?

Children: ____________________

Teacher: *(To 2nd child)* what's one thing you might do?

Child 2: ____________________

Teacher: *(Record first solution to left of line and immediately ask Child 1 for one possible consequence.)* What might happen next if *(repeat child's solution)?*

Child 1: ____________________

Teacher: *(Record consequence to right of line.)* Is it a good idea to (repeat child's solution)?

Children: ____________________

Teacher: Now listen carefully. *(to 2nd child)* what is something different you could say or do if you do not want to use the old bean bag?

Child 2: ____________________

Teacher: *(Record child's second solution and immediately elicit a consequence to that solution.)*

Children: ____________________

Teacher: *(If children suggest grabbing someone else's bag or bargaining for someone's bag, ask)* how would *(other child)* feel if he/she has to use the old bean bag?

Children: ____________________

Teacher: How would you feel if you made *(other child)* feel *(repeat child's second solution)?*

Children: ____________________

Teacher: *(Continue simply pairing solution and one consequence without further help in evaluating solutions.)*

In our initial trials with the program, we found that aggressive boys tended to give more aggressive solutions to social problems after training. During that training, we had accepted aggressive and destructive solutions along with other ideas, expecting that these would ultimately have to be evaluated along with other solutions. However, we found the increase of aggressive solutions worrisome and thought that perhaps we had failed to put enough emphasis on ways of evaluating outcomes and on standards for evaluating quality of responses. This caused us to rethink the preliminary games dealing with the evaluation of outcomes, as is discussed in the following section.

Increasing the Repertory of Evaluation Strategies

In the Shure and Spivack programs, early discussions center on taking a picture and trying to tell how the characters feel, what happened, and what might happen next. The major lessons dealing with consequences focus on "safety"; it is not a good idea to pull the cat's tail because he might scratch you; it is not a good idea to play in front of the swings because you might get hurt if someone hits you. In many other games, solutions are evaluated implicitly on the basis of effectiveness. Clearly, if getting what you want is the only way of evaluating a solution, aggressive and destructive solutions can be considered effective.

We felt it would be beneficial to be more explicit about ways of evaluating outcomes and emphasize at least four ways of telling if a solution is a "good idea" based on its consequence. These criteria for evaluation were (1) how it makes you and others feel, (2) fairness, (3) safety, and (4) effectiveness. Since this has been developed most completely in the classroom program, the illustration for this lesson is drawn from the classroom program.

Day 16—30 minutes Social 5: Is it a good idea?

Rationale: To develop four criteria for evaluating solutions to interpersonal conflicts: (1) how it makes you and other people feel, (2) fairness, (3) safety, and (4) effectiveness.

Student Objective: The student will learn the four evaluation criteria and will learn the lyrics to the song "Helping" from Marlo Thomas' album *Free to Be You and Me.*

Teacher Objective: The teacher will ask students for different plans that would be good ideas for each ineffectively solved situation.

Materials: David C. Cook Publishing Co. Pictures:

1. "Respect Ownership"—*Children and the Law*
2. "Relationships Between Sisters and Brothers, Part Two"—*Learning About Human Relationships*
3. "Electricity"—*Safety*

The Instructo Corporation Pictures:

4. "Boy with Dog"—*Understanding Our Feelings*

"Helping" from Marlo Thomas' album *Free to Be You and Me,* Arista Records

Teacher: Today we're going to do more pretending. We need to think of lots of different plans and we'll see if our plans are good ideas or not good ideas.

Teacher: *(Picture 1)* Joey helped his mother by cleaning his room and by sweeping the walks, so she paid Joey a quarter. Was it a good idea for Mother to give Joey a quarter for his help?

Children: ______________________

Teacher: How did Mother feel when she saw Joey's clean room?

Children: ______________________

Teacher: How did Joey feel while he was working at home?

Children: ______________________

Teacher: *(Show "Happy" cue card and put it on blackboard ledge.)* Is it a good idea or not a good idea for Joey to help his mother?

Children: ______________________

Teacher: Why?

Children: ______________________

Teacher: Yes, it is a good idea because it made Joey and Mother happy. One way to decide if our plan is a good idea is to think how it might make us and other people feel.

Teacher: *(Picture 2)* Lenny's big brother took his toy away. Was it fair for Alex *(big brother)* to grab the baby's toy and hide it?

Children: ______________________

Teacher: *(Show "Fair" cue card and turn it upside down to indicate this action was not fair.)* How does the baby feel?

Children: ________________

Teacher: Is it a good idea or not a good idea to take away a baby's toy? *(Some children have suggested it is a good idea if the baby was playing with a dangerous toy. Pursue all responses.)*

Children: ______________________

Teacher: It was not a good idea to take the toy away because it make the baby sad and because it was not fair. So a different way to decide if our plan is a good idea is to think if it is fair.

Teacher: What's a different way Alex could play with his baby brother?

Children: ______________________

Teacher: Is it a good idea or not a good idea to ___________?

Children: ______________________

Teacher: Why?

Children: ______________________

Teacher: It is a good idea because it is fair. *(Turn "Fair" cue card right side up to indicate the fairness of this act.)*

Teacher: *(Picture 3)* Mother is ironing with a hot iron. Jerry is playing with his truck under the ironing board. What might happen next?

Children: ______________________

Teacher: Is it a good idea or not a good idea to play under the ironing board?

Children: ______________________

Teacher: Why?

Children: ______________________

Teacher: *(Turn "Safe" cue card upside down.)* A third way to judge if a plan is a good idea is to think if it is safe.

Teacher: Where is a safe place for Jerry to play?
Children: ________________
Teacher: *(Turn "Safe" card right side up.)*
Teacher: *(Picture 4)* Tony trained his big dog. Now his dog lies down so Tony's friends can pet him. His dog runs after sticks and brings them back to Tony and his friends. Is it safe to play with Tony and his trained dog? *(There may be disagreement about the safety. Guide children to understand that if you play gently with the collie it should be safe. Children who fear big dogs may not be relieved.)*
Children: ________________
Teacher: *(Ask one child to hand you the card that says "Safe".)* Is it a good idea or not a good idea to have fun with Tony's trained collie dog?
Children: ________________
Teacher: Let's listen to a song called "Helping." *(Play "Helping" tape from Marlo Thomas' record,* Free to Be You and Me.)
Teacher: You be copy cats. Agatha Fry, she made a pie.* *(Continue through song, gesturing appropriately. At end, give signal to stop copy cat.)*
Teacher: Agatha Fry made a pie. Christopher John helped bake it. Christopher John wanted a piece. What did he do so he could have a piece of pie?
Children: ________________
Teacher: Was it a good idea or not a good idea to help Agatha bake the pie?
Children: ________________
Teacher: His plan was a good idea because it helped him get what he wanted. Agatha Fry wanted to play with Christopher John, but Christopher John had to mow the lawn. What plan did Agatha Fry use so Christopher John could play with her?
Children: ________________
Teacher: What might happen when Agatha Fry and Christopher John finish working on the lawn?
Children: ________________
Teacher: Is it a good idea or not a good idea to help Christopher John rake the lawn?
Children: ________________
Teacher: It was a good idea because it helped Agatha get what she wanted: her plan worked. Jennifer Joy wanted to be Zachary's friend. Zachary had to clean the rug, so what did Jennifer Joy do next? *(Hint with shaking rug motion, if necessary.)*
Children: ________________

Teacher: Is it a good idea or not for Jennifer to help Zachary? Why?
Children: ______________________
Teacher: Jennifer Joy made a toy for her friend Zachary. What did Zachary do next?
Children: ______________________
Teacher: Was it a good idea for Zachary to break the toy?
Children: ______________________
Teacher: *(Turn upside down whichever cue card children refer to.)* Will Jennifer Joy be friends with Zachary since he broke her toy?
Children: ______________________
Teacher: What's something different Zachary could do so Jennifer will be his friend?
Children: ______________________
Teacher: You be copy cats *(Memorize last two verses, then play tape one time through.)*
Teacher: Now we have four ways to help us decide if our plans are good ideas or not. What are the four things we can think about to judge our plans?
Children: ______________________
Teacher: *(Elicit self-evaluation in terms of listening, thinking what is a good idea or not a good idea, and learning.)*

To emphasize the evaluation process even further for aggressive children, an entire lesson was devloped to deal with "fairness." Our observations suggested that concern over what is or is not fair constitutes a major preoccupation of school-aged children. The fairness lesson attempted to deal with these feelings directly. It is recognized that the following dialogue does not include evaluation of fairness on the basis of higher order concepts of justice or rules made for the common good. However, it is expected that older children would be able to develop their own list of alternative ways of evaluating outcomes and to recognize concepts of social order and justice in evaluating fairness.

Day 13 Social 7: Fairness

(Use mounted Rosenzweig P–F pictures and Dragon and Wolf puppets.)

Teacher: Today we are going to talk about fairness. Let's look at this picture. *(Show # RPF 1—scooter.)*
Teacher: This boy took the girl's scooter away from her. Was that a fair thing for him to do?
Children: ______________________
Teacher: Why not?
Children: ______________________

Teacher: What is the problem? What does the boy want to do?
Children: ____________________
Teacher: What could he say or do that would be fair so he can ride the scooter?
Children: ____________________
Teacher: Why would that be fair?
Children: ____________________
Teacher: How does the girl feel *(least verbal child)?*
Child: ____________________
Teacher: Is that fair?
Child: ____________________
Teacher: Let's pretend that *(one child's name)* has Wally *(hand wolf puppet to less demanding child. This action will no doubt provoke a spontaneous social situation that should be dealt with.)* And I have Dilly. You have this toy that Dilly wants. So Dilly grabs it. *(Use Dilly to grab at Wally.)* Is that fair?
Children: ____________________
Teacher: Why not?
Children: ____________________
Teacher: What does Dilly want?
Children: ____________________
Teacher: *(Hand Dilly to non-involved child.)* __________, Tell Dilly something he could do or say to Wally that would be fair.
Child: ____________________
Teacher: *(Put puppets away.)* Let's look at another picture. *(Show RPF #2—boys with toy soldiers.)* Pretend this boy, Peter, has four soldiers and this boy, Jack, has two soldiers and a cannon. Pretend that Peter wants the cannon. Is it fair for him to take it away from the other boy?
Children: ____________________
Teacher: *(If "no" is given)* __________, what does Peter want?
Child: ____________________
Teacher: What would be a fair thing he could do or say?
Children: ____________________
Teacher: *(Show RPF #3—father buying doll for girl.)* Father says, "Sally, I'll buy that doll for you since you were my helper today." Is that a fair thing for Father to say?
Children: ____________________
Teacher: *(If yes)* Why? *(If child says it is not fair, ask:)* Why not? and what would be a fair thing for him to say or do?
Children: ____________________
Teacher: *(If yes)* Why? *(If child says it is not fair, ask:)* Why not? What would be a fair thing for him to say or do?

are borderline in their development of verbal mediation skills and who may use the "Think Aloud" experience to develop and consolidate their skill in commanding and directing their own behavior toward personally and socially constructive goals.

References

Achenbach, T. M. 1975. A longitudinal study of relations between associative responding, IQ changes, and school performance from grades 3 to 12. *Developmental Psychology, 11,* 653-54.

Camp, B. W. 1976. Stability of behavior ratings. *Perceptual and Motor Skills, 43,* 1065-66.

Camp, B. W. 1977. Verbal mediation in young aggressive boys. *Journal of Abnormal Psychology, 86,* 145-53.

Camp, B. W. 1976. Problems in research with The Think Aloud Program. Paper presented at the Second National Conference on Cognitive Behavior Therapy Research, New York, New York, Oct. 1976.

Camp, B. W. In press. Two psychoeducational training programs for aggressive boys. *Hyperactive Children: The social ecology of identification and treatment,* ed. C. Whalen and B. Henker. New York: Academic Press.

Camp, B. W. and Bash, M. A. 1978a. The classroom "Think Aloud" program. Paper presented at the American Psychological Association Convention, Toronto, Canada, August, 1978.

Camp, B. W. and Bash, M.A. 1978b. Think aloud: Group manual (Revised). Denver, Colorado: University of Colorado Medical School, November, 1978.

Camp, B.W., Blom, G. E., Herbert, F., and Van Doorninck, W. J. 1977. "Think Aloud": A program for developing self-control in young aggressive boys. *Journal of Abnormal Child Psychology, 5,* 157-69.

Camp, B. W., Zimet, S. G., Van Doorninck, W. J., and Dahlem, N. W. 1977. Verbal abilities in young aggressive boys. *Journal of Educational Psychology, 69,* 129-35.

Hetherington, E. M. and McIntyre, C. W. 1975. Developmental psychology. *Annual Review of Psychology, 26,* 97-136.

Jensen, A. R. 1966. Verbal mediation and educational potential. *Psychology in the Schools, 3,* 99-109.

Kohlberg, L., LaCrosse, J., and Ricks, D. 1972. The predictability of adult mental health from childhood behavior. In *Manual of Child Psychopathology,* ed. B. B. Wolman. New York: McGraw-Hill.

Loevinger, J. 1976. *Ego development.* San Francisco, Jossey-Bass.

Maier, N. R. F. 1963. *Problem-solving discussions and conferences.* San Francisco: McGraw-Hill.

Meichenbaum, D. 1975. Theoretical and treatment implications of developmental research on verbal control of behavior. *Psychologie Canadienne/Canadian Psychological Review, 16,* 22-27.

Meichenbaum, D., and Goodman, J. 1971. Training impulsive children to talk to themselves: A means of developing self-control. *Journal of Abnormal Psychology, 77,* 115-26.

Miller, L. C. 1974. School behavior check list: An inventory of deviant behavior for elementary school children. *Journal of Consulting and Clinical Psychology, 15,* 169-77.

Palkes, H., Stewart, M., and Kahana, B. 1968. Porteus maze performance of hyperactive boys after training in self-directed verbal commands. *Child Development, 39,* 817-26.

Prentice, N. and Kelly, F. J. 1963. Intelligence and delinquency: A reconsideration. *Journal of Social Psychology, 60,* 327-37.

Razran, G. 1961. The observable unconscious and the inferrable conscious in current Soviet psychophysiology: Intereoceptive conditioning, semantic conditioning and the orienting reflex. *Psychological Review, 68,* 81-147.

Shure, M. B. and Spivack, G. 1974. A mental health program for kindergarten children: A cognitive approach to solving inter-personal problems. Philadelphia: Community Mental Health/Mental Retardation Center, Department of Mental Health Sciences, Hahnemann Medical College and Hospital.

Vygotsky, L. F. 1962. *Thought and language.* Cambridge, Mass.: M.I.T. Press.

Watson, D. L. and Hall, D. L. 1977. Self-control of hyperactivity. La Mesa, California: Pupil Services Division, La Mesa-Spring Valley School District.

White, S. H. 1970. Some general outlines of the matrix of developmental changes between five and seven years. *Bulletin of the Orton Society, 20,* 41-57.

1974; Spivack, Platt, and Shure, 1976; Shure, 1979). And this was true of boys whose mothers may have given them the same advice as mothers of girls (Shure and Spivack, 1978b). We also found that adjusted children can think of forceful ways to obtain a toy as well as the poorly adjusted, but could also think of more nonforceful ways. So the idea is not to take away from poor adjusters what they already know, but to help them to think about what they can do and then to discover that there's more than one way.

In thinking of alternative solutions, the question is whether a child can generate in his own mind different ways to solve a problem. If a girl asks her sister to let her play with her doll and her sister says no, can she think of other ways to get her sister to let her play with it? If she can think of only one or two ways, she might soon become frustrated. This could lead her to react aggressively, or she might avoid the problem entirely by withdrawing, behavior which could become more frequent if problem after problem remains unresolved.

This girl might hit her sister, not as an impulsive reaction to frustration, but after deciding that hitting is one way to get it. If this is the case, the new question is whether she also thought about the potential consequences of her hitting and whether that might have influenced her decision to hit. She might have foreseen that her sister could hit her back and not let it concern her. She may go ahead and do it anyway. Perhaps she can not think of anything else to do.

It is possible that inhibited youngsters experience failure so often that they need to withdraw from other children and from problems they cannot solve. In any case, they have no need to think about what to do. Other than watching or playing by themselves, they rarely do anything at all.

We do know that good problem solvers are better adjusted than poor ones, and we believe it's because they experience less frustration. They are more likely to succeed because if their first option fails, they can turn to a different, more effective one and when they cannot have what they want, they can handle the frustration by thinking of other ways to deal with their feelings or satisfy their desires. Not only are such children less nagging and demanding on adults, but adults are less nagging and demanding on them. They do not need to be told what to do. They can think for themselves.

Ability to conceptualize alternative solutions was measured by what we call the Preschool Interpersonal Problem Solving, or PIPS Test (Shure and Spivack 1974).

Children were given two problems: (1) how to get to play with a toy another child has, and (2) how to keep mother from being angry after having broken something of value to her. The idea was to elicit as many solutions as the child could think of to each problem. Before training, young children are not used to giving more than one answer to the same question, so we switched toys and child characters after one relevant solution was given. To the child it was a different story, but to us it was asking for a new solution to the same problem. The same procedure was done with the mother-problem type. To the mother problem, most responses include "fix it," "get her a new one," "say I'm sorry." My favorite solution is, "Get her mommy a drink and she'll feel better."

Consequential thinking was measured by using the same technique as the PIPS Test. For example, the child was shown stick figures of two children, a picture of a toy, and then told, "Johnny just grabbed this toy from Jim." The child was then asked, "What might happen next?" or, if necessary, "What might Jim do or say when John grabs the toy from him?" After one relevant consequence, the characters and toys were replaced by new ones and the procedure repeated. A second group of stories depicted character children taking something from an adult without asking first (Shure and Spivack 1975a).

To test the mediational effects of interpersonal cognitive problem-solving (ICPS) skills on adjustment, we experimentally altered these skills through training, and then observed changes in the degree to which the child displayed specific aspects of impulsivity or inhibition in the classroom. Children are reinforced for thinking of different ideas, not for having stated a "good one." They are praised for thinking about "what might happen next," not for verbalizing the "right" answer. In problem-solving techniques of training, the important thing is not what the child thinks, but that he thinks.

To achieve this level, the child must first master certain language and cognition skills, and then be taught how to use them in solving real interpersonal problems.

First I will give some highlights of how we trained mothers to work with their child at home. The program script (in Shure and Spivack, 1978b) is a modification of earlier ICPS curricula developed for use by teachers of four-year-olds (Shure and Spivack, 1971; also in Spivack and Shure, 1974), and of kindergarten youngsters (Shure and Spivack, 1978a).

The Training Program

Just as Roeper and Sigel (1967) could successfully train four-year-olds to conserve by first teaching them the individual components of the conservation tasks (such as simple demonstrations of reversibility), we included in our formal lessons concepts we judged to be prerequisite to the final problem solving skill to be learned. The early games consisted of basic word concepts needed to establish an association for their later use in problem solving.

Thinking about the negation through use of the word "not" becomes important in order that a child can later decide what and what *not* to do, and whether something is or is *not* a good idea. With the games centered on people and interpersonal relations, one game the mother played was to say, "Tommy *is* a boy. Tommy is *not* a girl. Let's think of lots of things Tommy is *not.*" Then the mother asked her child to tell what he is and lots of things he is not. The word "or" was taught so that the child could later think, "I can do this *or* I can do that."

Associations with the words "same" and "different" were important so that the child could think of different ideas and different things that "might happen if . . . ." The child could also learn to recognize that, for example, "hitting and kicking" are the same idea because they are both "hurting." The words "same" and "different" were first taught by encouraging the child to do the same thing the mother was doing (rolling her hands), then something different (such as patting her head). While many of the children may understand these concepts, their constant repetition in the early games helped to establish their use within the framework of interpersonal relations. Unlike language programs per se, these words were not taught as an end in themselves, but rather to set the stage for their role in problem-solving thinking.

Once words were identified that designate people's feelings, "happy," "sad," "angry," it was possible to teach that people have feelings and that feelings change. Games were devised to find out how people feel. In addition to later recognition that different people can feel different ways about the same thing, sensitivity to the preferences of others is also important in deciding what to do. This kind of perspective taking, sometimes called role taking, would help a child who wants a toy from his friend to think about what would please that friend, and what would not. The child learns that different people can like different things, and that that is O.K. He learns that he can think about what people like and how they feel by watching what they do, hearing what they say, or by simply asking them.

The idea that everybody does not choose the same thing is important, in that many young children frequently assume others would choose what they would like. This exercise used pictures of foods, forms of transportation, animals, or places to be. The child was first asked what he or she would choose if given the choice of playing in the park or being sick in bed. Then the child was asked what he or she thought another child might choose. Some chose being sick in bed because "Mommy brings me presents." In problem solving, it is important to find out things about another person, and the child was always asked, "How can you find out?" If no other child was present, the mother picked up a family face puppet and in the voice of the puppet character said, "Which one do you think I would choose? How can you find out?" To emphasize the necessity of finding out, the puppet character always chose the opposite if the child made an assumption about his choice. If the child said, "the cat," the puppet would say, "I would chose the dog. See, you had to find out."

These games were followed by emphasis on "why-because" and on "might-maybe" through use of pictures, puppets, and simple role-playing techniques. A picture is shown of a girl crying and the mother says, "How is this girl feeling?" After the child says, "sad," the mother follows with, "She might be sad because...." Pointing to another child in the picture, the mother asks, "What can this boy do to make her feel happy again?" When the child answers, she says, "That might make her happy. Can you think of something different he can do?" For this and all other materials, we used commercial pictures—any appropriate materials can be used.

After having mastered the word concepts and pre-problem-solving thinking skills, the children were ready for the games and dialogues that teach interpersonal problem-solving thinking.

For example, a picture was shown depicting a girl feeding animals, and a boy looking on. Although no problem was inherent in the picture, we made one up. The child was told that the boy wants the girl to let him feed the animals, but she will not let him. The mother then asked, "What can the boy do so the girl will let him feed the animals?" After the child offered an idea, such as "ask her," or "push her," the mother would follow with, "That's one way. Can you think of something different he could say or do?" Not only were forceful solutions such as "push her out of the way," "hit her," or "snatch the food" probed for new ideas, so too were non-forceful ones.

When the child ran out of ideas, the mother would pick up the puppet and say: "I wish I could think of an idea. Can you help me?" But neither the mother nor her puppet character suggested any solutions. If necessary for a nonresponder, the mother would give the child a chance to be the puppet.

To encourage consequential thinking, the child was also guided to think about "what might happen next" if the child's suggestion should be carried out. If needed, the child was guided with a more specific question, such as, "What might the other child *do* if . . . ," or "What might the other child say?" All solutions were evaluated *by the child* in the same way regardless of content. With the tools the child now has, he or she can decide whether an act is or is not a good idea because of what might happen next.

The total length of training was 10 weeks, and the mothers met with us weekly to learn the games and techniques.

In addition to formal training, mothers were taught how to use our approach when real problems arose. Four-year-old James asked his friend John to give him his truck back. John said "No, I'm still playing with it." He had been playing with it a long time, and James, angry and frustrated, tried to grab it. Before training, mothers are often just as preoccupied with their needs as their child is with his. James' mother, for example, handled the grabbing problem this way:

M: Why did you snatch that truck from John?
C: 'Cause it's my turn!
M: Give it back, James.
C: I don't want to. It's mine.
M: Why don't you play with your cars?
C: I want my firetruck!
M: You should either play together or take turns. Grabbing is not nice.
C: But I want my truck now!
M: Children must learn to share. John will get mad and he won't be your friend.
C: But, Mom, he won't give it to me!
M: You can't go around grabbing things. Would you like it if he did that to you?
C: No.
M: Tell him you're sorry. (Shure and Spivack, 1978b, p.32)

While this mother did "explain" consequences to her child, nothing was communicated that would teach her child how to think. Preoccupied with teaching her child to share, she did the thinking for him. When she asked James why he snatched the truck from John, she might have followed up on what he said to find out more about the problem. But she probably would have told him to give it back no matter how James answered her question. She was thinking about what was important to her, not what was important to him. Parents often complain that their child doesn't listen to them, but how often do children feel the same way about their parents?

Here is how a mother handled a problem similar to that of James, after training. We call the technique "problem-solving dialoguing." Ralph grabbed a racing car from his friend.

M: What happened? What's the matter?
C: He's got my racing car. He won't give it back.
M: Why do you have to have it back now?
C: 'Cause he's had a long turn. (Shure and Spivack, 1978b, p. 36)

In eliciting the child's point of view, this mother learned something that she would not have learned possible had she simply demanded that he share. She learned that, in fact, her son had shared his toy. The nature of the problem now appeared different.

M: How do you think your friend feels when you grab toys?
C: Mad, but I don't care. It's mine!
M: What did your friend do when you grabbed the toy?
C: He hit me. But I want my toy!
M: How did that make you feel?
C: Mad.

M: You're mad and your friend is mad, and he hit you. Can you think of a different way to get your toy back so you both won't be mad and so he won't hit you? (Shure and Spivack, 1978b, pp. 36-37)

What Ralph would say at this point is not the critical issue. What is critical is that in such dialoguing Ralph is guided to think about the problem, and what happened when he acted as he did. This mother focused on the child's view of the problem—wanting his toy back. She avoided imposing her view, or disapproval, of his act of grabbing.

The words are not enough. It's the whole approach. The child needs to be guided in how to think about a problem, and it does take time, patience, and warmth. This is not to say that parents should never get angry with a child. Anger is a problem in itself with which a child has to learn to cope, if he is encouraged to think that way to begin with, and if anger and emotional outbursts are not the predominant forms of dealing with the child.

When teachers used this problem-solving approach with inner-city four-year-olds in day care, children improved significantly in both thinking skills and behavioral adjustment, and most importantly, a direct link was established (Shure and Spivack, 1980). Children who most improved in their skills, especially in finding an alternative solution, and to a lesser extent in consequential thinking, were the same children who most improved in social adjustment. Changes were not related to initial IQ or IQ change, suggesting that children within a wide IQ range (70-120+) were able to benefit. This added support to our position that these ICPS skills function as significant mediators of social adjustment. And following through kindergarten and first grade, the positive effects of training lasted at least two years. Not only did initially aberrant children who became adjusted tend to stay that way, but those who were adjusted to begin with were more likely to stay that way than control children never exposed to training. This is very exciting, because it means that the program has preventive effects as well as the ability to help children who already display varying degrees of aberrance (Shure and Spivack 1975b; 1979). The need for such programming is evident when we saw that the percentage of children judged to be adjusted steadily declined from the beginning of nursery to the end of first grade, and George Spivack and Marshall Swift (1977) have further data suggesting some behaviors in adjusted children regress still further by the end of third grade in typical inner-city settings. In more seriously disturbed youngsters, Zax and Cowen (1976), reporting on the Rochester Primary Mental Health Project, noted that children with early identified dysfunctions, left untreated, did poorly in the first few years and were already quite impaired by the third grade.

Earlier I mentioned that we found the extent to which mothers explained consequences, made suggestions, and showed their child how to do things relates to their daughters' behaviors. We also discovered that these techniques related to ICPS skills in girls, and it was these thinking skills that turned out to be the most significant mediators of adjustment. In boys, ICPS skills also relate to their behavior, and they were no less efficient in their thinking skills than girls. It was the relationships between mothers' handling of problems and children's ICPS skills that occurred only for girls. This happened in two separate studies (Spivack and Shure 1975; Shure and Spivack, 1978b). What all this amounts to is that boys and girls have about the same level of thinking skills, and in both sexes these skills play a key role in their behavior. We saw this in the teacher-training studies from the direct link. However, while girls appeared to learn these skills from their mothers, we do not know exactly where our fatherless boys learned them.

A mother's child-rearing style includes more than methods of discipline. If, for example, a mother told her child she would talk to the teacher about the child being hit, her response was scored just as low as a spanking for misbehavior with no explanation. In both cases, the mother does not bring the child into the process of thinking through the problem or about what he did. To us, if a mother tells her child to hit back, or not to hit back but to tell the teacher instead, she may be giving different advice, but she is using the same approach; she is thinking for the child. If the child says he is afraid to hit back, or that if he tells the teacher, his friend will get after him, parents may still insist because they are trying to teach the child what they think is best from their point of view. It often happens that the child does not have to think further about what to do, only about how to do it. Before training, very few parents asked their child for his or her ideas about how to solve the problem or what might happen as a result of what was done.

When children were trained by their mothers, they improved in both ICPS skills and behavior relative to controls. However, improvement in the solution skills of impulsive youngsters was not as great as it was when children were trained by their teachers. Because we recognized that these mothers may not have understood the rationale behind the "dialoguing" and that many were relatively deficient in their thinking skills, we decided to add a new dimension to the mothers' training. A second group of mothers was given ICPS training of their own. At strategic points throughout the script, we inserted exercises for parents. When a mother was helping her child consider his own and others' feelings and the effects of his actions on others, the mother was also encouraged to think about feelings and how her actions affect others, including her child. For example, a mother told the group what her child does that might make her angry, then what she does that might make her child feel the same way. She was asked to think about how she can tell how her child feels, other than by seeing he is crying or laughing. Group discussion included questions such as: "Can you think of an example when your child said something that made you aware he was feeling a different way than you thought? What happened? Why did you think that?"

As the mother guided her child to think of solutions to problems relevant to him, she also thought of solutions to problems relevant to herself, particularly when a child would create a problem for her. Thus parents learned ICPS skills of their own and learned to guide their children to think through and solve actual problems that arise during a typical day. For the child, the goals were the same as in the teacher-training studies. For mothers, the goals were: (1) to increase awareness that the child's point of view may differ from her own; (2) to discover that there is more than one way to solve a problem; (3) to discover that thinking about what is happening is, in the long run, more beneficial than immediate action to stop it; and (4) to provide a model of problem-solving thinking. A thinking parent might inspire a child to think.

Children often want their mother's attention at inconvenient times. Typical is wanting a story read. When a mother says, "I'm busy, you'll have to wait," or explains what she is doing, or even suggests an alternative activity, she is thinking only of her point of view—mainly to get the child out of her hair. The child may nag and demand, and a power play begins. In recognizing the child's point of view, the mother can help the child see hers as well. If, for example, she is on the phone, she can follow with: "If I stop talking to my friend, how will she feel?" After the child answers, the mother can say, "Can you think of something different to do now until I'm finished talking on the phone?" A child who thinks of his or her own idea is less likely to resist.

Mothers' improved ability to solve hypothetical adult problems (such as how to keep a friend from being angry after showing up too late to go to a movie) did *not* relate to her child's improved ICPS skills, but her ability to solve hypothetical problems about children (or about children and their parents) did. Mothers who could learn to think of sequenced steps to reach a hypothetical goal, who could see potential obstacles (that problem solving is not always smooth sailing), and who tended to perceive a story child as able to contribute to the resolution of a problem, were also most likely to apply problem-solving dialoguing with their child when real problems would arise, partly because they could now understand and accept their child's point of view. Together, these new skills affected the child's ability to solve problems. The findings suggest that a mother's improved thinking ability and childrearing style contribute significantly to the child's ICPS skills, yet covariance analyses suggested it was still the child's ICPS skills that functioned as the most significant direct mediator of his or her behavior.

The present group of mother-trained youngsters increased in solution thinking significantly more than the previous group trained by mothers not receiving systematic ICPS training. While both of these mother-trained groups improved more than controls, these findings suggest that greater impact on the child occurs when the mother as well as the child are taught how to think (Shure and Spivack 1977; 1978b).

Over the two-year period, 40 mothers have demonstrated they can successfully apply the ICPS program script with their children. The 20 mothers in the final study have given us information that may explain why boys as well as girls benefit from this kind of intervention at home (at pretest, relationships were for girls only). Trained mothers acquire thinking skills above and beyond those which even the best problem solvers could exhibit initially. Before training, better problem solvers tend to offer suggestions to the child about what he should do, and perhaps explain why. For whatever reason girls pick up on what their mothers say; ICPS thinking of boys and girls are affected in a similar way when the children are guided to think for themselves, and when the mother understands these objectives.

Importantly, children exposed to ICPS programming at home improve their behavior as observed in school, an environment different from that in which training took place. We believe this happens because children learn how to think and can generalize their skills to more than one situation. That ICPS and behavior change in children trained by their mothers were so similar to those trained by their teachers is particularly encouraging. It is important to know that inner-city mothers, many of whose thinking skills were deficient at the start, could improve not only their abilities but also the abilities of their child in only three months time.

A question asked of the research is whether behavior really changes because of the child's improvement in ICPS skills, or possibly because of special attention given to them by their mothers. We believe it is the former because the findings are logical and consistent. Linkages between thought change and behavior change emerge only with processes shown to correlate prior to training. Whether children are trained at school (by their teachers) or at home (by their mothers), alternative-solution thinking is the most strongly related to impulsive and inhibited behaviors before training, most receptive to change after it, and most significantly related to change in parenting skills. Improvement in a child's solution skills related to change in the mother's ability to think about problems relevant to him, not in problems only relevant to her. Consequential thinking, though not as dramatic, showed similar consistency. Finally, improvement was in skills emphasized in training, not in those that were not. Such consistency was not found with other measured behaviors and other measured thinking skills. If improvements were due to mere attention, the obtained relationships and change in thinking skills would have been random. A placebo-attention group in the teacher-training studies confirmed our notion that attention groups do not change ICPS skills or behavior in the same way as does ICPS training (Shure, Spivack and Gordon 1972).

Of course, we are making no claim that ICPS skills are the only mediators of behavior. Emotions can block out any attempt to think at any given moment. Other interpersonal thinking skills may also play a role in the child's behavior. Role taking, for example, relates to behavior, though we have just learned that in four-year-olds, that means being able to identify emotions, an ability that enriches the more powerful mediator, solution thinking. At this age, this makes sense: knowing how someone feels does not guarantee the child will then know what to do about it. One question is how much role taking in older children, who are capable of higher stages of perceiving perspectives different from their own, plays a part in behavior relative to ICPS skills. Or, are our mothers deficient in problem solving skills more deficient because their perspective-taking skills are less advanced than better problem solvers, as Selman and Jaquette (1977) might predict?

We have also learned by interviews with both mothers and fathers of children 6–16 that parents of older children talk to them in very much the same style as do our inner-city mothers of four-year-olds, and how unusual the problem solving approach is. The content of particular problems and what parents do or say may differ, but the extent to which a parent encourages the child to think does not change because a child gets older or because he is a member of the middle class.

While we found that kindergarten children can benefit from ICPS training in about the same amount of time as can four-year-olds (Shure and Spivack, 1979), this kind of training for still older children may take a little longer. In a program combining role taking and ICPS training for fourth- and fifth-graders, Elardo and Caldwell (1979) were able to decrease impatience, and increase respect and concern for others, willingness to share experiences with the group, and self-control. These and other behavior changes occurred, however, only after the program script (Elardo and Cooper, 1977) was fully incorporated into the school curriculum for the entire year, and the teachers consistently applied the approach (through informal follow-up dialogue techniques) when real problems arose (Elardo and Caldwell, in preparation). Others have found obstreperous behaviors like classroom disruptiveness to be slower to change, as Larcen (in Allen, et al., 1976) has discovered. Ellis Gesten and his colleagues (1979), and Mary Rotheram (this volume) have been applying ICPS training with elementary school-age children and have suggestions for optimal training for children after the age of five.

In addition to applying the ICPS approach to relatively normal youngsters, our kindergarten curriculum has been used with varying degrees of success with retarded-educable children 6-12 years of age (Healey, 1977), and in combination with Meichenbaum and Goodman's (1971) self-instructional techniques, it has been implemented with hyperaggressive youngsters (Camp and Bash, 1975; 1978; this volume). Further discussion of the ICPS approach with older children is presented in Shure, in press b.

Clearly, there are implications here for training other members of *any* family, if that could be possible. With the help and encouragement of Marshall Swift, Director of Part F and Consultation and Education at the Hahnemann Community Mental Health/Mental Retardation Center, wc were able to train staff to work with mothers (Shure, 1976). In one of the sessions, an interesting story was told. A child cracked a car window while trying to open it. The mother told a trainee that her husband was amazed that she was dialoguing with their daughter (age 4) about the problem, and that the child was offering solutions. Before, the father would have yelled, the daughter would have cried, and there would have been silence during the rest of the trip.

From what we have learned, the mediating effects of ICPS skills on children's behavior, and out findings that impact is heightened when both the mother and child are taught how to think, have clear implications for the problem-solving approach, and optimal mental health programming for parents and their young children.

References

Allen, G., Chinsky, J., Larcen, S., Lochman, J., and Selinger, H. 1976. *Community psychology and the schools: a behaviorally oriented multilevel preventive approach.* Hillsdale, N. J.: Earlbaum.

Baumrind, D. 1971. Current patterns of parental authority. *Developmental Psychology Monograph,* (No. 4).

Camp, B. N., and Bash, M. A. 1975. *Think aloud program group manual.* Denver: University of Colorado Medical Center.

Camp, B. N., and Bash, M. A. August 1978. The classroom "think aloud" program. Presented at the meeting of the American Psychological Association, Toronto.

Elardo, P. T., and Caldwell, B. M. 1979. The effects of an experimental social development program on children in the middle childhood period. *Psychology in the schools, 16,* 93-100.

Elardo, P. T., and Caldwell, B. M. In preparation. Project Aware: A school program to facilitate the social development of kindergarten-elementary children. Little Rock: University of Arkansas.

Elardo, P. T., and Cooper, M. 1977. *Project Aware: a handbook for teachers.* Reading, Mass.: Addison-Wesley.

Gesten, E. L., Flores De Apodaca, R., Rains, M., Weissberg, R. P., and Cowen, E. L. 1979. Promoting peer-related social competence in schools. In *The primary prevention of psychopathology,* ed. M. W. Kent and J. E. Rolf, Vol. 3: *Promoting social competence and coping in children.* Hanover, N. H.: University Press of New England.

Healey, K. 1977. An investigation of the relationship between certain social cognitive abilities and social behavior, and the efficacy of training in social cognitive skills for elementary retarded-educable children. Unpublished doctoral dissertation, Bryn Mawr College.

Hoffman, M. L. 1963. Parent discipline and the child's consideration for others. *Child Development, 34,* 573-88.

Hoffman, M. L. 1971. Father-absence and conscience development. *Developmental Psychology, 4,* 400-406.

Hoffman, M. L. and Saltzstein, H. D. 1967. Parent discipline and the child's moral development. *Journal of Personality and Social Psychology, 5,* 45-57.

Meichenbaum, D. H., and Goodman, J. 1971. Training impulsive children to talk to themselves: A means of developing self control. *Journal of Abnormal Psychology, 77,* 115-26.

Roeper, A., and Sigel, I. E. 1967. Finding the clue to children's thought processes. In *The young child,* ed. W. Hartup and N. Smothergill Washington, D.C.: National Association for the Education of Young Children.

Sears, R. R., Macoby, E. E., and Levin, H. 1957. *Patterns of childrearing.* Evanston, Ill.: Row, Peterson.

Selman, R. L., and Jaquette, D. 1977. Stability and oscillation in interpersonal awareness: A clinical-developmental analysis. In *The XXV Nebraska symposium on motivation,* ed. C. B. Keasy. Lincoln: University of Nebraska Press.

Shure, M. B. 1976. Staff training in a preventive mental health program. Research and Evaluation Report No. 47 and Consultation and Education Report No. 11. Philadelphia: Department of Mental Health Sciences, Hahnemann Community Mental Health/Mental Retardation Center.

Shure, M. B. 1979. Training children to solve interpersonal problems: A preventive mental health program. In *Social and psychological research in community settings: designing and conducting programs for social and personal well-being,* ed. R. F. Munoz, L. R. Snowden, and J. G. Kelly. San Francisco: Jossey-Bass.

Shure, M. B. In press a. Childrearing and social competence. In *Handbook of social skills,* ed. M. Argyle. London: Methuen.

Shure, M. B. In press b. Social competence as a problem solving skill. In *Identification and enhancement of social competence,* ed. J. D. Wine and M. Smye. New York: Guilford Press.

Shure, M. B., Newman, S., and Silver, S. May 1973. Problem-solving thinking among adjusted, impulsive and inhibited Head Start children. Paper presented at the meeting of the Eastern Psychological Association, Washington, D.C.

Shure, M. B., and Spivack, G. 1971. *Solving interpersonal problems: a program for four-year-old nursery school children: training script.* Philadelphia: Department of Mental Health Sciences, Hahnemann Community Mental Health/Mental Retardation Center.

Shure, M. B. and Spivack, G. 1974. *Preschool interpersonal problem-solving (PIPS) test: manual.* Philadelphia: Department of Mental Health Sciences, Hahnemann Community Mental Health/Mental Retardation Center.

Shure, M. B. and Spivack, G. 1975a. *A mental health program for preschool and kindergarten children, and a mental health program for mothers of young children: an interpersonal problem solving approach toward social adjustment.* A Comprehensive Report of Research and Training. No. MH-20372. Washington, D.C.: National Institute of Mental Health.

Shure, M. B., and Spivack, G. August 1975b. Interpersonal cognitive problem solving intervention: The second (kindergarten) year. Paper presented at the meeting of the American Psychological Association, Chicago.

Shure, M. B., and Spivack, G. March 1977. Interpersonal problem solving intervention for mother and child. Paper presented at the meeting of the Society for Research in Child Development, New Orleans.

Shure, M. B., and Spivack, G. 1978a. *A mental health program for kindergarten children: training script.* Philadelphia: Department of Mental Health Sciences, Hahnemann Community Mental Health/Mental Retardation Center. Revised Edition.

Shure, M. B., and Spivack, G. 1978b. *Problem solving techniques in childrearing.* San Francisco: Jossey-Bass.

Shure, M. B., and Spivack, G. 1979. Interpersonal cognitive problem solving and primary prevention: Programming for preschool and kindergarten children. *Journal of Clinical Child Psychology, 2,* 89-94.

Shure, M. B., and Spivack, G. 1980. Interpersonal problem solving as a mediator of behavioral adjustment in preschool and kindergarten children. *Journal of Applied Developmental Psychology, 1,* 29-43.

Shure, M. B., Spivack, G., and Gordon, R. 1972. Problem-solving thinking: A preventive mental health program for preschool children. *Reading World, 11,* 259-73.

Slaby, D. A. 1976. Day treatment and parent training programs. Seattle: Department of Behavioral Sciences, Children's Orthopedic Hospital and Medical Center.

Spivack, G., Platt, J. J., and Shure, M. B. 1976. *The problem solving approach to adjustment: a guide to research and intervention.* San Francisco: Jossey-Bass.

Spivack, G., and Shure, M. B. 1974. *Social adjustment of young children: a cognitive approach to solving real-life problems.* San Francisco: Jossey-Bass.

Spivack, G., and Shure, M. B. April 1975. Maternal childrearing and the interpersonal cognitive problem-solving ability of four-year-olds. Paper presented at the meeting of the Society for Research in Child Development, Denver.

Spivack, G., and Swift, M. 1977. "High Risk" classroom behaviors in kindergarten and first grade. *American Journal of Community Psychology, 5,* 385-97.

Zax, M., and Cowen, E. L. 1976. *Abnormal psychology: changing conceptions,* 2nd ed. New York: Holt, Rinehart and Winston.

4

Social Skills Training Programs in Elementary and High School Classrooms

Mary Jane Rotheram

Daily, children and adolescents are faced with problem situations that demand assertiveness and sophisticated interpersonal skills. A teacher mistakenly reprimands the wrong child for talking and disrupting the class. What and how does the innocent victim respond? Perhaps an adolescent girl wants to ask a boy in class for a date. How does she approach him? Should she say she likes him, or is that pushy? And what is the response likely to be? How do adolescents convince an employer that they are the best for a job? Do they try to sell themselves or to be honest about past inexperience? How can they stop being nervous?

These situations raise monumental problems for children lacking the skills and self-confidence to act assertively. In a manner similar to adults, children must be able to decide what they want from others and to communicate their needs clearly. They should know when to say "no" to friends, family, and classmates. Those who cannot assert themselves often develop one of two patterns. Children who cannot ask for themselves will often begin to shrink from the world, feeling that others do not give to them because they are not worth caring for. Children believe that if people really cared, they would know what they want. As they withdraw, their ability to talk with others decreases even more. A cycle of decreasing self-esteem and competence is started. Teachers and parents are generally satisfied at such an undemanding relationship.

In contrast, a second group of children learns that the world must satisfy their needs and demands immediate compliance. While children do not get everything, at least they win occasionally. Teachers dread aggressive children and jump to put them in their rightful places through heavy punishment. The children's fears are reinforced. Unless they push, they will never be heard. Such maladaptive behavior patterns are reflections of typical negative spirals established early in childhood. These patterns will be crucial to the children's life satisfaction, self-worth, and school adjustment (Spivak, Platt and Shure 1976), and even academic competence (Rotheram, Armstrong, and Booraem 1978).

The present program is a cognitive behavioral model used to teach social skills to young children and adolescents in the classroom. With these skills, children learn to assert themselves with others. The goal of the program is to increase the child's freedom in dealing with others. The child is taught to be aware of what is happening inside himself and to evaluate how people in the environment are responding. The child is given information on rules of the socially approved means to reach his goals and the verbal and nonverbal skills to interact successfully in the world. With these skills, it is expected that the number of positive interchanges the child experiences with others will significantly increase. He will feel better about himself, develop higher self-esteem, and be better able to satisfy his needs. The child increases his chances of good social adjustment.

These assertions on the strong positive impact of social skills training need to be closely examined. While Jahoda hypothesized the relationship among interpersonal skills, social adjustment, and mental health as early as 1953, data confirming the direct relationship among these factors have been slow to emerge. The lack of supporting evidence can be traced to the fact that each component of social skills has been researched as a unidimensional variable. Social skills is a multidimensional concept composed of many factors which interact constantly within the individual and in the social context. In general, however, two separate bodies of literature have been generated addressing two major components of social skills: the cognitive and the behavioral. To examine the importance of social skills, it is necessary to look at each body of literature individually.

Cognitive Factors

Research on cognitive factors involved in social skills has centered primarily on interpersonal problem-solving skills (Spivack, Platt, and Shure 1976) and on abilities to make social inferences and cognitive self-talk (Meichenbaum 1975). Research on these individual components has found positive relationships between each factor and social adjustment. However, intervention programs aimed at manipulating any one variable have been unsuccessful in producing positive change lasting beyond several weeks.

The problem-solving process has been most clearly delineated by D'Zurilla and Goldfried (1971). The process requires an awareness of choices in responding to a situation and an ability to choose the most effective alternative. A five-step model was proposed:

1. general orientation or problem set,
2. problem identification and formulation,
3. generation of alternatives,
4. decision making,
5. evaluation.

These steps were formulated from research on impersonal problems, such as perceptual tasks. In interpersonal problems, particularly with children, the pioneers in the field have been Spivack, Shure, and Platt (1971). Concentrating on the decision-making stage of the D'Zurilla and Goldfried model, Spivack et al. (1971, 1974, 1977) have identified four types of thinking required to solve interpersonal problems efficiently: (1) ability to conceptualize alternative solutions to interpersonal problems, (2) step by step goal planning and implementation, (3) consequential thinking, and (4) awareness of cause-effect relationships. These stages are subcomponents of D'Zurilla and Goldfried's decision-making phase.

Researchers have not examined the D'Zurilla model with children; however, a considerable literature is available on Spivack and Shure's (1974) interpersonal problem solving. In third and fourth grade, a child's expertise in generating alternatives and means-end thinking has been related to group functioning in the classroom as rated by teachers on the Devereux Social Behavior Rating Scale (Elardo and Caldwell, in preparation) and, in general, healthy adjustment (Spivack and Shure 1977). Evidence of the relationship between problem solving and behavioral performance on a simulation problem-solving task has been less consistent. Larcen (in Allen, Chinsky, Larcen, Lockman and Selinger 1976) found a positive relationship. McClure (1975) failed to demonstrate the relationship. No attempt has been made to establish a direct link between cognitive problem skills and behavioral improvement. Among adolescents, the ability to generate alternatives (Spivack and Levine 1973) and means-end thinking (Platt and Spivack 1974; Platt, Saura, and Hannon 1973) have also been found to relate to healthy adjustment. The abilities to identify problems, evaluate consequences, and assess cause-effect relationships have been found to be less important in the older age group. No attempts have been made to intervene or train cognitive problem-solving skills in adolescents and examine resulting behavioral adjustment.

A second cognitive prerequisite for the development of social skills has been social inferential ability: the ability to identify emotional states in another person and to imagine yourself in their position, that is, to take another's role. Both these skills have been related to prosocial or altruistic behavior in young children (Hartup 1970; Rothenberg 1970). Izard (1971) found sensitivity to another person's emotional states associated with peer popularity, a discriminating variable for future mental health (Roff 1961; Roff, Sells, and Golden 1972; Cowen et al. 1973). Baseline studies have demonstrated a relationship between role taking and cognitive problem skills (Larcen et al. 1974; Sobol 1974). Intervention programs in interpersonal problem solving demonstrate concomitant changes in role taking (Elardo 1974; Elardo and Cooper, in press; McClure 1975). Elardo and Caldwell (1976) found inconsistent improvement in actual social role taking, but observed improvement in classroom adjustment as measured by the teachers in the Devereux Elementary School Behavior Rating Scale (Spivack, Platt and Shure 1977). McClure (1974), comparing a variety of intervention modes to enhance role taking, found behavioral changes in cognitive problem solving immediately following treatment, but these changes disappeared within four months. Larcen's intervention program for role taking (in Allen et al. 1976) was found to enhance capacity to generate alternatives, but again, behavioral changes were very inconsistent across children.

Among adolescents, perspective or role taking has been related to healthy adjustment (Platt et al. 1974; Feffer and Jahelka 1968; Schnall and Feffer 1970; Sucholiff 1970; Platt and Spivack 1973). No intervention studies are available. In general, while baseline studies on two specific cognitive skills, problem solving and social inferential ability, have been found to relate to later social functioning, intervention programs attempting to change cognitive factors have been unable to demonstrate positive changes in behavioral functioning.

Cognitive-behavioral theorists (Meichenbaum 1974) emphasize the importance of covert behaviors. i.e., how we talk to ourselves, as determinants of our social behavior. While little research with young children exists, there have been two thrusts in this research with adolescents. Schwartz and Gottman (1974) assessed positive and negative cognitive self-statements of college students as the students role played assertion situations. Low assertive subjects were found to give a balance of positive and negative self-statements before entering the assertion situations. In contrast, high-assertive subjects covertly rewarded themselves for the upcoming performance. A second area has been with cognitive self-talk. Novaco (1975) demonstrated that behavioral rehearsal of cognitive coping statements was an effective intervention with aggressive delinquents. While the research on covert self-monitoring and self-coping talk is sparse, the potential importance of these factors is large.

Behavioral Factors

A second approach to social skills has been aimed at assessing interpersonal behavioral skills. In young children, activities such as communicating to an adult listener (Asher and Parke 1975; Flavell et al. 1968; Blucksberg and Krausse 1967) or interacting with peers (O'Connor 1969, 1972; Rubin 1972;

Walker and Hops 1973) have been studied and related to peer popularity. As noted above, peer popularity in childhood has been repeatedly associated with indices of later mental health. Grossman and Levy (1974) conducted a factor analysis of coping behavior in preschool children and consistently found assertive behavior to be a primary factor in adjustment. Dorman (1973) has related assertive behaviors to cognitive performance on IQ tests for five-year-olds.

Intervention programs using modeling with dolls (Chittenden 1942) or modeling films and role playing interpersonal situations (Pitkanen, 1972, 1974) have been successfully used to increase discriminations of socially appropriate behavior. Oden and Asher (1977) used a three-step intervention model for teaching children how to make friends. The process involved receiving instructions on making friends with an adult, playing with peers, and receiving follow-up feedback from the adult after the play period. Oden and Asher found no significant differences between experimental and control groups in behavioral observations of classroom behavior or sociometric ratings. Using skits to teach social skills, Chennault (1967) found initial increases in peer acceptance which were not maintained. These results parallel findings of other researchers (Lilly 1971, Rucker and Vincenzo 1970), who found initial gains in social behaviors to be quickly lost. As with cognitive programs, generalizations of behavioral changes beyond a few weeks have not been found.

In contrast to the work with young children, there is no research assessing behavioral deficits among adolescents. However, there have been several intervention programs. Sarason and Ganger (1971) developed modeling scripts to teach delinquents how to apply for jobs and deal with employers. The dicated significant changes in the delinquents' social behavior. No followup dicated significant changes in the delinquents social behavior. No follow up was made on the delinquents' success in securing jobs. Stuart (1971) has shown that behavioral contracting with adolescents can lead to changes in family interactions. Schwitzgebel (1972, 1974) demonstrated the efficiency of employing adolescents as research subjects using successive approximation to engage the adolescents as clients in therapy. In general, behavioral techniques have been applied with adolescent populations, but little data has been gathered that demonstrates program effectiveness.

Children's emotional responses, such as anxiety, have been ignored in the literature. In adult social skills programs, anxiety is recognized as an inhibitor of assertive responses (Lange and Jakubowski 1976; Lieberman, King, and de Risi 1977). Clinical evidence of the importance of emotional expressiveness and control of anxiety for developing social skills in adults is plentiful (Liebert 1976; Rotheram and Armstrong 1977), while few studies have examined the role of emotions in children's skill development (Cox and Gunn 1978).

To summarize the literature, the components which make up social competence can be categorized as follows:

1. Cognitive factors
   a. Problem-solving ability emphasizing alternative generation and means-end thinking
   b. Discrimination of socially desirable behaviors
   c. Self-monitoring through self-reinforcement and self-punishment

2. Behavioral factors
   a. Verbal behaviors such as positive statements to self and other, friendship initiation and feedback
   b. Nonverbal behaviors such as posture, voice tone, latency, gestures, and eye contact

3. Emotional factors
   a. Monitoring and assessment of positive and negative emotional states
   b. Methods of relaxing or control of negative emotional states

Each of these factors has a positive relationship to social functioning and future adjustment; however, manipulating any one variable has consistently proven fruitless. The integration of cognitive and behavioral factors has been virtually ignored, although the importance of an integration has been suggested by a number of writers. For example, early research examining the influence of the cognitive sense of the other person on prosocial behavior in children yielded equivocal findings (Shantz 1975). Barrett and Yarrow (1974) found significant interactions between cognitive and behavioral variables. Prosocial helping behavior was found to be a function of both assertive interpersonal skills and the cognitive ability to make social inferences. Without pre-existing assertiveness skills, social inferential ability did not significantly influence prosocial behavior. With social skills, the training in role taking did make a significant difference. The combination of cognitive and behavioral components in the individual is crucial, particularly in intervention programs.

As noted in the introduction to this book the concept of social competence is a multidimensional one. This concept, often labeled as assertiveness in adults or social skill in children, refers to an ongoing interaction between individuals and their environments. In response to environmental inputs, a child must employ cognitive-social inferential ability and data from his own emotional reactions in order to define the situation and emit a behavioral response. Each response is one link in a sequence of ongoing interactions with the environment. The evaluation of the response as adaptive or nonadaptive is a function of the individual's intention and the reaction from those in his environment. Thus, a program to teach social skills must synthesize the components into an interaction strategy that the child can use and must include a strategy for learning as well as for discrete skills.

In fig. 4.1, the steps in a social interaction strategy have been outlined. In conjunction with each step, the adaptive, cognitive, behavioral, and emotional responses necessary to execute the process effectively are listed. The developmental nature of each component, and the relevance of different factors at varying ages, are as yet undetermined. In fact, the general importance of each component has not been specified. A strategic model of social functioning suggests that any component could disrupt adaptive functioning and lead to ineffective interpersonal interactions. A spiraling effect is easily established in either a positive or a negative direction. For example, negative self thoughts lead to poorer performance and increased anxiety. The unsuccessful intervention programs detailed earlier would be expected to fail and demonstrate no effects beyond 2-3 weeks. Habitual response patterns quickly extinguish newly acquired changes in one component. An assertive interpersonal style demands cognitive, behavioral, and emotional coping skills that are interdependent. The social skills programs presented in this chapter are aimed at integrating cognitive, behavioral, and emotional control factors in teaching children and adolescents a new strategy for interpersonal interactions.

Trainers make value decisions defining appropriate and inappropriate behaviors when working with young children. Good social skills are socially acceptable behaviors as defined by the person, situational cues, and the observers. Assertive behavior is the generally agreed upon definition of socially appropriate behavior. Lying between passive and aggressive behaviors on a number of continua (see fig. 4.2), assertive behavior is perceived as the optimal response. Adult social skills trainers emphasize that they are teaching assertiveness as an option. Passive and aggressive responses are acceptable choices an individual might make (Cotler and Guerra 1976; Alberti and Emmons 1976; Rotheram 1978). Children, particularly young children, lack the information to choose to act assertively or have already fully developed repertoires of passive and aggressive responses. The goal of social skills training is to develop the option to act assertively. The trainers teach children cultural norms for assertiveness, social awareness, and behavioral skills.

Several situations have been identified as commonly necessitating assertive behavior. These are initiating new relationships and delivering and receiving verbal positives and negatives. Students role play situations involving these problem areas in assertive social skills programs.

Model of Strategy for Social Interactions	*Cognitive*	*Adaptive Skills* *Behavioral*	*Emotional*
1. Problem orientation	1. Social inferential ability		1. Self-monitoring of internal discomfort
2. Negative emotional response	2. Labeling of negative emotion (e.g., anxiety, depression, excitement) and assessing intensity of response	2. Ability to control behavioral response.	2. Labeling of negative emotion (e.g., anxiety, depression, excitement) and assessing intensity of response
3. Cope with negative emotional response	3. Identify covert self-punishment, catastrophic thinking, intervene with coping self-talk, self-reinforcement	3. Control of nonverbal responses, use of time out	3. Relax physiologically
4. Problem solve (a) clarify goal (b) generate alternatives (c) evaluate select alternative	4. (a) state one goal in one sentence, (b) divergent thinking, (c) social inferential ability to assess realistic consequences of behavior	4. (a) direct requests, refusals, (b) behavioral repertoire to implement any alternative	4. Assessment and ability to control new emotional states that arise
5. Respond behaviorally	5. Belief you have right to be assertive, self-esteem in ability to respond	5. Verbal skills (disclosures, I statements, requests, refusals), nonverbal skills (eye contact, voice tone, latency level, facial expression)	5. Relaxation techniques
6. Evaluate	6. Self-reinforce, goal set	6. Request feedback from environment	6. Monitor and assess internal state

Fig. 4.1. Model for social interaction process with associated prerequisite cognitive, behavioral, and emotional responses for effective interpersonal style

Nonverbals	*Passive*		*Assertive*		*Aggressive*
Eye contact	Looking at floor	20% eye contact 80% looking around room	eye contact 70-80% occasional break	95% eye contact	Glaring 100% eye contact, no breaks
Voice level	inaudible	low tone, weak	audible, clear decibel range	loud, not matching average	yelling
Voice tone	whining	apologetic	modulated, no meta-messges; matches request or refusal	irritated, negative	angry, demanding
Posture gestures	hunched shoulders, hands behind back	turned sideways, head at right angle to shoulders, weight directly on feet	weight off balance, head and shoulders straight, hands raised	fists clenched, arms folded across chest, resting on heels	leaning forward, fists shaking, arms flailing
Personal space	7 feet	4 feet	1½ to 3 feet	1 foot	6 inches
Verbal Behaviors					
Requests	This is sure a mess.	If you aren't busy and think you might have time, maybe you'd like to clean this mess.	I would like you to clean this mess.	You should clean this up.	Clean up this.
Refusals	Well, I am pretty busy...Well, okay.	Well, I don't think I'll have time. I'll let you know, maybe.	I don't want to play ball with you now.	No way.	No, why would I play with a jerk like you.
Feeling range	Satisfaction	Hurt	Excitement, hurt, anger, ecstasy, irritation, scared.	Anger, excitement	Rage

Fig. 4.2. Continua of passive assertive/aggressive verbal and nonverbal behaviors

Elementary School Intervention: Grades 3-6.

Children develop patterns of social behavior by the age of eight (Rothbart 1966). The patterns are sex typed (Sears, Maccoby, and Levin 1969) resulting in males exhibiting more aggressive behavior than females (Bandura, Ross, and Ross 1971; Macoby and Wilson 1957; Muste and Sharpe 1958). Females more frequently engage in behaviors labeled dependent, passive, and conforming (Crutchfield 1955; Kagan and Moss 1962; Rothbart 1966). Emotional expressiveness in males, particularly emotions such as fear and hurt, are expected to be suppressed during middle childhood (Kagan 1964). On problem-solving tasks, differences in approach styles between girls and boys already exist (Smith 1933; Kagan 1964).

To introduce most effectively the content of a cognitive behavioral assertion program with young children, a simulation game is used (Rotheram 1977). As Flowers (1975) has indicated, simulations lead to fewer dropouts and are fun and highly reinforcing to children. Most important, simulations aid generalization of learning. Generalization is particularly important given the failure of research on intervention programs to demonstrate effectiveness beyond a few weeks. The program employs the coaching model of McFall and Twentyman (1973) in which shaping and behavioral rehearsal are central. Classrooms are divided into teams of 6-10 children. Each team includes an equal number of child actors, a director, and a paraprofessional leader. The paraprofessional leader, or "Supercoach," presents the team with an interpersonal problem. The team problem solves the situation and rehearses the solution. The child actors acquire verbal and nonverbal assertive behaviors, through role playing and receiving feedback in the form of one-inch by one-inch color-coded tokens delivered by the directors. Directors concentrate on problem solving and acquiring discrimination skills. Over a 12-20 week period, didactic instruction is used in conjunction with the game to provide information on meeting other people, complimenting others, and handling anger.

The content provided in the children's social skills package can be divided into seven sections (see fig. 4.3). With children practicing the skills in the classroom, each section may take from four to eight lessons to master. While this program has been evaluated using 24 sessions, 4 sessions for each section, this was not enough practice for many children. This is particularly true for children with learning disabilities. The number of sessions required to master the content of each section varies depending on the population. The seven sections are reviewed below.

Section	*Didactic Introduction*	*Role Play Sample*	*Nonverbal Behavioral Focus*	*Interpersonal Problem Solving*	*Thought Rehearsal*
1.	Define passive, assertive, aggressive. Role play for class.	You took a permission slip home to your parents so you can participate in a special school program. Your parents have not signed it. What do you want?	Eye contact, voice loudness	Clarifying clear goals—1 sentence	Verbalize cognitive states most people feel when behaving passive, assertive, aggressive, e.g., passive, "I'm not worth it."
2.	"Feeling Thermometer" or SUDS. An anxiety scale from 0-100.	A boy crowds in front of you in a cafeteria line. You don't like it. What can you do? What else?	Posture, voice tone	Generating alternatives	Verbalize positive self-thoughts at low SUDS.
3.	"Strokes," giving and receiving compliments. Self-reinforcement.	Giving compliments to all group members, including yourself; you like your ballet lessons. What can you do? What else?	Facial expressions	Generating alternatives	Verbalize positive and negative self-thoughts. Intervene with positive after each negative.
4.	Making friends	Interviewing stars from TV, meeting someone on a bus, telling friend he hurt your feelings. What is likely to happen?	Personal space	Means-ends evaluation	Role play catastrophic fantasy of worst outcome of making a friend
5.	"Playing Cool," controlling anger by taking time out	You have been working hard on a test. Your teacher yells at you that you are cheating. What are you saying to yourself? What can you do? What is likely to happen?	Gestures	Evaluate Consequences	Role play coping self-talk
6.	"The Big Switch," accepting a negative from someone else and self-reinforcing.	You have forgotten to do your homework and your teacher's angry with you. What are you saying to yourself? What can you do? What will your teachers do?	Latency	Evaluate consequences	Role play coping self-talk
7.	Strategy learning with new problems.	Request and refusal situations.	Consolidate	Review	Consolidate

Fig. 4.3. Agenda for assertion training interventions

Orientation

An orientation talk familiarizing teachers and parents with assertiveness is critical. The children will not be practicing new skills in a vacuum. Children need reinforcement for their new behaviors (Stuart 1971; Armstrong 1977). To assure reinforcement for new assertive behavior, an orientation session or workshop for teachers and parents is important. Expectations for positive changes can be set. Potential problems can be identified. In particular, some teachers or parents want passive children. Children who ask questions, make requests, or spontaneously express feelings are punished. In this case the trainer must make an ethical decision on the benefits or harm that may result for the child from the intervention.

With children, social skills training is presented as part of the normal school curriculum. The label of "being weird" or "there's something wrong with us" must not be attached to the intervention. The normalization of the process is a crucial entry problem. In one project where students were removed from the class, the question of why they were selected remained the main topic of conversation for eight weeks. In the orientation session, the definition of social skills is presented and a sample simulation game is modeled for the class. Large blank poster boards with the words "assertive," "passive," and "aggressive" across the top are used. Children must generate behaviors associated with these labels. For example, passive means shy, scared, talking low, looking at floor, afraid, embarrassed, hunched over, shaking, or quiet. Assertive is standing tall, looking at someone, smiling, asking, saying no, or feeling good about yourself. Aggression is being angry, yelling, stamping, hitting, shouting, being mean, getting out of control, spitting, or screaming. Role plays of passive, assertive, and aggressive behavior in a classroom situation are modeled. Students are asked to identify the components of passive, assertive, or aggressive responses. The children are instructed that they will learn how to be assertive by practicing and playing a new drama game while working as a team of actors and directors. The simulation game can be demonstrated using a modeling or stimulus videotape of children playing the game or by using a group of children from the class.

Assessment and Group Composition

The class will then be divided into teams composed of six to ten children. The number of children on the team varies primarily as a function of the teacher's or consultant's skills in group management. Teams should be balanced for sex, both males and females, and composed of passive, assertive, and aggressive members. Positive models of assertive behavior help the group process and facilitate role playing.

Cognitive Interpersonal Problem Solving Skills can be assessed using the Means-Ends Problem Solving Test (Spivack and Shure 1974). Administered individually, stories are read to the children. The stories lack either the middle or end sections. To evaluate the child's ability to generate alternatives, a problem is presented and the child creates as many different solutions as possible. Given the beginning and end of a story, the child is asked to use means-end thinking to generate what happened in the middle. Consequential thinking is assessed by asking children to complete unfinished stories and to project consequences for different behavioral sequences.

To identify spccific behavioral deficits, initial assessment tools are the Children's Assertiveness Test (Rotheram, Armstrong, and Booraem 1978), a version of the Goal Seeking Test (Rotheram 1974, 1977), or role-playing situations (Cox and Gunn 1978). These instruments are reviewed in the following paragraphs.

1. The Children's Assertion Test is composed of 20 situations the child is likely to experience in his or her life. From a multiple choice selection of passive/aggressive/assertion alternatives, the child chooses a likely response. The format is similar to the Adolescent Assertiveness Discrimination Test (Schumacher 1974) and the Adult Self-Expression Scale (Gaye, Galassi, and Galassi 1976). Test-retest reliability is .89 at one month and .76 at one year.

2. The Goal Seeking Assertion Test has been adopted from research on aggressive behavior (Rotheram 1977). A group of four children are given a list of 16 hobbies, foods, or TV programs subgrouped into sets of four each. Each child is assigned a subset of four favorite hobbies, TV, or foods and instructed to convince the group to accept the items on his sublist as the group's five favorites. The child's goal is preset—to convince the group to accept as many of his or her assigned favorites as possible. Prior to starting the test, children are asked how many they think they will be able to convince the group to accept. Following the test, the children rate their behavior on a scale of one to ten. Four types of information are, therefore, generated from this test:

A. A behavioral measure of self-esteem using the self-reported expectation of success.
B. Assertion score—the number of choices the child was able to convince the group to accept.
C. An assessment of the child's ability to realistically assess his or her performance by subtracting the achieved outcome from his or her expectations. In research with aggressive delinquents, the outcome or actual number of choices the individual convinced the group to accept and the delinquent's realism in predicting his own behavior were prime determinants of aggressiveness (Rotheram 1977).

Teams of six to ten children are formed and divided into actors and directors. The supercoach or an adult supervisor presents an interpersonal problem situation to the group. For example, the coach says, "Your mother is waiting in the car while you run into the store for a carton of milk. You're late for a Cub Scout meeting, and your mother is upset about it already. After you get the milk off the shelf, you find every checkout line has 20 people in it. What do you want?" Sample situations can be found in figure 4.4. The actors clarify the goal in one sentence. In our sample problem the goal is "to get the milk as quickly as possible." Students generating goals such as "I don't want to make my mom mad" would be asked to restate their goals in terms of what they did want or what it would take for him or her to accomplish this. Having clarified the goal, the team would role play a way of implementing the goal. In this case, asking to get in the front of a line would be a probable role play. The scene would be set. One child of the actor team would then become a person in line, another child would play the checker, and the target actor is Amelia or Arnold Assertive, who wants to move to the front of the line. The target actor would be coached to ask assertively, "May I go in front of you?" The actors switch roles freely. If a child experiences difficulty in the role play, the supercoach asks another child to model the desired behavior. The target actor practicing assertiveness rotates every ten minutes.

The directors learn discrimination skills. Each must (1) evaluate the goal clarity and appropriateness of the goal, (2) give feedback to peers on the behavior skills during the role play, and (3) learn to ask the actor to evaluate his own performance first, before giving feedback. To cue the actors and clarify the discriminations, the directors distribute green (assertive), red (aggressive), and blue (passive) tokens to the actors. Similar to the warm-up period, the tokens accompany verbal feedback to the actor and are not given instead of the verbal feedback. A target director is chosen and rotated every ten minutes. The target director's task is to hold the tokens for the team of directors and to function as the captain of a team. Before delivering any tokens, the target director huddles with his teammates and with the other directors to get information to make his decision. One director serves to record the tokens so that no cheating occurs. Often the directors are assigned different jobs by the supercoach. For example, one director is watching eye contact and another is in charge of goal clarity. The actors and director teams switch roles every half hour.

The supercoach has yellow tokens that are delivered for behavioral management in the group and to signal and reinforce accurate discriminations by the directors. Only yellow tokens are used by the supercoach, and these are clearly secondary reinforcers. No negative or punishing tokens are used. The leader uses a behavioral teaching model that rests on principles of successive approximation. The games are positive experiences for the children. A child who raises her eye contact rate from 10 percent to 40 percent during a role play is reinforced for the increase. In the next rehearsal, the 40 percent will hopefully rise to 60 percent and then 80 percent. Perfect assertive performances are not expected or demanded by the supercoach. The child is encouraged to try on new behaviors and rewarded for trying. For some children, the new behaviors may swing to opposite ends of the assertion continuum. Passive children become aggressive and then temper their aggression to assertion. Children are developing behavioral options and realizing that they have alternatives. The assertive choice is generally the one most likely to be rewarded by society. The child learns this by testing in the group. The leader facilitates this process through rewarding the children and makes this reward clear with the yellow tokens.

Section Two

Having mastered the mechanics of the game and initial discriminations of the assertion continuum, attention is focused on developing an awareness of anxiety states and methods of emotional self-control. A feeling thermometer or temperature gauge is introduced. The concept of a feeling thermometer is an easy way for children to understand Wolpe's (1958) Subjective Units of Discomforts Scale (SUDS). Children develop individual ratings of their own responses on a scale from 0 to 100 in different stressful situations. For example, a feeling thermometer of 100 is telling your dad you don't want to go to the basketball game with him. A 30 is telling a teacher that you were not talking. A feeling thermometer for the whole class is constructed. Children are able to construct a hierarchy in discriminating anxiety situations at 10 point intervals on the scale. Many children initially report only two SUDS scores—0 and 100. They flip-flop to different ends of the continuum. They are unaware of physiological signals of low levels of anxiety. When they do become aware, as their SUDS hit 100, they are either immobilized or striking out. Increased ability to differentiate their emotional reactions enables the children to deal with their problems while the problems are still minor issues. In the didactic presentation, the nonverbal correlates of varying levels of anxiety are emphasized. For example, at 100 your hands are shaking, your face gets red, you start to sweat. Also, it is explained that this is a subjective scale; people's SUDS are their own.

Two people can have very different SUDS in a situation. For example, "telling my friends I don't want to play ball" may generate SUDS of 50 for one child, but may be 20 SUDS for his friend. A discrimination is also made between anxiety and excitement. Since the child's body feels the same, the child is unable to discriminate physiological reactions. Anxiety and excitement are often confused. Getting an ice cream and being disciplined by the principal might elicit similar physiological responses. The child feels his

Section Four

Initiating contacts in the classroom and with friends is rehearsed. While adult social skills programs have complicated, step-by-step, structured interactions for initiating friendships (Smith 1973), a children's program must be much more direct. A child's approach is a straight, "Hi! Would you like to play with me?" Friendships are built around shared activities such as playing ball. The child's nonverbal behavior is the area most likely to need attention—eye contact, positive facial expression, and posture. Homework assignments center on meeting two new friends during the week.

For initiations with adults and for request situations, two different skills were emphasized—asking open questions and developing specificity in the request. Role-playing interviews with television stars have been an overwhelming success in teaching children to ask open questions. Open questions are those that begin with the words "how," "why," and "what." Responses to these questions generally elicit more than a one-word answer and the child receives free or extra information that was not specifically requested. In contrast, questions that begin with the words "when," "where," "do you" or "did" are likely to yield one-word responses. The children play the role of a reporter interviewing such stars as Starsky and Hutch, the Bionic Woman, and the Six Million-Dollar Man. The child's job is to find out as much information from the television star as possible and, generally, with great enthusiasm. A second prerequisite skill is acquiring the ability to be as specific as possible in requests. Role play scenes are carefully chosen to demand specificity, for example, arranging to meet a friend on Saturday at 10:00 in Shadow Park by the flag pole. Children are instructed to check and reaffirm information by using repeat back (Smith 1975). With this technique, the child asks to "tell me what we decided to be sure we agree." This technique is quickly adopted by teachers in the classroom.

The interpersonal problem-solving component of the program teaches children to evaluate alternatives by employing means-end thinking. After the alternatives have been listed on the board, each actor assesses how successfully the action will meet the intended goal. For example, the child is in the store and there are long lines in each aisle; the stated goal is to buy the milk as quickly as possible. The nonexhaustive list of alternatives are:

- stealing the milk under a coat
- waiting in line
- asking someone near the front of one line to buy the milk
- asking to step to the front of a line
- not buying the milk here, going to another store
- yelling, "Fire," and having everyone run out

- asking the manager to open a new line to check you out
- not buying the milk at all
- asking the mother to come in and buy the milk

The actors examine each alternative and hypothesize how each act will satisfy the goal. "Stealing the milk" may be efficient; however, it does carry substantial negative consequences if caught. "Waiting in line" does not reach the goal, but is easy to do. "Asking someone to go in front of them" is a viable assertive alternative. The goal is reached and no unpleasant effects are likely to be generated. In turn, each alternative is evaluated by the actors. Actors also decide whether the alternatives are passive, assertive, or aggressive. The target actor chooses the scene to be role played. Directors cue the correct evaluations with tokens and are in turn reinforced by the supercoach.

Personal space is defined and assessed for children. Assertive distance is estimated at between 18 and 36 inches. Each child's "comfort zone" is assessed in the group. In the middle of a six-foot by six-foot square on the floor, a child stands and other members of the group approach individually one foot at a time from different directions (Whalen et al. 1975). The child is asked to signal when other members are close enough for his or her comfort. When the child is initiating an action, assessments of personal space can be made by asking the target child to approach each group member or the adult supercoach until the child is close enough, as the supercoach stands in the grid. A desensitization procedure can be instituted for a child with extraordinarily large personal space. During the exercise, each child assesses emotional discomfort or anxiety on the SUDS scale. Like the SUDS anxiety scale, personal space is unique and subjective. Children learn to notice their own and their peers' nonverbal cues when the comfort zone is invaded. For example, fidgeting with hands and blushing are cues of discomfort.

Section Five

At the same time children in Indiana were using "Keeping Cool Rules" (Cox and Gunn 1978), children in California were learning "Playing Cool" (Rotheram, Armstrong, and Booraem 1978). These sessions focus on self-control procedures for anger and include self-initiated behavioral time-outs and cognitive self-coping talk (Meichenbaum 1976). Dealing with situations in which the child feels angry or has negatives to deliver is easier than receiving negatives; therefore, self-control of anger is dealt with first. Time-out is generally used as a forced withdrawal of potential reinforcement enforced on a child by being in segregated places alone.

To develop self-control of anger, children are taught to initiate a time-out or break for themselves when they feel high anxiety or a desire to aggress. Instead of a withdrawal from potential reinforcement, a cooling-off period

Section Seven

During this phase, the learning in previous lessons is consolidated. Problem situations are used from the students' homework sheets. For each problem, the entire strategy model for assertive behavior is employed. Students clarify a goal. Negative emotional states are assessed and relaxation techniques employed, if necessary. The goal is set. A number of alternatives are generated, and evaluated, and a course of action set. The action is role played with both self-talk, and verbal and nonverbal behavior. The student evaluates his own behavior and receives feedback from others. The children run the group independently without a need for the supercoach by this time.

Research

The effectiveness of the social skills program outlined above has been evaluated (Rotheram et al. 1977). Two hundred and eighty children, 153 male and 130 female from fourth and fifth grades at a lower-class middle school, participated in the study. One hundred and six children received the social skills training packet described above for two hours a week for twelve weeks. Teams were composed of six children. The only difference in format was that no homework was assigned.

Fifty-eight children received training aimed at increasing classroom participation by using a self-confidence simulation game (Flowers and Marston 1972). In small groups, students play a variant of the television game show, College Bowl. Competing on three-person teams against three classmates, they answer questions on hobbies and academic classroom material. Students were assigned to teams with classmates of similar confidence levels. Confidence was operationally defined as attempting to answer questions. Past research indicates that when grouped with same-level responding peers, low and average-level responders increased their participation rate. After successful competition experience with peers of the same response level, the children are gradually integrated into groups with the higher-level responders. The initially low responders continue to attempt and successfully answer questions at a high response rate. These in-game behaviors had been found to generalize to the classroom. This game was also played two hours a week for 12 weeks by the children. A no-treatment control group was also examined.

The effectiveness of three intervention programs (social skills training, self-confidence training, and no treatment) at two grade levels (fourth and fifth) with male and female participants was evaluated (see fig. 4.5). Measures of problem-solving skills, assertiveness on a self-report inventory and behavioral tasks, self-esteem, teachers' ratings of behavior problems and achievement, peer popularity ratings, and grades were assessed.

Grade Level		Intervention		
		Social Skills	Self-confidence	Control
Fourth	Male	n = 14	n = 32	n = 23
	Female	n = 17	n = 34	n = 28
Fifth	Male	n = 12	n = 21	n = 24
	Female	n = 13	n = 23	n = 26

Fig. 4.5. Outline of research project evaluating the effectiveness of social skills training, self-confidence/college bowl simulation, and no-treatment control for fourth and fifth grades (n = 280)

The results of posttest measures of the problem-solving and assertion skills indicate positive changes as a function of the social skills intervention package. In problem-solving tasks, the number of passive and aggressive alternatives are significantly reduced in the social skills intervention. For the fifth grade social skills group, the number of assertive alternatives is significantly increased. The self-report inventory of assertive behavior shows significantly fewer passive alternatives chosen by the social skills group. This parallels the results of the behavioral assertion measure where the social skills group is significantly less submissive. Neither the self-report nor the behavioral measure indicated significant increases in assertive responses; the changes were in terms of decreasing passivity. While data is only available on the self-report measure a year later, all groups show an overall drop in assertive choices. The decrease in social skills groups (x = .06) is significantly less than the other groups and, also, has not decreased significantly from the previous year. There is a significant decrease in the control classes in assertive choices. This may indicate that training during this period may serve to inhibit losses in assertiveness that may be likely to occur from a developmental model.

The impact of the social skills package for executing immediate changes in the classroom environment is not clear. The self-confidence/college bowl game yielded the most changes. Significant increases in the number of teacher positives and the overall number of interactions were found in the self-confidence groups. There was a significant increase in student initiated interactions with the teacher in both college bowl and social skills classes. There was simultaneously, however, a decrease in the number of questions asked in the social skills classes. It would appear the college bowl game was more efficient in changing in-class behavior. This might be expected, since this game was directed at classroom behaviors such as answering questions and hand raising. It may be that behavioral changes from the social skills intervention would be more evident in measures where the quality of the interaction was rated or peer interaction was recorded. Grade level appeared an important variable in classroom changes. There was a significant increase in initiations and overall interactions and a decrease in teacher negatives in fourth as compared to fifth grade.

While the behavioral observations did not yield positive differences in the social skills classes, the teacher's perceptions did change. The teachers reported significantly fewer behavior problems among the social skills intervention group. Most impressive in these findings is that a year later, with new teachers who did not know what intervention the children had received, there were still significantly fewer behavior problems reported for the children receiving the social skills intervention.

The influence of the training on popularity is not clear. Sociometric ratings with peers of the number of friends and most popular children yielded no significant findings. This parallels results by O'Connor (1969). He found that sociometric ratings were not a sensitive instrument and did not reflect changes that were evident in behavioral observations. We had no behavioral measures of peer interactions. Teachers did report significant pretest-posttest increases in popularity in the fifth grade self-confidence classes and the fourth grade social skills groups immediately following treatment. A year later, new teachers' ratings of the popularity of the students in the social skills classes show significant increases in popularity compared to the other groups. No significant changes in self-esteem were found through pretesting and posttesting or at one year follow-up.

Changes in grades were examined to assess the relationship of social competence to academic competence. Immediately following the intervention, significant increases were found in the self-confidence/college bowl classes compared to other groups. A year later both the social skills and college bowl classes demonstrated significantly higher increases in grade point average. However, the social skills group had risen significantly more than any other group, almost a full grade point. The lag time in the positive influence of the social skills package in influencing grades would be expected. The college bowl game is directed at children gaining self-confidence in an academic setting. The results indicate that this simulation effectively reached its goal with a resulting change in grade point average that is maintained. The social skills target area is relationships with others and interpersonal problems. It was hoped that competence in these areas would generalize to other areas. This generalization would take longer, and our results indicate such a generalization did occur by the following year.

This project attempted to assess the impact of a cognitive behavioral social skills training package on a number of variables. Many more questions were raised by the data than were answered. One highly significant finding emerged: compared to other intervention programs that addressed either a cognitive or behavioral component of social skills (Elardo and Caldwell, in preparation; Oden, Asher, and Pitkanen 1977; Larcen et al. 1975; McClure 1975), the positive results of the present package were even more noticeable a year later. The program did appear to effect self-reported assertiveness in teacher perceptions and grades. The exact factor or factors responsible for the lasting change is less clear. One clear possibility is that the strategy model employed emphasized both t havioral and cognitive factors. Future research is needed to address this issue.

Social Skills Training With Adolescents

Adolescence has been described as the decade of turmoil and upheaval (Hall 1916). Certainly, the developmental tasks during that period are substantial. Major changes occur in physiological functioning with implications for physical as well as psychological adaption. Erickson (1960) has shown how the need to establish an independent identity separate from the nuclear family is paramount. The adolescent is in a transition stage within the culture—half child and half adult—with no clear-cut standards for the in-between age (Eisenberg 1965). The most universal changes, however, are in the relationships with others whom the adolescent is engaging. Goals, activities, and the degrees of intimacy change. The support group realigns during adolescence—from parents to peers and from same-sex to cross-sex linkings (Bandura 1964). The rules for operating in relationship become much more complex. Popular ten-year-olds form friendships with a simple, "Hi, want to play with me." Teenage friendships employ adult rules—asking open questions, finding common interests, deciding goals in the relationship, requesting contact.

These many changes often generate stress and anxiety and lead to low self-esteem during this critical developmental period (Ringness 1971). Coping skills are likewise reduced, both in social skills and in life competencies in academic or athletic settings (Ringness 1967; Jackson and Getyls 1971). The stress of adolescence is seen as a maturational life crisis. It used to be a popular idea that the storm and stress of this period was productive. The friction enabled the adolescent to break from his parents and establish himself separately. Recent research contradicts this notion. Gronlund and Anderson (1971) have shown that socially competent and outgoing adolescents tend to be the best adjusted in later life. Ringness (in Meuese 1971) has demonstrated that those who are high achievers in college and later life did not experience a tumultuous adolescence but continued to be achievers throughout the period.

This research and the fact that so many of the problems experienced by adolescents are relationship oriented suggest that social skills training may be a particularly useful intervention. Social skill training can (1) aid in learning adult rules on relationships and interaction skills in relationships, (2) help adjustment to new role demands through increasing problem-solving skills, (3) alleviate anxiety through relaxation training and skill acquisition, and (4) increase self-esteem through new self-monitoring techniques.

Using a theoretical orientation similar to the children's assertiveness program, the model has been adapted for high school populations (Rotheram and Armstrong 1977). While the content to be transmitted in the social skills packet is the same, the method of delivering the package is very different. In fact, initial differences in the type of assertion problems experienced and the adolescent's sophistication in group processes (Rotheram and Armstrong 1977) have led to the development of very different programs for ninth and twelfth grade classes. Adolescents with learning disabilities will be addressed separately.

Assessment

Adolescent versions of cognitive interpersonal problem-solving tests have been developed by Spivack and Levine (1963) and Platt and Spivack (1970, 1975). Assessments of role taking can be made with the battery developed by Feffer and Gourevitch (1960). These tests have highly reliable testing and scoring procedures. As with the children, stories missing either beginning, middle, or end sections are read. The adolescent must employ different types of reasoning or sensitivity to others' roles to construct missing sections of the story.

Self-report assessment of behavioral assertion skills can be made with a number of measures: the Adolescent Assertiveness Discrimination Test (Schumacher 1974), the Rathus Assertion Scale (1973); the Adult Self-Expression Scale (Gaye, Gallassi, and Gallassi 1976), the Problem Focus Checklist (Paulson 1973). None of these scales has substantial data on reliability and validity. The general format of these inventories is to present a number of typical situations involving assertiveness. Adolescents are asked to rate either the degree of discomfort they would experience in being assertive or to choose their typical response among passive/assertive/aggressive alternatives.

Two behavioral simulations have been developed. First, the goal-seeking task described under assessment for children can be used. In a group of four peers, adolescents are instructed to convince the group to accept their individual choices on a group list. The only shift is the category of items to be decided upon by the group. Instead of hobbies or food, lists of rock groups or pictures of women have been used. As with the children, this task yields measures of behavioral self-esteem, effectiveness in goal seeking, reality of expectations, and an opportunity for behavioral observation of peer interactions. Self-esteem and reality measures have proved particularly important in dealing with aggressive populations (Rotheram 1974). In addition, the level of group interaction skills is crucial to deciding the presentation format of the assertion program. This technique is particularly useful for allowing observation of these skills.

A second behavioral simulation was developed by Salter (1949) for adults. It can also be used with adolescent populations (Rotheram and Armstrong 1977). Role play situations are constructed with a stimulus person whose responses are preprogrammed. Request and refusal situations are employed and the interaction is videotaped. From videotape, measures of a number of nonverbal and verbal behaviors can be made (Hersen et al. 1973)—eye contact, voice latency, gestures, and posture. Meichenbaum (1975) has also pointed out how these role plays provide information on cognitive factors such as how the adolescent self-reinforces or self-punishes throughout the situation. Schwartz and Gottman's (1974) list of cognitive self-thoughts can be administered in conjunction with the behavioral simulation. Anxiety responses can also be more realistically assessed by the client and observed on videotape (Meichenbaum 1975). As with the children, the behavioral assertion measures, the goal seeking discussion, and the role play serve two functions. While providing data, they also can be used in the intervention phase as stimulus material to demonstrate behavioral deficits to the adolescent.

In designing social skills programs for adolescents, our research team experienced four failures. While having exciting and enthusiastic leaders and involving material to present, attendance by the fourth week had dropped 50-70 percent on each of our first four projects. Major reassessment of the assertion issues for the population were needed. After our assessment, the importance of the developmental nature of social skills and initial assessment became clear. These results are summarized, since they had major impact on the structuring of the social skills program.

To evaluate overall assertiveness, Schumacher's (1973) Adolescent Assertiveness Discrimination Test was employed. The results for 40 adolescents, 20 males and 20 females in ninth and twelfth grades, are shown in table 4.1. As can be seen, females decrease significantly in assertiveness from ninth to twelfth grade ($F = 4.9$, $p < 0.05$), and males increase ($F = 5.9$, $p < 0.05$). Males decrease significantly in passivity ($F = 3.9$, $p < 0.05$), while females increase ($F = 6.3$, $p < 0.05$). Note the magnitude of the change in males' passivity, from 11.5 in ninth grade to 2.3 in twelfth grade. Females decrease significantly in aggressiveness from ninth to twelfth grade, with no change in males' aggressiveness during the period.

back on the instructor's performance. These presentations are made as funny and entertaining as possible. Props are used to characterize "El Jerko Delux," the most unassertive person in the high school. After two weeks, triad role plays of structured situations by students can be initiated. In these triads, one student is practicing assertiveness. Another is the stimulus person in the role play. The third student functions as a coach. The students are not asked to present problems from their life, but to role play and problem solve particular issues presented by the instructor. The instructor brings situations pertinent to the didactic content presented that day. For example, to coincide with didactic information on refusing others, the teacher may ask students to role play a door-to-door salesman, policeman selling tickets for the charity ball, and a friend who wants to borrow money. I emphasize that students are not asked to disclose problems from their personal lives. For ninth graders, this appears to be too anxiety provoking. These triads are instructed to deliver only positive feedback on performance, with at most one suggestion on a specific way to improve the role play performance. For example, "I liked your eye contact and your voice. Next time use your hands to emphasize your point." No negative feedback is permitted.

After four or five weeks, a behavioral group may be formed. The presentation, however, continues to be an informational program on social skills. The students are working as a group to master content, and on acquiring and implementing social skills. They are not discussing personal problems in the social skills area. Again, the content of the group focuses around the same issues as the children's groups. Each week new didactic information is presented with concomitant cognitive, behavioral, and emotional components. Red (aggressive), blue (passive), and green (assertive) tokens are held and delivered by all group members. Tokens accompany all feedback among group participants. As noted above, by employing tokens in the group, student-student interaction is facilitated, the activity level of the group increases, and students more easily acquire discrimination skills (Flowers 1975). Tokens facilitate the emergence of students as peer coaches. This is a crucial variable for learning in the groups.

The sequence of each session closely resembles Lieberman, King, De Risi, and McCann's (1975) program for adults:

1. Elicit assertive success experiences
2. Present didactic content, such as, how to initiate relationships
3. Role play new situations (scenes provided by leader)
4. Receive feedback from group
5. Continue role play and feedback
6. Give positive feedback on group process and effectiveness
7. Do homework assignments

This group takes approximatley five weeks to introduce into a ninth-grade class. Once the group is functioning, 90 percent of the time is being devoted to out-of-group problems with parents and teachers. Group cohesion builds as students bind together to conquer a common enemy. Typical positive feedback between group members might be, "I can tell you are going to be assertive when you apply for the job—GOOD!"

In contrast, twelfth-grade students are enthusiastic and want peer interaction in a group setting on the first day of social skills training. Not providing twelfth graders with peer interactions, in our experience, leads to boredom and apathy. The students want to give feedback, especially positive, and quickly form cohesive groups. While ninth graders comment on a good job, twelfth graders proclaim, "I like you a lot." Their feedback is more personal. The students want and request practice with the content of the assertion package on themselves. Instead of role playing delivering positives to others, the twelfth graders are comfortable and delight in exchanging compliments in the group. (Ninth graders panicked at such a prospect). The students want to initiate new relationships among themselves, and the typical school curriculum does not facilitate the process. Scenes for role plays are generated by the students from their own lives. Twelfth graders' group skills are much more sophisticated and make the instructor's job much easier.

As with the younger children, presenting the social skills package as a component of the typical school curriculum is crucial. In one 12-week intervention conducted by experienced Ph.D. psychologists, adolescents with behavior problems were preselected from the classroom and told to attend social skills training in a separate class. Eleven weeks later, students continued to ask, "Why me?" There was a high dropout rate. Using the same leaders and techniques three months later, but keeping the students in the classroom, led to no dropouts and an enthusiastic response. Instead of an extra burden, students were getting a welcome break in the classroom routine. In addition, conducting the training in the classroom generally assures that some positive models of assertiveness are present. This facilitates the group process and skill acquisition.

The assessment data and clinical experience suggest that the entry is the most crucial problem with adolescents. Once a cohesive relationship has been established, few problems result. Developing this relationship is a difficult process and requires clinical skill. As with the children, a pyramid learning approach is employed. Early acquired learning is built in later stages. Remember, however, a strategy is being taught for approaching social situations and problems. We are not trying merely to transfer information on the socially appropriate assertive response.

Since the methodology of the seven sections is similar to that used with younger children, that content will not be reviewed here. In the program didactic information, rehearsal through drilling and small group interaction are used to facilitate assertiveness. Attention is focused on clear requests and referrals, initiating relationships, expressing and receiving positive and negative feeling. The high school students assimilate the didactic information much more quickly than the children. The groups can then concentrate on such issues as job interviewing and work related problems.

Adolescents with Learning Disabilities

These adolescents experience many problems in social relationships. Among their peers, this group is more often the target of jokes and negative feedback. Aggression problems are frequent and the students must learn to deal effectively with this. School and adult relationships have been equally negative, leaving these students with low self-esteems and poor social skills. Developmentally, the assertion issues of children with learning disabilities are more typical of adolescents three to four years younger. Ninth-and twelfth grade adolescents with learning disabilities concentrate role play situations with parents. While these were the initial scenes addressed, methods of effectively dealing with peers are included.

The group interaction skills among this population are poor. The setting needs to be tightly structured with clearly defined roles for the participants. In contrast to typical adolescent groups where the students are encouraged to assume leader functions, the instructor takes charge and directs the activity in the learning-disabilities group. Without calling the procedure a game, the format of the children's social skills package is more appropriate for this population. The group is divided into actors and directors with clearly assigned tasks. Each director has a specific nonverbal behavior to monitor, such as eye contact or voice. Each actor is involved in the role play. No attempt is made to elicit personal disclosure from the adolescent's life. The scenes are role played and tokens are used to teach discriminations and for behavioral management in the group. The only alteration from the children's structure is that all group members receive tokens to distribute. Instead of didactic presentation of concepts of social skills for an entire class, the material is presented in the small group where the tokens are used to repeat and drill the content. Repetition of the concepts in as many ways as possible is necessary. Role play, token cueing, dedactic instruction, and repeating back, are used for a variety of situations.

With learning-disabilities students, it is necessary to limit the groups to four to six same-sex members with two co-leaders, one male and one female. Behavior problems are frequent in adolescents with learning disabilities. While one co-leader concentrates on social skills instruction, one leader needs to be available for behavior management. The learning-disabilities students are not as sophisticated in peer relationships, particularly the males. In cross-sex groups, the students limit the topics of discussion, are unwilling to role play or try on any new behavior that might be labeled silly, and attempt to impress their opposite-sex peers. All this results in monumental problems for behavior control, and we advise limiting groups to members of the same sex. In contrast, a co-leader of the opposite sex in the group does appear to facilitate the group process. First, since many students have problems with their parents, the opposite-sex leader allows a chance for the adolescents to test their perceptions with adult, nonparent models. Being older, and therefore unavailable for a romantic relationship, the opposite-sex leader is a safe target with which to try new behaviors. High school students are unwilling to role play members of the opposite sex. The co-leader offers a potential role play partner who is a successive approximation of peer relationship. These students often have a long history of negative relationships with adults. The supportive atmosphere of the group and reinforcement used by co-leaders often leads to the first positive adult peer relationships for these students.

Timing appears to be the most curcial variable in dealing with learning disabilities. The latency of the students' responses—their thoughts as well as their behavioral and emotional responses—is often too short. The integration of the cognitive, behavioral, and emotional components cannot be executed until the habitual maladaptive responses can be extinguished. In identifying a variable such as crazy or intense negative self-thoughts, the thoughts occur so quickly that students are not aware initially that they cognitively processed the situation. Emotional responses such as intense anger occur instantaneously before any reality testing of the situation. To interrupt the pattern, the role play situations must be designed to slow down the tempo of responding. In a role play, the strategy model presented earlier is employed. After presentation of the problem, negative emotional responses are checked and either cognitive coping self-talk (Meichenbaum 1974; Novaco 1975) or relaxation training procedures initiated. The problem-solving process is instituted with the group to clarify a one-sentence goal, to generate alternatives without giving negatives, and to select one to be implemented. The implementation is role played. During the role play, constant breaks are made to see what the protagonist is thinking: Does the student have negative self-thoughts? Has the goal changed? An enforced two-second delay is placed between the students' responses. The leader counts aloud, "one, two," before each response. This forces the student to re-evaluate his reaction, and it has been found to be a very effective technique. This two-second delay is also effective with younger children.

In dealing with the common aggression problems found in the population, the BARB technique (Kaufman and Wagner 1972) time-out and the self-talk procedures (Novaco 1975: Meichenbaum 1975) are most effective. The BARB is a desensitization procedure that can be used by the group leader to increase adolescents' tolerance to negative feedback. After cueing him to anticipate the negative, the leader delivers false, low-level negative statements. The youth must first look at the leader and say anything to him in a normal tone of voice. Using successive approximation, the leader increases the level of the negative feedback, drops the cue prompt, and the students must learn to respond with assertive verbal and nonverbal responses. The group members are later included in the BARB procedure, and the adolescent is unsure whether the negative is real or an instruction as part of the desensitization procedure.

Time-out is used as a self-control device. Adolescents place themselves on time-out, a withdrawal from the interaction, whenever they need to problem solve or employ cognitive self-coping talk. A standard line, "Give me a few minutes to think about that," is taught. In intense anger situations, the time-out is initiated by disclosing discomfort and making a commitment to return at a specified time—for example, "I am too upset to talk about this now. I'll come back in 10 minutes and we can discuss this."

Research

The effectiveness of social skills training with adolescents was initially evaluated by Rotheram and Armstrong (1977). Twenty-six ninth-grade (15 male and 11 female) and 34 twelfth-grade students (16 male and 18 female), at a middle-class high school, received a 10 week assertiveness training package for two hours per week. Within the assertion condition at each grade level, half the students participated in groups that were rated as significantly more cohesive than their peers on the basis of leader and group ratings. These students were compared on a variety of measures with a no-treatment control group of 20 ninth- and 34 twelfth-grade students. A comparison was made among cohesive assertion training, noncohesive assertion training, and control group. The results indicated a significant increase in assertiveness on self-report (Schumacher 1974) and behavioral measures (Hersen, Eisler, and Miller 1974) and a decrease in teachers' rating of behavioral problems in the cohesive assertiveness training group. No positive changes were found in the noncohesive assertiveness training or control group. In fact, there was a significant increase in aggression and passivity on the self-report assertiveness inventory in the noncohesive assertive groups. These findings do point to the importance of cohesion in adolescent social skills training groups, as well as the effectiveness of the intervention when there is a cohesive group.

Discussion points

Control. Interpersonal control is an issue when dealing with adolescents. First, adolescents often initiate a testing process. Who has the power to decide how and what someone is going to do? Engaging the adolescent around these issues is the single most destructive process in social skills training. Unlike children, who can be physically placed in a time-out room for disruptiveness, adolescents must be treated differently. Adolescents can behave in any way they want, and the leader has little control over the outcome. If adolescents do not want to learn how to be assertive, they will not and the instructor cannot force them.

Self and interpersonal control are also relevant for twelfth graders, but at a different level. Children do not know the social rules or consequences, or lack the assertive option in their behavior repetoire. The primary goal of training is to transfer the information and develop skills. By 17 or 18 years of age, the average adolescent knows or is cognitively aware of the social rules. This is particularly true in a middle-class setting. The primary goal of the assertion program is not to teach or transfer information about the rules, but to free the adolescent from the cognitive or emotional inhibitors or behavioral mislearning that has occurred. This shift in emphasis is a crucial one. It allows adolescents the potential to make an extra dimensional shift in their understanding of assertiveness, and requires further explanation.

Salter (1949) originally defined assertiveness as expression of self in whatever way desired. Now, cognitive behavioral therapists have refined the understanding of social interaction to specific cognitive behavioral packages which tell us the socially appropriate assertive behavior in a variety of situations (Lange and Jakobowski 1976; Cotter and Guerra 1975). While originally designed to increase an individual's options, assertiveness training now provides us with a new set of rules to follow. Instead of dropped voice and eyes, we must now look at someone and talk between 5 and 10 decibels. This is confirmed by the social skills trainer's injunction to "be assertive." To shift from the cognitive behavioral definition of assertiveness as a set of behaviors on the middle of a set of a continuum, to Salter's (1949) defintion of expressiveness, requires a shift in perceptual sets. This shift involves the perception of behavioral options in the world—passive and aggressive as well as assertive (Rotheram 1978). For example, approximately 40 percent of the female adolescent population cannot yell on request, not even the alphabet. For these girls, assertive behavior is not a real choice, because assertive behaviors such as expression of feelings and requests are not in their behavioral repertoire. The knowledge that there are other options is a crucial variable in facilitating a shift for the adolescent from acquiring the cognitive-behavioral components of assertiveness to expressive assertiveness. Executing the shift produces the integration of all components—cognitive, behavioral and emotional—and dramatic behavioral changes are noted.

To sidestep the interpersonal control issues typical of adolescent period, to aid in a release from paradoxical injunction to "be assertive", and to jump from Lange and Jakubowski's (1976) cognitive behavioral definition of assertiveness to Salter's (1949) definition, paradoxical techniques can be successfully employed with adolescents. The trainer's approach to working with challenges must be that, "I can't make you be assertive. You can choose to be assertive or not. You have the power to determine what, when, or how you choose to respond. You decide what is assertive and what isn't." In addition, trainers can reinforce the perception of assertiveness as an option by asking for and eliciting passive and aggressive behavior. In role playing a problem, the trainer may ask for the most passive response imaginable. The adolescent is asked to become Casper Milktoast or Agatha Aggressive. As he role plays, there is no performance criterion. He is free, or even encouraged, to be incompetent and make mistakes. Often this is the most assertive role play experience of the rehearsal period. Also, the adolescents goals are crystallized in this imperfect production. Homework assignments to engage in passive or mildly aggressive behaviors are a third method of facilitating the extra-dimensional shift. These assignments make the adolescent painfully aware of the internal dialogue and low self-esteem associated with being nonassertive.

Consultation Models. The original impetus for developing the present cognitive behavioral social skills model was a consultation request to a regional mental health team from a school with widespread behavior problems and underachievement. Barbara Smith (1974) employed assertion training with school administrators as a consultation strategy to gain entrance into the school systems. Having gained trust at the administrative level, she could gain access to field personnel, and eventually, the target child population. In the present project, a very different consultation strategy was employed. The ultimate target of the intervention was the children. A primary goal was to train personnel in the school district who could continue to provide services after the mental health team has completed the consultation. The literature on consultation points to the frequent failure of teachers and administrators to apply knowledge gained in training workshops. An initial workshop given to teachers a year earlier had failed to execute a transfer into the classroom. While excited and hopeful during the workshop, the teachers found classroom implementation overwhelming. The teachers began to discount the value of the intervention. While it was personally beneficial to the teachers, they knew the consultant had not had to face 30 mixed-up kids. King's (1978) data on discrimination of innovation therapeutic techniques suggest that the interventions must be demonstrated and modeled for the trainees. In this case, a five-step process was required.

1. Conduct an initial workshop with teachers to inform and to excite them

about the intervention. This also helps to minimize sabotage to the program.
2. Demonstrate statistically the efficiency of using social skills with children.
3. Thoroughly train teachers and counselors in didactic material outside classroom.
4. Provide on-site consultation to teachers as they reimplement the program themselves.
5. Branch up the administrative hierarchy.

This process was successfully completed using the social skills training program outlined above. This report and data were developed at stage two of the process. In addition, three agencies received benefits from the projects:

1. The schools initiated requests for services to mental health. The school received training for over 400 elementary and high school children and 25 teachers and administrators over a two-year period.
2. Mental health coordinated and provided consulting services. The agency received positive publicity in the community and the following year received a paid consultation contract with the district.
3. A major university received field and research training for 35 undergraduate and graduate students who assisted mental health in implementing the program. A package program was developed and tested. The data provided evidence on the efficiency of the intervention for teachers and administrators.

Research. At the present time, energy must be focused on the developmental nature of interpersonal social skills. Preschool children make friends very differently from third-grade children, who are again differentiated from sixth graders. Age-appropriate baseline measures of assertiveness are needed. A study on this topic is in progress at the present time. From the data available on children, it appears that social skills training will influence such variables as grades. The relationship between social and academic competence is an important issue necessitating further investigation.

Summary

A cognitive behavioral social skills training program to be applied to third- through sixth-grade children and high school students was presented. The program focused on teaching a strategy for solving interpersonal problems combined with the behavioral skills and emotional self-control to implement the problem solving. The cognitive skills included Spivack and Shure's (1977) interpersonal problem solving program, self-monitoring of covert reinforcement and punishment, and social inferential ability. Behavioral skills including both verbal and nonverbal behaviors gained through role playing, modeling, cuing, reinforcement, assessment techniques, relaxation training, and cognitive self-data procedures were taught to provide emotional self-control to the children. Differences in the format of presentation to children of different ages were reviewed. Research on the effectiveness of the interventions was summarized.

References

Alberti, R. E. and Emmons, M. C. 1976. *Your perfect right, 2nd ed.,* San Luis Obispo, Calif.: Impact Press.

Allen, G., Chinsky, J., Larcen, S., Lochman, J. and Selinger, H. 1976. *Community psychology and the schools: A behaviorally oriented multilevel preventive approach.* Hillside, New Jersey: Earlbaum.

Asher, S. R. and Parke, R. D. 1975. Influence of sampling and comparison processes on the development of communication effectiveness. *Journal of Educational Psychology 67,* 64-75.

Bandura, A. 1964. The stormy decade: fact or fiction. *Psychology in the School, 1,* 224-31.

Bandura, A., Ross, D., and Ross, S. A. 1961. Transmission of aggression through imitation of aggressive models. *Journal of Abnormal Social Psychology, 63,* 575.

Barrett, D. E. and Yarrow, M. R. 1977. Prosocial behavior, social inferential ability and assertiveness in children. *Child Development, 48,* 475-81.

Blucksbert, S. and Krauss, R. M. 1967. What do people say after they have learned to talk? Studies on the development of referential communication. *Merrill-Palmer Quarterly, 13,* 309-42.

Bond, F. T. 1974. Enhancement of self-concept through elicitation of positive self-assertive statements and positive social reinforcement. *Dissertation Abstracts International, 34,* 3979A-3980A

Chennault, M. 1967. Improving the social acceptance of unpopular educable mentally retarded pupils in special classes. *American Journal of Mental Deficiency, 72,* 455-58.

Chittenden, G. E. 1942. An experimental study in measuring and modifying assertive behavior in young children. *Monographs of the Society for Research in Child Development, 7,* no. 1 (serial no. 31).

Cowen, E. L., Pederson, A., Babigian, H., Izzo, L. A., and Trost, M. A. 1973. Long term follow-up of early detected vulnerable children. *Journal of Consulting and Clinical Psychology, 41,* 438-46.

Cox, R. and Gunn, W. 1978. Assessment of social skills in children. Presented at the Seventh Annual Meeting of the Houston Behavior Therapy Association, Houston, Texas, 1978.

Crutchfield, R. S. 1955. Conformity and character, *American Psychologist, 10,* 191.

Dorman, L. 1973. Assertive behavior and cognitive performance in preschool children. *Journal of Genetic Psychology, 123,* 155-62.

D'Zurilla, T. J., and Goldfried, M. R. 1971. Problem-solving and behavior modification. *Journal of Abnormal Psychology, 78,* 107-26.

Eisenberg, L. 1965. A developmental approach to adolescence. *Children, 12,* 131-65.

Elardo, P. T. 1974. Project Aware: A school program to facilitate the social development of children. Paper presented at the Fourth Annual H. Blumberg Symposium, Chapel Hill, North Carolina.

Elardo, P. T. and Caldwell, B. M. 1974. Project aware: A school program to facilitate the social development of kindergarten elementary children. Unpublished manuscript.

Elardo, P. T. and Caldwell, B. M. 1976. An examination of the relationship between role-taking and social competence. Paper presented at Southeastern Conference on Human Development, Nashville.

Erikson, E. 1960. Youth and culture, *Children, 7,* 43-49.

Feffer, M.H. and Gourevitch, V. 1960. Cognitive aspects of role-taking in children. *Journal of Personality, 28,* 383-96.

Feffer, M. H. and Jahelka, M. 1968. Implications of the decentering concept for the structuring of projective content. *Journal of Consulting and Chinical Psychology, 32,* 434-41.

Flavell, J. H., Botkin, R. T., Fry, C. L., Wright, J. W. and Jarvio, P. E., 1968. *The development of roletaking and communication skills in children.* New York: Wiley.

Flowers, J. 1975. Simulation and role-playing methods. In *Helping People Change: A Textbook of Methods,* ed. F. H. Kanfer and A. P. Goldstein. Elmsford, New York: Pergamon Press.

Flowers, J. V. and Marston, A. R. 1972. Modification of low self-confidence in elementary school children. *Journal of Educational Research, 66,* 30-34.

Flowers, J., Rotheram, M., and Kenney, B. 1974. Behavioral group therapy and the behavioral training of group therapists: A symposium paper presented at the Western Psychological Association, San Francisco.

Getzel, J. W. and Jackson, P. W. 1971. The highly intelligent and the highly creative adolescent: A summary of research findings. In *Adolescent behavior and society: A book of readings,* ed. R. E. Muess. New York: Random House.

Gronlund, N. E. and Anderson, L. 1971. Personality characteristics of socially accepted, socially neglected, and socially rejected junior high school pupils. In *Adolescent behavior and society: A book of readings.* ed. R. E. Muess. New York: Random House.

Hall, G. S. 1916. *Adolescence.* New York: Appleton.

Hartup, W. W. 1970. Peer interaction and social organization. In *Carmichaels manual of child psychology,* ed. P. Mussen. Vol. 2. New York: Wiley.

Hersen, M., Eisler, R. M., and Miller, P. M. 1973. Development of assertive responses: Clinical, measurement and research considerations. *Behavior Research and Therapy, 11,* 505-21.

Kagan, J. 1964. Acquisition and significance of sex typing and sex role identity. In *Review of child development research,* ed. M. Hoffman and L. Hoffman. Vol. 1. New York: Russell Sage.

Kagan, J., and Moss, H. A. 1962. *Birth to maturity: The Fels study of psychological development.* New York: Wiley.

Kaufman, L. M., and Wagner, B. R. 1972. BARB: A systematic treatment technology for control disorders. *Behavior Therapy, 3,* 84-90.

Lange, A. and Jakubowski, J. 1977. *A cognitive-behavioral approach to assertiveness training.* Champaign, Ill.: Research Press.

Larcen, S. W., Chinsky, J. M., Allen, G., Lochman, J., and Selinger, H. V. 1974. Training in child sociological problem solving strategies. Paper presented at Midwestern Psychological Association, Chicago.

Lieberman, J., King, L., DiRisis, W., and White, J. 1977. *Personal effectiveness.* Champaign, Ill: Research Press.

Lilly, M. S. 1971. Improving social acceptance of low sociometric status, low achieving students. *Exceptional Children, 37,* 341-47.

Maccoby, E. and Wilson, W. 1957. Identification and observation learning from films. *Journal of Abnormal Sociology and Psychology, 55,* 76-87.

McChure, L. F. 1975. Social problem-solving training and assessment: An experimental intervention in an elementary school setting. Unpublished dissertation, University of Connecticut, Storrs.

McFall, R. M., and Twentyman, C. T. 1973. Four experiments in the relative contribution of rehearsal, modeling, and coaching to assertion training. *Journal of Abnormal Psychology, 81,* 199-218.

Meichenbaum, D. 1974. *Cognitive behavior modification.* Morristown, N.J.: General Learning Press.

Meichenbaum, D. 1976. Toward a cognitive theory of self-control, in *Consciousness and self-regulation,* ed. G. Schwartz and D. Shapiro. Vol. 1. New York Plenum Press.

Meichenbaum, D. 1976. A cognitive-behavior modification approach to assessment. In *Behavioral assessment: A practical handbook,* ed. M. Hersen and A. S. Bellack. Elmsford, New York: Pergamon Press.

Mussen, P. H., Early sex role development. 1969. In *Handbook of socialization theory and research,* ed. D. Goslin. Chicago: Rand McNally.

Muste, M. H., and Shape, D. F. 1947. Some influential factors in the determination of aggressive behavior in preschool children. *Child Development, 18,* 11.

Novaco, R. W. 1974. A treatment program for the management of anger through cognitive and relaxation controls. Unpublished doctoral dissertation. Indiana University, Bloomington, Indiana.

Novaco, R. W. 1975. *Anger control: The development and evaluation of an experimental treatment.* New York: Lexington Books.

O'Connor, R. D. 1969a. Modification of social withdrawal through symbolic modeling. *Journal of Applied Behavior Analysis, 2,* 15-22.

O'Connor, R. D. 1969b. Modification treatment of nonbehavioral disorders. Paper presented at 41st Annual Meeting of Midwestern Psychological Association, Chicago, May.

O'Connor, R. D. 1972. *Social learning and communication: A psychological approach to mental health.* New York: Holt, Rinehart and Winston.

Oden, S., and Asher, S. R. 1977. Coaching children in social skills for friendship making, *Child Development, 48,* 495-506.

Platt, J. J., and Spivack, G. 1972. Problem-solving thinking of psychiatric patients. *Journal of Consulting and Clinical Psychology, 39,* 148-51.

Platt, J. J., and Spivack, G. 1975. Manual for the means-ends problem-solving procedure. *Journal of Clinical Psychology, 31,* 15-16.

Ringness, T. A. 1967. Identification patterns motivation, and school achievement of Bright Junior High School. *Journal of Educational Psychology, 58,* 93-102.

Roff, M. 1961. Childhood social interactions and your adult bad conduct. *Journal of Abnormal and Social Psychology, 63,* 333-37.

Roff, M., Sells, B., and Golden, M. M. 1972. Social adjustment and personality development in children. Minneapolis: University of Minnesota Press.

Rothbart, M. K., and Maccoby, E. E. 1966. Parents' differential reaction to sons and daughters. *Journal Personality Social Psychology, 3,* 237-43.

Rothenberg, B. 1970. Children's social sensitivity and the relationship to interpersonal competence, interpersonal comfort, and intellectual level. *Developmental Psychology, 2,* 335-50.

Rotheram, M. 1974. Stylistic patterns of aggressive behavior among incarcerated delinquents. Paper presented at Western Psychological Association Annual Conference, Los Angeles.

Rotheram, M. 1977. Differences in aggressive response style among four groups of delinquents. *Dissertation abstracts international.*

Rotheram, M., and Armstrong, M. 1977. Assertiveness among high school students. Paper presented at Western Psychological Association, Seattle.

Rotheram, M., Armstrong, M. and Booraem, C. 1978. Ecobehavioral analysis of social skills training. Unpublished manuscript, Ohio State University.

Rubin, K. H. 1972. Relationship between egocentric-communication and popularity among peers. *Developmental Psychology, 7,* 364.

Rucker, C. H., and Vincenzo, F. M. 1970. Maintaining social acceptance gains made by mentally retarded children. *Exceptional Children, 36,* 679-80.

Sabol, D. E. 1974. The effects of psychosocial awareness classes on self-esteem, behavior, and academic achievement in the elementary grades. *Dissertation abstracts international,* 271A.

Salter, A. 1949. *Conditioned reflex therapy.* New York: Creative Age Press.

Saranson, I. G. 1968. Verbal learning modeling and juvenile delinquency. *American Psychologist, 23,* 254-66.

Saranson, I. G., and Ganger, V. J. 1971. Modeling: An approach to the rehabilitation juvenile offenders. Final report to the social and rehabilitation service of the Department of Health, Education, and Welfare, June 1971.

Schnall, M., and Feffer, M. 1970. Role-taking task scoring criteria. Unpublished manuscript. Yeshiva University, New York

Schantz, C. V. 1975. The development of social cognition. In *Review of child development research.* ed. E. V. Hetherington. Vol. 1. Chicago: University of Chicago Press.

Schumacher, M., and Pyrinski, C. 1974. Group assertion training for institutionalized delinquents. A paper presented to the Western Psychological Association, Los Angeles, Calif.

Schwartz, R., and Gottman, J. 1974. A task analysis approach to clinical problems: A study of assertive behavior. Unpublished manuscript, Indiana University.

Sears, R. R., Macoby, E. E., and Levin, H. 1957. *Patterns of child rearing.* New York: Harper and Row.

Smith, M. E. 1933. The influence of age, sex and situation on the frequency and form and function of questions asked by preschool children. *Child Development, 3,* 201.

Smith, M. 1975. *When I say no I feel guilty.* Los Angeles: Dial Press.

Spivack, G., and Levine, M. 1963. Self-regulation in acting out and normal adolescents. Report M-4531, National Institute of Health, Washington, D.C.

Spivack, G., Platt, J., and Shure, M. 1976. *The problem-solving approach to adjustment.* San Francisco: Josey-Bass Publishers.

Spivack, G., and Shure, M. B. 1974. *Social adjustment of young child: A cognitive approach to solving real-life problems.* San Francisco: Josey-Bass.

Stuart, R. B. 1971. Behavioral contracting within the families of delinquents. *Journal of Behavior Therapy Experimental Psychiatry, 2,* 1-11.

Suchotliff, L. 1970. Relation of formal thought disorder of the community deficit of schizophrenics. *Journal of Abnormal Psychology, 76,* 250-57.

Walker, H. M. and Hops, H. 1973. The use of group and individual reinforcement contingencies in the modification of social withdrawal. In *Behavior change, methodology, concepts and practice,* ed. L. C. Hardy and E. J. Mash. Champaign, Ill.: Research Press.

Whalen, C. K., Flowers, J., Rotheram, M., and Tressbet, T. 1975. Behavioral measures of personal space in children, Man, Environment, and Systems. *V. T., 5,* 396-403.

Wolpe, J. 1958. *Reciprocal Inhibition Therapy.* Stanford, Calif.: Stanford University Press.

5

Interpersonal Skills in the Schools: Assessment and Curriculum Development

Roger D. Cox
William B. Gunn

It is generally recognized that the ability to interact successfully with both peers and significant adults is one of the important developmental milestones of a child's elementary school years. The development of those interpersonal skills, however, has not traditionally been assumed to be the responsibility of the educational system (Strain, Cooke, and Apolloni 1976; Lazarus 1973). The primary function of formal education has always been to provide academic skills for the child. The school's role in the socialization of children has most often been viewed as important, but limited. School provides the child with the opportunity to experience peer and adult interactions under the supervision of responsible, concerned educators in a healthy physical environment (see Hartup 1976). The development of adaptive, socially acceptable interaction skills has always been presumed to occur without formal structured training. The varieties of informal training assumed to accomplish the task of "socializing" have included such influences as the modeling of parental social behaviors, parental discipline for socially deviant responses, and attention, approval, and reinforcement for appropriate responses. In addition to the role of the parents and family, some secondary responsibility for the socialization of children in interpersonal areas has often been accepted by religious or civic organizations, such as scouting organizations and church groups. One final socializing influence on children, considered by some to be the most important, is the interaction with peers, an experience which Hartup (1976) argues is not a superficial luxury to be enjoyed by some children and not by others, but also a necessity of childhood socialization.

Fortunately, the majority of children develop at least minimally acceptable interpersonal skills under this loosely knit, informal system of social instruction. Recently, however, evidence has been reported which causes concern for those children for whom this system of socialization is not adequate. Research now suggests that many children go through their school years with few or no friends. For example, in one study, Gronlund (1959) found that 6 percent of third to sixth graders have *no* classroom friends, and an additional 12 percent have only one friend. Additional concern for such children is aroused when one reviews the findings of studies that have examined the relationship between low-level peer relationships and other adjustment problems. Children who are socially isolated or who have problems interacting with others are: (1) more likely to drop out of school (Ullmann 1957) (2) more likely to be later identified as juvenile delinquents (Roff, Sells, and Golden 1972), and (3) more likely later to have mental health problems (Cowen et al. 1973). Other researchers have demonstrated additional relationships between low social ability and both bad-conduct discharges from military service (Roff 1961) and overall school maladjustment (Gronlund and Anderson 1963). While it is always wise to consider the interpretation of such retrospective studies cautiously, the number of studies which continue to support the idea that low social skill children are at high risk with regard to healthy adjustment in such diverse areas compels attention.

Though schools have not included formal instruction of social skills for children, the interpersonal behavior of students within the school environment significantly affects the instruction of academic skills. Teachers frequently complain about the increasing discipline problems within schools that hamper their ability to provide quality academic instruction. In addition to the discipline problems created by disruptive students, educators and clinicians are becoming increasingly aware of both social and academic deficiencies associated with withdrawal and isolation of school children (Hops, Walker, and Greenwood 1977). While restructuring traditional academic curricula to include broader "social" areas such as interpersonal skill development will create additional burdens on educational staff, the early identification of low social skill children followed by appropriate remedial intervention programs should bring significant long-term benefits to both children and educators.

It would also appear that in light of the dramatic changes that can be observed in the "typical" American family, the review of educational objectives and priorities may need to occur immediately. The American family is changing; the nuclear family with father, mother, and one or more children residing together decreases in overall percentage each year. As family patterns change, it is not presently possible to predict the types of changes which will result for children growing up in such families. It is apparent from available research done on single-parent families that the children of such families are at some risk concerning their social and emotional development (see Hetherington, Cox, and Cox 1977, 1978). Each year the numbers of such children increase. In 1975 alone, there were more than one million divorces, and in each an average of 1.22 children were involved. According to recent estimates, there are more than 10 million children presently growing up in families without a father. In contrast to the increasing divorce rate, the marriage rate has begun to drop. The 1975 ratio of divorces to marriages was about 1:2, with 1,026,000 divorces and 2,126,000 marriages. While no one can completely predict the effects of such a dramatic change in society on its children, it does appear that the formal educational system should begin now to prepare itself for a generation of children who may have special needs concerning their social and emotional development.

The purpose of this chapter is to describe the rationale and procedures which are currently being utilized to identify low social skill children within school settings and to provide intervention designed to improve interpersonal functioning.

The Identification of the Low Social Skill Child

Once the decision has been made to attempt social skill intervention training in the school system, it is necessary to develop an assessment strategy to identify low skill children. Recently, the most popular assessment procedure has been some form of sociometric rating based on peer popularity or friendship (Gottman, Gonso, and Rasmussen 1975; Asher, Oden and Gottman 1976). While it is reasonable to assume that a socially deficient child is likely to be unpopular and/or seldom chosen by peers in a friendship rating, such a procedure measures a result or "outcome" of social skill deficiency. It does not specify or identify measurable behaviors of skills that are descriptive of the "process" of becoming a low skill child. Even researchers who favor such sociometric types of buddy ratings point out that friendship is simply one dimension that can be rated. McCandless (1976) suggests that a competence dimension can and should be added to such evaluations. It is our opinion that while increases in dimensions do broaden the perspective of such measures, the sociometric rating is simply not suited to the purpose for which it is being used. In our opinion, sociometric ratings by peers, teachers' ratings of behavior, and parents' ratings should, at best, be *con-*

sidered as useful in establishing discriminant validity for the specific measures of interpersonal ability selected for either assessment procedures or training. That is, since selection of specific skills related to increased social ability in children is at present an intuitive process, it is advisable to correlate performance on the tasks chosen as operational definitions of "social skill" with some other criterion of successful social ability such as sociometric rating of popularity (see Gottman et al. 1975). Other criteria which can be used in the same way to establish discriminant validity between tasks selected for measurement and independent indications of social ability are referral for emotional maladjustment and teacher or parent ratings of social behavior.

In developing the assessment procedure for identifying low social skill children, we have included two social domains of the child's life. The first domain consists of a variety of interpersonal-conversational situations. Specific skills and abilities associated with a child's performance within those conversational situations are recorded for analysis. The second domain consists of several situations in which the child becomes a participant in a two-person disagreement (that is, interpersonal conflict). Again, specific abilities and skills have been identified and are recorded for analysis. While these two domains, that is, conversational and interpersonal conflict situations, have been included in the assessment because of their relevance for a clinical population of children, independent support for the inclusion of such scenes in social skill evaluation with children has recently been reported (greeting scenes—Gottman et al. 1975; interpersonal conflict scenes—Bornstein, Bellack and Hersen 1977).

Within these two types of situations, our attempt to conceptualize social skillfulness has resulted in the identification of three separate but related response capabilites. First, the child who fails to respond appropriately to interpersonal situations may not possess the cognitive knowledge of appropriate behaviors required within the situation. To develop this cognitive knowledge, the child must have "attended" to previously modeled appropriate responses by others, while also having the capacity to "retain" and symbolically encode such behavior for future reference (see Bandura 1977). The child who lacks knowledge of "how one responds" to specific interpersonal situations may have failed to develop the necessary knowledge in one of several ways. First, he may have failed to attend to appropriate models who have demonstrated adaptive responses. Secondly, he may have attended but lacked the ability either to encode the symbolic representation of the event, or to retrieve the stored memory representation. Or thirdly, he may have not had the opportunity to observe an "appropriate" model due to the unavailability of a competent model or the poor quality of available models.

The second response capability which is required for a child to behave "skillfully" is in the area of the motor reproductive processes (see Bandura 1977). Even if the child has successfully coded the cognitive information concerning how to respond in a situation, it is possible that the motor reproductive abilities to carry out the actions are underdeveloped. To explain this ability, let me provide an analogy based on the ability to land a huge 747 airplane in a dense fog. While most readers of this manuscript are not pilots, it is certainly possible to imagine that step-by-step instructions on performing an instrument landing could be memorized and recited verbatim, should that be necessary. At this point, then, the individual who has memorized the landing procedure possesses the symbolic coding and cognitive information necessary to land the 747 using only instruments in a fog. But few, if any, reasonable adults who possessed knowledge of the steps required, the levers to be pulled and pushed, and the adjustments to counteract wind factors would be willing to attempt such a feat, for the motor reproductive skills, that is, the actual "doing" of the behaviors, have not been practiced or rehearsed. Children in interpersonal situations may face a similar type of problem. The necessary information about "responding" has been symbolically coded and is available to the child. But the actual "action sequence" has not been practiced and rehearsed. The child, then, has the cognitive competence to perform, but lacks the necessary motor skills to successfully complete the sequence of behavior.

The third response capability refers to the emotional response which may occur when the child is placed in interpersonal situations. The child may have the necessary knowledge, and may have practiced the motor skills required; still, the child has difficulty because of emotional responses that are incompatible with performing the appropriate behaviors. Perhaps this emotional response capability can best be conceptualized as an emotional continuum, characterized by Bronson (1969) as emotional reactivity. At one end of the continuum is the child who, when faced with interpersonal situations, is overcome by anxiety and perhaps even unable to respond at all. Even when the first two response capabilities are well formed and functional, some children have problems controlling the anxiety associated with interpersonal situations. To illustrate, I can remember one child that we had trained to cope with a variety of difficult interpersonal situations. While having lunch with the social skills training staff one day, however, this child discovered that he had been given a spoiled desert at a fast food restaurant where we were all eating. The boy looked sheepishly at us and said, "I know what I should do, but I'm really nervous about doing it." He took several deep breaths and approached the cashier with the spoiled desert trembling in his hand. The cashier called the manager and after a brief discussion, the child returned to the table with his refund. He was greeted with congratulations at his effective use of his newly acquired skills. We asked him why he had gotten a cash refund instead of having them give him another desert. "Because," he replied, "I'm still so scared about this that I was afraid I'd throw up if I ate anything else." For some children, the anxiety response may remain long after both knowledge and motor performance abilities have been strengthened.

At the other end of the continuum of emotional reactivity is the child with personal characteristics of impulsiveness, lack of self-control, little forethought about the response that should be made, and an inability to resist temptation (see Grim, Kohlberg, and White 1968). These children are not overly anxious when placed in interpersonal situations, but lack the reflective capacity necessary to bring their responses in line with newly acquired social abilities. For both types of children, of course, the goal of social skills training is to move them toward the middle of this dimension. The importance of attempting to accomplish that emotional movement can perhaps best be illustrated by Hartup's recent discussion of the findings of over 20 studies which report a positive relationship between good emotional adjustment and popularity (Hartup 1970, 1976).

Though it is certainly desirable for any assessment of interpersonal skillfulness to be responsive to all three response capacities, measuring these abilities in an independent fashion is not easy. Consider the difficulties of measuring the knowledge of a yound child concerning a difficult interpersonal situation (for example, another child takes away a toy from the target child). The most direct method of determining the knowledge that the child has about appropriate responses is simply to ask. In adult research assessing assertive skills, a questionnaire is often used to accomplish this objective. With most of these instruments, subjects respond to a series of 30-50 items that call for a decision about a specific response to the situation (Rathus 1973; Gambrill and Richey 1976). The response usually consists of a simple "yes" or "no." In some of the more sophisticated devices, the selection of a number is required (for example, one to five, indicating the degree to which the statement is descriptive of the subject; a one indicates "I never do that," a five means "I always do that."). Though the possibility exists of simply rewording such an instrument by making the questions more appropriate for children, major problems with this approach have precluded selection of this solution. For instance, as worded, most questions ask the subject to describe his or her actual behavior when in the specified situation. With a child, this leads to a high probability of having two different types of valuable information confounded. The knowledge of desirable actions can be confounded with his actual behavior when placed in those situations. Since children have a desire to appear socially desirable and will often respond as they think the experimenter wants them to, it is unlikely that information gathered with such a technique reliably reflects actual behavior. A more serious problem with the approach, however, is the model of social skillfulness that is implied by the format of the paper-and-pencil measure.

Even though the more sophisticated questionnaires allow for "some of the time" answers (that is, numbers two-four on the one-five scale), it is implied that the ability to make a single response within a social situation identifies the subject as skilled. For instance, in the Gambrill and Richey Inventory, one question asks the subject if he or she is able to "ask a person who is annoying you in a public situation to stop" (Gambrill and Richey 1976; item 40). Though this is a necessary first step to solving this conflict situation, asking once for a behavior change is not always sufficient to effect change. In fact, in our research, it has been found that it is after the first response fails to elicit a desired goal that the actual limits of a person's social ability are tested (Cox, Gunn, and Cox 1976).

The assessment procedure that we have developed is designed to test the limits of the child's responsiveness in interpersonal situations. A series of eight interpersonal scenes have been devised with four designed to assess the child's ability to initiate and maintain conversation and the second four designed to determine how the child responds to interpersonal conflict situations. The Appendix contains the instructions and scripts used in the assessment package.

The children assessed with this procedure are taken to an experimental room equipped with video tape recorder, TV monitor, microphone, table and selected games. The scenes are described to each child and the subjects are instructed to act as they would if this actually happened to them.

In our first attempt to validate the measure, we compared performance of 16 male students from a public school setting, grades four through six, with 16 male subjects from a residential program for children with behavior problems (Cox, et al. 1976). Following completion of the assessment, taped scenes were scored according to the following categories:

Nonverbal Behaviors
(Scored on all eight scenes)

Eye Contact
Body Posture
Loudness of Voice
Fluency, i.e., negative scores for stuttering, stammering, or voice breaks

Verbal Behavior: Greeting Scenes
(Scored only for greeting scenes and conversational scenes)

Greeting	Subject gave his name and made a salutation. Subject acknowledged the other person giving his name.
Request Information	Subject asked a question about the other person.
Statement	Subject made a general conversational statement.

Verbal Behavior: Interpersonal Conflict Scenes	
Polite Request	Subject asked for a change in other's behavior.
Emphatic Request	Subject told the other to change behavior.
Request Reason	Subject asked for motive of other person.
Argument/Denial	Subject refuted statement made by other person.
Reason	Subject gave a reason why the other person should comply with his request for change.
Nonphysical contingency	Subject expressed nonphysical event that would occur if other person did not change behavior.
Appreciation	Subject acknowledged behavior of other person with some appreciation.
Compliance	Subject complied with other person and failed to try to obtain behavior change.

The comparison of performance in two groups of male children resulted in several interesting results. We have found that the nonverbal categories scored on all scenes serve as a sensitive measure of the child's "nervousness" in the situations. A child who has difficulty making or holding eye contact, or who fidgets or shuffles his feet during the scene, generally gives the appearance of being in some discomfort. On three of the nonverbal measures scored in the evaluation, the males with behavior problems were scored as significantly less skillful than were the nonproblem boys. Eye contact was significantly lower for problem boys, body posture was stiffer with a higher frequency of fidgeting, and voice fluency was poorer for the problem boys, who were more likely to stutter, stammer, or suffer breaks in vocalization. Only loudness of voice failed to result in significant differences between the two groups, performance, as both groups of subjects spoke with an appropriately loud volume.

While this finding was not unexpected, it should be emphasized that the problem boys had not been referred for their inability to control anxiety. In fact, without exception, the boys had been referred for acting out hostility, lack of self-control, and unwillingness to follow directions. Thus, they appear to fall under the category of explosiveness rather than placidity (see Bronson 1966). Yet all their nonverbal behaviors were indicative of individuals who are having a strong emotional reaction.

Comparison of the two groups using the verbal categories associated with greeting and conversational scenes revealed no significant differences in performance. In other words, both groups of boys showed a similar pattern of greeting strangers, requesting information about the stranger, and making statements about themselves. This finding contradicts the reported difference in similar greeting scenes between popular and unpopular children found by Gottman et al. (1975). While additional research is needed to explore this discrepancy, it is entirely possible that the populations studied may have different characteristics. In two of the four greeting and conversation scenes used by Cox et al. (1976), however, the confederate actor responds favorably to the subject and agrees with the child's wishes or compliments the child on a job well done. The nonproblem males were significantly more likely to show appreciation for such comments than were the boys with behavior problems. Eleven of the 16 problem children made no statement of appreciation or thanks throughout the filming of the scenes. Thirteen of the 16 nonproblem children made at least one appreciative comment.

The scenes in which the child's ability to deal with interpersonal conflict was tested also resulted in differential performance between the two groups of boys. While both groups of boys were about equally likely to ask the other person politely to change his behavior, the behavior-problem children were significantly more likely to demand strongly a behavior change than were the nonproblem boys. The problem boys were also more likely to refute directly the previous statement of the confederate actor than were the nonproblem children (for example, Confederate: "I found the dollar and I'm going to keep it." Behavior-problem child: "No, you're not"). It seems to us that this category is of particular importance, since it results, in effect, in a direct confrontation or power struggle between participants. In contrast to this power-assertive approach, the nonproblem boys were significantly more likely to ask the confederate for the reason for his stubbornness (request reason), and also were more likely to give their own reason for expecting the confederate to engage in behavior change (reason). In addition, the nonproblem boys were significantly more likely to respond toward the end of a conflict scene with a statement that we called a nonphysical contingency (such as, "If you don't stop doing that, I'll have to get the teacher"). Note that we called it nonphysical to exclude any threatening gesture or statement which we scored as an emphatic request.

Finally, the behavior-problem boys were more likely simply to comply and voluntarily stop the scene before time was called than were the nonproblem children. We found this particularly fascinating, since one interpretation was that the problem children were "less assertive" than the nonproblem boys. From observation of the subjects, however, it appears that the most reasonable interpretation to place on this final difference is that the problem boys were more likely to use up their repertoire of verbal responses than were the nonproblem boys.

Utilizing Assessment Results in Curriculum Development

Though the results of assessment were informative and tended to support the utility of the assessment procedure, the most important function of the

6. Move to another location.
7. Threaten to go inform an authority figure about the problem.
8. Go find the authority figure and follow through with step seven.

It is important to note that for many children targeted for social skills training, the goal is not to teach them to respond to interpersonal conflict situations, but rather to teach them to respond to conflict with a measured response that does not have components of "aggression." We have found the rules to be good guidelines both for the child who overresponds by aggressing when in conflict as well as for the child who is anxious and does not know what response to make.

We found that after training children to use the keep-cool rules for about a month, our teaching staff was able to refuse to intervene in interpersonal conflict unless the complaining child was able to recite to the staff member which of the keep-cool rules he or she had tried to use to solve the problem. In other words, if a child approached a teacher and complained that another child had taken her pencil and wouldn't give it back, the teacher would ask which rules had been tried, other than number eight, which was to bring the matter to the attention of a teacher. Typically, we found that if a child could respond with three or four of the rules that had been tried before seeking assistance, intervention could usually be made in favor of the complaining child. Resorting to aggression was always considered a non-skillful response, as was running to the teacher without first trying to resolve the issue through the use of several of the rules. We should emphasize also that the rules, though taught as a hierarchy, were not considered to be rigid or fixed. For example, if another child physically attacked the subject child, particularly if that attack was unjustified and harsh, the child was taught to evaluate the seriousness of this action and respond with a rule that suited the situation (such as, "If you hit me again, I'm going to get the teacher.")

It is our experience that by defining terms with specific behaviors and listing rules as guidelines for responding that children can be taught to increase their cognitive knowledge of socially appropriate responses. In addition, we have also found that reviewing definitions of terms or rules provides an opportunity for modeling of the behaviors as they are reviewed. Thus, the motor performance of the child can also be improved as well. Discussion by the staff is directed toward both the consequences of the modeled behavior as well as the "quality" of the performance given by the role-play volunteer. Positive feedback is emphasized, and children as well as staff members are encouraged to acknowledge the appropriate aspects of the model's behavior. Criticism is also allowed, with the restriction that the comments constructively inform the model of specific responses that could have been included in his performance to improve the quality.

Goals of the Social Skills Training

The training sessions have three general goals which serve as overall objectives for each child. The first goal is to train each child to be an effective, competent role player. Role play provides each child with the opportunity to develop the necessary motor skills required to respond in the natural "real-life" environment. Role play also serves an important function of desensitizing the child to responding in interpersonal situations in front of an audience. Another major benefit of teaching the child to role play in the training sessions is that it helps develop the child's ability to observe the behavior of others. It is impossible for a child to imitate the behavior of another person adequately without spending time and effort focusing on the particular mannerisms and behaviors of that person. So an early part of the training sessions focuses on the ability of the child to role play another person, even if the content of the role play situation is not interpersonal. One technique that allows the training session to be nonthreatening and still productive is to have the child role play the behavior of his favorite teacher or staff member. This technique allows the child to role play a person who presumably demonstrates many of the prosocial responses (such as smiling, complimenting others on improvement, and offering assistance) that are desirable in the child.

The second goal is to focus on the behaviors necessary to greet and maintain conversations with others. During this training, particular attention is placed on the nonverbal aspects of responding, such as eye contact, body posture, personal distance from others, and facial expressions to indicate listening. The child is instructed in ways to approach and greet strangers, both adults and other children. It should be noted that the approach taught differs depending upon the status of the stranger. He or she is taught how to deliver compliments effectively and how to make statements of appreciation when appropriate. Conversation skills are also taught during this phase. Students are taught to use the previous remark of the conversant to cue their next response. They are given some guidelines for initiating and maintaining interesting conversations. Specifically, they are instructed in techniques designed to entice the conversant into talking about himself or herself. They are taught scripts which give them structure in asking appropriate questions about the interests, family life, and sports activities of the other person. Greeting and conversational scenes are role played in social skills club meetings to rehearse the motor skills/performance ability as well. Providing instruction in verbal and nonverbal components of conversation and greeting scenes prior to training in interpersonal conflict resolution has proved to be the most effective sequence of training. While there is some difficulty for many of the children in coping with the emotionality of all of the targeted interpersonal scenes, the conversation and greeting scenes do not have the added component of tension associated with interpersonal conflict. Therefore, training in greeting and conversational scenes prior to advancing to the more emotionally difficult interpersonal conflict scenes has proved to be an effective training strategy.

The final goal concerns the child's ability to cope with and solve interpersonal conflict. Our conclusions concerning the low-skill child's response to such situations is in basic agreement with other researchers who have studied this problem (Spivack and Shure 1964; Staub 1971). Spivack and Shure (1974) have suggested that low-skill children have a deficiency in their ability to generate alternative responses to difficult interpersonal situations. In contrast to the approach we describe, however, their training program encourages the children to generate and try their own solutions to these conflict situations. While these authors report that with extended training, the children do show decreases in aggressive responses, it appears to us that for many low-skill children the approach forces a low-skill child to learn by "trial and error." We find that the alternative strategy of teaching a series of behaviors loosely arranged in a hierarchy the keep-cool rules provides a basic structure within which the child can learn to utilize flexibility in responding to these situations.

Increasing Generalizations of Acquired Skills

The ultimate goal of any training program is to provide behavior change that generalizes to the child's social environment. It has been our experience that changing the behavior of the children within the social skills training sessions is a necessary but not sufficient goal. Without additional efforts by training staff to foster generalization when the children leave the training sessions, there is a tendency for the children to consider the learning "context bound," that is, appropriate for the social skills class but not used later. In order to increase generalization from training sessions to the natural environment, we have developed and used several procedures. The first procedure involved a written note by staff presented to the child. The note, called a "good note" by both children and teachers, was awarded whenever the child was discovered in the natural environment utilizing any of the specific skills that were objectives of the social skills training. If they witness a child using appropriate social skills in interpersonal situations, staff members are to take the child aside and personally write him or her a "good note." In the "good note," the particular behavior is described and the consequences of such behavior are emphasized. The note is read to the child and signed by the teacher. The child is instructed to carry the note with him or her until the next social skills class. At the next meeting, the note is presented to the class in front of all attending members, and the child is awarded special recognition.

Another procedure which has proven effective in increasing generalization has allowed specific targeted areas of concern to be identified and shaped for each child. A four-by-six-inch card is carried by the child. Listed on the card are the particular social behaviors that have been identified, with the help of the child, as those which need improvement. Staff members are encouraged to begin any session or class with the child by asking to see the card and making mental note of the behaviors which the child is attempting to improve. When a staff member observes the child demonstrating any of those targeted behaviors, the child is called aside and a notation on the card is made by the teacher, who then initials her entry. These notations can be something as simple as a checkmark or a "red dot" placed on the card with magic marker. Later, the child is able to exchange these checks or dots for a highly desirable activity, such as a field trip or lunch with a popular staff member.

One final procedure has been particularly effective in producing generalization of acquired social abilities. The class members are told that throughout the school day the staff has planted confederates who will be testing their newly acquired social skills. That is, they are told that a child who has been selected by the social skills training staff and given instructions may approach them and proceed to respond in a manner that creates conflict. They are told that these situations are "real-life tests" of their ability to use their newly acquired social skills. Under such instructions, the child is often alert to *all* interpersonal situations *as if* he or she might be the "real-life tests." While we typically do stage some situations with a "Candid Camera" approach to monitoring the event, the primary advantage of the procedure occurs primarily because the child is constantly looking for situations in which the trained skills might be utilized. The children return to class with stories about encounters with strangers or interpersonal conflicts that they were "positive" had been staged to test them. Special attention is given to students who report these situations, and they are often asked to role play their behavioral solutions for the class at its next meeting. All of these procedures have proven effective in the attempt to promote generalization of treatment effects.

Future Directions of Social Skills Training

Though the recent work of several investigators offers promise in improving the social skill level of socially deficient children, we are presently limited by our lack of sophistication in conceptualizing the area of social skills development. While a recent review has cogently summarized many of the methodological shortcomings of current efforts (see Combs and Slaby 1977), we would like to close this chapter with several comments about what we feel is the most serious of all problems that researchers and clinicians will face. The problem is a failure for present researchers to approach the problem of social skills from the developmental perspective. Such a failure has already resulted in the appearance of several attempts to scale down adult programs for use with children (Bornstein et al. 1977; Slaby 1976, cited in Combs and Slaby 1977). Unless social skill programs are based on a developmental model which recognizes intellectual, social, and emotional capacities of children of various ages, the likelihood that our intervention strategies will be designed to teach children to respond as "miniature adults" is high. When the researchers providing social skills training for adults do not have universally accepted standards of "socially acceptable behavior" (Eisler 1976), attempts to model programs for children on adult intervention strategies appear to be questionable.

Though difficult to accomplish, the solution to this problem is straightforward. Assessments in social skill functioning should include large-scale samplings of "normally skillfull" children across age levels. By including nonproblem children in social skills assessments, an empirical base can be established from which clinicians can develop intervention strategies. And, in fact, the failure to consider social skills within a developmental framework is only part of this problem. In addition, no research has provided differences in functioning of male and female children (see Maccoby and Jacklin 1976 for a notable exception). Information about how race, socioeconomic status, and intellectual capacity may interact with the development of social skills is not presently available. In order to provide needed information about these variables' relationship to social skills, the authors are presently investigating social skills functioning level for over 175 children aged 10-14 (grades four-eight) within a public school system. The study, when completed, will provide empirical data on the relationships between social skills and variables such as age, sex, socioeconomic status, achievement level, and race. While it is our opinion that the training of interpersonal social skills will always imply certain "value judgments" in selecting certain types of sequences of responses as "skillfull" and others as "maladaptive," we should always remain as close to a solid empirical data base as is possible. At present such data bases are simply unavailable. It is hoped, however, that other researchers will also extend the assessment of social skills to nonclinical nonproblem populations of children and increase our knowledge about developmental time frame and sequencing of interpersonal skills. Such research strategies will increase the quality of social skills intervention programs that are developed for use with the nonskilled child.

Appendix

Social Skills Script

"Hello, how are you? Today, we're going to play a kind of acting game. I am going to tell you where you are and what you are doing. That is the situation. I want you to think for a moment about this situation and then act just like you would if this were actually happening. O.K. Do you understand? For example, if I told you that I was your dad and that I was standing here, and you wanted to go outside, what would you do? (Make sure subject understands procedure.) O.K. Here's the first one."

I. *Target: Greeting A Stranger*

Instructions: "Outside is a person whom you have never met. He will come in. Greet him and talk to him as long as you can."

Experimenter is in the room, standing. He responds to the subject's statements but makes no other remarks. This will last for 45 seconds from the greeting. Experimenter makes only acknowledgment statements.

II. *Target: Interpersonal Conflict*

Instructions: "You are watching your favorite television program. What is your favorite? O.K. You are watching______, your favorite program."

Experimenter comes in the room after 15 seconds and turns the channel. He is to respond to the subject's statements with:

A. I don't like that program.
B. It figures you would watch it.
C. But I don't like that program.

Scene continues for 45 seconds.

III. *Target: Introduction*

Instructions: "In the next situation, you and I are friends. You and Bill, who is out in the hall, are friends. But Bill and I don't know each other. You are to introduce me to Bill and *keep the conversation going as long as you can.*"

Scene continues for 45 seconds from introduction.

Gambrill, E. and Richey, C. 1975. An assertion inventory for use in assessment and research. *Behavior Therapy, 6,* 550-61.

Gottman, J., Gonso, J., and Rasmussen, B. 1975. Social interaction, social competence, and friendship in children. *Child Development, 46,* 709-718.

Grim, P., Hohlberg, L., and White, S. 1968. Some relationships between conscience and attentional processes. *Journal of Personality and Social Psychology.* 239-49.

Gronlund, N. 1959. *Sociometry in the classroom.* New York: Harper and Brothers.

Gronlund, H., and Anderson, L. 1963. Personality characteristics of socially accepted, socially neglected, and socially rejected junior high school pupils. In *Educating for mental health,* ed. J. Seidman. New York: Crowell.

Gunn, W., and Cox, R. 1978. Utilizing teacher ratings of social skillfulness in the identification of low skill children. Unpublished manuscript.

Hartup, W. 1970. Peer interaction and social organization. In *Carmichael's Manual of Child Psychology,* ed. P. Mussen. Vol. 2. New York: Wiley.

Hartup, W. 1976. Peer interaction and the behavioral development of the individual child. In *Psychopathology and child development: Research and development,* ed. E. Schopler and R. Reichler. New York: Plenum Press.

Hetherington, E., Cox, M. and Cox, R. 1978. Beyond father absence: Conceptualization of the effects of divorce. In *The American family: Dying or development,* ed. Smart and Smart. New York: Plenum Press.

Hops, H., Walker, H., and Greenwood, C. 1977. PEERS—A program for the remediating social withdrawal in the school setting. Paper presented at Banff conference, Banff, Alberta.

Houff, K., and Cox, R. 1976. The training of interpersonal social skills in a population of behavior problem children. Paper presented at the Midwestern Association of Behavior Analysis, Chicago.

Lazarus, A. 1973. On assertive behavior: A brief note. *Behavior Therapy, 4,* 697-99.

Maccoby, E., and Jacklin, A. 1976. Assertion and how it grows: Early sex differences and similarities. Paper presented at the Society of Research in Child Development Western Regional Conference, Emerville, California.

McCandless, B. 1976. The socialization of the individual. In *Psychopathology and child development,* ed. E. Schopler and R. Reichler. New York: Plenum Press.

Rathus, S. 1973. A 30-item schedule for assessing assertive behavior. *Behavior Therapy, 4,* 398-406.

Roff, M. 1961. Childhood social interactions and young adult bad conduct. *Journal of Abnormal Social Psychology, 63,* 333-37.

Roff, M., Sells, B. and Golden, M. 1970. *Social adjustment and personality development in children.* Minneapolis, Minn: University of Minnesota Press.

Spivack, G., and Shure, M. 1974. *Social adjustment in young children,* San Francisco: Jossey-Bass.

Staub, E. 1971. The use of role-playing and induction in children's learning of helping and sharing behavior. *Child Development, 42,* 805-16.

Strain, P. S., Cooke, T. P., and Apolloni, T. 1976. *Teaching exceptional children: Assessing and modifying social behavior.* New York: Academic Press.

Ullmann, C. 1957. Teachers, peers, and tests as predictors of adjustment. *Journal of Educational Psychology, 48,* 257-67.

6

Structured-Learning Therapy: Overview and Applications to Adolescents and Adults

Robert Sprafkin, N. Jane Gershaw, and Arnold Goldstein

Our involvement in the development of social competencies, specifically the teaching of interpersonal, personal, and planning skills, began with concern over enhancement of such skills among long-term, institutionalized, lower-class, chronic psychiatric patients. Why begin with this difficult-to-treat population? Despite the proliferation of treatment approaches, the nation-wide push toward deinstitutionalization of chronic psychiatric patients and the widespread use of psychotropic medications, the plight of institutionalized psychiatric patients has remained a difficult one. Clearly the numbers of inpatients in psychiatric hospitals declined dramatically, from over 550,000 in 1955, when major tranquilizers were introduced, to less than half of that number within two decades. But what has happened to these newly deinstitutionalized patients? One-third of them fall into a "revolving door" pattern. Unable to stay outside of the institution for any period of time, they pass in and out of psychiatric hospitals at an alarming rate. The remaining two-thirds either return to the same facilities for increasingly longer stays, or end up leading essentially institutionalized lives, characterized by withdrawal, social isolation, apathy and dependency, in the quasi-mental hospitals of their run-down boarding houses, hostels, welfare hotels, and the like.

Antecedents of Skill Training

Why social skills training? Despite demonstration of skills relevant to their institutional survival such as withdrawal dependency and conformity, these institutionalized patients remained deficient in the skills necessary for independent living outside of the custodial confines of the hospital. As Paul (1969) and others have commented, it is often the development of social competency, self-maintenance, interpersonal interaction, and communication skills that patients need in order to have any chance of returning to the community with tenure.

Unlike many others within the social skills training movement, our interest developed from a deficit-oriented clinical tradition; it is also consistent with a growing psychoeducational thrust, both in and out of a clinical framework. This movement is a linear descendant of American academic psychology, and has been involved, since its inception, with the study of learning. In the 1950s, under the general rubric of behavior modifications, laboratory-based learning procedures were applied to the amelioration of problematic behavioral deficits (or behavior excesses). Typically, these approaches incorporated in their methods the specification of behavioral goals, the careful delineation of training or treatment procedures, and the careful assessment of outcome or behavior change. We have sought to reflect these same principles in our approach to enchancing social competence.

There is an even older traditional approach to the institutional treatment of psychiatric patients that appears to have influenced the development of social skill training within clinical settings. It is the movement known as *moral treatment,* which began in Europe around the turn of the eighteenth century, moved to the United States, and flourished for less than 75 years. It was characterized by its humane concern for patients in institutions, by its emphasis on environmental influences in shaping abnormal and normal behavior, and (most important for social skills training) by its use of educational methods for bringing about appropriate "mental discipline" (Sprafkin 1977). While the early adherents of moral treatment did not teach social skills directly, they did view provision of appropriate models of socially competent behaviors as an integral part of the rehabilitation of institutionalized patients. Also, direct teaching in classroom settings was an essential component of the treatment approach. While this mode of institutional treatment died in the United States by the end of the Civil War, its heritage seems to be resurrected in the image of current social skills training approaches.

Structured-Learning Therapy: Rationale

As noted above, our first target population for social skill training was chronic, adult psychiatric patients. Our immediate concern was to develop a treatment approach that was congruent with the expectations and learning styles of our particular clientele. Despite the profusion of approaches to psychotherapeutic intervention, the majority of existing therapies tend to be highly verbal, psychodynamic, insight-oriented, and, most important, largely incomprehensible to the long-term, withdrawn, nonverbal, low-income residents of psychiatric institutions.

If these patients are judged by mental health professionals to be purportedly "unsuitable for psychotherapy," and yet are clearly in need of psychological treatment, what should practitioners do with them to provide appropriate service? One earlier approach has been to assume that traditional, verbal, insight-oriented psychotherapies are necessary and sufficient, but that these long-term, chronic, lower-social-class patients simply do not know how to avail themselves of their benefits. Therefore, so the argument went, if these patients could be taught to appreciate and use the therapies properly—that is, if professionals could "make the patient fit the therapy"—then chances of psychotherapeutic success would be greatly enhanced. Unfortunately, with a few exceptions, attempts at teaching lower-class, chronic patients to participate adequately in middle-class verbal psychotherapies have not been very successful. Apparently, the expectations of the therapist as to what constitutes appropriate participation in psychotherapy and the expectations of the chronic patient as to what constitutes "treatment" are often too far apart to meaningfully bridge the gap.

In initially developing Structured Learning Therapy with a long-term, institutionalized, lower-class population, we sought to develop a therapy that was responsive to the treatment expectations and learning styles of such individuals. Rather than attempting to have the patient conform to the expectations of existing verbal psychotherapies, we sought to design a therapy to meet the patient's therapeutic preferences and channels of accessibility. By examining sociological and developmental psychology literature on child-rearing and learning styles for possible clues to the structure of such a therapy, we found real differences reported between the child-rearing practices and learning styles of the middle class and those of lower- or working-class individuals. These bodies of literature reveal that in middle-class child-rearing there is an emphasis placed upon intentions, motivation, self-control and inner states, which are also the qualities necessary to function as a "good patient" in verbal, insight-oriented psychotherapies. The middle-class child is thus trained early to participate in and appreciate the ground rules and procedures of verbal psychotherapy, should he or she need to do so later in life. In the lower-class home, on the other hand, there is much greater focus on behavioral control through compliance with external authority, on action rather than verbal behavior, and on consequences rather than intentions. This "basic training" does not appear to prepare the person well for verbal psychotherapy. We felt that an adequate psychotherapy must be responsive to these early-learned styles. That is, we concluded that psychotherapeutic intervention of such individuals must be concrete, brief, require imitation of specific, behavioral examples, be authoritatively administered, teach role-taking skills, involve immediate feedback, and include early continuation and frequent reinforcement of correct enactment of the behaviors taught (Goldstein 1973; Goldstein, Sprafkin and Gershaw 1976). The result was the development of the approach to treatment which we call Structured-Learning Therapy (SLT).

Structured-Learning Therapy: Procedures

Structured-Learning Therapy consists of four components, each of which is a well-established behavior change procedure. These procedures are modeling, role playing, social reinforcement, and transfer of training.

In each training session, a group of patients: (1) listens to a brief audiotape (or watches live persons) depicting specific skill behaviors shown to be helpful in dealing with common problems of daily living (Modeling), (2) is given extensive opportunity, encouragement, and training to rehearse or practice behaviorally the effective behaviors that have been modeled (Role Playing), (3) is provided corrective feedback and approval or praise as their role playing of the behaviors becomes more and more similar to the model's behavior (Social Reinforcement), and (4) discusses homework reports completed between sessions as one of a variety of procedures used to encourage the transfer of the newly learned behaviors from the training setting to their real-life setting (Transfer of Training).

Each Structured-Learning Group consists of trainees who are clearly deficient in whatever skill is going to be taught. The optimal size group for effective Structured-Learning sessions includes 6 to 12 trainees plus two trainers. For both learning and transfer to occur, each trainee is given ample opportunity to practice what he has heard or seen modeled, to receive feedback from other group members and the trainers, and to discuss his attempts to apply at home, on the job, or in the ward what he has learned in the therapy sessions

The skills we have taught through Structured-Learning Therapy fall into two major categories which we call "basic skills" and "application skills." For each skill, a modeling tape has been developed. The modeling tapes, described below, were designed in a manner to enhance trainee attention to the new material, as well as retention and the ability to reproduce that material.

First, on each tape, a high-status narrator introduces himself. He then gives the name of the skill to be modeled. After a general description of the skill, the narrator gives the behavioral definition of the skill. We have used the term "learning points" to designate the three to six behavioral steps that make up each skill.

Next, the narrator makes an incentive statement describing how and why use of the particular skill is rewarding. In a discrimination statement, the narrator indicates how and why skill absence may be unrewarding.

The next section of the modeling tape consists of the actual modeling displays. On each tape, ten vignettes of skill usage are portrayed. In each vignette, the complete set of learning points for that skill is employed. The vignettes encompass a broad range of content areas, with a strong emphasis upon content relevant to the lives of the trainee groups including both in-hospital and out-of-hospital situations. Repetition is relied upon to enhance learning. The actors who serve as models are similar to typical trainees in age, sex, and apparent socioeconomic status. In each vignette, the model receives social reinforcement for effective skill usage.

Each modeling tape is presented in this systematic fashion. Prior to engaging in any behavioral rehearsal, trainees are thus able to hear (1) an operational definition of the skill (in relatively simple language), (2) how and why to use the skill, and (3) a number of positive examples of the skill in use. Each example is presented in a manner designed to enhance transfer of training.

The basic skills for which we have developed modeling displays are listed in figure 6.1.

Series I. Conversations: Beginning Skills
- Skill 1. Starting a Conversation
- Skill 2. Carrying on a Conversation
- Skill 3. Ending a Conversation
- Skill 4. Listening

Series II. Conversations: Expressing Oneself
- Skill 5. Expressing a Compliment
- Skill 6. Expressing Appreciation
- Skill 7. Expressing Encouragement
- Skill 8. Asking for Help
- Skill 9. Giving Instructions
- Skill 10. Expressing Affection
- Skill 11. Expressing a Complaint
- Skill 12. Persuading Others
- Skill 13. Expressing Anger

Series III. Conversations: Responding to Others
- Skill 14. Responding to Praise
- Skill 15. Responding to the Feelings of Others (Empathy)
- Skill 16. Apologizing
- Skill 17. Following Instructions
- Skill 18. Responding to Persuasion
- Skill 19. Responding to Failure
- Skill 20. Responding to Contradictory Messages
- Skill 21. Responding to a Complaint
- Skill 22. Responding to Anger

Series IV. Planning Skills
- Skill 23. Setting a Goal
- Skill 24. Gathering Information
- Skill 25. Concentrating on a Task
- Skill 26. Evaluating Your Abilities
- Skill 27. Preparing for a Stressful Conversation
- Skill 28. Setting Problem Priorities
- Skill 29. Decision Making

Fig. 6.1. Structured-Learning Therapy: Basic skills for adult psychiatric trainees (*continued on next page*)

stage and making the trainee's task as clear as possible.

Once the stage is set, trainees enact the skill. The main actor as well as the co-actor and observers have skill cards on which are written the learning points. The trainers provide any added instruction or prompting required by the actors.

After each role play, the trainer provides the main actor with opportunity for social reinforcement and corrective feedback by encouraging comments from the observing trainees, as well as from the co-actor, on how well the main actor executed the role play. The trainers also provide the main actor with feedback on his performance. All trainees are instructed to keep a behavioral focus during this phase of the group. If it is indicated, a particular scene may be role played again after corrective feedback is given. In a forthright effort at transfer of training as the last step in each group, the trainer provides each trainee the opportunity to practice his newly learned material in his real-life environment. With aid of a variety of forms (which we have included in a workbook we call the Trainee's Notebook for Structured-Learning Therapy), the trainee is asked to fill out a portion of a "Homework Report," in which he contracts to practice his new skill in a real-life setting. Once he has done this, he completes the rest of the form, indicating the outcome of his efforts, and reports back to the group at the next meeting. After the assignment of homework, the group ends.

Once the trainees in a group have achieved a reasonable level of competence in the various basic skills of Structured-Learning Therapy, the task of the group becomes that of solving complex daily living problems by using various basic skills in combination. For instance, the task of finding a place to live may entail a basic skill sequence of (1) asking for help, (2) gathering information, (3) responding to persuasion, (4) negotiating, and finally (5) making a decision. We have developed an extended series of Application Modeling Tapes which are listed in figure 6.2. This series portrays daily living problems for which various basic skills can be sequentially combined. These tapes are not, however, modeling tapes in the usual sense. They provide examples of how a particular person might effectively solve the application problem. After playing an appropriate Application Modeling Tape, the task of the trainer is to develop, through discussion with an individual trainee, a list of basic skills that meet *his* specific needs in solving the application problem at hand. Next, the trainee role plays the basic skills in sequence. Feedback discussion and homework assignments follow.

Skill 38: Finding a Place to Live (through formal channels)
Skill 39. Moving In (typical)
Skill 40. Moving In (difficult)
Skill 41. Managing Money
Skill 42. Neighboring (apartment house)
Skill 43. Job Seeking (typical)
Skill 44. Job Seeking (difficult)
Skill 45. Job Keeping (average day's work)

Fig. 6.2. Structured-Learning Therapy: Application skills for adult psychiatric trainees (*continued on next page*)

Skill 46. Job Keeping (strict boss)
Skill 47. Receiving Telephone Calls (difficult)
Skill 48. Restaurant Eating (typical)
Skill 49. Organizing Time (typical)
Skill 50. Using Leisure Time (learning something new)
Skill 51. Using Leisure Time (interpersonal activity)
Skill 52. Social (party)
Skill 53. Social (church supper)
Skill 54. Marital (positive interaction)
Skill 55. Marital (negative interaction)
Skill 56. Using Community Resources (seeking money)
Skill 57. Using Community Resources (avoiding red tape)
Skill 58. Dealing with Crises (inpatient to nonpatient transition)
Skill 59. Dealing with Crises (loss)

Fig. 6.2. *(continued)*

Our involvement in the development of Structured-Learning Therapy has not remained exclusively with low-income, chronic, institutionalized psychiatric patients. As seems to be the natural history of any psychotherapy, its success and popularity fosters its utilizations with populations other than those for whom it was initially developed. This appears to be the case with Structured-Learning Therapy. In our own application of Structured-Learning techniques to different populations, we have tried to be cognizant of the unique characteristics of each population that might necessitate a modification of the therapy-training techniques. That is, we do not want to fall into the trap of premature closure—of creating yet another psychotherapeutic dogma. If so, then we too would be forced to "make the patient fit the therapy," which is clearly not our aim!

Our first application of Structured-Learning techniques to populations other than adult psychiatric patients was with those professionals and paraprofessionals who work with our patients in various therapeutic roles. We have used Structured-Learning procedures to teach empathy to hospital attendants (Sutton 1970), to ministers (Perry 1970), and to nurses (Goldstein and Goudhart 1970). The same procedures have been used to enhance self-disclosure toward personnel (Lack 1971), and the attention of hospital staff toward lower-class alcoholic and schizophrenic inpatients (Friedenberg 1971; Walsh 1971).

In our more recent work with hospital and clinic staff, we have been particularly concerned with the training of SLT trainers using Structured-Learning techniques (Goldstein, Sprafkin, and Gershaw 1976). That is, we use Structured Learning to teach Structured Learning. Concretely, we expose groups of potential trainers to modeling displays (audio tapes) of various segments of SLT sessions: introducing Structured-Learning Therapy to a new group, leading role playing, eliciting feedback, assigning homework, and dealing with resistive behavior. Trainers-in-training then assume patient roles, constitute a group, and take turns leading the role-played group as co-trainers. Next, they are provided feedback on their performances by other trainers-in-training and by their supervisors. Finally, as a forthright effort at transfer of training, they are sent out to run their own patient groups under supervision. Thus, the four major components of Structured-Learning Therapy are embodied in the training of Structured-Learning trainers.

Structured Learning has also been applied to other clinical and nonclinical populations. These populations include: aggressive adolescents in regular schools and institutional settings, police, supervisors in industry, child-abusing parents, and normal adults (through self-instruction). In each instance of applying Structured Learning to a different population, the four basic components were retained, but some modification was made in order to adapt the technique to the particular characteristics of the group being addressed. Such adaptations have included changes in the selection of skills to be taught, the medium for presenting the modeling displays, the selection of relevant models, and the amount and kind of participation required of trainees. Some examples of those adaptations are presented below.

Aggressive Adolescents

Dealing with the interpersonal competency needs of adolescents in regular schools and in residential treatment settings required some major modification of the SLT procedures. First, although many of the skills that were used with adult psychiatric patients were also appropriate for use with teenagers (with the wording of the learning points modified in some instances), some new skills were needed. As can be seen in the skill list presented in figure 6.3, there is a forthright effort in the adolescent series to teach skills dealing with feelings, stress, and prosocial alternatives to aggression.

Group I. Beginning Social Skills

1. Listening
2. Starting a conversation
3. Having a conversation
4. Asking a question
5. Saying thank you
6. Introducing yourself
7. Introducing other people
8. Giving a compliment

Group II. Advanced Social Skills

9. Asking for help
10. Joining in
11. Giving instructions
12. Following instructions
13. Apologizing
14. Convincing others

Group III. Skills for Dealing with Feelings

15. Knowing your feelings
16. Expressing your feelings
17. Understanding the feelings of others
18. Dealing with someone else's anger
19. Expressing affection
20. Dealing with fear
21. Rewarding yourself

Group IV. Skill Alternatives to Aggression

22. Asking permission
23. Sharing something
24. Helping others
25. Negotiating
26. Using self-control
27. Standing up for your rights
28. Responding to teasing

29. Avoiding trouble with others
30. Keeping out of fights

Group V. Skills for Dealing with Stress
31. Making a complaint
32. Answering a complaint
33. Sportsmanship after the game
34. Dealing with embarrassment
35. Dealing with being left out
36. Standing up for a friend
37. Responding to persuasion
38. Responding to failure
39. Dealing with confusing messages
41. Getting ready for a difficult conversation
42. Dealing with group pressure

Group VI. Planning Skills
43. Deciding on something to do
44. Deciding what caused a problem
45. Setting a goal
46. Deciding on your abilities
47. Gathering information
48. Arranging problems by importance
49. Making a decision
50. Concentrating on a task

Fig. 6.3. Structured-Learning Skills For Adolescents
Source: From Sprafkin, Gershaw, Goldstein and Klein 1978

In addition to modifying the skills to be taught to adolescents, adaptations were also made in the mode of presentation of modeling displays. While the majority of adult psychiatric patients are quite passive and thus able to attend adequately to audio-taped modeling displays, teenagers raised on television seemed to need both auditory and visual stimulation to capture their attention. Thus, our preference has been to present vivid filmstrip and audio-tape modeling, often supplemented by live modeling, in order to capture the interest of adolescent trainees.

Another modification we have used with teenagers is to utilize the power and attractiveness of the natural peer leaders. As anyone who has worked with teenagers will confirm, no adult can possibly have the influence of the teenage leader. Often it is possible to take advantage of that influence by having the (adult) trainer employ the peer leader as a co-trainer for some of the Structured-Learning sessions. Since the peer leader is likely to be influential both inside and outside of the classroom setting, the involvement of the peer co-trainer also enhances the likelihood of transfer of training to out-of-class settings.

Other Trainee Populations

Structured Learning has also been used, to a much more limited extent, with child-abusing parents. As with other target populations, our goal has been to develop the particular skills in which this group appears to be deficient. These would include self-control skills, parenting skills, marital skills, and peer-oriented skills. It is our view that the actual act of child abuse is but one manifestation of skill deficiency in a number of areas.

Police work has been the target of yet another application of Structured-Learning techniques. Only recently have police officials, the general public, and mental health professionals acknowledged the complexity of the interpersonal skill needed by police to perform their usual and their unusual duties. A number of training programs have been conducted using Structured-Learning techniques to teach law enforcement officers to deal more effectively with situations, such as family disputes, which involve highly complex crisis-intervention skills (Goldstein et al. 1977). A related involvement with law enforcement officers has been the teaching of hostage-negotiation skills using Structured Learning (Miron and Goldstein 1978).

Structured-Learning techniques have also been used to teach supervisory skills to managers in industry (Goldstein and Sorcher 1974), and, more recently, the present authors have provided an effective means by which individuals seeking to improve their social skillfulness may utilize the Structured-Learning approach on a self-help basis (Goldstein, Gershaw, and Sprafkin 1979). In this modified version of Structured Learning, modeling is done by means of written examples portraying adequate skill use; role playing is self-administered (e.g., tape recorded), or done with the help of a trusted friend or spouse; feedback is provided through self-critique, observed reactions from others, or requested reactions from friends; and transfer is accomplished by means of various homework assignments, contracts, and/or reward systems.

Research Support and Implications

Clinical and educational interventions must not proceed on faith alone, however effective they appear to be. Hand in hand with our training and materials development efforts, we have conducted a 10-year research program designed to systematically examine the efficacy and limits of Structured-Learning. Our studies now number approximately 75, and have focused in stages upon each of the target trainee populations discussed earlier in this chapter—chronic adult psychiatric patients (Goldstein 1973), aggressive adolescents (Goldstein et al. 1978), hospital and clinic staff (Goldstein 1973), police (Goldstein et al. 1977), industrial managers (Goldstein and Sorcher 1974), child-abusing parents (Soloman 1977), and self-help populations (Goldstein, Gershaw and Sprafkin 1979).

While our experimental designs have varied, most of our studies have been factorial in structure, behavioral in criteria, and successful in outcome. By "successful," we wish to underscore that a very common result—across skills and across trainee populations—has been positive skill acquisition. Stated otherwise, by the end of either lengthy or even brief Structured-Learning participation, the vast majority of trainees do learn the skill being taught. While we are pleased with this consistent outcome, we are keenly aware that successful acquisition is a nonsurprising outcome of most therapy or educational interventions, nonsurprising because in certain comparative senses, success is "easy" in the nurturant, protective, supportive, reinforcing context of the training or therapeutic setting.

The more crucial test of success, the only arena in which training can truly matter, relates to the question of transfer. Do the skills learned in the training setting generalize to and maintain in the transfer setting, the home, school, factory, and street? In recent years this question has become the major focus of our Structured-Learning research program.

We have drawn heavily from research in laboratory, industrial, and educational contexts, taking from these settings procedures which there seem to function as effective transfer enhancers and tested their efficacy in the context of Structured-Learning skill training. In this manner, transfer-enhancement efforts via general principles, identical elements, stimulus variability, overlearning, and performance feedback have each been operationalized and tested. In a recent publication (Goldstein and Kanfer 1979), it was estimated that across therapeutic interventions the average transfer rate is 20 percent! That is, approximately one-fifth of all therapy patients reporting improvement at the termination of treatment, regardless of type of treatment, are able to report maintenance of such gains upon later follow-up. Our best estimate is that the comparable transfer rate for Structured Learning is 45 percent. We feel the positive differential here favoring Structured Learning grows directly from our systematic incorporation into ongoing training of concrete, transfer-enhancing procedures.

We are certain that we and others can do even better. Systematic skill training through structured learning and similar psychoeducational interventions began with the 1970s. Such intervention, as a developing movement, is doing well and can, we feel, do even better as it attends more and more to concern with making new competencies endure.

References

Friedenberg, W. P. 1971. Verbal and nonverbal attraction modeling in an initial therapy interview analogue. Unpublished master's thesis, Syracuse University.

Goldstein, A. P. 1973. *Structured learning therapy.* New York: Academic Press.

Goldstein, A. P., Gershaw, N.J., and Sprafkin, R. P. 1979. *I know what's wrong, but I don't know what to do about it.* Englewood-Cliffs, N.J.: Prentice-Hall.

Goldstein, A. P., and Goudhart, A. 1973. The use of Structured Learning for empathy-enhancement in paraprofessionals psychotherapist training. *Journal of Community Psychology, 1,* 168-73.

Goldstein, A. P., and Kanfer, F. H. 1979. *Maximizing treatment gains.* New York: Academic Press.

Goldstein, A. P., Monti, P. J., Sardino, T. J., and Green, D. 1977. *Police crisis intervention.* Elmsford, New York: Pergamon Press.

Goldstein, A. P., Sherman, M., Gershaw, N. J., Sprafkin, R. P., and Glick, B. 1978. Training aggressive adolescents in prosocial behavior. *Journal of Youth & Adolescence, 7,* 73-92.

Goldstein, A. P., and Sorcher, M. 1974. *Changing supervisor behavior,* Elmsford, New York: Pergamon Press.

Goldstein, A. P., Sprafkin, R. P., and Gershaw, N. J. 1976. *Skill training for community living.* Elmsford, New York: Pergamon Press.

Lack, D. Z. 1971. The effect of a model and instructions on psychotherapist self-disclosure. Unpublished master's thesis, Syracuse University.

Miron, M., and Goldstein, A. P. 1978. *Hostage.* Elmsford, New York: Pergamon Press.

Paul, G. L. 1969. Chronic mental patient. Current status—future directions, *Psychological Bulletin, 71,* 81-94.

Perry, M. A. 1970. Didactic instructions for and modeling of empathy. Unpublished doctoral dissertation, Syracuse University.

Soloman, E. 1978. Structured learning therapy with abusive parents. Unpublished doctoral dissertation, Syracuse University.

Sprafkin, R. P. 1977. The rebirth of moral treatment. *Professional Psychology, 8,* 161-69.

Sprafkin, R. P., Gershaw, N. J., Goldstein, A. P., and Klein, P. 1978. *Trainer's manual: Skill training for adolescents.* Syracuse, N.Y.: Structured Learning Associates.

Sutton, K. 1970. Effects of modeled empathy and structured social class upon level of therapist displayed empathy. Unpublished master's thesis, Syracuse University.

Walsh, W. 1971. The effects of conformity pressure and modeling on the attraction of hospitalized patients toward an interviewer. Unpublished doctoral dissertation, Syracuse University.

7

Parent-Adolescent Conflict: A Skill-Training Approach*

Arthur Robin

It is 11:30 on a Saturday night and Mr. and Mrs. Jones, filled with a strange combination of indignation and anxiety, are sitting near the door of their home. Fourteen-year-old Betsy is already one hour late in returning from a party. Suddenly, the door opens and it's Betsy.

Mr. Jones: Betsy, why are you one hour and two minutes late? I thought we told you to be home by 10:30!

Mrs. Jones: We didn't know what happened to you. We were so upset!

Betsy: But Dad, my ride was delayed. The guy was supposed to drive me home didn't show up, so this guy Bill took me.

Mrs. Jones: I thought Barbara's father was supposed to drive you and Barbara home.

Betsy: But, you see . . .

Mr. Jones: Don't try to deny this one. You've been caught lying this time. Where were you since 10:30?

Betsy: At the party, of course.

Mrs. Jones: Are you sure? You said that last week and then we found out that you were out driving with some boys.

Mr. Jones: We'll find out soon enough. This is the third week in a row that you've come in late with some excuse. Don't you care about our feelings? You obviously don't. I'm getting sick and tired of your hanging out until all hours of the night

*This chapter was adapted from the article "Problem-solving communication training: A benavioral approach to the treatment of parent-adolescent conflict" in *The American Journal of Family Therapy, 7* (2), 69-82. Permission to reprint granted by the publisher.

with that bad crowd and doing who knows what. You're grounded for two weeks.

Mrs. Jones: Your father's right . . .

Betsy: What's an hour? You just don't understand. You treat me like I'm a baby. Well, I'm all grown up. All my friends can stay out till midnight, and I'm the laughing stock of the neighborhood. (Tearfully) They call me "Baby Betsy."

Mr. Jones: Your friends' parents don't really care about them if they let them stay out so late. . .Things could happen. . .

Betsy: Things could happen (sarcastic mimic). Little you know. And if you really cared about me, you would want me to stay out so I wouldn't be laughed at by everyone.

Mr. Jones: Enough. Cut out the disrespect this minute, young lady, or I'll make that one month of grounding. . .

Betsy: Threats, threats, threats. That's all you know how to do. What kind of parents are you? You don't understand me at all. I hate you both!

Mr. Jones: That's six weeks that you are grounded.

Betsy: I won't take this. I'll run away. . .

Mr. Jones: Just you try.

Mrs. Jones: Your father is right. You really ought to show Dad more respect.

This argument illustrates several features of parent-adolescent conflict. Betsy and her parents argued over a specific issue—curfew. Betsy wanted to stay out later than her parents wished. Her parents ordered her to obey a curfew that met their needs without seriously addressing her problem. As a consequence, Betsy disobeyed their rules. When she didn't comply, her father yelled, accused, and threatened punishment; and Mrs, Jones sullenly supported her husband's position. Betsy reciprocated their accusatory onslaught with sarcasm, denials, complaints, and criticisms. During this interchange, all of the family members attempted to impose their wills on the others without considering solutions which might be mutally acceptable. They displayed clear-cut deficits in their ability to resolve disagreements concerning specific issues. These deficits took the form of excessively negative problem-solving communication behavior.

Perhaps the dispute over curfew was less important than the general theme which it illustrated—Betsy's growing independence from the family. As a young child, Betsy generally accepted her parents' rules and the family served as the central source of reinforcement in her life. Over the past year, there has been a drastic change. Her peers have replaced her parents as the most significant source of reinforcement and socialization. In order to participate fully in her peer culture, Betsy has wished to excercise more control over rules and regulations governing her behavior. When her parents resisted her growing independence from the family, they interfered with her source for obtaining important reinforcement, and she reacted in an extremely defensive, hostile manner. Mr. and Mrs. Jones, in turn, became frightened by their sudden loss of decision-making authority. They wished to retain control over decisions, such as curfew, until they felt they could trust Betsy's ability to exercise "good judgment." They interpreted her resistance to their attempts to maintain control as another example of her "bad judgment" and used it as justification for refusing to grant her additional decision-making power. In turn, their refusal elicited additional rebellious behavior from Betsy. And the cycle worsened over time. In essence, both the parents and the adolescent displayed deficits in those skills that are needed to cope with the natural developmental phenomenon of a child's growing independence from the family. The parents displayed deficits in independence-granting skills and the teenager displayed deficits in independence-seeking skills.

The case of the Jones family illustrates how parent-adolescent conflict may be conceptualized as a "family skill deficit." One major developmental task of adolescence is achieving independence from the family (Conger 1977; Douvan and Adelson 1966). As with any novel task, certain skills and attitudes are required for successful disengagement of a child from p arental controls. Developmental psychologists who have studied the skills and attitudes that contribute to adolescents' achieving independence from their parents with a minimum amount of conflict have concluded that:

> Democratic practices, with frequent explanations by parents of their rules of conduct and expectations, foster responsible independence learning in several ways: (1) by providing opportunities for increasing autonomy, guided by interested parents who communicate with the child and exercise appropriate degrees of control; (2) by promoting positive identification with the parent, based on love and respect for the child, rather than rejection or indifference; and (3) by themselves providing models of reasonable independence, that is, autonomy within the framework of a democratic order. In contrast, the child of autocratic or indifferent parents is not presented with models of responsible, cooperative independence; he or she is not so likely to be encouraged by parental acceptance to identify with adults; and he or she is not given age-graded experiences in the orderly assumption of responsible autonomy. . . .[Conger 1977, pp. 240-41. Copyright, Harper and Row. Used with permission.]

Democratic methods of resolving disagreements promote less conflict and greater observational learning of responsible independence-seeking behavior than authoritarian methods. In order to resolve a conflict democratically, family members must be proficient in the use of the following skills: (1) communicating their views of the problem in a nonthreatening manner; (2) listening to and understanding each other's views of the problem; (3) suggesting alternative courses of action, which might meet each other's needs; (4) projecting the effects of various actions on each person's problems; and (5) negotiating solutions which maximally meet each other's needs (Gordon 1970). In other words, family members must be proficient at a variety of cognitive interpersonal problem-solving and communication skills (Spivack, Platt, and Shure 1976).

Two important social-learning principles of reciprocity and coercion complement this developmental skill analysis and help to explain how conflict develops when parents and teenagers resolve disagreements through the use of authoritarian, power-based methods (Patterson 1976; Patterson and Reid 1970). The principle of reciprocity asserts that there is an equity in the giving and receiving of positive and negative consequences in most social interactions. If a parent positively reinforces an adolescent's behavior in 50 percent of their interactions, the parent, in turn, will receive roughly the same proportion of positive reinforcement from the adolescent. If a parent punishes an adolescent's behavior in 90 percent of their interactions, the parent will receive roughly the same proportion of punishment from the adolescent. The principle of coercion asserts that when a person A makes an aversive demand of person B, person B will often escape the aversive situation by complying with the demand. If B does not comply with A's demand, B's noncompliance is punished by an increase in the intensity of the aversive stimuli presented by A. If B complies, B's compliance is negatively reinforced by removing the aversive demand. When B complies with A's demand, A's aversive demanding behavior is positively reinforced. For example, if Betsy demands that her parents permit her to come home after midnight, they might reinforce her demanding behavior by complying with her request. Her parents, in turn, would escape her aversive demand. However, if they do not comply with her demand, she may punish their noncompliance by coming home late without their permission.

The principles of reciprocity and coercion can be extended to independence-related conflicts between parents and teenagers. Some parents may positively reinforce their adolescents' requests for additional freedom concerning specific issues by democratically resolving disagreements in a mutually satisfactory manner. Their adolescents, in turn, may reciprocate by exercising their increased decision-making authority responsibly and positively reinforcing their parents' independence-granting behavior. By contrast, other parents may punish their adolescents' requests for autonomy by ignoring these requests and decreeing rules in an autocratic manner. Their adolescents, in turn, may reciprocate in a similarly authoritarian manner, ignoring their parents' rules and punishing their parents' autocratic behavior. In certain instances, a parent may demand that an adolescent comply with certain rules. If the adolescent complies, the parent's demanding behavior is positively reinforced and the adolescent escapes a coercive situation. If the adolescent does not comply, the parent's demanding behavior is punished and the parents may escalate the demand or reciprocate with more intense punishment for the adolescent's noncompliance.

There are enormous individual differences between families in the use of democratic and authoritarian conflict-resolution techniques and in the level of reciprocity and coercion (Alexander 1970). Families such as the Joneses display deficits in the use of democratic conflict-resolution techniques that lead to repeated sequences of coercive negative interactions characterized by high proportions of reciprocity of punishment. Families proficient in the use of democratic conflict-resolution techniques interact more appropriately and display high proportions of reciprocity of positive reinforcement. The developmental social-learning framework outlined above suggests that skill acquisition programs designed to ameliorate parent-adolescent conflict should foster changes in basic, systematic family interaction patterns.

Behavior therapists have designed and evaluated effective interventions for remediating skill deficits with a variety of clinical populations, including unassertive adults, depressed psychiatric patients, and socially unskilled college students (Hersen and Eisler 1976). Family therapists have designed and evaluated effective interventions for modifying negative interaction patterns with a variety of family problems (Alexander and Parsons 1973; Haley 1976). Presumably, analogous interventions can be proven effective for remediating parent-adolescent skill deficits and modifying negative interaction patterns. The remainder of this chapter will review the Problem-Solving Communication Training Program, a skill acquisition program which has been designed to remediate family skill deficits with parents and adolescents and to modify negative, systematic family interaction patterns. First, an overview of the program will be given; second, a methodology for the assessment of parent-adolescent conflict will be presented; and third, relevant research evaluating the technique will be summarized. A detailed clinical manual describing the step-by-step implementation of problem-solving communication training is presented in the Appendix to this chapter.

Overview of the Treatment Program

The Problem-Solving Communication Training Program consists of three components: problem solving, communication training, and generalization programming (Robin 1976).

Problem Solving

Problem solving follows the four-step model presented in figure 7.1 and is designed to provide a democratically oriented heuristic for structuring attempts at conflict resolution.

I. Define the Problem
   A. Each person states what words and actions of the other are creating a problem for him/her.
   B. Each person paraphrases the others' statements and pinpoints the contrasting views of the problem.
II. Generate Alternative Solutions
   A. Family members take turns listing possible solutions.
   B. Family members adhere to three rules of brainstorming.
      1 . List as many ideas as possible.
      2 . Don't evaluate ideas, either overtly or covertly.
      3 . Be creative and freewheeling; suggest crazy ideas.
   C. One person writes down the ideas.
III. Decide upon the Best Idea
   A. Family members take turns evaluating each idea by:
      1 . Projecting the consequences of ech idea for each person.
      2 . Stating why it is a good or bad idea.
      3 . Making an overall judgement of each idea and recording a "plus" or "minus" for each person next to the idea.
   B. Family members select the "best" idea as the solution by:
      1 . Looking for any ideas rated "plus" by all.
         a. Select one idea.
         b. Combine several ideas.
      2 . If none is rated plus by all, looking for ideas rated "plus" by the most individuals. Negotiate by:
         a. Generating a list of compromises using brainstorming.
         b. Evaluating the compromises as in III-A.
         c. Agreeing to a compromise.
IV. Plan to Implement the Selected Solution
   A. Family members specify who will do what, when, where, how, and to what criteria.
   B. Family members write down the details in a contract.

Fig. 7.1. Problem-solving model

Defining the Problem. Family members all recognize the existence of a conflict and state the nature of the problem explictly from their respective points of view. An adequate problem definition is concise, nonaccusatory, and appropriately assertively. To insure accurate exchange of problem definitions, family members are required to paraphrase each others' viewpoints concerning the problem. Whenever there are discrepancies between the paraphrased and the original statements, speakers are urged to clarify their' views.

Generating Alternative Solutions. Family members take turns suggesting ideas for solving the problem, adhering to three rules of brainstorming: (1) defer judgment; (2) quantity, not quality of ideas counts; (3) be creative and freewheeling. the therapist interrupts premature evaluations, suggests novel solutions if participants "run dry" or take too rigid a stance, and ensures equal participation by all family members. Ideas are typically recorded on a problem worksheet. When the therapist judges that the family has sufficient ideas for evaluation (minimum of six to eight ideas), they progress to decision making.

Decision Making. Family members independently evaluate each solution by (1) projecting its positive and negative consequences and (2) assigning it an overall rating of "+" or "−," depending upon whether its benefits outweigh its detriments. The individual's overall evaluations are recorded on the problem worksheet under separate columns for each family member. A lively exchange of opinion is encouraged in order to clarify the consequences of the solutions and to help family members appreciate each other's perspectives. Often, additional solutions are suggested during decision making, and these are evaluated along with the original solutions. Afterwards, family members carefully examine the worksheet for ideas rated "+" by everyone, and one such idea is adopted or several are combined. If a consensus has not been reached, family members negotiate a compromise agreement based on the ideas rated "$" by the most individuals. The therapist plays a highly directive role during negotiation of compromise agreements by encouraging family members to consider each other's needs and by clarifying the extent to which particular solutions would solve each person's problem.

Planning Implementation. Details specifying who will do what, when, where, and how to fulfill the agreement are discussed. The family members establish behavioral criteria and monitoring systems for evaluating compliance with the solution. Then, the selected solution is written at the bottom of the problem worksheet. The therapist helps the family clarify the details that need to be discussed and suggests alternative ways of monitoring compliance with the solution.

Communication Training

Communication training is designed to teach parents and teenagers appropriate skills for expressing their ideas and feelings assertively but unoffensively and for receiving ideas and feelings expressed by others attentively and accurately. Negative communication habits such as accusations, interruptions, lectures, put-downs, overgeneralizations, commands, sarcastic expressions, and inattentive postures are replaced with positive communication habits such as verification of meaning, passive listening, active listening, I-messages, appropriate eye contact, and appropriate nonverbal posture. The therapist remediates deficiencies idiosyncratic to each family by noting their occurrence during a problem-solving discussion and requiring family members to "replay the scene" and replace the negative behaviors with positive behaviors. Modeling, instructions, and intensive behavior rehearsal are used as needed to shape positive communication behavior. Several communication patterns are targeted per session. Over successive problem-solving discussions, a variety of communication skills are taught.

Generalization Programming

During the opening and closing ten minutes of each session, homework assignments are reviewed and assigned, respectively, in order to program use of problem-solving communication skills in the natural environment. Three types of tasks are assigned.

First, family members are instructed to implement solutions to specific issues negotiated during problem-solving discussions. This type of assignment often includes collection of supporting data by charting and graphing.

Second, family members are instructed to conduct additional problem-solving discussions at home. These discussions are audio taped for review by the therapist. At the beginning, relatively mild conflicts are assigned for home discussion. Later, complex topics are assigned. Often, a family is asked to complete a discussion started during a session. Additional family members are included in home discussions as necessary for particular topics.

Third, family members are instructed to apply component problem-solving communication skills in daily interchanges with each other. Such assignments are tailored to the circumstances of each family and are designed to modify recurrent negative-interaction patterns noted by the therapist.

Procedures for Training

Skill-acquisition training takes place over seven to twelve one-hour sessions, preceded and followed by a two-hour assessment session. At the beginning of the first intervention session, the rationale for problem solving is presented, outlines of the four-step model are distributed, and a topic is selected for an initial discussion. The presentation of the rationale is restricted to four or five minutes because most teenagers rapidly tune out extended theoretical lectures and because families learn the procedures as they problem solve specific issues. The initial topic for discussion should be a significant but not severe conflict, and should be a problem chosen by the adolescent. It should be amenable to concrete definitions and compromise solutions since it serves as a vehicle for skill acquisition. Topics such as curfew, chores, bedtime, or playing the stereo too loudly typically meet these criteria better than talking back, smoking pot, choice of friends, or dating. The therapist models each step of problem solving and then asks the family members to imitate him or her, using the written outline as a guide. When they stray from the outline, instructions, prompts, behavior rehearsal, and feedback are used to correct their verbalizations. However, since a primary goal of the first session is to conduct an entire discussion and send the family home with a successfully negotiated solution for implementation, the therapist restricts corrections to macroscopic errors in performance. Later sessions provide the opportunity for microscopic dissection of subtle stylistic factors.

At each successive session, an additional conflict is problem solved. The therapist gradually increases the subtlety of his or her corrections for deficient problem-solving communication behaviors. Several communication skills are targeted for modification at each session. At the start of the session, the therapist announces the skills to be corrected and models their appropriate use. Then, he or she intervenes whenever inappropriate instances of these skills occur. During the last two sessions, the therapist fades out the corrections and minimizes the use of written aids, encourages family members to progress naturally from step to step, and helps them to recognize when they are getting bogged down.

Assessment Methodology

A variety of self-report and behavioral measures are used to assess parent-adolescent relations and the success of the treatment program (Prinz 1977; Weiss and Robin 1978). During a first two-hour assessment session, which precedes the first treatment session, the family participates in a behavioral assessment interview (45 minutes) and a series of standardized measures is administered (75 minutes). During a second 75-minute assessment session, which follows the last treatment session, the standardized measures are readministered. During a third 75-minute assessment, which takes place ten weeks after the completion of the last treatment session, the series is again readministered.

Interview

The behavioral assessment interview follows the outline given in figure 7.2 which is based upon the guidelines suggested by Goldfried and Davison (1976), modified for use with families. First, the therapist greets the family, noticing how they choose to arrange themselves in the interview and any nonverbal communication which takes place during this process. Second, the therapist asks each family member to describe the problem from his or her perspective. The therapist is relatively nondirective during this opening stage of the interview. As the family members tell their stories, the therapist begins to ask increasingly specific questions designed to pinpoint deficits in positive and excesses in negative problem-solving communication behavior. Whenever possible, questions are phrased in a way which prompts interactions among the family members and which provides information. For example, if family members begin to display the negative communication behavior that they are describing, the therapist may choose to interrupt them with a question such as, "Is this the type of thing that happens at home when you talk with each other?" This strategy helps to provide an in-session sample of behavior, helps to validate their self-reports, and permits a quick assessment of "authority pecking orders" in two-parent families, that is, who talks most, whether they listen and respond to each other, and so forth.

The following types of questions have proved useful in pinpointing negative-interaction patterns:

1. What happens when parents and adolescent attempt to discuss a specific disagreement?
2. Does one person refuse to participate in the discussion?
3. Do parents make accusations which set the occasion for defensive reactions by the adolescent?
4. Does one person hold strong, rigid beliefs which he or she attempts to impose on the others?
5. Do family members go around in circles, get off the topic, behave in a confrontive manner, and generally get bogged down in details, without ever concluding the discussion?
6. What issues are the primary sources of contention?
7. To what extent do specific disputes concern the teenager's activities outside the home as opposed to requests to help out with activities within the home?

When the therapist has determined the content and topography of a family's maladaptive interaction patterns, then he or she proceeds to assess associated environmental antecedents and consequences. Under what conditions can a family resolve conflicts harmoniously? What aggravates or alleviates the intensity of conflict? What are the effects of negative interchanges and specific disputes upon each family member? In a similar fashion, the therapist assesses the remaining topics on the outline, including relevant historical information, positive family characteristics, past attempts to cope with the problems, expectations regarding treatment, and goals for change. The details of these portions of the interview will not be discussed here; instead, the reader is referred to the sources for additional information concerning family and behavioral interviewing.

Goldfried and Davison (1976); Haley (1976); Morganstern (1976); and Meyer, Liddell, and Lyon (1977). It has been found that a general picture of family functioning can usually be obtained in a single, 45-minute interview. Although additional assessment interviews may yield more detailed information, it has been noted that adolescents become restless during multiple information-gathering sessions. Consequently, it is best to permit additional details about family functioning to emerge during the first few treatment sessions.

Self-Report Inventories

Three self-report checklists developed by Prinz (1977) complement the behavioral assessment interview and serve as dependent measures in research evaluations of problem-solving communication training. Parents and adolescents independently complete each checklist. When both parents are participating in treatment, the adolescent fills out separate versions of each checklist for his or her relations with mother and father.

Issues Checklist. The Issues Checklist assesses the degree of conflict on 44 potential parent-adolescent issues during the preceding four weeks. It includes issues such as curfew, dating, chores, going places without parents, smoking, drug use. Three scores are obtained for each family member from the Issues Checklist: (1) the quantity of issues discussed; (2) the mean anger-intensity level of the discussions (five-point scale ranging from calm to angry), and (3) the weighted average of the frequency and intensity-anger level of the discussions.

Conflict Behavior Questionnaire. The Conflict Behavior Questionnaire, which is composed of 75 two-point items (yes-no), assesses each person's appraisal of the other's communication behavior and each person's appraisal of the dyadic interaction during the preceding three weeks. It includes such items as, "My child sulks after an argument," "My mother usually listens to what I tell her," "We enjoy doing things together," and "At least once a day we get angry at each other." Each item is rated "yes" or "no," depending upon whether the individual judges it to be mostly true or mostly false. Two scores are obtained for each family member by summing across appropriate items: (1) appraisal of the other person's behavior, and (2) appraisal of the dyadic interaction.

Home Report. The Home Report, which is composed of 11 two-point (yes-no) items and one five-point rating scale ("only talked nicely to each other" to "only argued"), assesses the degree of daily conflict and argument at home. It includes such items as, "My mom yelled at me today," "My child was generally pleasant to me today," and "My dad wanted me to do families participating in outpatient therapy and from families whose adolescents were attending a day school for emotionally disturbed youth. Nondistressed dyads were volunteers from the community who had not been in treatment for parent-adolescent relational problems for one year prior to their interview. During a two-hour home visit, each dyad completed the Issues Checklist, Conflict Behavior Questionnaire, and two audio-taped problem discussions, which were coded with the modified Marital Interaction Coding System, an earlier version of the PAICS. Table 7.1 summarizes the mean scores on the Issues Checklist, Conflict Behavior Questionnaire, and modified MICs for this sample and also gives the mean scores on the Issues Checklist and Conflict Behavior Questionnaire for Prinz's sample. Univariate analyses indicated that the distressed dyads scored significantly more negatively than the nondistressed dyads on the Conflict Behavior Questionnaire and the Issues Checklist. In addition, distressed dyads emitted a significantly lower proportion of positive problem-solving communication behavior than nondistressed dyads during the two discussions, but there were no differences between groups on negative or neutral problem-solving communication behavior.

Taken together, the two studies described above showed that the Issues Checklist, Conflict Behavior Questionnaire, Home Report, Interaction Behavior Code, and modified Marital Interaction Coding System successfully discriminated distressed from nondistressed parent/adolescent dyads. Future research will need to address additional questions concerning these measures. For example, what is the reliability of the measures over time? Can the test of concurrent validity be replicated with triads and larger family units? To what extent do parents and adolescents diverge in their self-reports of the same events? Can these measures discriminate different levels of parent-adolescent distress? Do they possess construct validity? At the present time, clinicians can rely upon these measures and use the data in table 7.1 as a "rough guide" to their interpretation. In addition, clinicians can obtain useful information for planning treatment by inspecting responses to individual items on the self-report questionnaires.

Factors Influencing the Success of Treatment

The course of treatment is rarely as smooth as it appears in the manual. Unanticipated crises arise, appointments are missed, homework assignments are not completed, and individuals attempt to sabotage treatment. The therapist must be prepared to cope flexibly with unexpected interferences. As in any behavior therapy treatment, it is exceedingly difficult to strike an appropriate balance between the use of structured techniques and a tendency to disregard previously established structure and respond to the immediate clinical needs of each family. For some families effective treatment will follow, roughly, the guidelines in the manual; for others, effective

Table 7.1 Means for Distressed and Nondistressed Dyads on the Issues Checklist, Conflict Behavior Questionnaire, and Modified Marital-Interaction Coding System

Score	Weiss and Robin (1978) Distressed n=14	Weiss and Robin (1978) Nondistressed n=14	Prinz (1977) Distressed n=38	Prinz (1977) Nondistressed n=40
Issues Checklist				
Maternal Quantity of Issues	23.86	14.93[2]	19.71	19.29
Maternal Intensity of Issues	2.12	1.65[1]	2.60	1.74[2]
Maternal Intensity by Frequency	1.30	.51[2]	1.72	.60
Adolescent Quantity of Issues	17.57	17.00	24.31	19.71[1]
Adolescent Intensity of Issues	2.24	1.74[1]	2.46	1.86[2]
Adolescent Intensity by Frequency	.90	.66	1.45	.59[1]
Conflict Behavior Questionnaire				
Maternal Appraisal of Adolescent	22.86	8.29[2]	28.89	7.88[2]
Maternal Appraisal of Dyad	7.93	3.00[2]	11.29	2.26[2]
Adolescent Appraisal of Mother	14.64	7.43[2]	19.88	6.18[2]
Adolescent Appraisal of Dyad	7.00	2.86[2]	9.55	3.19[2]
Modified Marital-Interaction Coding System				
Proportion Positive Maternal Behavior	.04	.18[2]	--	--
Proportion Negative Maternal Behavior	.50	.46	--	--
Proportion Neutral Maternal Behavior	.46	.36	--	--
Proportion Positive Son Behavior	.05	.28[2]	--	--
Proportion Negative Son Behavior	.58	.49	--	--
Proportion Neutral Son Behavior	.37	.31	--	--

[1] $p<.05$
[2] $p<.01$

treatment may violate many of the most sacrosanct guidelines. Three years of experience in treating about 100 families with the problem-solving communication training program has helped to identify factors which influenced the success of treatment. They are: (1) the level of involvement of family members in treatment, (2) the degree of balance maintained by the therapist, (3) the functional analysis of basic family interaction patterns, and (4) the degree of rigidity-resistance exhibited by family members.

Level of Involvement. Successful intervention requires a commitment to change and a high level of involvement by all family members. Most teenagers are at best unenthusiastic and at worst overtly hostile about family treatment. They often attend treatment sessions under duress from their parents. In the initial screening session, it is the therapist's job to make clear the benefits of treatment for the teenager, that is, the parents will be asked to change in directions desired by the adolescent, and the therapist is not simply another adult attempting to impose alien values on the adolescent. The possible stigma attached to attending a mental health program also must be discussed before many teenagers will agree to participate. Extensive use of reflective listening techniques and clear-cut presentation of factual information about the problem-solving communication training program and psychological treatment in general can help to assess and alleviate many adolescents' anxieties about participating. An individual private conference can be held with a teenager to discuss frankly the teenager's concerns without the pressure created by the parents' presence. When the adolescent's resistance to participation is judged to be an act of rebellion against parental coercion, this resistance can sometimes be overcome by conducting a problem-solving discussion on a topic chosen by the teenager and reaching an agreement by the end of the first session. Thus, the adolescent will have the opportunity to observe how the therapist restrains parental authoritarianism and to experience successful resolution of a specific dispute. In other cases, paradoxical suggestions may help overcome strong resistance to participation (Haley 1976). Many adolescents are willing to try several sessions with the understanding that they can withdraw if they dislike the program. However, if the teenager is unwilling to make a clear-cut commitment to attend at least two or three sessions, it is questionable whether the family can benefit from the program. Approximately 10 percent of the adolescents who attend initial screening sessions have refused to participate.

In order to maintain involvement during sessions, the therapist should watch for signs of restlessness and boredom. As soon as a family member appears inattentive, the therapist should ask the family member a question or make a provocative statement designed to draw the person into the conversation.

Balance. Maintaining neutrality in a credible manner is crucial for a therapist who is conducting problem-solving communication training. If a family member perceives the therapist to be taking sides, the family member may become uncooperative. In the first session the therapist should announce that he or she will serve as a mediator, favoring neither parents nor adolescents. Then, the therapist should sit facing the entire family and attempt to distribute comments equally among family members. When giving corrective feedback concerning deficient problem-solving communication behavior, the therapist should attempt to couch statements in terms of the dyadic relationship instead of individual deficiencies. For example, if a father is talking in an accusing, sarcastic manner to his son, the therapist might say, "Mr. Smith, your last comment sounded accusatory to me. Mike, that's the type of comment I was talking about a few minutes ago when I said that you get defensive in response to things your parents say." In the choice of topics for problem-solving discussions, the therapist should alternate across sessions between topics considered problems by the adolescent and topics considered problems by the parents. A balance should also be maintained between topics involving additional freedoms sought by the teenager and topics involving additional responsibilities sought by the parents. When family members' comments suggest that they perceive the therapist to be playing favorites, their perceptions should be discussed immediately before the problem-solving discussion is resumed.

Functional Analysis of Family Interaction Patterns. Throughout the first two or three treatment sessions, the therapist attempts to "map out" significant functional relationships between verbal and nonverbal behaviors of various family members. It is assumed that the dysfunctional communication behavior exhibited at intake serves to maintain the systemic homeostasis within the family, and that before change can occur, it is necessary to undersand these homeostatic functions. Does the father make the final decisions? Does the mother defer to her husband's judgment? Are the mother and father struggling with each other for control of their adolescent? Is the teenager a "spoiled brat" who exercises power over meek, unassertive parents by rebelling? Are family members well-matched in terms of their verbal skills? Does the teenager take advantage of disagreements between his or her parents to control their behavior? Is one parent covertly encouraging rebellious behavior by the adolescent to "get at" the other parent? Thoughtful observation of family members' interchanges provides answers to many of these questions. After formulating hypotheses about significant functional relationships, the therapist plans long-range strategies to change these relationships in adaptive directions. The strategies dictate, to a certain extent, the choice of issues for problem solving, communication habits for modification, and tasks for homework assignments.

Further consideration of the Jones family mentioned at the beginning of the chapter will be used to illustrate a functional analysis. Mr. Jones made the final decisions concerning important family matters. His wife supported her husband's decisions and rarely challenged his authority. When Betsy attempted to gain greater independence over decisions such as curfew, she was challenging her father's authority. He reacted in a harsh, punitive manner, eliciting additional coercive, rebellious behavior from Betsy. This cycle worsened over time, until father and daughter had backed each other in rigid, opposing positions concerning issues such as curfew. Each perceived the actions and words of the other in terms of a struggle for power. The therapist planned to teach Mr. Jones and his daughter to share decision-making authority. To achieve this goal, Betsy had to be taught to request additional decision-making power without threatening her father. Mr. Jones had to be taught that it is natural for an adolescent to seek independence from parental control and that he could grant her additional decision-making authority without severely detrimental consequences. It was planned to maintain his "authority" by placing him in charge of distributing power to Betsy rather than exercising power against her. Consequently, extreme, polarizing statements by either family member were targeted for modification during early sessions. Independence-related topics were the primary material for the problem-solving discussions. Homework assignments included tasks in which the therapist allocated decision-making authority to Betsy; she was to report the results of her decisions to her father who could comment and advise her, but not change her decisions. If he was dissatisfied with the consequences of her decisions, he was to report to the therapist in the next session rather than overrule his daughter at home. Problem-solving communication training served as a catalyst for producing these changes in family functions. Without careful attention to the functional analysis of family interactions, problem-solving communication training may not produce durable improvement in parent-adolescent relations.

Rigidity, Flexibility, and Resistance. The degree of rigidity displayed by family members has proven a useful clinical indicator of the level of distress of the family and the difficulty of producing change through structured treatment programs. Rigidity is operationalized as the pervasiveness, arbitrariness, and strength of a person's belief systems concerning significant family issues and functions. A father who believes that "girls should never date before age 17" is taking a more rigid position than a father who believes "girls may date before age 17 with certain boys under certain circumstances." Rigidity, as the term is being used here, resembles irrational thinking, as described by Ellis and Harper (1975).

The therapist informally rates each family member's level of rigidity. Cases in which one or more family members takes a rigid stance concerning a variety of family issues have been more difficult to treat than cases in which family members adhere to flexible belief systems. Parents with rigid belief systems often resist attempts at reaching compromise solutions, sabotage homework assignments, and in extreme cases, challenge repeatedly the rationale for a problem-solving approach and the competence of the therapist. Such parents indicate that the purpose of treatment is to teach their unruly children to obey them, and if this goal is not accomplished, they drop out.

Clinical experience and social psychological research have suggested that direct confrontation is not the appropriate approach for coping with rigid behavior and attitudes. Instead, the contingencies maintaining the rigid behavior and attitudes should be assessed, and a shaping program instituted to modify these contingencies. A useful working hypothesis has been that rigid parental responses serve as avoidance behavior, that they help the parents avoid the occurrence of some "ultimate aversive consequence" perceived to follow if the rigid attitude is relaxed. Throughout the sessions, the therapist can look for hints as to what the "ultimate aversive consequence" might be in a particular case. When a hypothesis has been formulated concerning the consequence, it can be integrated into the problem definition stage of a problem-solving discussion. Then, solutions can be proposed which take the expanded definition of the problem into account. In practice, this strategy can work, but it requires a great deal of clinical sensitivity when implemented. The therapist must listen for a statement which provides an opening for the introduction of a hypothesis about rigid behavior and attitudes. Two cases will serve to illustrate this strategy for coping with rigidity:

Mr. Levin believed that his daughter Kathy should come home by 10:30 p.m. until she reached age 16. When questioned further, he could not give any reason for his belief other than, "She is too immature to stay out late." He added, however, that he would permit her to stay out until 11:30 p.m. after she reached age 16. The therapist pointed out that since Kathy's 16th birthday was in three months, perhaps her curfew should be extended by one and one-half minutes per day from the present until her birthday. The ridiculousness of the suggestion prompted Mr. Levin to consider that his rule appeared arbitrary. He then expressed his "real" concern that his daughter might drive around with the boys and become precociously involved in sexual activities if she stayed out later. Promiscuous behavior, possibly resulting in pregnancy, was the "ultimate aversive consequence" for Mr. Levin. When his concern was communicated clearly to Kathy, she was able to suggest solutions which provided him with appropriate reassurances. His "rigid attitude" softened, and a compromise about a curfew was reached.

Mr. and Mrs. Kordowski insisted that their sixteen-year-old son Randy attend church with them every Sunday. With prompting from the therapist, Randy communicated to his parents for the first time in his life that he was agnostic and that he considered it hypocritical to continue attending religious services. His parents were devastated. Mrs.

the home application assignments or the generalization programming session described above in the manual. Before and after the treatment sessions, the dyads participated in an assessment session in which they were administered retrospective checklists and audio-taped discussions of two topics. They were instructed to discuss and attempt to resolve the two topics for ten minutes apiece. One topic was a standard, hypothetical problem (bedtime) while the other topic was a real, family-specific conflict. The audio-tapes served as a measure of the acquisition of problem-solving communication skills; the self-report checklists served as measures of parent-adolescent relations at home.

Trained observers listened to the audio-taped discussions and reliably tabulated the frequency of four positive problem-solving behaviors—problem definition, solution listing, evaluation, and agreement—and the frequency of negative behavior—commands, curses, and threats. Problem-solving scores were computed for parents and adolescents by summing the frequency of the four positive problem-solving behaviors. Figure 7.3 presents the mean frequency of problem-solving behavior for parents and adolescents in the treatment and wait-list groups before and after treatment. The mean frequency of problem-solving behavior increased dramatically for parents and adolescents in the treatment group relative to the wait-list group, reflected in the highly significant group by time interactions on both problems. Analyses of the distributions of change scores for each group indicated that all of the dyads in the treatment group improved while only two of the dyads in the control group improved.

It had been predicted that the frequency of dyadic negative behavior would be high at preassessment, and that after training it would decrease more for the treatment group than for the control group. However, the frequency of negative behavior was low at preassessment (Hypothetical problem: treatment group mean = 1.75, wait-list group mean = .67; real problem: treatment group mean = 1.00, wait-list group mean = 1.00), leaving little room for improvement. At post assessment there were no negative behaviors in the problem-solving discussions of the treatment group and 1.00 and 2.33 negative behaviors in the hypothetical and real problem-solving discussions of the wait-list group, respectively. The group by time interaction approached significance on the real problem but was not significant on the hypothetical problem. It was concluded that parents and adolescents receiving treatment had acquired problem-solving skills.

The retrospective checklists did not provide clear-cut evidence of reduction in parent-adolescent conflict at home. On the Communication Habit Survey, Part A, a list of 39 family-specific issues, parents and adolescents rated on a five-point Likert Scale the degree of argument during the past two weeks concerning each issue. Mean scores were computed for parents

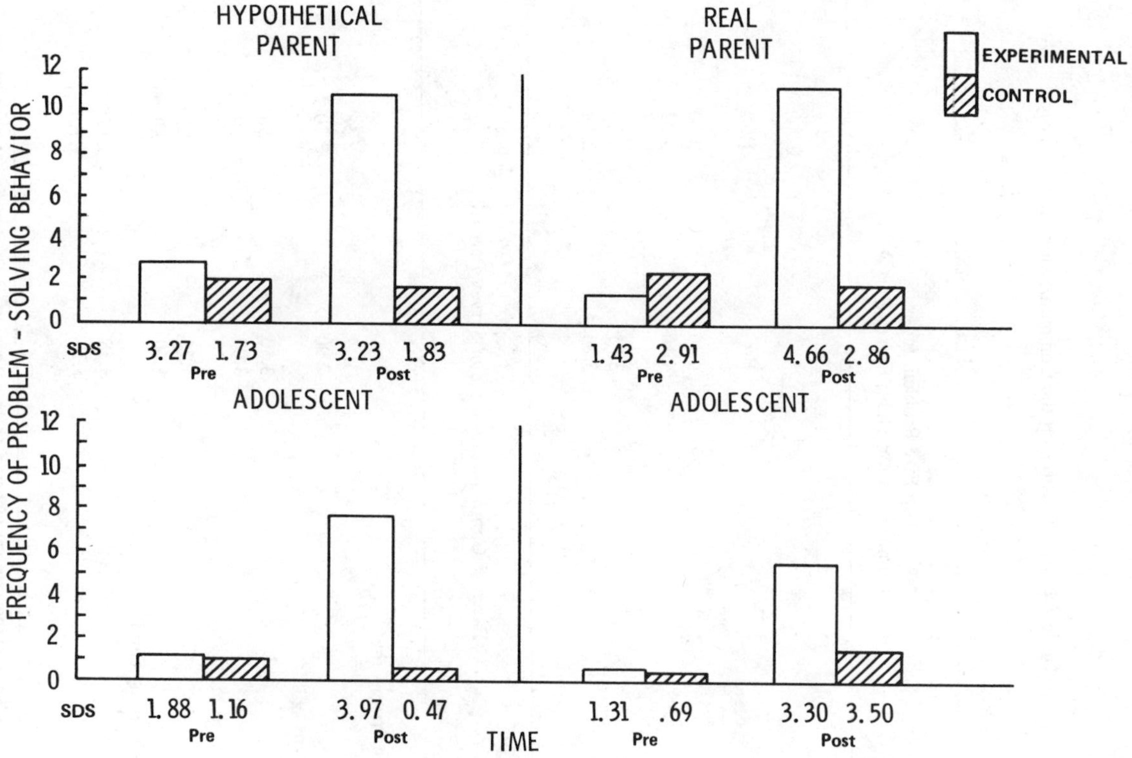

Fig. 7.3. Mean frequency of problem-solving behavior for parents and adolescents in the experimental (treatment) and wait-list (control) groups. The numbers printed below each panel are the standard deviations

and adolescents across the five most intense conflicts and are summarized in table 7.2. Although the mean conflict scores decreased as predicted, the group by time interactions did not achieve statistical significance. Parents' scores showed a trend towards significance.

Table 7.2 Mean Scores on the Communication Habit Survey

Top Five Problem Index Communication Habit Survey Part A	Pre	Post
Parents		
PSCT*	4.10	2.60
WL*	4.16	3.32
Adolescents		
PSCT	3.95	2.20
WL	3.86	2.58
Parents' Communication Habit Survey Part B		
My child interrupts me		
PSCT	3.42	2.58
WL	2.90	3.30
I interrupt my child		
PSCT	3.50	2.50
WL	3.00	3.30
My child lies to me		
PSCT	1.75	1.25
WL	1.60	1.80
I can confide in my child		
PSCT	3.58	3.17
WL	3.20	3.70

*PSCT = problem-solving communication training group; WL = wait-list control group.
Source: From study by Robin (1975).

On the Communication Habit Survey, Part B, a list of 28 statements characterizing positive and negative communication behavior at home, parents and adolescents rated on a five-point Likert scale the applicability of each statement to their interactions during the past two weeks. Each item was analyzed separately. Significant improvements favoring the treatment group were obtained on only four items for parents. No significant effects were obtained for adolescents. A more detailed discussion of the questionnaire data can be found in Robin (1975).

The results of the first evaluation of the problem-solving communication training program suggested that although parents and adolescents acquired problem-solving communication skills, there was little consistent improvement in conflict resolution and communication behavior at home. Several factors may have contributed to the lack of generalization of the problem-solving communication skills to the home setting. First, the therapists did not devote any session time to discussing home applications of the problem-solving communication skills. Although several dyads anecdotally reported attempts to use newly acquired skills at home, no systematic attempt was made to encourage such application. Second, three of the five sessions were devoted to discussing hypothetical conflicts and two were devoted to discussing real conflicts. Two sessions may have been insufficient for teaching families to apply problem solving with real problems and for helping families to resolve significant currently distressing conflicts. Third, fathers were not included in the intervention. This may have made it difficult for dyads to generalize what they had learned to naturalistic family situations. Fourth, the program had not been extensively piloted prior to the study. Therefore, many of the procedures necessary to maintain involvement, analyze systemic interaction patterns, and overcome resistance by family members had not yet been developed. Fifth, the measures used to assess change at home were unvalidated.

In order to remedy the deficiencies discussed above, the generalization programming and assessment technologies described earlier in the chapter were developed. Additional pilot trials were conducted which included fathers, and intervention strategies were devised to overcome common implementation problems. Then, two additional outcome studies were conducted.

Foster (1978) replicated the evaluation by Robin et al. and also investigated the effects of the procedures that were designed to enhance generalization to the home. Twenty-eight families experiencing parent-adolescent conflict (25 triads and three dyads) were matched according to pretreatment conflict severity scores on the Conflict Behavior Questionnaire and were randomly assigned to either a wait-list control or one of two treatment groups. Each family participated in a preassessment session, seven one-hour treatment sessions, and a postassessment session. The two treatment groups were also reassessed six to eight weeks after the end of treatment. One treatment group (skill training) received seven sessions of training in problem-solving communication skills. Treatment followed the procedures used in the Robin et al. study, except that Foster's therapists spent one session on assessment and goal setting and six sessions on problem solving real problems. Unlike Robin's intervention, which placed a heavy emphasis on learning the problem-solving strategy through the use of hypothetical problems, Foster's intervention placed more emphasis on resolving currently distressing problems. The other treatment group (skill training plus generalization programming) received the same training plus the generalization-programming procedures, which included homework assignments of graduated difficulty and weekly discussions of factors affecting the use of problem-solving skills at home. All of the treatment sessions were audio taped, and ratings of these tapes with a therapy-process code found that the therapists did conduct skill training and skill training plus generalization-programming training appropriately.

Multidimensional measures were used to assess change. The measures included: (1) ratings of a single ten-minute audio-taped discussion of a significant family problem, coded with the Interaction Behavior Code and a frequency-based problem-solving code similar to that used in Robin et al. (1977); (2) the Issues Checklist; (3) the Conflict Behavior Questionnaire; (4) the Home Report; (5) the Decision-Making Questionnaire; and (6) self-report ratings of family-specific goals and communication targets. In addition, a composite score was derived from the questionnaires and from the ratings of the audio-taped discussions by applying a discriminant function (Prinz 1977). For triads, questionnaires were completed separately by the mothers and fathers. Data were analyzed separately for mothers and fathers. The data were submitted to stratified block repeated measures analyses of variance with three factors: group (wait-list, skill training, skill training plus generalization programming), time (pre- and postassessment), and blocks (severity at preassessment). Separate analysis of the treatment groups were conducted to evaluate the follow-up data.

The results of the pre- and postassessment comparisons were mixed. The treatment groups did not improve significantly more than the wait-list group on the ratings of the audio-taped discussions on either the Interaction Behavior Code or the problem-solving code. However, there were trends towards significant treatment effects for negative maternal and adolescent behavior on the Interaction Behavior Code. This trend was a reflection of improvement by the skill training plus generalization group and deterioration by the other two groups. Thus, unlike Robin et al.'s (1977) study, there was no consistent evidence in Foster's study that families acquired problem-solving communication skills. The lack of significant differences on the ratings of the audio-taped discussions may have been due to the great variability among families within each group, especially at preassessment, which suggested that some of the families in the present sample already possessed some of the problem-solving skills tapped by the codes.

Several significant treatment effects were indicated by the analyses of the responses to the self-report questionnaires. Both treatment groups were superior to the wait-list group at postassessment, but did not differ from each other on the mother's intensity and the mother's-intensity-by-frequency scores of the Issues Checklist. On the Conflict Behavior Questionnaire, there was a trend towards a significant treatment effect on the mother's appraisal of dyadic conflict. Also, adolescents in the skill training group were superior to the other two groups at postassessment on the appraisal of maternal conflict and the appraisal of dyadic conflict scores of the Conflict Behavior Questionnaire. There was a trend towards a significant treatment effect on the composite score, accounted for by positive changes in the skill training plus generalization programming group. Finally, both treatment groups were superior to the control group but were equal to each other at postassessment on global ratings of improvement on family-specific goals and communication targets. No other treatment effects were found on the self-report questionnaires.

The interpretation of results was complicated by the fact that the wait-list control group improved on many of the measures, producing many main effects of time. In addition, there were several significant differences between groups at preassessment, with the wait-list group scoring most disturbed. (Analyses of covariance were used to analyze the postassessment data when there were between-group differences at preassessment, with the preassessment scores serving as the covariate). This suggested the possibility that greater regression effects operated for the wait-list groups than for the two treatment groups. In any event, when significant treatment effects were not found, this was typically due to improvement by the wait-list group rather than to lack of improvement by the treatment groups.

At follow-up, most of the gains were maintained or increased slightly, although the lack of an untreated control group at this point in time precluded attributing maintenance effects to the treatment procedures. Contrary to predictions, on several measures the skill-training group continued to improve significantly from postassessment to follow-up, while the skill-training-plus-generalization programming group did not. Mothers and adolescents in the former group reported less dyadic conflict on the Conflict Behavior Questionnaire, and mothers achieved lower intensity and intensity-by-frequency scores on the Issues Checklist.

The results of this investigation provided additional evidence for the effectiveness of the problem-solving communication training program but also raised a number of provocative questions. The significant improvements of both treatment groups on selected scores from the Issues

Checklists and Conflict Behavior Questionnaires as well as on global ratings of treatment goals and communication targets suggested that there were some generalized reductions in parent-adolescent conflict at home. The lack of significant effects on the remaining self-report measures suggested that the reductions in conflict were by no means universally evident. However, it was difficult to interpret these negative results since they were partially due to improvement by the wait-list group. Additional research is needed concerning normative fluctuations in parent-adolescent relations in distressed and nondistressed families over extended periods of time.

The lack of significant treatment effects on the ratings of the audio-taped discussions was disappointing. It constituted a failure to replicate the results obtained by Robin et al. (1977). The discrepancies between the results of the two studies may be due to one or more of the following factors: (1) methodological differences in the discussion tasks and instructions to the families, (2) differences in the content of the treatment sessions, and (3) differences in the amount of emphasis placed on practicing problem-solving skills versus resolving currently distressing problems. Since Foster's therapists, emphasized resolution of currently distressing problems more than Robin's therapists, who emphasized acquisition of problem-solving skills, perhaps it shouldn't come as a surprise that Foster obtained greater change on measures of communication and conflict at home and Robin et al. obtained greater change on measures of skill acquisition. Future research should determine the balance between these two emphases needed to produce optimal change in both behavior areas.

Finally, the lack of differences at postassessment between the skill training and skill-training plus generalization-programming groups suggests that the generalization procedures had little impact. It can, however, be argued that the test of the generalization procedures should be discounted, since the behavioral measures provided minimal evidence that the skills to be generalized were acquired. The surprising differences in favor of the skill-training group over the skill-training plus generalization-programming group at follow-up suggest that the generalization-programming procedures may have had an iatrogenic effect on maintenance. Additional research is needed to determine the replicability and reasons for these possibly iatrogenic effects of the generalization-programming techniques.

Given the evidence that problem-solving communication training can produce some skill acquisition and some generalized reduction in parent-adolescent conflict at home, the question arises whether the effects of the program are due to its structured components or due to demand characteristics, expectation effects, and nonspecific therapist variables. A third clinical outcome study was recently undertaken to determine the importance of the structured elements of problem-solving communication training and to provide additional evidence of generalized change in parent-adolescent relations at home (Robin 1977, 1979). The problem-solving communication program was contrasted with a less structured "best alternative treatment" condition and a wait-list control group. A "best alternative treatment" condition was used instead of an attention-placebo control because of the ethical and practical problems associated with attention-placebo controls (O'Leary and Borkovec 1978).

Thirty-three families, with teenagers who ranged in age from 11 to 16 (mean age = 13.5), requested help for parent-adolescent conflict at a private mental health clinic. Families were matched on severity of conflict, sex of the adolescent, and number of participating parents, and then were randomly assigned to problem-solving communication training, best alternative treatment, or wait-list control. Within each condition families were assigned to therapists on the basis of scheduling convenience.

Each family attended an initial two-hour assessment session, seven one-hour treatment sessions, and a final two-hour assessment session. Wait-list families received treatment following the second assessment session. Treatment families were re-assessed ten weeks after completing the program.

Families in the problem-solving communication training group were taught problem-solving, communication skills, and generalization-programming skills following the manual outlined earlier in this chapter. One doctoral and three masters-level psychologists served as therapists. Five therapists (one psychiatrist and four masters-level mental health professionals), who were providers of short-term family therapy, conducted the best alternative family therapy. These therapists indicated in interviews and on questionnaires that they did not use problem-solving communication training, but characterized their approaches as "eclectic," "family systems," or "psycho-dynamic." The therapists agreed to treat families in the research project in the same way that they treated their other cases.

Great efforts were taken to insure comparability across treatment conditions on all of the variables except treatment methods. Therapists were given equal access to information and were instructed to have all participating family members attend each session. At the end of the first therapy session, families were given a brief questionnaire, which assessed their expectations for therapeutic change, to complete at home and mail back to the research staff. There were no differences between treatment conditions on either parents' or adolescents' expectations for change.

The assessment measures for the study included: (1) the Issues Checklist, (2) the Conflict Behavior Questionnaire, (3) the Home Report, and (4) audio-taped discussions of two family-specific conflicts coded with the Parent-Adolescent Interaction Coding System (Robin and Fox 1978). Treated families were also administered an attitude survey (nine-point Likert scale) at postassessment.

Since the results of this study have not been completely analyzed, the follow-up measures and the ratings of the audio-taped discussions will not be reported in this chapter. Pre-post scores on the Issues Checklist, Conflict Behavior Questionnaire, and Home Report were submitted to three-group (problem-solving, best alternative family therapy, and wait-list) by two-time (pre and post) analyses of covariance, with the three matching variables serving as covariates. In the case of triads, scores were averaged across parents for the analyses. Table 7.3 summarizes the results.

Table 7.3 Mean Scores on the Issues Checklist, Conflict Behavior Questionnaire, and Home Report
From Robin's (1977 and 1979) Study

		Pre	Post	Significant Effects
Issues Checklist				
Parents[1]				
Intensity of Conflict	PSCT[2]	2.4	1.8[4]	Time × Treatment
	NBFT	2.1	2.0	p < .005
	WL	2.2	2.5	
Weighted Average of Intensity × Frequency	PSCT	2.7	2.0[4]	Time × Treatment
	NBFT	2.4	2.2	p < .01
	WL	2.6	2.7	
Adolescents[3]				
Intensity of Conflict	PSCT	2.4	2.1	
	NBFT	2.2	1.9	
	WL	2.4	2.4	
Weighted Average of Intensity × Frequency	PSCT	2.8	2.6	Time
	NBFT	2.7	2.0	p < .01
	WL	2.8	2.6	
Conflict Behavior Questionnaire				
Parents				
Appraisal of Adol.	PSCT	28.5	17.7[4]	Time p < .001
	NBFT	23.0	19.0	Time × Treatment
	WL	26.4	24.7	p < .02
Appraisal of Dyad	PSCT	11.4	5.6[4]	Time p < .001
	NBFT	8.5	6.4	Time × Treatment
	WL	10.9	9.7	p < .006
Adolescents				
Appraisal of Parents	PSCT	18.9	17.0	
	NBFT	20.3	15.8	
	WL	15.4	14.0	
Appraisal of Dyad	PSCT	10.6	8.5	Time p < .003
	NBFT	10.5	6.7	
	WL	7.9	7.4	

Table 7.3 *(continued)*

		Home Report		
Parents[5]				
Daily Conflict	PSCT	3.0	2.7	
	NBFT	2.9	2.3	
	WL	2.7	2.9	
Argument Ratio	PSCT	1.9	1.6	
	NBFT	1.6	1.6	
	WL	1.7	1.6	
Adolescents[6]				
Daily Conflict	PSCT	3.4	2.8	
	NBFT	3.6	2.5	Time $p < .03$
	WL	2.6	2.3	
Argument Ratio	PSCT	2.3	1.9	Time $p < .04$
	NBFT	2.1	1.7	
	WL	1.7	1.5	

[1] N = 11(PSCT), 11(NBFT), 11(WL)
[2] PSCT = Problem Solving Communication Training Program
NBFT = Nonbehavioral Family Therapy
WL = Wait-List Control
[3] N = 11(PSCT), 10(NBFT), 11(WL)
[4] Significant differences between PSCT and WL at post.
[5] N = 8(PSCT), 8(NBFT), 9(WL)
[6] N = 7(PSCT), 7(NBFT), 8(WL)

For parents, there were significant treatment by time interactions on the Issues Checklist and Conflict Behavior Questionnaire, but not on the Home Report. A priori contrasts indicated that on both measures the problem-solving communication training group was significantly lower than the wait-list group at postassessment but that there were no differences between the best alternative family therapy and wait-list groups. For adolescents, there were no significant treatment by time interactions on any of the measures, althought there were significant main effects of time on most of the measures. T-tests were used to compare groups on the attitude survey. Parents consistently rated problem-solving communication training more positively than best alternative family therapy. There were significant differences on their ratings of improvement in communication with their adolescent, improvement in their relationship with their adolescent, improvement in parent-adolescent discussions, and the extent to which the program fulfilled their expectations. Adolescents rated the two types of treatment equally.

The results of this study indicated that problem-solving communication training produced significant reductions in parent-adolescent conflict while the "best-available" alternative treatment did not. Parents receiving problem-solving communication training reported significant reductions in conflict and significant effects of treatment on parents' appraisal of adolescents' behavior on the Conflict Behavior Questionnaire. Neither study obtained significant effects of treatment on the Home Reports or the adolescents' Issues Checklists. However, Foster obtained significant effects of treatment on the adolescents' Conflict Behavior Questionnaire while Robin did not. In addition, Robin's wait-list control group displayed less of a tendency to improve from pre- to postassessment than Foster's wait-list group, perhaps accounting for the differences between the pattern of significant results in the two studies.

Taken together, the three clinical outcome studies reviewed above suggest that the problem-solving communication training program: (1) facilitates acquisition of problem-solving communication skills, and (2) produces generalized reduction in conflict at home. In addition, it appears that the obtained improvements are due to the specific treatment components rather than demand characteristics, expectation effects, or therapist variables. However, the results of these three studies were not uniformly positive or completely consistent with each other. Suggestions for future research aimed at improving the problem-solving communication training approach will be considered in the remaining portion of the chapter.

Future Directions

Future research and applications of problem-solving communication training should be addressed to three concerns: theory, assessment, and treatment.

Theory. A social-learning developmental skill model of parent-adolescent conflict was outlined at the beginning of this chapter. However, only one study provides empirical support for this model (Alexander 1970). Future research should evaluate the social-learning developmental skill model. To what extent do the principles of reciprocity and coercion characterize parent-adolescent interactions? Do distressed parent-adolescent triads display greater significant improvement in their adolescents' behavior at home and their interactions with their adolescents? In addition, they were more satisfied with the outcome of treatment than parents receiving the best alternative family therapy.

Adolescents, however, did not report either significant reductions in conflict or significant improvement in their parents' behavior at home and their interactions with their parents. Thus, parents and adolescents agreed that the best alternative family therapy was ineffective, but disagreed about the effectiveness of problem-solving communication training. Several interpretations of this inconsistency are: (1) Either parents or adolescents are inaccurate reporters of treatment outcome, and this study could not determine whose perceptions were inaccurate. (2) Parents and adolescents used different criteria when completing the checklists (parents may have been less stringent than adolescents in evaluating outcome, or events labeled "improvement" by parents may not have been labeled "improvement" by adolescents). (3) Parents acquired problem-solving communication skills but adolescents did not. (4) Because of the nature of the developmental stage of adolescence, teenagers are harsh judges of family relations and are extremely unwilling to admit that conflict has been reduced. Future research is needed to determine which of these hypotheses is correct. The present study points out the importance of collecting outcome measures from both parents and children in clinical research with families.

Many of Robin's results on the self-report questionnaires were consistent with the findings of Foster's (1978) study. Both Robin and Foster found significant effects of treatment on parents' intensity and intensity-by-frequency scores on the Issues Checklists and parents' appraisal of dyadic interaction scores on the Conflict Behavior Questionnaire. Robin also found reciprocity of punishment and less reciprocity of positive reinforcement than nondistressed triads. Do distressed triads display greater reciprocity of authoritarian decision making and less reciprocity of democratic decision making than nondistressed dyads? To what extent is democratic decision making related to low levels of conflict in families and autocratic decision making related to high levels of conflict in families?

In addition, several concepts introduced in this chapter stretch the boundaries of a social learning model and require further clarification. "Resistance," "rigidity," and "sabotage" are three such constructs. In this chapter, these terms have been used without clear-cut definitions. It will be important for future investigators to integrate these concepts into a social-learning model. For example, what does it mean to say that a family is "resisting change" by failing to complete a homework assignment? Perhaps "resistance" can be operationalized in terms of avoidance behavior. There may be certain consequences of changing family interaction patterns perceived to be aversive by individual members of the family. If family members wish to avoid these aversive changes, they might avoid completing the homework, which has been construed as part of the change process. When, however, would a change in family interaction patterns be considered aversive by a member of the family? And when would the family seek therapy if some of its members wished to avoid change? Perhaps some family members' negative communication behaviors are being positively reinforced.

For example, in the Smith family, the father and daughter "resisted change" by failing to complete their homework assignments, although the mother attempted to complete the assignments. It was learned that Mr. and

Mrs. Smith argued intensely with each other concerning a variety of issues, including their daughter Sally's behavior. These arguments took the form of verbal onslaughts by Mrs. Smith against her husband. Mr. Smith was unskilled at responding to his wife's verbal onslaughts. Instead, he punished his wife by subtly encouraging Sally to disobey rules imposed by Mrs. Smith. Sally learned to ignore her mother's rules when she wished additional freedom because her father would contradict her mother. Mrs. Smith's confrontations with Sally were a source of reinforcement to Mr. Smith. Essentially, the parents were using the daughter to punish each other's behavior. Sally was using her parents' disagreements to gain additional freedom from restrictions. Each family member was being reinforced for emitting inappropriate communication behavior. Under these circumstances, if either the father or daughter cooperated with attempts to change family interactions, he or she would lose an important source of reinforcement. Consequently, they resisted completing the homework assignment. The contingencies were structured to encourage failure to cooperate with the therapist.

Another direction for future theoretical analysis concerns the "skill deficit" aspect of the model of parent-adolescent conflict. To what extent do families lack skills? To what extent do families fail to use skills which are already in their behavioral repertoire? Are families deficient in behavioral or cognitive skills, or both? Spivack et al. (1976) have postulated that certain key cognitive-interpersonal problem-solving skills mediate behavioral adjustment, and that different cognitive skills are important at different developmental stages. They have postulated that alternative-solution thinking, consequential thinking, empathy, role taking, and social reasoning are particularly important mediators of adjustment in adolescence. To what extent do deficits in these cognitive skills mediate parent-adolescent conflict? When problem-solving communication training leads to improved parent-adolescent relations, are positive changes mediated by acquisition and increased utilization of relevant cognitive-interpersonal problem-solving skills? Or are the positive changes a direct result of behavioral skill training? Cross-sectional and longitudinal comparisons of distressed and nondistressed families on a variety of cognitive and behavioral measures are needed to answer these questions. In addition, it will be important to measure parents' and adolescents' cognitive-interpersonal problem-solving skills before and after families receive treatment (see Lapides 1978 for an example of this approach).

Assessment. Suggestions for additional research concerning the validity of the self-report and behavioral measures of parent-adolescent conflict were made in an earlier section of the chapter. Here, more general assessment issues will be considered.

First, there is a need for future researchers to devise a technology for obtaining direct samples of parent-adsolescent communication-conflict behavior in the natural environment. At present, audio-taped behavior samples are obtained in an analogue setting. These behavior samples may be reactive. For example, Weiss and Robin (1978) found that when mother-son dyads were asked to discuss two problems for ten minutes apiece, mothers exhibited more negative behavior during the second discussion than the first discussion. Distressed sons exhibited more negative behavior during the second discussion than the first, but this was not true for nondistressed sons. One interpretation of Weiss and Robin's results might be that mothers and distressed sons were constrained by the demand characteristics of the assessment situation and did not display their genuine response tendencies until they habituated to the setting during the second discussion.

Behavior therapists have often observed parents and young children in the home. However, direct observations in the home may be highly reactive and impractical with parents and adolescents. Also, the events of interest may be low base-rate behaviors not circumscribed in time. It may be possible to use the observational strategy developed by Johnson, Christensen, and Bellamy (1976). With the permission of a family, a tape recorder can be concealed in the home and can be activated at random intervals throughout the day.

A second assessment concern is the need for standardized tools to measure functional relationships between parents and adolescents' responses. The self-report and behavioral assessment devices provide a static, cross-sectional picture of family functioning. They do not provide information concerning time-based contingency relationships between various responses. Clinicians presently rely upon interviews for such information.

A measure of functional relationships might be developed by surveying a large number of distressed and nondistressed families to determine common behavioral sequences between parents and adolescents. Then, interactional tasks might be devised which serve to bring out each interactional sequence. An assessor could ask a family to complete a relevant task and observe the degree to which they exhibit the function measured by the task. For example, one function might be, "Mother mediates disputes between the father and son." The father and son might be given opposing positions of an issue to discuss. The mother might be given a neutral position. Then, the assessor might audio-tape the discussion and rate the extent to which the mother serves as a mediator. Alternatively, family members might be taught to self-monitor "mother's mediating behavior" at home for one week.

Treatment. The less than completely successful results of the clinical outcome studies suggests that the treatment program is in need of further refinement to produce more consistent results. Families vary greatly in the degree of conflict which they exhibit at intake. However, the treatment procedures do not vary much as a function of the presenting level of distress of the family. Clinical impressions suggest that the current treatment program has been most consistently successful with mild to moderate levels of parent-adolescent conflict. Severely distressed families often possess so many negative communication skills that it is extremely difficult to teach them to resolve conflicts using the problem-solving model. Such families may require more than seven sessions of treatment. A "pre-problem-solving training period" might be useful in such cases. During pre-problem-solving training, the therapist might meet individually with each family member to shape appropriate communication behavior and modify rigid, negative attitudes. It might be useful for severely distressed parents and adolescents to practice using problem-solving communication skills with unrelated teenagers and adults in a group setting before attempting to use these skills in their own families. Further research is needed to determine the best mixture of techniques for helping families with different levels of distress.

Analyses are also needed to examine the contribution of various components to the overall effectiveness of problem-solving communication training. How important is the four-step model of problem-solving? What combination of feedback techniques is most effective for the modification of negative communication habits. What changes might be made in the generalization programming techniques to improve their effects? Since large-scale factorial-design research is costly and impractical, it might be desirable for investigators to develop a single-subject methodology for answering questions about the components of the treatment program (Hersen and Barlow 1976).

Finally, researchers might examine parameters within the family which influence the success of treatment. What is the relative effectiveness of problem-solving communication training with dyads, triads, and larger family units? What is the relationship between marital conflict and parent-adolescent conflict? How is parent-adolescent conflict different in younger and older adolescents? How do birth order and sex of the adolescent influence the effectiveness of treatment?

At present, the clinician has available a demonstrably effective method of treating parent-adolescent conflict. By following carefully the suggestions outlined in this chapter, the clinician is likely to achieve success in reducing most parent-adolescent conflict. With the continuation of research outlined here, the problem-solving communication training program may well become the treatment of choice for parent-adolescent conflict.

Appendix: Treatment Manual for Parent-Adolescent Conflict Program

This manual provides detailed instructions for conducting problem-solving communication skill training. The instructions are organized in the form of a session-by-session treatment manual. Certain aspects of the procedures will differ from one family to the next. For example, the therapist tailors communication skill training to the particular negative communication habits displayed by each family. The manual will note such points of choice and present illustrations with typical cases. Seven sessions of treatment are outlined for a mother-father-adolescent triad. Certain families may require a fewer or greater number of sessions. It is assumed that an initial assessment has been completed and that the therapist has access to the Issues Checklists. The reader should consider this manual as a set of guidelines that can be modified to accommodate the needs of each family.

Session One

Goals

1. Introduce problem solving.
2. Conduct one problem-solving discussion.
3. Send the family home with a solution to implement.

I. Provide introduction to and rationale for problem-solving communication training.

A. Emphasize that parents and teenagers need to learn how to resolve problematic issues and how to communicate more effectively; they need to learn what to say and how to say it.

B. State that you will teach them a specific method to reach mutually agreeable solutions to particular disagreements, and they will practice using this method at home. You will also help them solve several significant problems, but you won't help them solve all of their specific disputes during the sessions.

C. Inform them that they will be required to attend sessions as a family and will be expected to apply problem-solving communication techniques at home.

D. State that during each session they will solve one problem by following the method that you will outline. You will serve as a "stage director" by guiding their discussions, making suggestions, and reviewing the adequacy of their problem-solving communication behavior.

E. Solicit family members' reactions to your rationale. Be sensitive to verbal and facial reactions that indicate that they do not understand what you said or are uneasy with your rationale. Respond to their uneasiness without being confrontive or defensive. You should be modeling ap-

propriate ways to handle criticism as well as answering any questions.
Note: It is very important to use simple, straight forward language in talking with the family. Adolescents, especially, are turned off by "fancy vocabulary" and flowery sentences.

F. Obtain family's permission to audio-tape or video-tape the sessions. If they give permission, turn on the equipment.

II. Select problem to be discussed.
   A. Ask them for a moderately intense disagreement, not for the most serious conflict. It should be intense enough to be a meaningful issue.
   B. Try to select a problem which the adolescent wants to see resolved in order to maximize his or her participation.
   C. If the family does not readily suggest a topic, select a topic with a moderate intensity score (two or three) from their Issues Checklists.

III. Distribute copies of the problem-solving outline to each family member (table 7.1).
   A. Inform them that they should retain their copies of the outline for use at home.
   B. Note that you will not review the entire outline after distributing it. You will call attention to each step as the family reaches that step of the discussion.

IV. Proceed to problem definition.
   A. State the attributes of an adequate problem definition and provide a model based upon the topic which was selected.
      1. An adequate problem definition describes explicitly what the other person is doing or saying that creates a problem for the speaker. It tells why the other person's behavior is problematic to the speaker. It is nonaccusatory and concise. It addresses behaviors and situations, not attributes of persons.
      2. Examples:
         a. "My problem is that I want to stay out until midnight on weekends to party with my friends, but my curfew is 11:00 p.m. This bothers me because I miss out on fun by having to leave parties early."
         This is an adequate definition because it states what the other person does that creates a problem for the speaker and why.
         b. "My problem is that you are too strict about curfew."
         This is an inadequate definition because the speaker accuses the listener of being too strict and because it is not specific about what she means by "too strict."
         c. "My problem is that you are irresponsible when it comes to taking care of your room."
         This is an inadequate definition because the speaker accuses the listener of being irresponsible without defining the term.
         d. "I'm upset about the dust on the floor, the clothes on the bed, and the messy papers on the desk in your room because it embarrasses me when my friends visit and see your room."
         This is an adequate definition because it specifies the behaviors

of the listener which upset the speaker and clearly indicates why these behaviors bother the speaker.

B. Ask one family member to define the problem from his or her perspective. Tell the others to listen carefully because they will be asked to paraphrase the speaker's definition.
   1. Let whoever suggested the topic define his or her problem first.
   2. When the definition is inadequate, correct it and ask for a restatement from the speaker. Correct only gross performance errors.
C. After the person has stated his or her perspective of the problem, ask one of the listeners to paraphrase the definition to verify his or her understanding of the speaker. Illustrate paraphrasing with a clear-cut example.
   1. Example:
      a. Problem definition: "I'm upset because when I ask for help around the house, you refuse to help me. This upsets me because there are so many chores to do and so little time to do them in."
      b. Paraphrase: "So you are annoyed that I refuse to help you with the chores, and this annoys you because of the great amount of work there is to be done."
D. Ask the person who gave the problem definition to verify the accuracy of the paraphrase. If it was accurate, the speaker should acknowledge this. If it was inaccurate, the speaker should restate the problem definition, and ask for an additional paraphrase.
E. Continue problem definitions and paraphrases until father, mother, and adolescent have all expressed their perceptions of the problem and are all satisfied that the other family members accurately received their communications.
F. Conclude this stage of problem solving by noting that each person has defined the problem in a different manner, but that despite the differences, their definitions complement each other. Note that respecting each other's right to express different views of the problem is important, and that providing such respect does not have to imply agreeing with those views.

V. Generation of alternative solutions.
   A. Describe the goal of this stage of problem solving as generating a variety of suggestions for ways to solve the problem.
   B. Review three rules of brainstorming that will govern generating ideas.
      1. List as many ideas as possible.
      2. Defer evaluation of ideas.
      3. Be creative and outrageous in the solutions that are suggested.
   C. Appoint one family member as a secretary and distribute a blank problem-solving worksheet (see fig. A-1). The secretary's task is to write down solutions as they are suggested. If the adolescent appears uninvolved in the discussion, it is sometimes helpful to appoint him or her as secretary, to ensure at least a minimum level of participation and attentiveness.
   D. Ask the family to take turns suggesting ideas.
   E. Acknowledge each suggestion and praise their efforts, but don't evaluate

the specific suggestions which they give.

F. Enforce the rules of brainstorming by interrupting premature evaluations of ideas, suggesting outlandish ideas, and encouraging rapid-fire suggesting of multiple solutions.

G. If parents and/or adolescents "run dry" after listing several ideas, introduce one or more of the following guidelines for constructing additional solutions:

1. What is the basic conflict concerning this problem? Can solutions address that conflict?
2. Is a trade possible?
3. Can the physical environment be rearranged to solve the problem?
4. Can cues be provided to help each family member remember to act differently?
5. Who has to make the most drastic change in behavior to solve this problem? What can be done to make it easier for that person to make this change?
6. Can the problem be solved by changing the way one or more family members think about the problematic situation?

H. Continue listing solutions until the family has accumulated between six and eight ideas.

Note: A light-hearted mood can facilitate creative solution listing. You can suggest humorous ideas to help lighten the mood.

VI. Evaluation and Decision Making.

A. Provide a rationale: "Next, we are going to decide upon the best idea. I'm going to ask each of you to say whether each idea is good or bad and why. Remember, you should consider whether the idea will solve the problem and whether you could really carry it out. If you like an idea, we will record a 'plus' for you on the worksheet. If you dislike an idea, we will record a 'minus.'"

B. Model consequential thinking with the first idea on the problem worksheet.

1. Idea: "We could hire a maid to clean up the room."
2. Evaluation: "That seems like a good idea because then I won't have to clean it up myself; but, it would cost money to hire a maid. I don't have the money so it's really not a good idea. I give it a 'minus.'"

C. Ask each family member to evaluate the first idea. As each person states his or her evaluation, a "plus" or "minus" should be recorded in the appropriate place on the problem worksheet (table 7.2).

D. Direct the family to continue to evaluate the listed solutions. Prompt, guide, praise, and shape appropriate evaluative statements.

1. Family members often truncate evaluative statements; they indicate their opinion without giving a reason. Insist upon reasons in order to teach consequential thinking.
2. Additional solutions may emerge during the evaluations of the listed ideas. Encourage the family to add these additional ideas to the worksheet.
3. You should not impose your personal evaluations of solutions upon the family.

Family_______________________ Date___________

Problem_______________________

Original Solutions	Evaluations					
	Adolescent		Mother		Father	
	+	−	+	−	+	−

1. ______________________________
2. ______________________________
3. ______________________________
4. ______________________________
5. ______________________________
6. ______________________________
7. ______________________________
8. ______________________________
9. ______________________________
10. ______________________________
11. ______________________________
12. ______________________________

Compromise Solutions ______________________________

1. ______________________________
2. ______________________________
3. ______________________________
4. ______________________________
5. ______________________________

Selected Solution ______________________________

Fig. A.1. Problem-solving worksheet

E. After all of the solutions have been evaluated, review the worksheet to determine if any ideas were rated "plus" by everyone.
   1. If they reached consensus on one or more solutions, ask them to select one or to combine several. Ask the secretary to record the adopted solution on the bottom of the worksheet. Then, proceed to Implementation planning (VII).
   2. If there was no consensus, begin negotiation training.

F. Negotiation training.
   1. You play an extremely directive role in helping the family reach a mutally acceptable compromise.
   2. Select as a potential compromise the solution on which the family came closest to agreement (typically the one with two plus signs).
   3. Have each person restate his or her evaluation of this idea and point out the area of disagreement between them.
   4. Ask them to list variations on this idea that could serve as compromises.
   5. Ask them to evaluate the potential compromises, making it clear that each person will have to give something up to get something in return.
   6. If they do not reach an agreement, determine why. Is one person afraid of losing face by giving in? Do the parents fear that if they give in on this issue, that the adolescent will escalate demands on other issues? Is one person retaliating against the others because of a past grievance? Was the problem defined inadequately?
   7. Ask them questions and make reflective statements in a way which makes explicit your opinion about what is preventing them from compromising. Provide reassurances to alleviate their concerns about compromising. Suggest a trial solution to be renegotiated at the next session.
   8. Be as persistent and directive as necessary in overcoming their resistance to a compromise solution.
   9. When a solution has been reached, ask the secretary to record it on the bottom of the problem worksheet.

VII. Implementation planning.

A. Prompt family members to consider exactly how the solution will be implemented.
   1. Who will do what, when, where, how, etc?
   2. Clarify the criteria for solution compliance.

B. Develop a plan for monitoring solution compliance.
   1. Informal reports or event records are usually sufficient.
   2. Explain charting procedures when necessary.

C. Anticipate difficulties that might arise when they implement the solution and plan strategies to overcome these difficulties. Roleplay parts of the solution which involve verbal interchanges.

VIII. Assign homework.

A. The family should implement the solution which was reached during the problem-solving discussion.

B. The family should complete the problem-solving exercise sheet (fig. A.2) as a means of refining the skills.

C. You should put the assignment for the family in writing.

IX. Closing social amenities.

A. Administer the "dead man's" test, i.e., ask the adolescent to repeat the homework assignment.

B. Answer any questions the family may have.

X. Complete the parent-adolescent therapist session note form illustrated in figure A.3.

Fig. A.2. Problem-solving exercise: Session one homework

Name ______________________________ Date ______________

The purpose of this worksheet is to give you practice with the steps of problem solving. Write out the answers as best you can. Bring the sheet to your therapist at your next session; the therapist will go over it with you.

I. Defining the Problem.

A good definition of the problem tells what the other person is *doing* or *saying* that *bothers* you and *why* this bothers you. The definition is short, neutral, and does not blame the other person. Below are several definitions. Read each one. Then, say whether it is good or bad. If it is bad, write down a better definition.

A. *Mother:* My problem is that I don't like to see your room dirty; all the clothes are on the bed and the dust is two-inches thick. I'm upset when my friends come to visit and see the room looking that way.

1. Is this a good definition of a room-cleaning problem?
______YES ______NO

2. If you said no, write a better definition: ___________________________

____

____

____

B. *Daughter:* I hate you, mom. You just are a real pain. I'm missing out on all the fun because you make me come home by 9 p.m. on weekends.

1. Is this a good definition of a coming-home-on-time problem?
______YES ______NO

2. If you said no, write a better definition: ___________________________

____

____

____

C. *Father:* Son, the real problem with you is that you don't respect your elders. Kids just don't know the meaning of respect today.

When I was your age, I would never talk to my father the way you talk to me.

1. Is this a good definition of a talking back problem?
   ______YES ______NO
2. If you said no, write a better definition: ________________________

____

____

____

D. *Son:* I get angry when you bug me 10 times a day about taking out the trash and feeding the dogs. I'm old enough to do these things without being reminded.

1. Is this a good definition for a chores problem?
   ______YES ______NO
2. If you said no, write a better definition: ________________________

____

____

____

E. Below, a mother and a daughter define their problem about playing the stereo too loud. Notice how each accuses and blames the other; this is a poor way to define the problem. Read their definitions. Then, write a better definition for each person.

Mother: You are ruining your ears with that loud stereo. You just don't have good taste in music. How can you stand all that loud noise? I can't and what's more, I won't stand for it.

Daughter: Don't talk to me about taste in music. You sit around all day listening to 1940 junk music. No one listens to that stuff anymore. And get off my back about the loud stereo. I'll play it as loud as I like so I can enjoy my music.

Better Definitions:

Mother: ____

____

____

____

Daughter: ____

____

____

____

II. Listing Solutions.

A. List as many ideas as you can.

B. Be creative and free.

C. Anything goes.

D. Don't say whether ideas are good or bad now. This comes later. Make believe you are trying to solve a telephone problem. A mother is upset because her son talks on the phone two hours a night and runs up bills. The son says his friends live too far away to visit on weekdays; he calls them instead. Make a list of 10 ideas to solve this problem. Put down anything you can think of. Try to be creative.

List of solutions.

1. ______________________________

2. ______________________________

3. ______________________________

4. ______________________________

5. ______________________________

6. ______________________________

7. ______________________________

8. ______________________________

9. ______________________________

10. ______________________________

If you run out of ideas, here are some hints:

a. Is a trade-off possible?
b. Can they change anything around the house to help?
c. Is a change of place or time possible?
d. What about other ways to talk to friends?

III. Picking the best idea—Decision Making.

When you decide upon the best idea, you should state the good and bad points of each idea on your list. Then, rate each idea "+" or "−." Ask yourself about each idea:

A. Will this idea solve my problem?
B. Will this idea solve the other person's problem?
C. Will this idea really work?
D. Can I live with it?

Consider the telephone problem we discussed above. Make believe one idea was "buy a second telephone."

A. An adolescent might evaluate this as follows:
Well, this idea meets my need to talk to my friends, and my mother might get off my back for talking on her phone too much. I'll give it a "+." "+".

B. A parent might evaluate it as follows:
It is true that this would get my adolescent off my phone, but it would not solve the problem of high bills—we would have to pay for two phones. Now, if my adolescent wants to get a job to pay for the new phone, that's different. As is, I rate this idea "−."

Now, write out evaluations for the first two ideas on your list for the telephone problem on the last page. For each idea write out an evaluation from the parent's side and a second evaluation from the adolescent's side.

Idea #1.
Parent's Evaluation: ______________________________

____

____

____

Adolescent's Evaluation: ______________________________

____

____

____

Idea #2.
Parent's Evaluation ______________________________

____

____

____

Adolescent's Evaluation ______________________________

____

____

____

Fig. A.3. Parent-adolescent therapist session notes

Family ______________________________ Session # 1 2 3 4 5 6 7

Therapist ______________________________ Date______________

Problem Issue ______________________________

Solution ______________________________

1. Did they do their homework? YES SORT OF NO DOES NOT APPLY
   Comments:

2. Did they report any attempts to use problem solving at home? YES NO DOES NOT APPLY
   A. How many (including homework)? ________

Fig. A.3. *(continued)*

B. If yes, how did it work out?

very well	______
moderately well	______
so-so	______
moderately poorly	______
very poorly	______
I didn't get a full report	______

3. Did they report any attempts to implement previously negotiated solutions at home?

YES NO DOES NOT APPLY

A. If yes, how did it work out?

very well	______
moderately well	______
so-so	______
moderately poorly	______
very poorly	______
I didn't get a full report	______

4. Communication skills dealt with during this session:

5. Participation:	*Disaster*	*Poor*	*Mediocre*	*Good*	*Excellent*
A. Mother	1	2	3	4	5
B. Father	1	2	3	4	5
C. Adolescent	1	2	3	4	5

6. In a paragraph, describe the course of the session, noting any strengths, weaknesses, etc.

7. Were scheduled activities covered? YES NO

Explain if NO:

8. Homework assigned:

9. Special recommendations for next session:

10. Overall rating of session:

1	2	3	4	5
Disaster	Poor	Mediocre	Good	Excellent

11. Other impressions:

Session Two

Goals

1. Review homework thoroughly.
2. Conduct a second problem-solving discussion.
3. Intervene to modify one negative communication habit.
4. Prepare the family to conduct a problem-solving discussion at home.

Session two is a pivotal session because you have the first opportunity to judge the family's ability and willingness to complete homework assignments. Families who complete homework assignments often improve more than families who do not. Without doing the homework, a family is unlikely to integrate newly acquired problem-solving communication skills into their daily interchanges. In this session, you review the completed homework thoroughly or explore the reasons why the homework was not completed. In addition, you begin to modify negative communication habits and continue to refine problem-solving behavior. One problem-solving discussion is conducted. If the solution to last week's problem was successfully implemented, a new topic is introduced. Otherwise, last week's topic is renegotiated.

I. Review homework.
   A. Find out if the *two* homework assignments were completed.
   B. If the family implemented the solution at home, praise their efforts and then:
      1. Ask each person for a brief report of the outcome of the implementation of the solution to the problem. Was the outcome satisfactory? Did new, unexpected problems arise? Review the data that were collected and suggest that the family continue to implement the successful solution.
      2. If the family was dissatisfied with the implementation, indicate that the topic will be renegotiated in several minutes.
   C. Review the completed problem-solving exercises. Concentrate on the first two pages, on which the family practiced problem definitions. Ask family members to exchange papers and read each other's answers aloud. Praise adequate answers and correct inadequate answers. When family members give many incorrect answers, they may not understand problem definitions. Clarify the critical attributes of an appropriate problem definition.
   D. If the family did not complete either assignment, assess the reasons why. If one or both of the assignments were partially completed, you should also follow these procedures. Do not treat failure to complete assignments lightly.
      1. Did the adolescent refuse to participate?
      2. Did a family member who is not participating in the training program sabotage the homework?
      3. Did the family become frustrated before giving the solution a fair try?
      4. Was the procedure for implementing the solution insufficiently detailed?
      5. Did the family "forget" or simply fail to attempt to complete the assignment?

E. Take action to correct the situation which led to a failure to complete the homework. Reassign the homework. Either make suggestions for completing the assignment and continue the session, or adjourn until the family completes the assignment. Follow the guidelines below:

1. If the adolescent refused to participate, hold a private conference with the adolescent to assess the source of the resistance and to enlist cooperation for completing future assignments. Then, continue the session.
2. If a family member who is not participating in the training program sabotaged the homework, discuss the possibility of including that person in future problem-solving discussions either at home or in the office sessions. Discuss tactics for presenting agreements to other family members in a nonthreatening manner. (The most important point is not to impose solutions on others. Rather, they should be involved in a brief discussion of a solution and permitted to provide input prior to implementation.) Then, continue the session.
3. If the family tried a solution and gave up before there was sufficient opportunity for the solution to work, attribute the "failure" to insufficient practice or poor problem solving rather than personal inadequacies of the family members. It is important to place "failure" in a problem-solving framework. For example, you might find that the consequences of the adopted solution were inaccurately projected. Then, renegotiations can occur without accusations. Continue the session with the renegotiation.
4. If the implementation procedure was insufficiently detailed, help the family to specify the details adequately. Often, one person conveniently "forgets" a crucial detail. Written contracts are useful prompts when agreements are forgotten or remembered incorrectly. After specifying the details adequately, continue the session.
5. If the family did not attempt to complete the homework, determine whether environmental circumstances made completing it difficult (e.g., a father was suddenly called out of town on business, the adolescent spent the entire week at a grandparent's house.) If environmental events did interfere, reassign the same task for the next week and continue the session. If environmental events did not interfere, failure to attempt to complete the assignment may be a sign of poor motivation for change. Don't give them a lecture which puts you in the role of a "good parent" and the family in the role of a "naughty child." Instead, express your disappointment that they have missed an important opportunity to help improve family communication, and note that this program is carefully sequenced in such a way that completion of each homework assignment is necessary before you proceed to the next session. Consequently, you cannot conduct session two today, but will have to adjourn until next week, when you expect that they will have compeleted the homework. Then, adjourn. Use this extreme option only if the family has made no effort to complete the assignment. Most families will try to complete the homework in response to this contingency.

II. Target a negative communication pattern for change.

A. Below is a list of communication excesses and deficits often found with this population and some suggested alternative responses.

Problem	Possible Alternatives
• interruptions	listening; raising hand when wanting to talk; briefer statements
• accusations, blaming ("You did ______")	I-statements ("I feel _____ when _____ happens")
• overgeneralizations ("always," "never")	objective statements ("Sometimes," use qualifiers)
• lecturing, "shoulds"	"I would like ______," statements that project consequences
• sarcastic tone of voice	neutral tone of voice
• child doesn't talk	reflective listening, ask child what he/she wants
• monopolizing conversation	brief statements, take turns talking
• zapping, putdowns	I-statements
• commands	suggestions
• getting off the topic	catching self and coming back to problem *as defined*
• bring up the past	stick to future changes, come up with solutions to correct past negative outcomes.

B. On the basis of your behavioral assessment, select those communication behaviors which are problematic for a particular family. There are no specific guidelines governing the order of intervention of communication behaviors. However, it is generally useful to intervene to modify high-frequency negative communication behavior first. Later, low-frequency, subtle negative communication behavior can be modified. Parents' accusatory statements and adolescents' defensive responses have been most frequently targeted for modification in session two. Pick one communication behavior for each family member for modification in this session.

C. Indicate to parents and adolescent which negative communication pattern you have targeted for modification. Model the negative response and discuss its detrimental effects on family relations. Then, model a suggested alternative response and discuss its beneficial effects on family relations. Ask them to rehearse the positive alternative behavior. Afterwards, tell them that you will interrupt any displays of the negative response and require the alternative positive response.

III. Select a topic for problem solving.

A. If the solution implemented at home was unsuccessful, renegotiate this problem.

B. If the solution implemented at home was successful, choose a second moderately intense conflict based on their suggestions or their Issues Checklists. If the adolescent chose the topic in the last session, then a parent should choose the topic for this session. In general, it is important to balance the source of topics over successive sessions.

IV. Conduct a problem-solving discussion.

A. Go through the four steps of problem solving as outlined under session one.

B. Praise correct performance and correct inappropriate problem-solving behavior and the targeted negative communication habit. In this session you should make as many corrections as necessary, and not restrict corrections to gross performance deficits. The emphasis in this session is on skill acquisition. It is more important to shape appropriate problem-solving communication behavior than to reach a solution to the topic during the session. The most common correction procedures are listed below, with guidelines for their use.

1. Direct Feedback. You stop the discussion, indicate which statement or behavior was inappropriate and why, and ask them to emit an alternative, positive response. This should be the first tactic you use when you wish to correct inappropriate problem-solving communication behavior.
2. Prompts. You do not stop the discussion or indicate which statement or behavior was incorrect. Instead, you momentarily interrupt the conversation and request an elaboration or clarification of a statement. Prompts are appropriate when a response is partially correct.
3. Instructions, Modeling, and Behavior Rehearsal. You demonstrate the appropriate response and instruct the family member to imitate you. Feedback is given, and the response is practiced until you judge its performance as adequate. This tactic is useful when direct feedback and prompts have not produced a correct response. This tactic is usually needed when the correct response is not in the individual's repertoire.
4. Shaping. You break a correct response into its components and use modeling, behavior rehearsal, and feedback to teach each component in a hierarchical fashion. Each component is a successive approximation to the terminal response. Shaping is useful when the individual displays difficulty imitating a model of the entire response. It has been used most often to teach problem definition statements to low-functioning adolescents. Since shaping is a time-consuming procedure, it should be used sparingly.
5. Socratic Discussion. You stop the discussion when person A has emitted a negative statement directed at person B and ask person B how that remark felt. Typically, person B will indicate that he or she was upset, angry, annoyed, etc., by the remark. You then ask person A whether eliciting an angry reaction was intended. Often, person A responds negatively. Finally, you ask person A to correct the situation

by rephrasing the negative remark. This tactic has many variations, but its key ingredient is to lead the speaker to "have insight" into the effects of his or her behavior on others without directly stating the effects. Socratic discussion is useful when an individual is extremely defensive and/or rigidly opposed to changing the negative communication habit.

6. Role Reversal. In order to teach a person to view a problem or behavior from another person's perspective, you may ask parents and adolescent to reverse roles and "replay the scene." Sometimes it is useful to ask each person to give an exaggerated rendition of the other person's behavior. Afterwards, you ask each person to indicate his or her reaction to role reversal. They often learn what it is like to receive the negative communications which they send to other family members. Role reversal has been used to teach consequential thinking. For example, when one adolescent did not appreciate why her mother had difficulty maintaining a sympathetic attitude towards her when the daughter repeatedly complained about her social life, the therapist asked the dyad to reverse roles and replay a typical sequence of complaints. The daughter had difficulty responding sympathetically to the mother's role-played complaints. As a consequence, the daughter began to complain less.
7. Audio-taped and/or video-taped Feedback. You stop the discussion and play back the audio-tape and/or video tape. This form of feedback is used to help modify subtle stylistic factors such as voice tone or nonverbal posture. Since it takes more time than the other correction procedures, it should be used sparingly.

C. When the problem-solving discussion has been completed, summarize the strengths and weaknesses of the family's problem-solving communication behavior at this point in time.

Note: A problem-solving discussion will sometimes not be completed by the end of the session. In such cases, you can assign the remainder of the discussion for homework. However, if you judge that the family's skills are not yet sufficient to complete the discussion at home without a confrontation, ask them to complete the discussion during the next treatment session.

V. Assign Homework.

A. The family should implement the solution to the problem discussed during session two and should continue to implement the solution to the problem discussed during session one.

B. The family should set aside one hour at a mutually convenient time and conduct a problem-solving discussion on a new topic at home. Guidelines for the home discussion are:

1. In the first home discussion, relatively mild disagreements should be discussed to maximize the likelihood of a successful outcome. Later, more intense disagreements can be resolved at home.
2. If a discussion deteriorates into an argument, the family should stop and bring the topic up for consideration at the next session.

3. One person should be given responsibility for organizing the discussion and guiding transitions from step to step. Often, a parent would be assigned this responsibility.
4. Home discussion should be audio taped whenever possible for review by the therapist.
5. Additional family members not participating in treatment can be invited to join home discussions concerning issues that involve them.
6. Problem solving should be tailored to the natural communication style of the family at home. Some families enjoy the formal step-by-step structure with the listing of solutions in writing and the formal evaluation of each idea on the list. Other families operate in a much more informal manner and are unlikely to continue to use a procedure which requires writing down solutions and closely following an outline. For these families, home discussions can be more informal, with a minimum of writing and a blending of the problem-solving steps. It is important that the home discussions be structured so that the probability that they will become a regular part of the family's life after the end of treatment is increased.

C. Parents and adolescent should informally correct each other's emission of the negative communication behavior modified during session two whenever it is emitted at home.

D. Write out the homework assignment.

VI. Complete a parent-adolescent therapist session note form (fig. A.3).

Sessions Three, Four, and Five

Goals

1. Problem solve one new topic per session or renegotiate one old topic per session.
2. Modify one additional negative communication skill per family member, per session.
3. Review home applications of problem-solving communication training and plan additional home applications.

Overview. Each of these sessions follows a similar format: review homework assignments, establish a communication deficit or excess for modification, conduct a problem-solving discussion, intervene to modify a negative communication behavior, and assign additional homework. Over successive sessions you intervene to modify subtler communication patterns and require more precise problem-solving behavior. In addition, issues which elicit intense conflict (intensity scores of four or five on the Issues Checklist) are resolved.

I. Review of Homework

A. Determine how much of the assignment was completed. Praise them if most of the assignment was completed. Otherwise, assess the reasons for lack of completion by following the guidelines presented above for session two.

B. Review the home problem-solving discussion. Ask each family member to give a brief report of what happened at each step of problem solving. Consider as many of the following questions as you can since you will use this information to plan future discussions.

1. Were they able to give clear, nonaccusatory definitions of the problem?
2. Did they list a variety of solutions? Who suggested most of the ideas? (Ask to see their problem worksheet.)
3. Did they systematically evaluate each solution?
4. Were they able to reach an agreement?
5. Did they implement the solution?
6. How well did the solution work?
7. Which negative communication habits interfered with their discussion? How angry did they get with each other during the discussion?
8. Did each family member consider the discussion and solution "fair" or did one family member dominate the others (notably parents dominating teenagers)?
9. If the home discussion was a "disaster," why? Was there a skill deficit, temporary loss of control by one person, sabotage by one person, lack of effort by all, fight for control by several family members, etc?
10. Who guided the discussion? How well did this work out?

C. If a particular skill deficit or negative communication pattern was evident during the home discussion, plan to intervene during upcoming sessions to remedy that deficit or modify that communication pattern. In any case, collect the audio tape of the discussion, listen to it during the week to confirm their reports, and give them brief feedback about the discussion at the beginning of the next session.

D. Assess whether each of the previously negotiated solutions is continuing to be implemented effectively. Praise their efforts for successful solutions. Analyze the reasons for failure with unsuccessful solutions:
   1. Who ceased to implement their part of the solution? Under what conditions? With what effects?
   2. Did a nonparticipating family member sabotage the solution or did environmental events cause it to fail?
   3. Did the family try to renegotiate on their own?
   4. Was there a major family crisis or fight which set the stage for ceasing implementing a wide variety of solutions?

E. If the solution was not renegotiated at home, do parents and adolescent wish to renegotiate it during this session? If not, what can be done to restart the previously effective solution?

F. In what ways did parents and adolescent informally apply problem-solving communication skills during daily interchanges? Praise their successful applications and examine the reasons for unsuccessful applications.
   1. How often did they apply components of problem-solving and communication training?
   2. Which skills were most helpful? Least helpful?
   3. Did they perceive their applications as "natural" or "contrived"?
   4. In what way do problem-solving communication skills need to be tailored to the family to increase informal applications?

Note: You may not have time to review the homework as thoroughly as outlined here. Select one homework task for thorough review each week and survey the remaining tasks. Vary the task reviewed in detail over sessions three, four, and five. Use your judgment in deciding which families need more emphasis on which tasks.

II. Target one negative communication pattern for change for each family member.

A. Select behaviors from the list given under session two (II-A), and announce that you will stop their discussion every time the targeted behavior is emitted.

B. Model an alternative, positive behavior and ask the family to rehearse it.

III. Problem-solving discussion.

A. Select a topic from one of four sources:

1. Unfinished topics from a previous session.
2. Topics which were unsuccessfully or incompletely resolved at home.
3. Topics which are related to a previously successful solution which subsequently failed.
4. Topics from the Issues Checklist (intensity of four or five) or ones suggested by a family member.

Note: Often, there will be many conflicts that compete for immediate attention. Previously successful solutions may fail during the same week that family crises arise or home discussions end in a stalemate. In fact, certain families appear to be in a perpetual state of crisis. You must use your own judgment in determining the priority of topics for problem solving and not permit family members' panicky reactions to dictate the topics. You should consider the parents' and adolescents' current level of skills and the usefulness of certain topics for bringing out negative communication patterns and/or family functions which you wish to modify. For example, if you decided to modify a mother's overprotective attitude towards her fourteen-year-old son, it would be wiser to select a topic involving the son's freedom outside the home (such as curfew or dating) than a topic involving chores, cleaning up the room, or taking out the garbage.

B. Guide the family through the four steps of problem solving, correcting inappropriate responses as they are emitted.

1. As the sessions progress, you should begin to fade out your corrections and prompts. You might try appointing one family member as "stage director" to guide the transitions from step to step of problem solving.
2. Teach family members to prompt each other and move forward when they begin to get "bogged down."

IV. Assign Homework. There are three types of tasks for homework, each of which you have previously assigned at least once: implementation of solutions, problem-solving discussions, and informal applications of component communication skills during daily interchanges. Ideally, you should assign all of these tasks after sessions three, four, and five. In practice, the family may be unwilling or unable to complete three tasks in one week. Assign as many of these tasks as you judge can be completed. Write out their assignments.

A. Implementation of solutions. Implement all previously negotiated solutions.
B. Problem-solving discussions. Conduct at least one discussion at home and audio tape it if possible.
C. Informal application of skills during daily interchanges. You must tailor this assignment to each family. The goal of the assignment is to integrate positive communication skills into their natural conversation so that disagreements can be prevented from escalating into confrontations. You should design a task based upon previously targeted negative communication habits. Family members are asked to monitor their own and each other's responses and provide feedback at critical junctures. An example will be given for the Smith family.
   1. Negative Interaction Pattern. Mr. Smith often accused his unassertive son Timmy of lying. Mr. Smith made the accusations in a hostile, inflammatory fashion. Timmy denied the accusations and clammed up. This frustrated Mr. Smith, who stepped up the accusations, which were followed by further denials from his son. Eventually, Mr. Smith punished Timmy whether or not Timmy actually had lied.
   2. Preparation for Assignment. The therapist targeted hostile accusations by the father and clamming up by the son for change during session three. Intensive modeling and behavior rehearsal were used to teach the father to modify his voice tone and method of expressing his disapproval of his son's behavior. The son was taught to respond assertively to an accusation and to give his father feedback about voice tone.
   3. Assignment. At least once a day Mr. Smith was to make a critical remark concerning Timmy's behavior in a nonaccusatory manner. Timmy was to give his father feedback about his voice tone and then respond assertively to the content of the remark. Mrs. Smith was to monitor the implementation of this assignment.

V. End each session with a statement summarizing the progress made to date and outlining the tasks remaining for future sessions.

VI. Complete a parent-adolescent therapist session note form (fig. A.3).

Session Six

Goals

1. Plan strategies for using the newly acquired skills in the natural environment.
2. Review home applications of problem solving and assign additional home applications.

This session is devoted to generalization programming. Its organization should be flexible and should be adjusted to meet the needs of each family. Below are three alternative suggestions for the content and organization of the session. You should review the progress of each family during the first five sessions and choose the most appropriate format. Reviewing and assigning homework, as described for sessions three, four, and five, precedes and follows discussing the generalization programming issues. (In certain cases, the generalization programming session may even be scheduled prior to the sixth week of the program.)

I. Crisis management training.

Parents and teenagers encounter many crises. A crisis typically occurs when a parent and adolescent confront each other after the adolescent has broken a rule that is considered important by the parents. Examples are: (1) an adolescent comes home at 3:00 a.m. when curfew was midnight; (2) a parent apprehends an adolescent who has been drinking beer or smoking marijuana; (3) an adolescent fails several subjects at school and has cut several classes. During crises, family members tend to lose control and make extremely hostile, polarizing remarks, which interfere with effective conflict resolution. Crisis management training is designed to prepare parents and adolescents to use problem-solving communication skills to cope with unexpected crises.

A. Identify the types of crises encountered by the family. By the sixth session, you will most likely have much of the information you will need. However, you should consider asking the following questions:
   1. Do all family members become embroiled in most crises, or is at least one person available to serve as a mediator?
   2. Do crises follow particular patterns of negative communications, e.g., parental accusations elicit adolescent denials, which elicit further accusations and harsh punishment, which culminates in adolescent rebellion?
   3. Are there discernible cues of an impending crisis which can serve as discriminative stimuli for implementing crisis management techniques?

B. Ask the family to relate a recent sample of a crisis situation. Obtain a detailed report of each person's behavior during the crisis. You will use their example to develop crisis management techniques.

C. Guide the family in listing alternative courses of action that each person could follow in the sample crisis situation. You should play a more active role in the listing of solutions for crises than you have played in regular problem-solving discussions since you may be able to suggest useful coping techniques not applied by the family in the past. In general, prompt them to consider ways to defuse out-of-control behavior and emotionality to a level at which rational discussion can take place.
   1. Can one person use reflective listening to defuse another person's anger?
   2. Can family members isolate themselves from each other for a brief "cooling off" period?
   3. Can an individual not directly involved in the crisis serve as a mediator?
   4. Can individuals use self-control techniques to avoid "blowing up"?

D. Ask the family, after they list several solutions, to evaluate the solutions and to decide upon the best crisis management strategy.

E. Ask the family to role play the sample crisis and to attempt to implement the agreed-upon strategy. The family should practice as many elements of the strategy as are feasible in a simulation.

F. Have the family discuss their reactions to the simulation, and give them feedback about their crisis management skills, as exhibited during the simulation.

II. Involving additonal family members in problem-solving discussions. Problems often involve family members who are not participating in treatment. The generalization programming session can be used to teach the family how to involve additional siblings in problem solving. The family is instructed in advance to invite the sibling to attend this session. If the sibling accepts the invitation, the family is instructed to provide the sibling with a nonthreatening explanation of the problem-solving model and a copy of the outline prior to the session (fig. 7.1)

A. Begin the session by establishing rapport with the sibling. Ask the sibling to discuss his or her views of family relations. Then, have the adolescent explain each step of problem solving to the sibling. Introduce the topic to be problem solved, and assign one parent responsibility for leading the discussion. The parent guides the family through the four steps of problem solving.

B. Provide the parent with feedback about the performance as a discussion leader.
Correct inappropriate problem-solving behavior.

C. However, do not attempt to modify many of the negative communication skills emitted by the sibling since you only have a single session to work with this individual.

Note: Several siblings may be invited to participate in a generalization-programming discussion. Although successful discussions have been held with as many as four youths, such discussions become unwieldy and difficult to control. Few issues are interesting enough to maintain the attention of three or four adolescents for an entire hour.

III. Remediation of individual behavioral deficits and excesses. One family member may display severe deficits in appropriate behavior, severe excesses in inappropriate behavior, or extremely rigid, inappropriate attitudes. Because it may have been difficult to modify those behaviors and attitudes during the family sessions, a private meeting can be held with this person during the generalization-programming session.

A. Private sessions with individual family members will vary from family to family. Representative examples follow:

1. Overprotective parental behavior and attitudes. Some parents severely restrict their teenagers' freedom because they are afraid that their children will get into serious trouble despite the fact that their teenagers rarely misbehave. As a consequence, such parents retard their adolescents' acquisition of responsible independence behaviors. Overprotected adolescents may fail to acquire age-appropriate social skills and may become overly sensitive to disapproval from their parents. Several general guidelines are useful for modifying overprotective behavior and attitudes.

a. Provide the parents with factual information concerning normal adolescent development, the growing need for independence from the family, etc.

b. Use your authority to sanction responsible independence-seeking behavior as "normal."

c. Attempt to assess the reasons for the parents' overprotective behavior. Often, the parents experienced severe trauma and/or deprivation when they were adolescents, and they wish to prevent such negative consequences from happening to their children.

d. Use cognitive restructuring and rational emotive techniques (Ellis and Greiger 1977) to help parents modify unrealistic attitudes.

e. Establish a shaping program which requires the parents to give gradually increasing amounts of freedom to their teenagers, and which has built-in reassurances to assuage the parents' concerns about potentially dire consequences of the freedom.

2. Perfectionistic behaviors and attitudes. Certain parents expect their teenagers to behave perfectly and achieve lofty academic, social, and vocational goals. Such expectations are unrealistic and conflicts develop when an adolescent fails to achieve parental goals.

   a. Cognitive restructuring can be used to help parents to modify perfectionistic attitudes.

   b. Gordon's (1970) concept of "ownership of the problem" can be introduced to help parents to realize that it is inappropriate for them to impose their own academic, social, and vocational goals on their children. Help parents to understand how they can instill their aspirations in their children by serving as positive role models rather than by giving endless lectures and setting rigid restrictions.

3. Exceedingly negative self-evaluations. Some adolescents lack self-confidence and engage in a high rate of self-derogatory remarks. They may be overly concerned with "defects" in their appearance or social-intellectual skills.

   a. Use cognitive restructuring and self-instructional techniques to modify the negative self-evaluations (Meichenbaum 1977).

   b. Use assertiveness training to remediate social skill deficits (Hersen and Eisler 1976).

   c. Teach parents to use positive communication skills to convey acceptance of the adolescents despite perceived "defects." For example, assume that Mary puts herself down frequently because she is "bow-legged." Her mother can be taught to use reflective listening to help Mary express her anger that she was born "bow-legged," while her brothers were not, and her concern that this "defect" makes her less attractive and worthwhile. Reflective listening can be modeled and then the mother can be guided in applying the technique. Mary can then be given an abbreviated version of the rationale for cognitive structuring (Goldfried and Davison 1976, pp. 162-65) and taught to challenge the unreasonable belief that her self-worth is linked to her appearance. It can be noted that each person has pleasing and displeasing physical characteristics, and a list of Mary's pleasing physical features can be complied. Mary can then be assigned the task of standing in front of a mirror each morning and reviewing her positive physical features.

IV. At the end of session six, you should complete a parent-adolescent therapist session note form (fig. A.3).

Session Seven

Goals

1. Problem solve one topic.
2. Intervene to modify one additional negative communication habit for each family member.
3. Fade out the therapist's prompts during the problem-solving discussion.
4. Conduct a review of home applications of problem-solving skills.
5. Tie up "loose ends" and terminate.

I. Review of homework. Same as in sessions three, four, and five.

II. Problem-solving discussion. Same as in sessions three, four, and five, with the expection that the family members should be asked to guide the discussion without your assistance. Prompt them to correct each other's behavior.

III. Prepare for termination.
   A. Ask the family for feedback concerning their perceptions of changes that took place during the program.
      1. Did parent-adolescent communication at home improve?
      2. To what extent did they attribute improvement in communication to the program?
      3. What useful skills did they learn?
      4. Which skills do they intend to continue to use in the future?
      5. How adequately prepared were they to resolve specific disagreements?
      6. What were the strengths and weaknesses of the program?
   B. Give the family feedback about the changes which you have perceived.
   C. Suggest areas that need additional work and outline continued home applications of problem-solving communication skills.
   D. If the program has been unsuccessful with a family, it is best to discuss it honestly and to try to discover what factors led to the lack of success. You may wish to refer them for additional treatment.

IV. Write a parent-adolescent therapist note form (fig. A.3).

Notes

The author wishes to acknowledge the following individuals and organizations: K. Daniel O'Leary, whose support helped in the initial development of the treatment program; Sharon Foster, whose ideas contributed to parts of the treatment manual; Ronald Prinz, who developed the assessment methodology; Joan Weiss, who helped edit the chapter; and the University of Maryland Computer Sciences Center, which supported analyses of the data presented in this chapter. Preparation of the manuscript was partially funded by Public Health Service Grant MH-31,000-01. The opinions herein, however, do not necessarily reflect the position or policy of the granting agency.

References

Alexander, J.F. 1973. Defensive and supportive communication in normal and deviant families. *Journal of Consulting and Clinical Psychology, 40,* 223-31.

Alexander, J.F., and Parsons, B.V. 1973. Short-term behavioral intervention with deliquent families: Impact on family process and recidivism. *Journal of Abnormal Psychology, 81,* 219-25.

Bright, P. 1978. Case studies of problem-solving communication training with parents and adolescents. Unpublished master's thesis, University of Maryland, Baltimore County.

Conger, J.J. 1977. *Adolescence and youth: Psychological development in a changing world,* 2nd ed. New York: Harper and Row.

Douvan, E. and Adelson, J. 1966. *The adolescent experience.* New York: Wiley.

Ellis, A., and Harper, R.A. 1975. *A new guide to rational living.* Hollywood, Calif.: Wilshire Book Company.

Ellis, A., and Grieger, R. 1977. *Handbook of rational emotive therapy.* New York: Springer Publishing Company.

Fogg, R. 1972. *Some effects of teaching adolescents some creative, peaceful approaches to international conflict.* Unpublished doctoral dissertation, Harvard University.

Fogg, R. 1975. *The creative, peaceful class of conflict management approaches and a repertoire of several dozen types.* Unpublished manuscript, State University College at Buffalo, Buffalo, New York.

Foster, S. 1978, *Family conflict management: skill training and generalization procedures.* Unpublished doctoral dissertation, State University of New York at Stony Brook.

Fox, M., and Robin, A.L. 1978. *The application of behavioral technology to observer training: a preliminary study.* Paper submitted for presentation, 1978.

Goldfried, M.R., and Davison, G.C. 1976. *Clinical behavior therapy.* New York: Holt, Rinehart, and Winston.

Gordon, T. 1970. *Parent effectiveness training.* New York: Wyden.

Haley, J. 1976. *Problem-solving therapy.* New York: Harper and Row.

Hersen, M., and Barlow, D.H. 1976. *Single case experimental designs.* Elmsford, New York: Pergamon Press.

Hersen, M., and Eisler, R.M. 1976. Social skills training. In *Behavior modification: principles, issues and applications,* ed. W.E. Craighead, A.E. Kazdin, and M.J. Mahoney. Boston: Houghton Mifflin.

Johnson, S.M., Christensen, A., and Bellamy, G.T. 1976. Evaluation of family intervention through unobtrusive audio recordings: Experiences in "bugging" children. *Journal of Applied Behavior Analysis, 9,* 213-19.

Lapides, K.B. 1978. *A study of the impact of problem-solving training on a cognitive problem-solving skill: The ability to take others' perspectives.* Unpublished master's thesis, University of Maryland, Baltimore County.

Meichenbaum, D. 1977. *Cognitive-behavior modification.* New York: Plenum Press.

Morganstern, K.P. 1976. Behavioral interviewing: The initial stages of assessment. In *Behavioral assessment: a practical handbook,* ed. M. Hersen and A.S. Bellack. Elmsford, N.Y.: Pergamon Press.

Meyer, V., Liddell, A., and Lyons, M. 1977. Behavioral interviews. In *Handbook of behavioral assessment,* ed. A.R. Ciminero, K.S. Calhoun, and H.E. Adams. New York: Wiley.

O'Leary, K.D., and Borkovec, T.D. 1978. Conceptual, methodological, and ethical problems of placebo groups in psychotherapy research. *American Psychologist, 33,* 821-30.

Patterson, G.R. 1976. The aggressive child: Victim and architect of a coercive system. In *Behavior modification and families,* ed. E.J. Mash, L.A. Hamerlynck, and L.C. Handy. New York: Brunner/Mazel.

Patterson, G.R. and Reid, J.B. 1970. Reciprocity and coercion: two facets of social systems. In *Behavior modification in clinical psychology,* ed. C. Neuringer and J.L. Michael. New York: Appleton-Century-Crofts.

Prinz, R.J. 1977. *The assessment of parent-adolescent relations: Discriminating distressed and non-distressed dyads.* Doctoral dissertation, State University of New York at Stony Brook, 1976. *Dissertation Abstracts International, 37,* 5370B.

Prinz, R.J., and Kent, R.N. 1978. Recording parent-adolescent interactions without the use of frequency or interval by interval coding. *Behavior Therapy, 9,* 602-604.

Robin, A.L. 1976. *Communication training: an approach to problem solving for parents and adolescents.* Doctoral dissertation, State University of New York at Stony Brook, 1975. *Dissertation Abstracts International, 36,* 5814B.

Robin, A.L. 1977. Parent-adolescent problem-solving training. PHS MH 31,000-01. Grant proposal funded by the Public Health Service, Washington, D.C.

Robin, A.L. 1979. A controlled evaluation of problem-solving communication training with parent-adolescent conflict. Paper presented at meeting of the Eastern Psychological Association, Philadelphia, April 1979.

Robin, A.L. In press. The parent-adolescent problem-solving communication training program. *Adolescence.*

Robin, A.L., and Fox, M. 1978. The parent-adolescent interaction coding system: Coding manual. Unpublished manuscript, University of Maryland, Baltimore, Maryland.

Robin, A.L., Kent, R.N., O'Leary, K.D., Foster, S., and Prinz, 1977. An approach to teaching parents and adolescents problem-solving communication skills: A preliminary report. *Behavior Therapy, 8,* 639-43.

Spivack, G., Platt, J.J., and Shure, M.B. 1976. *The problem solving approach to adjustment.* San Francisco: Jossey Bass.

Weiss, J.G., and Robin, A.L. 1978. The behavior assessment of parent-adolescent problem-solving communication skills. Paper presented at the meeting of the American Psychological Association, Toronto, August 1978.

Weiss, R.L., Hops, H., and Patterson, G.R. 1973. A framework for conceptualizing marital conflict, a technology for altering it, and some data for evaluating it. In *Behavior change: Methodology, concepts, and practice,* ed. A Hamerlynck, L.C. Handy, and E.J. Mash. Champaign, Ill.: Research Press.

8

Couples Become Parents: A Behavioral Systems Analysis of Family Development

John P. Vincent, Gerald E. Harris, Nancy I. Cook, and C. Patrick Brady

Susan and Craig stare quietly toward the television set. Both seem sullen, bewildered, and exhausted. They can't understand what's happened to them. Only months ago everything was going their way. Both are in their late twenties, attractive, and well educated. He is a social worker in a local community mental health center; she is comptroller for a small independent oil firm. Both had felt fulfilled, challenged, and appreciated in their work. They had just finished remodeling a lovely two-story brick home. Susan drove a BMW, Craig, a Porsche. They enjoyed a wide circle of friends, had season tickets to the opera, and were competitive in mixed doubles. They were happy and contented with one another and looked forward to having a family, sharing holidays, and growing old together.

Everything seems different now. Craig feels pressured and hassled at work. Recently he began an outside consultantship and finds himself to be overextended and ineffective. He has assumed more responsibility at home, but feels resentful and unappreciated. They just don't seem to have the fun they used to have. Quarrels start with the slightest provocation. Susan has quit her job. She feels reproved and cut off from her friends and outside interests. When she looks in the mirror, she sees an older Susan, one with pale skin and dull eyes. But most of all, she feels overwhelmed. There is a quiet murmur in the adjacent room. Susan looks to Craig, he to her. She rises slowly, wearily, and walks in front of the television on her way to tend their one-month-old son, Matthew.

Having one's first child is a complicated mixture of joy and agony. Learning to become a parent is one of the many tasks in life that is taught by trial and error. Although we all acknowledge the importance of families in shaping our very existence as human beings, how families successfully evolve is one of nature's deeply guarded secrets.

This chapter presents a framework to help understand the factors that affect a couple's transition to parenthood. The first section reviews background research focused on reproductive complications, parent-infant relationships, and marital satisfaction over the life cycle. The second section presents a behavioral systems model of marriage that conceptualizes the mechanisms of change as couples accommodate to a first child. Implications both for identification of couples "at risk" in becoming successful parents and for preventive services for these couples are discussed in the final section.

Background Literature

Three broad areas of literature have contributed to our understanding of the developmental changes in beginning families: (1) the impact of marital factors on reproductive complications, (2) the nature of early interaction between caregiver and infant, and (3) marital satisfaction over the life cycle. A selective review of these areas provides a background in attempting to unravel the interplay of marital and infant variables in family development. For more extensive discussion of these topics, the interested reader should consult Sameroff and Chandler (1975), Escalona (1974), Anthony (1974), and Miller (1976).

Reproductive Complications

Clear relationships have been demonstrated between maternal emotional states, difficulties during pregnancy, and complications with labor and delivery. Early investigators found that anxiety in particular was related to a higher incidence of both psychosomatic complaints during pregnancy (Schaefer and Manheimer 1960, Zemlick and Watson 1953) and abnormal reactions during labor (Davids, DeVault and Talmadge 1961; Rosengren 1961). Although many of these earlier studies can be faulted on methodological grounds, a significant relationship between anxiety and physical symptoms during pregnancy and birth have also been found in more experimentally sound studies (Lubin, Gardiner and Roth 1975; Zuckerman, Nurnberger, Gardiner, Vandiver, Barrett and den Breeijen, 1963).

Maternal emotional factors also have been linked with a variety of specific birth complications. Among women with a history of habitual abortion, Javert (1962) noted evidence of psychic conflicts, strong dependency needs, and poor emotional control. Prematurity has also been shown to be related to the psychological state of the mother. Mothers of premature infants have been described as anxious, immature, negative in their attitudes toward pregnancy, and prone to feelings of inadequacy (Blau, Slaff, Easton, Welkowitz, Springarn and Cohen, 1963). Pilowsky and Sharp (1971) found personality deviations in women who suffer from pre-eclamptic toxemia (PET). He described these women as introspective, depressed, languid, and brooding. The deleterious effects of maternal anxiety are further suggested by Dodge's (1972) findings that pyloric stenosis occurred more often in first-born children than would be expected solely on genetic grounds.

To explain the relationship between maternal emotional reactions and birth complications, many investigators have looked to the mother's personality. Women with so-called "neurotic personality traits" are more emotionally labile and therefore are assumed to be prone to somatization of anxiety. However, trait theories of this sort recently have been challenged on both conceptual and empirical grounds (see Mischel, 1968). By contrast, a few investigators have suggested that "situational" variables, such as the marriage relationship, may be related to reproductive complications.

Zuckerman et al. (1963) noted that "the significant correlation between the Taylor Manifest Anxiety Scale (MAS) and somatic expressions of anxiety and their relationship with the Marital Conflict Scale suggests the origin of this anxiety." Pilowsky and Sharp (1971) added that to cope with the stress of pregnancy, wives typically look to their husbands for support, especially in their first pregnancy.

The crucial importance of emotional support from husbands during pregnancy is underscored by the fact that single, separated or divorced women are more likely to develop PET (Pilowsky and Sharp, 1971). A relationship between emotional conflict and marital strife also has been demonstrated among married PET victims (Hetzel, Bruer, and Poidevin 1961). Based on data from the 16 PF test, Pilowsky and Sharp (1971) showed that husbands of PET women seemed incapable of providing emotional support to their wives, had low frustration tolerances, were immature, changeable in their attitudes, evasive on important issues and decisions, and failed to respond constructively to problem-solving situations. These attributes led the authors to conclude that during pregnancy, "when more support is called for, less will be forthcoming." In a study of childbirth pain, Davenport-Slack and Boylan (1974) found that a wife's desire for her husband's presence during delivery was related to shorter labor, less anesthesia, and more positive testimonial accounts of the birth. In another investigation, Dodge (1972) found that severe stress, most frequently marital conflict in the woman's last trimester of pregnancy, was related to the development of pyloric stenosis in the newborn.

Despite the evidence linking marital factors to birth complications, the findings must be interpreted cautiously. From a methodological standpoint, the major focus has been on the mother. Data concerning the father seldom have been collected, and no investigator has examined systematically the interaction between spouses directly. The validity and reliability of marital assessment procedures is also questionable. Consequently, hypotheses concerning the relationship between marital variables, maternal emotional reactions, and subsequent pregnancy and birth complications have not been amenable to adequate empirical study.

Parent-Infant Interaction

Interest in the postnatal period stemmed in part from the failure to account for long-term disability solely on the basis of initial birth complications (Sameroff 1975). For example, in studies which attempted to link anoxia at birth with later deficits in learning, the initial impairments at birth have virtually disappeared by school age (see, for example, Corah, Anthony, Painter, Stern and Thurston, 1965). To account for how initial vulnerability can be translated into eventual disability, most investigators have postulated the role of adverse environmental factors. Although socioeconomic conditions have been hypothesized as one such factor (for example, Werner, Bierman and French 1971), SES represents a rather vague constellation of variables which tells us little about the actual etiology. Factors which affect the quality of interaction that develops between parent and infant appear to be of crucial importance.

Through study of infant temperament (Thomas, Chess, and Birch 1968), the view emerged that the infant had an important role in shaping the nature of interaction with others. This is most evident in studies that used frame-by-frame analysis of video-taped interactions between caregiver and infant. Condon and Sander (1974) noted an obvious synchrony between an infant's body movements and the caregiver's speech. Brazelton, Koslowski, and Main (1974) delineated a cycle of attention-withdrawal in the mother-infant sequence: (1) *initiation*, in which the infant relates and by gazing gives the mother the first clues of readiness to interact; (2) *orientation*, in which the infant's eyes and face brighten and his body orients toward the mother; (3) *state of attention*, in which the infant communicates his readiness to the mother; (4) *acceleration,* in which the infant communicates through vocalizing, smiling, and tonguing; (5) *peak of excitement*, in which the infant makes efforts to control the degree of excitement and intensely fixes his eyes on the mother; and (6) *deceleration*, in which the infant may continue to vocalize, but with a dull, monotonous quality.

Stern (1974) developed a transitional probability matrix to analyze both the flow and the direction of the interaction between mother and infant. He concludes that the timing of the infant's gaze, initiations, and terminations are dependent on the interactive events from the mother's behavior.

Similarly, Als and Lewis (1975) found that the mother's sensitivity to the infant cyclical fluctuations is related to the nature of subsequent interaction. If the child is allowed to interact in a uniformly rhythmic fashion where he determines the sequence and the timing of the pattern, more frequent peaks of excitement are to be expected which in turn enhance the gratification between mother and infant. More importantly, if the mother attempts to impose her own rhythms on the infant in order to regulate the interaction sequence, then the points of contact between mother and infant are generally brief and often unsatisfying.

Stern (1974) found that the mother's emtional expressiveness influenced the flow of the mother-infant interaction. In these instances the infant appeared confused by changes in the mother's behavior. Brazelton, Tronick, Adamson, Aslo and Wise (1975) compared the infant's behavior to the mother's responsive and unresponsive face, and found that the infant became overwhelmingly distressed when confronted with an unresponsive face, made several attempts to attract her attention, and finally turned away in exhaustion from his futile attempts. Thus, the infant is delighted with the interaction game when he can control and predict the outcome. However, these investigations suggest that emotional upset on the mother's part tends to be transmitted to the child by making the interaction unpredictable, and thereby confusing the infant and making him upset.

It is also very clear that distress in the infant elicits similar reactions in the parent. Moss (1974), Ainsworth and Bell (1969), and Escalona (1953) indicated that infants communicate their needs with varying degrees of clarity, and that predictability of the infant's signals affects the prospects of higher-level communication. This is particularly true when the infant is irritable and the caregiver is ineffective in his attempts to console the child. The parent typically responds with frustration and withdrawal. While infants effectively elicit a maternal response by crying (Bell 1971; David and Appell 1961; Moss and Robson 1968), many mothers measure their parental competence by their ability to console the infant quickly. The mother's sense of failure is translated into a series of rapid experiments with numerous consoling techniques which generally overstimulate the infant and increase his tension and crying (Brazelton 1962).

Little attention has been directed toward factors which affect the parents' contribution to parent-infant interactions. We may assume that asynchronous interactions are more likely to occur when the emotional climate of the family reflects discord between husband and wife. Parental deficiencies in tracking the infant's behavior may in part reflect similar difficulties within the marital dyad. If spouses fail to perceive accurately behavior and affective states in each other, and tend to rely on aversive behavior change tactics, similar patterns may arise in interaction with the infant. Another possibility is that spouses involved in unrewarding marital relationships will compensate for their lack of fulfillment by turning to the infant, forcing him to respond, to show affection, and thus becoming intrusive with the infant.

While the infant literature hints that these interaction patterns may relate to the eventual development of child problems, neglect of the father's contribution as well as that of the marital relationship limits the applicability of these studies (Lamb 1975). Furthermore, these investigations have either examined prenatal or postnatal factors in relatively normal families. An analysis of the developmental spectrum from pregnancy through infancy within families who differ in their level of functioning is a necessary prerequisite for understanding how marital factors, reproductive complications, and disordered parent-infant reciprocity interact with one another.

Sociological Studies of Marital Satisfaction

Family sociologists have focused on the relationship between marital satisfaction and stages in the life cycle. Early studies showed a gradual decline over the course of marriage, which was interpreted to reflect "disenchantment" with the relationship (Pineo 1961; Blood and Wolfe 1960). Recent studies (see Rollins and Feldman 1970) have divided the life cycle into seven stages: (1) beginning families with no children, (2) child-bearing families with children under six, (3) family with school-age children under 13, (4) families with teenage children under 21, (5) families with children who are leaving home, (6) families in the middle years (empty nests), and (7) aging families in retirement years. Although findings from these studies are somewhat different, in general, most studies show that marital satisfaction is curvilinear, with high points observed with beginning families at one end of the continuum, and retirement families at the other end (Rollins and Feldman 1970; Rollins and Cannon 1974). Role strain (Burr 1972; Rollins and Cannon 1974), ease of role transition and change in companionate activities (Miller 1976) have been suggested to explain these changes in satisfaction over the life span. Some investigators also have noted that the curves are somewhat different for men and women (Spanier, Lewis, and Cole 1975), although Rollins and Cannon noted that sex differences might be an artifact of the measurement procedures.

Life span research has consistently shown that a large decrement in marital satisfaction coincides with birth of the first child (Campbell 1975). Couples in childless marriages tend to report greater levels of satisfaction than comparable couples who have children (Feldmen 1965). Furthermore, reported stress tends to be highest in marriages with very young children (Campbell 1975). While these studies imply a causal relationship between having a child and marital dissatisfaction, a number of methodological problems may, in part, account for the findings. First, cross-sectional as opposed to longitudinal designs have been employed. Samples at different life stages may be incomparable in a variety of important ways. Second, the data are exclusively self-report, which raises questions concerning validity and reliability. It is quite possible that response biases, such as social desirability, may be age-related, with young persons having greater investment in portraying a positive view of their relationships. Third, marital satisfaction and satisfaction with other aspects of life are hopelessly confounded in such studies. Since we know that middle-aged adults frequently experience considerable emotional turmoil, it is impossible to disentangle the contribution of personal unhappiness from dissatisfaction with the marriage. Finally, individual differences between couples at each life stage are seldom reported. Consequently, we know little about what factors affect the range in satisfaction for persons within each life stage. Despite these methodological shortcomings, data on marital satisfaction over the life cycle suggests that childbirth is a major ingredient in marital dissatisfaction. Further work is needed, however, to identify the processes by which developmental changes across the life span lead to discord between partners.

A Behavioral System Model of Marriage

The research reviewed in the previous section suggests that the role of marital factors in the course of pregnancy, labor, delivery, and the early months postnatally is an important, but neglected, area of study. A behavioral systems or social-learning framework has provided a useful way to understand marriage relationships during periods of stress. This approach grew out of naturalistic studies of families with problem children (see Hawkins, Peterson, Schweid and Bijou, 1966; Patterson and Brodsky 1966), and was later applied to couples by Stuart (1967) and by Weiss, Patterson and their colleagues at the University of Oregon (Weiss, Hops and Patterson 1973). The behavioral systems framework involves an integration of concepts from social exchange and reinforcement theory (Jacobson and Martin 1976; Thibaut and Kelley 1959). Briefly, marital discord is assumed to be a function of breakdown in the amount of positive reinforcement exchanged between partners, faulty mechanisms of behavioral discrimination, and reliance on aversive strategies of behavior change. In addition to articulating a conceptual model of marriage, social-learning theorists have made significant contributions in marital assessment (Weiss and Margolin

1977). Intervention strategies also have been developed to help partners improve their skills in pinpointing problems, behavioral tracking, communication, and change negotiation. Case studies of behavioral couples therapy generally have shown improvement in various aspects of marital functioning (Margolin, Christensen, and Weiss 1975; Weiss, Hops and Patterson 1973). Controlled studies of outcome have also shown that couples in social-learning theory improve significantly more than those in either no treatment (Jacobson 1977) or nonspecific control groups (Jacobson 1978).

The Elements of Marriage

Weiss' (1978) paper on the behavioral system perspective represents the most extensive theoretical discussion of the model thus far. What follows is a modified version of Weiss' model, which highlights the elements of marriage most salient during a couple's transition to parenthood. According to this model, marriage is a socio-behavioral system, comprised of three overlapping spheres: (1) a cognitive sphere, (2) a behavioral-maintenance sphere, and (3) a sphere-regulating (restoring) sphere; see fig. 8.1).

MARRIAGE =

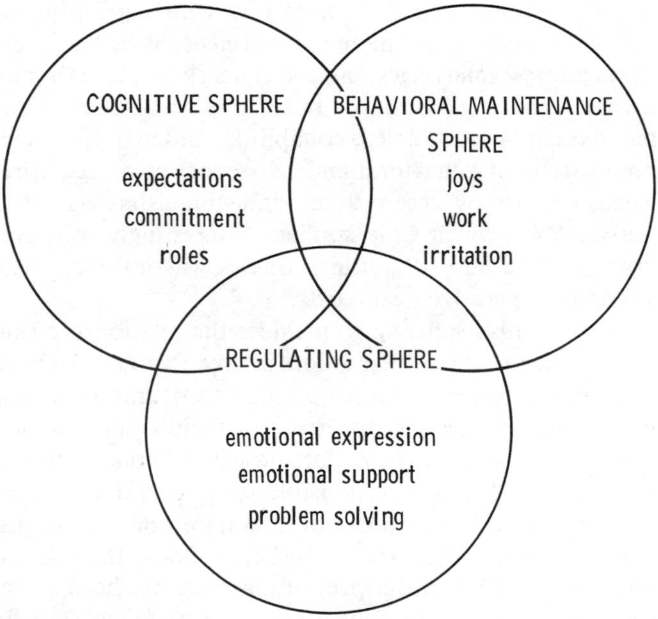

Fig 8.1. Three spheres of marital functioning

The Cognitive Sphere. Marital relationships are governed by a variety of factors that fall outside the province of traditional behavior viewpoints. Partners' assumptions and expectations about marriage often exert great power over the relationship. For example, many people believe that husbands are supposed to be the primary bread winner, wives are responsible for dusting the furniture, and both partners are to accompany one another to all social engagements. These assumptions about marriage usually are assimilated during childhood through a process of vicarious learning. Members of one's extended family, social contacts, and the media provide a model of how marriage is supposed to operate. This pattern of expectations is further shaped by experiences in relating to the opposite sex, and thus, by the time a couple marries, each partner has acquired a relatively fixed set of marital beliefs.

Feelings of commitment toward one's partner and the marriage relationship are an important part of the cognitive sphere. As Levinger (1965) pointed out, commitment is derived from attractions to the marriage, but also from certain barriers to termination, such as fear of community stigma, financial restraints, religious proscription, and children. When exit or termination costs are sufficiently high, the relationship will be maintained even in the absence of mutual attraction. Parenthetically, this kind of reasoning is used by those who favor toughening the divorce laws as a means of preserving the sanctity of marriage. Marriages which survive primarily because of high commitment have been termed by Weiss as "obligatory" marriages, and frequently include a number of so-called divorce-proof relationships. In his dissertation research, Cole (1975) compared a sample of married, cohabiting, and married who had first cohabited on a variety of behavioral and self-report measures of relationship accord. The three groups were virtually indistinguishable from one another on all the variables which Cole studied. Interestingly, however, satisfaction for both married and cohabiting couples was inversely related to the barrier strength of perceived exit costs.

The cognitive sphere also includes the relationship rules and roles which govern much of the interaction between spouses. These overt and covert agreements between spouses provide an overarching structure which organizes many of the task-directed and socio-emotional activities in the marriage. Relationship rules dictate how household work is allocated, who initiates sex, and who is responsible for taking out the trash. Other kinds of bargains are often struck. For example, one spouse (usually unwittingly) may behave incompetently in order to boost the self-esteem of the inadequate mate. While this aspect of marriage has been given little attention by social-learning theorists, it is a primary focus for clinicians who align themselves with general systems or strategic approaches to marriage (see Haley 1973; Watzlawick, Weakland and Fisch 1974; Watzlawick, Beavin, and Jackson 1967).

The Behavioral-Maintenance Sphere. The persistence of a marriage can be viewed in quasi-economic terms as a function of the costs and benefits of behaviors exchanged between partners (Adams 1963; Bagarozzi and Wodarski 1977; Homans 1974; Thibaut and Kelley 1959). Based on content analysis of the spouse observations checklist (Weiss and Issac 1976), Weiss (1978) suggested three main headings on which to array marital behaviors: appetite behaviors, instrumental behaviors, and byproducts. For this discussion, these three main categories are referred to here under slightly different terms: (1) marital joys, which include such benefits as affection, consideration, sex, and companionship, (2) marital work, which includes both costs and benefits involved in household tasks, decision making, financial management, and time allocation; and (3) marital irritants, which include costs associated with tolerating each other's personal habits, restrictions in individual freedom, and behaviors otherwise regarded as annoying (see table 8.1). Distinctions are drawn between behaviors (events) that transpire within the marriage relationship and those that occur outside the marriage. Outside joys refer to benefits derived independent from one's spouse, such as through social or family contacts, personal hobbies, or other individual pursuits. Outside work involves the benefits and costs derived from one's employment, school, or day-to-day obligations. Outside irritants include the nonspouse related events which are perceived as annoying. (See table 8.1).

Table 8.1 Elements of Behavioral Maintenance Sphere during the Prenatal Stage

	Joys	Work	Irritants
Marital	Affection Sex Consideration Companionship	Money Management Household Chores Time Allocation	Restrictions On Personal Freedom Personal Habits
Nonmarital	Social/Family Activities Independent Activities	Employment School Personal Management	Objectionable Interactions Day-to-Day Hassles

Exchanges within the behavioral-maintenance sphere are assumed to interface with an "affective barometer." Joys increment emotional satisfaction, irritants decrement satisfaction, and work affects satisfaction in both positive and negative ways. Weiss has referred to this function as the "pleasure sine wave." Viewed in this manner, partners are analogous to an on-line computer, in which events from one's marital and nonmarital environment provide the input channel which then is synthesized and expressed as emotional "output." On bad days where there are few benefits and many costs, anger, depression, and other unpleasant emotions typically are experienced. On days with a positive trade-off between benefits and costs, pleasant emotions usually follow. Given the ebb and flow of marital, as well as other contextual events, we must assume that this emotional barometer is in perpetual fluctuation. It is like having an open line to one's stockbroker to get the daily quotation from Dow Jones.

The other feature of the behavioral-maintenance sphere, at least the marital component, is that partners usually achieve equilibrium in the rate of exchange. This equilibrium has been referred to as "reciprocity," in that positives beget positives, negatives beget negatives (Patterson, Weiss, and Hops 1974). For most nondistressed marriages under stable conditions, reciprocity coefficients are generally positive. In contrast to early theories, Weiss (1978) pointed out that marital reciprocity seldom functions in a tit-for-tat manner. In fact, Murstein, Cerreto, and MacDonald (1977) have found that preoccupation with exchanges on that basis is often a sign of marital distress. While the rhythmical nature of many marital behaviors probably can be traced on a daily or weekly basis, Jackson (1966) observed that some reciprocity cycles will repeat themselves only after several years. For example, Sylvia allows Herman to attend law school for three years in exchange for Herman allowing her to choose the city, neighborhood and house where they live when he graduates.

Research findings generally have corroborated the relationship between marital exchanges and emotional satisfaction. In a classic study by Will, Weiss, and Patterson (1974) marital and nonmarital behaviors exchanged on a daily basis were shown to be related to the satisfaction which spouses reported. Using the Spouse Observation Checklist, seven couples counted the daily frequency of marital and nonmarital pleasing and displeasing behaviors over a fourteen-day period. Based on multiple regression analyses over days, daily satisfaction ratings were predicted quite well by the relative frequencies of pleasing to displeasing behaviors. For husbands, daily satisfaction was must strongly associated with their wives' instrumental behaviors. For wives, daily satisfaction was best predicted by husbands' appetitive (affectional) behaviors. For both spouses, negative behaviors (costs) decremented satisfaction to a greater extent than pleasing behaviors (benefits) incremented satisfaction. Nonmarital events accounted for approximately 8 percent of the variance in daily satisfaction ratings. The importance of spouse behaviors is also supported by findings of Birchler, Weiss, and Vincent (1975). In this study distressed and nondistressed partners recorded the frequency of pleasing and displeasing (P/D) spouse behaviors over a seven-day period. The average P/D ratio was 3:1 for distressed spouses and 19:1 for nondistressed spouses. The P/D ratios were also predictive of reported conflicts, interviewer ratings of marital adjustment and percentage of recreational activities involving spouses (Weiss, Hops, and Patterson 1973).

The theoretical importance of marital behaviors exchanged within the behavioral-maintenance sphere has been discussed at length elsewhere (see Gurman, Knudson, and Kniskern 1978; Jacobson and Weiss 1978). It is important, however, to underscore some important aspects of this sphere of marital functioning. First, the quality of marital behaviors can be perceived as a direct function of couple skill. In terms of marital joys, not all partners are equally adept in providing one another with gratification. Partners, who are clumsy sexually or nondemonstrative in terms of affection, may seriously limit the degree of emotional closeness which can be experienced in the relationship. Likewise, spouses with poor "executive" skills may be quite ineffective in household management, which increases the probability that transactions in this area will be perceived as irritating by their partners.

Second, the affective meaning of spouse behaviors is in the eye of the beholder. What one partner intends as an expression of caring may not be perceived that way by his spouse. For example, Henry may take his wife Priscilla to dinner as a way to show his appreciation. If she interprets this gesture to mean "he thinks I'm a lousy cook," she is likely to regard this event as rather unpleasant. Gottman, Notarius, Markman, Bank, Yoppi, and Rubin (1976) examined the intention and impact of spouse behaviors during participation in laboratory conflict-resolution tasks. It was interesting that the tendency to misattribute negative intention was more pronounced with distressed couples than with nondistressed couples. It is also true that the same behavior can have an opposite meaning on separate occasions. This feature of marital interaction has prompted some investigators to modify the Spouse Observation Checklist so that in addition to recording the frequency of spouse behaviors, each partner also specifies the affection valence of each behavior on a five-point scale from "very pleasing" to "very displeasing." Unlike previous versions of the SOC, which categorized spouse behaviors as either pleasing or displeasing on an a priori basis (see Birchler et al. 1975), this procedure allows partners to specify their own subjective reaction to the behavior.

Third, we speculate that the subjective meaning of spouse behaviors changes predictably over the life span. Early in relationships, the most important behaviors may be in the instrumental sphere. Later behaviors which confirm one's basic sense of worth may have the greatest impact on satisfaction. We know surprisingly little about how these developmental processes operate, and even less about how partners convey to one another that their priorities in what behaviors are important to them have shifted. It is possible that dissolution of marriage in mid-adulthood is based, in part, on circumstances, wherein one partner's behavioral preferences have changed, and the mate is either unaware of this, or is unwilling or unable to comply. Changing preferences across the life span may help explain Turkewitz and O'Leary's (1976) findings that behavioral therapy with couples worked best with younger couples (mean age = 29), while communication therapy worked best with older couples (mean age = 42).

While we assume that under stable conditions most couples achieve some degree of positive equilibrium in the behavioral-maintenance sphere, behavior exchange rates are in constant flux and are susceptible to at least two overlapping processes: (1) deterioration and (2) contextual disruption. Deterioration refers to a long-term, gradual reduction in the balance of marital benefits to costs. Represented graphically, one would see cyclical fluctuations in marital cost-benefit ratio on a daily or weekly basis, but when regressed on a linear plane, one would observe a gradual negative slope. There are perhaps many factors which affect deterioration. The reinforcing value of behaviors may erode, a process described by Jacobson (1978) as habituation. Parner's attributions concerning the meaning of particular behaviors may change. Likewise, partners may reduce their frequency of pleasing behaviors or increase their frequency of displeasing behaviors. Shifts could occur in the meta-relationship level, which alters the relative distribution of marital behaviors. A wife may no longer be content to run the household, and her efforts to renegotiate this relationship rule may have profound effects on how she and her husband behave toward one another. How long it takes before deterioration effects are apparent to partners is a function of several factors. The average level of cost-benefits at the highest point in the relationship, partner's use of denial or other cognitive strategies to reduce their awareness, or access to compensatory sources of gratification, all have bearing on how long it takes before partners will fully acknowledge that the quality of their relationship has deteriorated to any significant degree.

Contextual disruption refers to *outside* events which directly or indirectly change the nature of husband-wife interaction. Included among these events are change in jobs, change in residence, new relationships, death of a parent, or having a child. In each case, the exchange-patterns both inside and outside the marriage are disrupted, often in dramatic ways. A job change may require a woman to travel eight days out of the month, thus limiting the times available to interact with her husband. A family member may come for an extended visit and affect the distribution of time and behavior between the couple. Changing one's residence usually is accompanied by a sharp rise in household work and reduction in opportunities for social or recreational activities. Holmes and Rahe (1976) have shown that changes such as these can precipitate considerable stress, which in turn often leads to physical or emotional disturbance. The disruptive effects of having a child will be considered below.

The System-Regulating Sphere. For a variety of reasons, the need for change in relationships is inevitable. As suggested earlier, the cost-benefit ratio of marital behaviors is in constant flux and is also subject to long-term deterioration, as well as various forms of contextual disruption. The mechanisms by which partners attempt to correct this inbalance will be considered here as the system-regulating (restoring) sphere.

System-regulating processes occur at two levels, the subtle and the obvious. To discern the regulating processes at a subtle level requires great sensitivity and keen observation. If one views marital interaction in reinforcing terms, every transaction between partners would potentially alter the probability that given behaviors will occur in the future. Take a somewhat ludicrous example: Phyllis wants her husband, George, to take out the garbage. Early in the relationship, she simply requests, "George, would you please take out the garbage?" and he complies. Since George finds that taking out the garbage is quite aversive, over time we see that one simple request from Phyllis is not sufficient to get the job done. Where it once took a single plea, it now takes five, each a little more emphatic than the one before. If this continued over several years, George and Phyllis might appear in the marriage counselor's office with George complaining that Phyllis "bitches constantly." Viewed in reinforcement terms, this pattern of interaction is easy to understand. Phyllis' behavior is under the positive reinforcing control of George's compliance behavior. As he unwittingly delays his "reinforcement" until she emits a higher amplitude request, he illustrates that great power of intermittent reinforcement and extinction which forms the backbone of any well-executed operant shaping program. His behavior on the other hand is under the powerful control of negative reinforcement. As requests to take out the garbage become more aversive to him, he "learns" to terminate them by finally giving in. Interactions such as these are termed "coercive" by Patterson and his associates, and they figure quite prominently in interactions between unhappily married husbands and wives (Patterson and Hops 1973) as well as in interactions between parents and their aggressive children (Patterson and Reid 1970).

It is perhaps easier to understand system-regulating processes by focusing at the obvious level. In this case, our interest becomes the communication between partners which is directed toward restoring positive equilibrium in the marital system. Like general systems approaches to marriage (Ledderer and Jackson 1968), behavioral systems theorists regard all behavior as communication. When couples enter therapy complaining that they "don't communicate,'' this really means that they don't communicate *in ways that are positively adaptive.* This discussion will deal primarily with the overt aspects of communication involved in *purposive* attempts at change.

Communication can be viewed as a series of action-reaction sequences involving cognition and behavior. For illustrative purposes, communication can be arbitrarily divided into actor and reactor functions, acknowledging, of course, that both persons in an interaction are simultaneously actors and reactors (see fig. 8.2). It is interesting that most spouses typically see themselves only as reactors, which leads them to punctuate conflict interaction in self-serving ways. When spouses selectively attend to provocations in their partner's behavior, they feel perfectly justified in punitive reactions. They fail to realize, however, that punitive reactions are also provocative, and allow their partners to use exactly the same logic to justify their own indignant reactions.

	Spouse A (Actor)		Spouse B (Reactor)
	Sam		Alice
Encode	I am angry at the extra work my boss gave me today.	Decode	Sam is really upset about what happened at work today and would like me to give him a little support and reassurance.
Action	''Dear, would you talk to me for a couple of minutes. George really dumped on me today.''	Reaction	''Sure Sam. Sounds like you're really angry. Was Mr. Wilson his usual inconsiderate self?''
Relationship Request	I would like Alice to listen to me and be supportive.	Relationship	I can (will) listen to Sam and be supportive.

Fig. 8.2. Actor and reactor contributions to communication

In formulating a message, actors first *encode* at a cognitive level ''what I mean to say'' and ''what I want from the other person.'' This message is then translated behaviorally into *actions* involving ''what I actually say'' and ''what I want from my spouse.'' Requests for what the actor wants from the spouse are usually implied.

We must remember that messages also have other levels, including the context and meta-relationship statements which serve to reinforce higher order rules about the relationship (Ledderer and Jackson, 1968). The reactor's task at a cognitive level is to *decode* the message according to ''what did Spouse A mean'' and ''what does he want me to do in this conversation'' and ''can I comply with this request''; and then *react* at a behavioral level in terms of "how I actually respond to Spouse A's message," and "how I comply with Spouse A's request of me in this conversation." In effective communication, the message sent equals the message received, and reactions serve to facilitate discussion of the topic at hand. An example will help illustrate this process. Husband (actor) begins an interaction. He encodes the message, "I am angry at the extra work that my boss gave me today," and "I would like Alice to listen to me and be supportive." He acts, "Dear, would you talk to me for a couple of minutes. George really dumped on me today, and I'm mad as hell." Alice decodes, "Sam is really upset about what happened at work today and would like me to give him a little support and reassurance. This is something I can do and am also willing to do." She reacts, "Sure, Sam. Sounds like you're really angry. Was Mr. Wilson his usual inconsiderate self?" With the number of possible elements involved with any message like this, it is not surprising that many attempts at communication proceed unevenly, falter, and finally break down completely. The actor can be vague, unsure, or unaware of what he intends; he can act so that he obscures either the meaning of the message or what he wants from his spouse, or both. On the other hand, reactors can mishear the message, read in another meaning, or incorrectly decipher what the actor expects in the situation. Furthermore, the reactor's response may sidetrack the issue, ignore it all together, or in other ways impede the exchange of information.

Communications in the system-regulating sphere are generally of two varieties: emotional and problem solving. While there are elements of both problem solving and emotional expression in most "regulating" interactions, it helps to separate them arbitrarily to illustrate their properties. Skill in both kinds of communication is not acquired easily and usually requires mastery in areas of communication where partners have less investment. Weiss has termed these prerequisite skills "objectification," referring to the denotive aspects of communication. According to Weiss, objectification involves spouses making "reliable discriminations in their behavioral environments among (a) benefits received, (b) the situations which control behavior, and (c) discriminations among communication options." In clinical work with distressed couples, proficiency in objectification skills is critical to training in emotional problem-solving skills.

To communicate effectively in the emotional mode, actors must express their emotions in a clear, accurate, and honest manner. Congruence at the verbal and nonverbal level is important in signaling genuine emotional expression. Unskillful actors disguise their feelings in verbal harangue, fail to express them at all, except perhaps nonverbally, or otherwise fail to say what they really feel. Vincent, Friedman, Nugent and Messerly (in press) found that spouses' verbal behavior can be quite malleable depending on what kind of impression they are trying to convey. Nonverbal behaviors, however, are less subject to volitional control and more accurately reflect the emotional climate of the relationship. Skill at emotional expression is important for both pleasant and unpleasant emotions. In the system-regulating sphere, however, expression of unpleasant emotions tends to predominate.

Reactor skills vary depending on the nature of emotions being expressed and to whom they are directed. When the emotional content does not involve the reactor, some form of supportive understanding generally is called for. Emphatic nonjudgmental listening is well recognized as an important element in therapist-patient interactions (Truax and Mitchell 1971), as well as in marital interactions (Rappaport 1976). Unskillful reactors respond to emotional messages by personalizing them ("Oh, you're mad at me"), invalidating them ("you shouldn't feel that way"), ignoring them ("by the way, what's for dinner?"), or by treating them as a problem to be solved ("What you need to do is to develop a plan so this won't happen again. Now what you should do is..."). Perhaps the most difficult emotional messages are ones directed toward the reactor. Skillful reactors are able to stick to the issue, facilitate expression of feelings, and remain in the situation. Likewise, skillful reactors are able to avoid (or keep to a minimum) the temptation to invalidate, counterattack, defend, capitulate, detach emotionally, or escape from the situation. In many cases, skillful emotional communications can end effectively without the need for problem solving. As Weiss (1978) pointed out, however, if problem solving is necessary, discharge of unpleasant affect is a necessary step before partners can successfully move onto a problem-solving mode. To do so prematurely usually results in later eruption or emotion that forestalls effective negotiation of change.

Problem-solving discussions usually commence with an actor's request for change. Effective requests are ones which are clear, specific, and positively stated. The requests of unskilled actors are often vague ("I want you to be a good husband"), not articulated ("If she really loved me, she'd know that I like oral sex"), unfair ("I want you to go to the hockey game with me and have a terrific time"), or stated negatively ("I wish you'd stop being so rude in public"). Skillful reactors respond to change requests by communicating what they are willing or not willing to do without becoming defensive, justifying their behavior, switching the issue, counter requesting, ignoring, or otherwise avoiding the request. Effective problem-solving interactions often resemble bargaining or negotiating sessions in which partners alternate between what they want and what they are prepared to do, culminating in implementation of a mutually agreed upon plan for behavior change. In many ways, focus on the problem negotiation and behavior change has become the sine qua non of the behavioral systems approach (Jacobson and Martin 1976; Jacobson 1978). See Weiss, Patterson, and

Hops (1973), Weiss (1978), O'Leary and Turkewitz (1978), or Jacobson (1978) for a more complete discussion of the intervention implications of this approach.

Elements of the cognitive sphere bear on how effectively partners function in the system-regulating sphere. If partners hold assumptions that "emotional expression is bad" or "feelings must be rational," it is likely that they will encounter difficulty in mastering the skills involved with effective emotional communication. Furthermore, if couples have an unspoken agreement that one partner will be responsible for emotional expressions, and the other partner will tend to the organizational aspects of the relationship, it may be difficult for them to cooperate effectively in either emotional or problem-solving interactions. Perhaps it is for this reason that couples with egalitarian relationships are better candidates for intervention from a behavioral systems framework (Gurman, Knudson, and Kniskern 1978; Jacobson and Weiss 1978; Weiss 1978).

Children as Contextual Disruptors

Having one's first child has profound effects on the marital system. Even though children can be a great source of gratification, their presence tends to shift the distribution of time and behavior both inside and outside the marriage. All three spheres can be affected.

The Cognitive Sphere. The shift from couple to family is frequently accompanied by change in commitments, expectations and relationship rules. Spouses' commitment to the marriage relationship tends to increase, resulting sometimes in a trend toward an "obligatory," as opposed to a "beneficial" type of relationship (Levinger 1965; Weiss 1978). Likewise, partners' expectations for marriage are modified. Where at one time each may have expected a consistent flow of interpersonal gratification, with the advent of children parents soon learn to expect that less time will be devoted to pursuit of enjoyment, and more time will be directed toward managing the home (Cowan, Cowan, Cole and Cole, 1978). The couples' definition of roles and rules is often challenged. Blood and Wolfe (1960) noted that when children arrive, husband-wife roles tend to become more sex-role stereotyped. For couples in open or androgynous marriages, this change may violate the basic structure of the relationship.

The Behavioral-Maintenance Sphere. The cost-benefit distribution of partner behaviors is particularly sensitive to contextual disruption. While couples differ widely in the extent of disruption, some common trends can be predicted. In the marital component, joys tend to decrease. In part because of the taxing demands on time and energy, partners may be less affectionate with each other, spend less time in mutual companionship, and be less active sexually. Simultaneously, it is common for marital work to increase. During the period of role renegotiation, household management tends to be more chaotic and disorganized. In anticipation of the new baby, couples often take on additional burdens in this area, such as changing residence, remodeling the house, or redecorating a room. The physical and financial demands from these can be enormous. Accompanied by decreases in marital joys and increases in marital work, partners also are more likely to perceive a greater number of behaviors from one another as annoying or irritating.

A variety of important changes occur in the nonmarital arena. Husbands may feel more responsible toward work and are often compelled to increase their earning power to meet the new financial demands of the family. At the same time, they often reduce the time involved in pursuit of gratification outside the home and reallocate this time toward helping out with the new baby. It is usually the wife, however, who experiences the greatest change in the nonmarital area. If she is employed outside the home, she quits work, either temporarily or permanently. If work provided a sense of fulfillment and accomplishment, this change may be a tremendous loss. On the other hand, if work was burdensome, quitting to have a child may be a welcome escape from drudgery. Most young mothers also experience a dramatic reduction in outside joys, such as social activities and personal interests. This loss is offset if she has access to a strong support network of family or friends, but in most cases, this is not sufficient to compensate for restrictions in mobility and independence.

The new baby adds an entirely new sphere to the marital system, one which contributes added sources of joy, work, and irritation. Watching babies explore their environment, respond to the human face, and cuddle in their parents' arms is one of life's most endearing experiences. Unfortunately, for the first month or two of a baby's life, such experiences are often few and far between. New babies can seem oblivious to their parents' work, and taking care of them involves an enormous amount of time and energy. Furthermore, babies often are quite irritating, particularly if their behavior is poorly organized or they are fussy in temperament.

Viewed collectively, virtually every aspect of the marital system is disrupted by a new baby. Although infants provide considerable joy to their parents, the loss in gratification both inside and outside the marriage is often substantial. If one looks at the overall balance of costs to benefits, many young parents probably experience some degree of net loss. In this climate of mixed emotion, the task of new parents is to struggle with renegotiating the rules of their relationship and to restore positive equilibrium in the marital system.

The System Regulating Sphere. Given the demands for change during the transition to parenthood, couples' skills in regulating the marriage frequently are taxed to the limit. New parents may experience considerable emotional anguish. They often feel resentful, deprived, and ambivalent about the changes in their lives. Serious depressive reactions to childbirth are not uncommon (Dalton 1971). Ironically, at a time when both parents feel the greatest need for emotional support, neither spouse usually has much capacity for empathy and understanding.

The changes precipitated by having a child also call for good skills in problem solving and negotiation. In addition to revising many of the rules which govern the relationship, partners may have to seek alternative means to provide one another with gratification. Successful couples are probably able to reserve some time for one another, and avoid the common temptation to let the new baby pervade all aspects of marital life (Cowan et al. 1978).

There are wide individual differences in how much disruption new parents will experience. While there is no data on which elements are critical to this transition process, several interrelated factors can be hypothesized:

1. *The degree of marital accord before birth.* If couples have marital problems before the baby is born, we assume that things are likely to get worse after the baby is born. Most professionals recognize that the advent of children will not improve an already unsatisfactory marriage (Ledderer and Jackson 1978). Viewed within a behavioral systems model, such marriages are characterized by a low ratio of benefits to costs. Since we predict that childbirth is accompanied by a drop in benefits relative to costs, the positive reserves in a marginal relationship may vanish quickly.

2. *Appropriate expectations.* We assume that the disrupting influences of childbirth are greater when they are not anticipated. Couples who are forewarned as to what to expect take certain preparatory steps in anticipation of change. Furthermore, we assume that proper expectations give partners a conducive mind set that allows them to consider the disruption as predictable or normal, and avoid the common tendency to "catastrophize."

3. *Temperament of the baby.* Research on infant development has shown that babies vary widely in their temperament. Thomas, Chess, and Birch (1968) have identified three types of infants: easy, difficult and slow to warm up. Temperamental characteristics of the baby obviously place differing demands on parents in the amount of work that the baby requires as well as in the gratification which the parents receive. How well baby's temperament matches the parents' expectations has great bearing on how the infant's behavior will be perceived (Broussard 1970). Parents who expected their baby to be quiet, cuddly, and responsive may be quite unprepared when they discover that their baby is active, fussy, and unresponsive to affection.

4. *Degree of role shift.* When the basic role structure of marriage must be revised, couples may experience more disruption than otherwise. For example, Harold and Stephanie have a role-stereotyped relationship in which Harold is employed as the primary breadwinner, while Stephanie stays at home to manage the house. For this couple, having a child would probably require few changes in marital roles. On the other hand, Bob and Christine have an open marriage, where both are employed outside the home in pursuit of their own individual career goals. Each has an independent set of friends, and they divide the household responsibilities on an equal basis. For this couple, having a child would alter drastically many aspects of their relationship, at least temporarily.

5. *Change in marital and nonmarital costs and benefits.* While we assume that benefits will drop and costs will rise following the birth of a child, how much this occurs is a function of several factors. We can expect that the emotional turmoil which partners experience is a direct function of the change in cost-benefit ratios. If partners provide one another with sufficient caring, love, and consideration while keeping annoyances to a minimum, the transition to parenthood will be less disruptive.

6. *System-regulating skills.* From our perspective, couple skills in emotional expression and support as well as in problem solving are the most important factors in how much disruption couples will experience during this transition process. This factor is obviously related to the pre-existing level of marital accord, the ease with which roles are redefined, and the degree of shift in cost-benefit ratios of marital behavior. Helping couples improve their skills in this area is a major focus of intervention.

Clinical Implications

Identifying "At-Risk" Couples

Early detection of couples who potentially may have difficulty becoming parents is a necessary step in preventing later problems for family members. Determining the behavioral profile that distinguishes couples who later develop problems versus those who do not is a beginning step in the identification process. Theoretically, "at-risk" couples could be identified at either of two points in time: during pregnancy or during early postnatal months. Practically, however, identification during pregnancy is probably the most appropriate time, so that intervention could begin before destructive processes in the family become fully established.

During pregnancy, at-risk couples might exhibit one or more of the following patterns: (a) dissatisfaction with the present relationship, (b) unrealistic expectations toward having a child, (c) lifestyle that would be altered substantially by having a child, and (d) communication skill deficits which would impede the successful accommodation to change. While these factors are presently believed to be the most important early predictors, future research in the area can be expected to supplement and refine the list of factors that serve as primary precursors of emergent family problems.

The potential for later family disturbance might be identified soon after birth through evidence of the following: (a) a difficult baby, or one that does not fit parents' expectations, (b) parental difficulty in relating to the infant, (c) significant long-term disruption in the marriage relationship, or (d) serious emotional turmoil in either parent. The presence of one or more of these factors should alert professionals for potential difficulties in a couples' transition to parenthood.

An important question, regardless of whether identification takes place before or after the birth of the child, is which professionals should be involved in the process. This is a difficult issue. Obstetricians, pediatricians, or their nurses are the most likely candidates, but these professionals are not specifically trained to deal with nonmedical issues. Obstetricians focus primarily on the mother, pediatricians on the infant, and access to information concerning parenting or relationship variables is haphazard at best. Medical personnel have little, if any, training in how best to elicit clinically meaningful family information, or in how to use this information in providing care for their parents. In keeping with the trend to view childbirth holistically, it will be necessary to involve other professionals, such as psychologists or other mental health specialists, or to train medical personnel to deal effectively with nonmedical aspects of family development.

Intervention

It is ironic that while well organized programs are routinely available to teach couples how to deal with the physical aspects of childbirth, none exists to teach them how to cope with the emotional and relationship concomitants of having a child. Evaluations of natural childbirth education have shown these programs to be quite effective in relieving anxiety, reducing complications in labor and delivery, and in involving both parents in the birth process (Bergstrom-Waler 1963: Huttel, Mitchell, Fischel, and Meyer, 1972; Slusman 1975: Rising 1974). However, there are very few studies to date that document the effectiveness of educational programs aimed at the relationship aspects of having children. Cowan et al. (1978) involved eight couples in a supportive group program during a period from late pregnancy to six months after childbirth. Couples in the group experience reported a variety of changes during the transition period, especially in self-identity, role expectations, self-image, self-esteem, allocation of time and interpersonal communication. In contrast to a nonrandom comparison group, couples in the supportive group experience were more individuated and showed a greater disposition to address issues of communication. Furthermore, couples in the support group felt that the experience had been very worthwhile. They felt that they had learned a variety of new skills, and that the group had given them new perspectives concerning their roles as parents. While these self-report data are only suggestive, they do point to the potential benefits from support services for new parents.

A behavioral system approach to couples' therapy (Weiss 1978; Jacobson 1978; O'Leary and Turkewitz 1978) provides a useful starting point for designing an effective intervention program for young couples who are becoming parents for the first time. The following intervention model illustrates how the behavioral systems approach can be extended to meet the special needs of at-risk couples identified either early during pregnancy or in the first postnatal months. This model is designed in the clinical-research tradition and consists of an initial assessment, preventive and corrective intervention strategies, and a post assessment designed to measure the impact of treatment on various aspects of family functioning.

Initial Assessment. For either expectant or new parents, a multimethod assessment battery is adminstered in order to obtain a general picture of the couple's relationship. Global measures of marital functioning include a behavioral interview (Gottman et al. 1976), the Marital Adjustment Scale (Locke and Wallace 1959; Kimmel and Van der Veen 1974), and the Areas of Change Questionnaire (Weiss et al. 1973). An observational measure of couple communication skills is obtained by coding video-taped samples of problem-solving and emotional expression-support discussions, using a modified version of the Marital Interaction Coding System (Hops et al. 1974). In addition, behavioral reports of daily marital cost-benefit exchanges are obtained using the Spouse Observation Checklist (Weiss et al. 1973). Information from these measures not only provides a broad index of marital adjustment, but also pinpoints specific content areas within each relationship that require particular attention.

Instruments which tap information relevant to new or expectant parents is added to the standard marital assessment battery. Expectancy measures of "typical infant" behavior (Broussard 1970) and perceived lifestyle changes are administered to elicit information concerning realistic and unrealistic perceptions for change. If initial assessment takes place postnatally, two additional measures are administered. One is a behavioral self-report measure of daily parent-infant cost-benefit exchanges, similar in format to the Spouse Observation Checklist. The second is an observational measure of parent-infant reciprocity, using video-taped samples of father-infant and mother-infant interaction. A system similar to that developed by Brazelton et al. (1975) is used to code dyadic patterns of attention and facial expression.

Based on information from the initial assessment, a topographical profile of each couple's relationship can be formulated. Intervention directed toward general relationship issues, as well as the couple's specific areas of difficulty, then proceeds according to the strategies outlined below.

Communication Skill Training. Childbirth precipitates a variety of changes with the marital system, and it is important that couples are equipped to deal effectively with any problems that develop, as well as with the emotional consequences of the experience. As a preliminary step, information is provided concerning what changes typically occur in emerging families. Recognition that disruption is normal frequently serves an anxiety-relieving or stress-inoculation function, and helps facilitate a process by which couples pinpoint the kinds of changes that will occur or have already occurred in their own relationships. This exercise usually focuses couples' awareness on the need to renegotiate the rules for allocation of work and time, the steps for dealing with changes in gratification derived from companionship, social activities, and individual pursuits, as well as the importance of attending to the affective consequences of these changes. The specific problem areas generated from this exercise, as well as those identified during the initial assessment, provide the content for exercises in training skillful communicators.

Teaching couples to communicate effectively is, perhaps, best viewed as a two-step process. The first step involves emphasis on objectification behaviors, the prerequisites to good communication on higher levels. Simple expressive and receptive skills are best taught during interactions that are relatively neutral with regard to either emotional or problem content. Through use of modeling and behavioral rehearsal, couples can gain practice in maintaining eye contact, articulating ideas, listening reflectively, clarifying ideas, and communicating at a meta-level. Avoiding emotionally laden or problem issues is important at this step, so that couples can truly learn new skills without the easy temptation to fall back into old patterns involving negative interaction loops.

Once the basics have been mastered, training progresses to step two. At this level, couples acquire skills in emotional expression and support in problem solving by dealing with issues from their own relationships. Exercises in emotional expression and support involve translating nonverbal messages into verbal by substituting "I feel" for "you are" statements, using feeling reflections instead of defensive reactions, and avoiding mind reading, invalidation, and other nonfacilitative behaviors. Through video feedback, role playing, and modeling, couples can also be taught to make discriminations between relationship and nonrelationship emotional issues, to use "time out" and other conflict containment strategies, and to determine when emotional expressions must be followed by explicit attempts at problem solving.

Problem-solving training first involves teaching couples to pinpoint change requests in clear, specific and positive ways. By carefully exploring change options and what each partner is willing and not willing to do, workable plans for behavior change can be formulated and later implemented. While earlier versions of social-learning therapy relied heavily on written contracts to prompt behavior change (see Weiss, Birchler, and Vincent 1974), recent versions of the approach suggest that contracting need not be an integral part of effective therapy (Jacobson 1978). Through this type of communication training, not only do couples remediate specific problem issues in their relationships, they also acquire the necessary skills to deal successfully with new problems that arise.

Child Management Skills. While most of the behavioral systems approach is directed toward aspects of the marriage relationship, there is also a need to train couples in child management skills. This component of the program involves both didactic maternal and specific exercises. Many new parents have virtually no information concerning what to expect from a young infant. It is important to acquaint them with the early developmental milestones, facts concerning the normal range of infant behavior, and indications for medical attention. Through video and live demonstrations, parents can be taught the subtleties involved in handling and interacting with their infant. Suggestions concerning how to facilitate development of parent-infant reciprocity can be presented (see Brazelton et al. 1975). Likewise, parents can be taught alternative techniques to console the upset baby, as well as ways to enhance states of alertness and responsiveness to environment. Information concerning the several principles of behavior management may be very helpful to parents later as the infant grows older.

Evaluation. Because the success of this type of intervention is measured by its impact on the lives of young couples and their infants, thorough evaluation should be incorporated as an integral part of the program. Readministration of the assessment battery at the end of treatment and at follow-up should allow determination of whether aspects of the marriage and parent-infant relationship have been affected through intervention. In particular, one can examine whether problem issues identified at the outset of treatment have been successfully resolved, how marital costs and benefits have shifted, whether communication skills in emotional expression and support and in problem solving have increased through training, and the impact of intervention on parental perceptions of infant behavior, as well as on parent-infant reciprocity. For couples who participate in the intervention program during pregnancy, one might also include measures of pregnancy symptoms (Erickson 1967), complications during labor and delivery, and infant temperament and behavioral organization (Carey 1972; Brazelton

1973) to examine the impact of treatment on these variables.

Through appropriately designed outcome studies, one could assess whether intervention directed at teaching relationship and parenting skills has generalized effects on various aspects of family functioning, how these effects are compared to those associated with natural childbirth education or routine medical care, and whether the long-term payoff justifies the cost. As with any new program directed toward a heretofore unserved population, much research would be needed before definitive claims could be made concerning effectiveness.

Summary

Identification of factors affecting the transition to parenthood appears to be an important, but neglected, area of research. The struggles of couples as they become parents has been alluded to in studies of reproductive complications, infant development, and marital satisfaction over the life span, yet few systematic investigations have examined this process in detail. Behavioral systems theory provides a useful framework to understand marriage relationships, particularly as they are studied during developmental stages, such as childbirth. According to this model, the advent of children is associated with a variety of disruptions in the marriage. The extent of disruption is hypothesized to be a function of pre-existing levels of marital discord, parental expectations, temperament of the infant, change in husband-wife roles, and cost-benefit shifts in marital exchanges. The ultimate goal is to identify couples who are "at-risk" in successfully becoming parents and to provide effective services for these couples. Although as yet untested, the implication of this model is that by teaching parenting and relationship skills to new parents, they would learn the necessary tools to complete this critical family development task effectively.

References

Adams, J. S. 1963. Toward an understanding of inequity. *Journal of Abnormal and Social Psychology, 67,* 422-36.

Ainsworth, M. D. S., and Bell, S. M. 1969. Some contemporary patterns of mother-infant interaction in the feeding situation. In *Stimulation in early infancy,* ed. J. A. Ambrose. London: Academic Press.

Als, H., and Lewis, M. 1975. The contribution of the infant to the interaction with his mother. Paper presented at the Society for Research in Child Development, Denver, Colorado, April, 1975.

Anthony, J. E. 1974. Introduction: The syndrome of the psychologically vulnerable child. In *The child in his family: Children at psychiatric risk,* ed. E. J. Anthony and C. Koupernik. New York: John Wiley and Sons.

Bagarozzi, D. A., and Wodarski, J. S. 1977. A social exchange typology of conjugal relationships and conflict development. *Journal of Marriage and Family Counseling, 3,* (4) 53-60.

Bell, R. Q. 1971. Stimulus control of parent or caretaker behavior by offspring. *Developmental Psychology, 4,* 63-72.

Bergstorm-Walan, M. B. 1963. Efficacy of education for childbirth. *Journal of Psychosomatic Research, 7,* 131-46.

Birchler, G. R., Weiss, R. L., and Vincent, J. P. 1975. A multimethod analysis of social reinforcement exchange between maritally distressed and nondistressed spouse and stranger dyads. *Journal of Personality and Social Psychology, 31,* 349-60.

Blau, A., Slaff, B., Easton, D., Welkowitz, J., Springarn, J., and Cohen, J. 1963. The psychogenic etiology of premature births: A preliminary report. *Psychosomatic Medicine, 25,* 201-11.

Blood, R. O., and Wolfe, D. M. 1960. *Husbands and wives: The dynamics of married living.* Glencoe, Ill.: Free Press.

Brazelton, T. B., 1962. Crying in infancy. *Pediatrics, 29,* 579-88.

Brazelton, T. B., 1973. *Neonatal behavioral assessment scale.* Philadelphia: J. B. Lippincott Co.

Brazelton, T. B., Koslowski, B., and Main, M. 1974. The origin of reciprocity: The early mother-infant interaction. In *The effect of the infant on its caregiver,* ed. M. Lewis and L. A. Rosenblum. New York: Wiley Interscience.

Brazelton, T. B., Tronick, E., Adamson, L., Als, H., and Wise, S. 1975. Early mother-infant reciprocity. *Parent-infant interaction,* Ciba Foundation Symposium 33. Amsterdam: ASP.

Broussard, E. R., and Hartner, M. S., 1970. Maternal Perception of the Neonate as Related to Development. In *Child Psychiatry and Human Development,* Vol. 1, 16-25.

Burr, R. 1970. Satisfaction with various aspects of marriage over the life cycle: A random middle-class sample. *Journal of Marriage and the Family, 32,* 29-37.

Campbell, A. 1975. The American way of mating: Marriage si, children only maybe. *Psychology Today, 8,* 37-48.

Carey, W. B. 1972. Clinical applications of infant temperament measurements. *Journal of Pediatrics, 81,* 823-28.

Cole, C. M., and Vincent, J. P. 1978. Cognitive and behavioral patterns in cohabitive and marital dyads. Unpublished manuscript. University of Houston.

Condon, W. S., and Sander, L. N. 1974. Neonate movement is synchronized with adult speech: Interaction participation and language acquisition. *Science, 183,* 99-101.

Corah, N. L., Anthony, E. J., Painter, P., Stern, J. A., and Thurston, D. L. 1965. Effects of perinatal anoxia after seven years. *Psychological Monographs, 79,* 3.

Cowan, C. P., Cowan, P. A., Cole, L., and Cole, J. D. 1978. Becoming a family: The impact of a first child's birth on the couple's relationship. In *The first child and family formation,* ed. W. B. Miller and L. F. Newman. Chapel Hill, N.C.: Carolina Population Center.

Dalton, K. 1971. Prospective study into pueperal depression. *British Family Psychiatric Journal, 118,* 689-92.

Davenport-Slack, B., and Boylan, C. H. 1974. Psychological correlates of childbirth pain. *Psychosomatic Medicine, 36,* 215-23.

David, M., and Appell, G. 1961. A study of nursing care and nurse-infant interaction. In *Determinants of infant behavior,* ed. B. M. Foss. Vol. 1. New York: Wiley.

Davids, D., DeVault, S., and Talmadge, M. 1961. Anxiety, pregnancy, and childbirth abnormalities. *Journal of Consulting Psychology, 25,* 74-77.

Dodge, J. A. 1972. Psychosomatic aspects of infantile pyloric stenosis. *Journal of Psychosomatic Research, 16,* 1-5.

Erickson, M. T. 1967. Method for frequent assessment of symptomology during pregnancy. *Psychological Reports, 20,* 447-50.

Escalona, S. 1953. Emotional development in the first year of life. In *Problems of infancy and childhood,* ed. M. I. E. Senn. New York: Josiah Macy Foundation.

Escalona, S. 1974. Intervention program for children at psychiatric risk: The contribution of child psychology and developmental theory. In *The child in his family: Children at psychiatric risk,* ed. E. J. Anthony and C. Koupernik. Vol. 3. New York: John Wiley and Sons.

Feldman, H. 1965. Development of the husband-wife relationship. Unpublished manuscript. Cornell University.

Gottman, J., Notarius, C., Gonso, J., and Markman, H. 1976. *A couple's guide to communication.* Champaign, Ill.: Research Press.

Gottman, J., Notarius, C., Markman, H., Bank, S., Yoppi, B., and Rubin, M. E. 1976. Behavior exchange theory and marital decision making. *Journal of Personality and Social Psychology, 34,* 14-23.

Gurman, A. S., Knudson, R. M., and Kniskern, D. P. 1978. Behavioral marriage therapy. IV. Take two aspirin and call us in the morning. *Family Process, 17,* 165-80.

Haley, J. 1973. *Uncommon therapy.* New York: Ballantine Books.

Hawkins, R. P., Peterson, R. F., Schweid, E., and Bijou, S. N. 1966. Behavior therapy in the home: Amelioration of problem parent-child relations with the parent in the therapeutic role. *Journal of Experimental Child Psychology, 4,* 99-107.

Hetzel, C. S., Bruer, B., and Poidevin, L. O. S. 1961. A survey of the relation between certain common antenatal complications in promiparae and stressful life situations during pregnancy. *Journal of Psychosomatic Research, 5,* 175-82.

Holmes, T. H., and Rahe, R. H. 1967. The social readjustment rating scale. *Journal of Psychosomatic Research, 11,* 213-18.

Homans, G. 1974. *Social behavior: Its elementary forms,* 2nd ed. New York: Harcourt, Brace & World.

Hops, H., Wills, T. A., Patterson, G. R., and Weiss, R. L. 1971. Marital interaction coding system. Unpublished manuscript, University of Oregon.

Huttel, F. A., Mitchell, I., Fischer, W. M., and Meyer, A. E. 1972. A quantitative evaluation of psychoprophylaxis in childbirth. *Journal of Psychosomatic Research, 16,* 81-92.

Jackson, D. D. 1966. The marital quid pro quo. In *Family therapy for disturbed families,* ed. G. Zuk and I. Boszormenyi-Nagy. Palo Alto, Calif. Science and Behavior Books.

Jacobson, N. S. 1978. A stimulus control model of change in behavioral couples' therapy: Implications for contingency contracting. *Journal of Marriage and Family Counseling, 4* (3), 29-35.

Jacobson, N. S. 1977. Problem solving and contingency contracting in the treatment of marital discord. *Journal of Consulting and Clinical Psychology, 45,* 92-100.

Jacobson, N. S. Marital problems. 1978. *Psychiatric Clinics of North America, 1,* 227-89.

Jacobson, N. S. 1978. Specific and nonspecific factors in the effectiveness of a behavioral approach to the treatment of marital discord. *Journal of Consulting and Clinical Psychology, 46,* 442-52.

Jacobson, N. S., and Martin, B. 1976. Behavioral marriage therapy: Current status. *Psychological Bulletin, 83,* 557-78.

Jacobson, N., and Weiss, R. 1978. Behavioral marriage therapy. III. The contents of Gurman et al. may be hazardous to our health. *Family Process, 17,* 149-59.

Javert, C. T. 1962. Further follow-up on habitual abortion patients. *American Journal of Obstetrics and Gynecology, 84,* 1149-59.

Kimmel, D., and Van Der Veen, F. 1974. Factors of marital adjustment in Locke's Marital Adjustment Test. *Journal of Marriage and the Family, 36,* 57-63.

Klusman, L. E. 1975. Reduction of pain in childbirth by the alleviation of anxiety during pregnancy. *Journal of Consulting and Clinical Psychology, 43,* 162-65.

Lamb, M. E. 1975. Fathers: Forgotten contributors to child development. *Human Development, 18,* 245-66.

Ledderer, W. S., and Jackson, D. D. 1968. *The mirages of marriage.* New York: Norton.

Levinger, G. 1965. Marital cohesiveness and dissolution: An integration review. *Journal of Marriage and the Family, 27,* 19-28.

Locke, H., and Wallace, K. 1959. Short marital-adjustment and prediction tests: Their reliability and validity. *Marriage and Family Living, 21,* 251-55.

Lubin, B., Gardener, S. H., and Roth, A. 1975. Mood and somatic symptoms during pregnancy. *Psychosomatic Medicine, 37,* 136-46.

Margolin, G., Christensen, A., and Weiss, R. L. 1975. Contracts, cognition, and change: A behavioral approach to marriage therapy. *Counseling Psychology, 5,* 15-26.

Miller, B. C. 1976. A multivariate developmental model of marital satisfaction. *Journal of Marriage and the Family, 38,* 643-57.

Minuchin, S., Roseman, B. L., and Baker, L. 1978. *Psychosomatic families: Anorexia nervosa in context.* Cambridge, Mass.: Harvard University Press.

Mischel, W. 1968. *Personality and assessment.* New York: John Wiley and Sons.

Moss, H. A. 1974. Communication in mother-infant interaction. In *Study of communication and affect.* Vol. 1. *Non Verbal Communications,* ed. L. Krames, P. Pliner, and T. Alloway. New York: Plenum.

Murstein, B. I., Cerreto, M., and Macdonald, M. G. 1977. A theory and investigation of the effect of exchange-orientation on marriage and friendship. *Journal of Marriage and Family, 39,* 543-48.

O'Leary, K. D., and Turkewitz, H. 1979. The treatment of marital disorders from a behavioral perspective. In *Marriage and the treatment of marital disorders from three perspectives: Psychoanalytic, behavioral, and systems theory,* ed. T. J.

Paolino and B. S. McCrady. New York: Brunner/Mazel.

Patterson, G. R., and Brodsky, G. D. 1966. A behavioral modification programme for a child with multiple problem behaviors. *Journal of Experimental Psychology and Psychiatry, 7,* 277-95.

Patterson, G. R., and Hops, H. 1972. Coercion, a game for two: Intervention techniques for marital conflict. In *The Experimental analysis of social behavior,* ed. R. E. Ulrich and P. Mountjoy. New York: Appleton.

Patterson, G. R., Hops, H., and Weiss, R. L. 1977. Interpersonal skills training for couples in early stages of conflict. *Journal of Marriage and the Family, 37,* 295-303.

Patterson, G. R., and Reid, J. B. 1970. Reciprocity and coercion: Two facets of social systems. In *Behavior modification in clinical psychology,* ed. C. Neuringer and J. L. Michael. New York: Appleton.

Pilowsky, I., and Sharp, J. 1971. Psychological aspects of preeclamptic toxemia: a prospective study. *Journal of Psychosomatic Research, 15,* 193-97.

Pineo, P. C. 1961. Disenchantment in later years of marriage. *Marriage and Family Living, 23,* 3-11.

Rappaport, A. F. 1976. Conjugal relationship enhancement program. In *Treating relationships,* ed. D. H. L. Olson. Lake Mills, Iowa: Graphic Publishing Co.

Rising, S. S. 1974. The fourth stage of labor: Family integration. *American Journal of Nursing, 74,* 870-74.

Rollins, B. C., and Cannon, K. L. 1974. Marital satisfaction over the family life cycle: A reevaluation. *Journal of Marriage and the Family, 30,* 271-82.

Rollins, B. C., and Feldman, H. 1970. Marital satisfaction over the family life cycle. *Journal of Marriage and the Family, 26,* 20-28.

Rosengren, W. R. 1961. Some social psychological aspects of delivery room difficulties. *Journal of Nervous and Mental Diseases, 132,* 515-21.

Sameroff, A. J. 1975. Early influences on development: Fact or fancy. *Merrill-Palmer Quarterly, 21,* 267-94.

Sameroff, A. J., and Chandler, M. J. Reproductive risk and the continuum of caretaking casualty. In *Review of child development research,* ed. F. D. Horowitz, E. M. Hetherington, S. Scarr-Salapatek, and G. M. Siegel. Vol. 4. Chicago: University of Chicago Press, 187-244.

Schaefer, E. S., and Manheimer, H. 1960. Dimensions of perinatal adjustment. Paper presented at Eastern Psychological Association, New York City, April, 1960.

Spanier, G. B., Lewis, R. A., and Cole, C. L. 1975. Marital adjustment over the family life cycle: The issue of curvilinearity. *Journal of Marriage and the Family, 37,* 263-75.

Stern, D. N. 1974. The goal and structure of mother-infant play. *Journal of American Academy of Child Psychiatry, 13,* 402-21.

Stuart, R. B. 1969. Operant-interpersonal treatment for marital discord. *Journal on Consulting and Clinical Psychology, 33,* 675-82.

Thibaut, J., and Kelley, H. H. 1969. *The social psychology of groups.* New York: Wiley.

Thomas, A., Chess, S., and Birch, H. 1968. *Temperament and behavior disorders in children.* New York: New York University Press.

Truax, C. B., and Mitchell, K. M. 1971. Research on certain therapist interpersonal skills in relation to process and outcome. In *Handbook of psychotherapy and behavior change,* ed. A. E. Bergin and S. L. Garfield. New York: Wiley.

Turkewitz, H., and O'Leary, K. D. 1976. Communication and behavioral marital therapy: An outcome study. Paper presented at the Annual Meeting of the Association for the Advancement of Behavior Therapy, New York, Dec., 1976.

Vincent, J. P., Friedman, L. C., Nugent, J., and Messerly, L. 1979. Demand characteristics in observations of marital interaction. Unpublished manuscript, University of Houston, 1979.

Vincent, J. P., Weiss, R. L., and Birchler, G. R. 1975. A behavioral analysis of problem solving in distressed and non-distressed married and stranger dyads. *Behavior Therapy, 6,* 475-87.

Watzlawick, P., Beavin, J. H., and Jackson, D. D. 1967. *Pragmatics of human communication: A study of interactional patterns, pathologies, and paradoxes.* New York: W. W. Norton.

Watzlawick, P., Weakland, J. H., and Fisch, R. 1974. *Change: Principles of problem formation and problem resolution.* New York: Norton.

Weiss, R. L. 1978. The conceptualization of marriage from a behavioral perspective. In *Marriage and marital therapy: Psychoanalytic, behavioral and systems theory perspectives,* ed. T. J. Paolino and B. S. McCrady. New York: Brunner/Mazel.

Weiss, R. L., Hops, H., and Patterson, G. R. 1973. A framework for conceptualizing marital conflict, a technology for altering it, and some data for evaluating it. In *Behavior change—methodology, concepts, and practice,* ed. L. R. Hamerlynck, L. C. Handy, and E. J. Mash. Champaign, Ill.: Research Press.

Weiss, R. L., and Isaac, J. 1976. Behavior cognitive measures as predictors of marital satisfaction. Paper presented at the Western Psychological Association Meeting, Los Angeles, April, 1976.

Weiss, R. L., and Margolin, G. Marital conflict and accord. 1977. In *Handbook for behavioral assessment,* ed. A. R. Ciminero, K. S. Calhoun, and H. E. Adams. New York: John Wiley and Sons. 555-602.

Werner, E. E., Bierman, J. M., and French, F. E. 1977. *The children of Kauai.* Honolulu: University of Hawaii Press.

Wills, T. A., Weiss, R. L., and Patterson, G. R. 1974. A behavioral analysis of the determinants of marital satisfaction. *Journal of Consulting and Clinical Psychology, 42,* 802-11.

Zemlick, M. J., and Watson, R. J. 1953. Acceptance and rejection during and after pregnancy. *American Journal of Orthopsychiatry, 23,* 570-84.

Zuckerman, M., and Lubin, B. 1965. *Multiple affect adjective check list: Manual.* San Diego, Calif.: Educational Service and Industrial Testing.

Zuckerman, M., Nurnberger, J. I., Gardiner, S. H., Vandiver, J. M., Barrett, B.H., and Den Breeijen, A. 1963. Psychological correlates of somatic complaints in pregnancy and difficulty in childbirth. *Journal of Consulting Psychology, 27,* 324-29.

9

Simulated Interaction Training: Applications to Returning College Students

Patrick H. Doyle, W. Andrew Smith, Peter C. Bishop, and Mary A. Miller

A management trainee seeks to open a meeting with an enumeration of the agenda; before she can finish, however, a member of the group rises and begins to leave without explanation. She pauses to speak briefly to the would-be defector. Her demeanor and verbal skills are impressive; the person reoccupies his seat, ready to contribute to the meeting. Shortly after she resumes, two other individuals abruptly attempt to change the topic; again she adroitly manages those involved. Further on, still another problem arises when a subordinate indicates that he does not have his report ready. As before, her handling of this characteristic management problem is decisive and poised. This pattern continues throughout the meeting as she encounters typical managerial problems and astutely resolves them. Her behavior appears to mark her as a likely candidate for promotion; she is undeniably exhibiting effective leadership behavior.

As she concludes the meeting, the projector is turned off by the trainer and the persons with whom the trainee has been interacting fade into a white screen—the management trainee has been engaging in behavioral rehearsal with *video-taped images* shown on a large screen rather than with *live* people. She has just finished a session of simulated interaction training (SIT, pronounced S-I-T).

In simulated interaction training or SIT, trainees practice their responses to images enlarged to life size by projection onto a large screen. A script provided during the training directs the trainee's responses so they fit into the flow of events as in real-life encounters. While the trainee interacts with the screen images, a rater scores the effectiveness of his or her behavior and periodically provides feedback.

This treatment approach, it should be noted, basically conforms to the usual assertiveness training package of overt rehearsal followed by coaching. The difference lies in the rehearsal to screen rather than live figures. Thus far, research has tended to support the efficacy of such approaches, according to a recent review of the literature by Galassi and Galassi (1978), although there are many unresolved issues.

The SIT Approach

The trainee is positioned almost directly in front of and approximately three feet from the screen; this distance is comparable to those that North American cultures generally consider appropriate during social intercourse. He or she interacts with images originally videotaped at a distance which would make them life-size when projected onto screens measuring as much as 10 feet by 10 feet. During the training, the ambient illumination is reduced to minimize laboratory or office cues, thus directing attention to the screen, and at the same time preserving the brightness of the projected image. As shown in the schematic (fig. 9.1), the trainer or therapist is located on the side of the projector opposite the trainee or client, approximately halfway between the projector and the screen, and far enough from both the screen and the trainee to be able to conveniently view both for rating and feedback purposes.

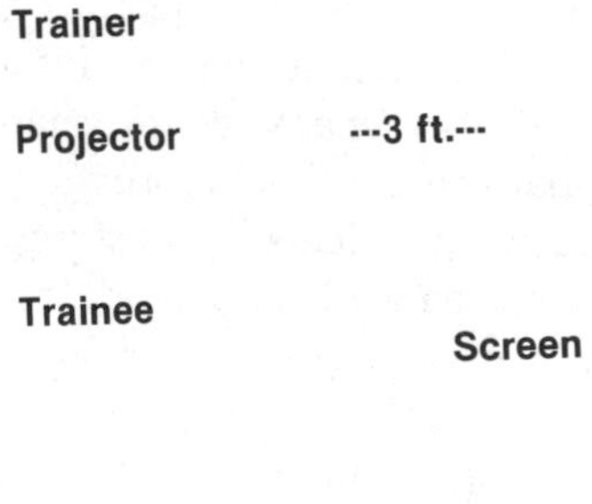

Fig. 9.1. Physical arrangements for SIT training

The simulations are prepared utilizing the subjective camera technique, whereby the camera view represents the perspective of a participant rather than an onlooker. In the finished product, the figures on the screen act toward the viewer who in turn makes his or her responses to them. For the sake of realism, the simulations are video-taped in color.

The scripts used are unique in a number of respects. Usual scripts provide for both camera and acting directions, with as much concern being placed on varying the camera angles as on the acting. However, since the purpose of the camera angle is to represent the perspective of a participant, the camera directions differ considerably from ordinary scripts. Obviously, there can be none of the usual shifting of perspectives, such as moving from a tight front shot to a distant side shot. Instead, the camera must portray the scene as a participant would see it. In particular, this means that movement, such as when the trainee walks from one end of a room to another, must be faithfully conveyed by the camera. A portable camera is carried at eye level and walked smoothly while focused, as would be normal, on various objects and people in the room. A wide-angle lens is also preferable to simulate the peripheral vision individuals normally experience.

The acting directions for SIT are no less out of the ordinary. Bearing in mind the video-tape simulation must include only the actions of the simulation figures in order for the trainee to actually participate during SIT sessions, the dramatic acting must be performed, to a large extent, to a silent camera lens rather than to another actor. In the earlier example of the management trainee, an actor played the role of the subordinate who did not have his report prepared on time. This role required that he repeatedly act as if he were addressed and then respond, though playing to a silent camera throughout. In practice, effective playing to a camera lens often requires performers to memorize both their lines and those of the trainee; only in this manner is it possible for the performer to be able to react as if the lines of the trainee are being heard.

Another complication for actors is the matter of timing the periods during which the trainee would be responding. The flow of the respective responses by the screen figures and the trainee must be effectively timed, or else the realism which the SIT system offers will be seriously eroded. If the delinquent report-preparer, mentioned previously, tends to respond in a clairvoyant fashion to the trainee before she has had time to express her thought, the verisimilitude of the training will be forfeited. Usually the timing of the silent sections of the simulation, which correspond to the dialogue of the trainee, is accomplished by the director silently mouthing or articulating the trainee's lines at the appropriate points to determine how much time should be allowed. The director then signals the actors when to deliver their lines or behave in some other manner. If the director sets a pace close to the norm for the particular region of the country, the timing of the silent sections will be quite effective, with the training interchanges subsequently occurring very realistically. Even where a trainee tends to vary from the norm in speaking, unless his or her speaking rate is considerably faster or slower than the norm, the reality of the exchange will be preserved. In real life, people's responses to one another are rarely perfectly synchronized.

There are occasions, however, when the timing would seem to have to be quite exact for each trainee. In telling a joke, for example, it would seem vital that the punchline delivered by the trainee coincide closely with the burst of laughter from the screen figures. Such problems as this can usually be resolved satisfactorily through the use of some ingenuity, though. Instead of having one relatively short spate of laughter, the acting director could cue it to start piecemeal towards the end of the silent period and build to a full chorus. In this manner, the final product would simulate realistic circumstances. There would be a rising laughter in the latter part of the telling of the joke, as if some people were anticipating the punchline. Ideally, the timing would be such that most persons would tend to finish slightly ahead of the climax of the laughter and only the most tardy storytellers would be able to extend their story beyond the period of rising laughter. Having the ultimate reaction occur in a matter of one or two seconds after the punchline, as would typically occur in this simulation, seems fairly common in real life and would probably be effective. Furthermore, by having people join in more or less one at a time with the laughing, there is a high probability that the trainee's punchline will indeed be closely followed by a fresh burst of laughter, albeit from the one or perhaps two people joining in at that point.

Illustrative Scenarios and Rationales

When adequate filming has been accomplished, the trainee faces circumstances which correspond remarkably to real life events. In the study to be reported herein, nine scenarios were produced that incorporated some classic conditions in which to practice assertive responses. In one scenario, the camera was positioned to provide the view of a member of an audience seated near the back of the room. In this simulation the trainee, or client, if conceptualized in more clinical terms, sees the backs of people's heads and a podium. The audience is acting as would be normal in waiting for the meeting to begin. Some people are talking while others are sitting quietly or looking around. Then a person steps to the podium and the audience focuses attention on the person about to speak. This person provides a short introduction to the main speaker. The speaker then assumes the podium and begins a discourse on her topic.

The speaker's voice is somewhat soft and consequently inaudible to those seated toward the back. Following his or her script, the client interrupts the speaker to indicate the problem and ask if she could speak louder. In making this request, the client has stood and attracted considerable attention from the audience. A number of people have turned around to view the client. In response to the client's request, the speaker nods her head in assent and talks more loudly as she proceeds. The client has resumed his or her seat as the audience listens.

Before continuing the scenario, it would be instructive to analyze the sequence of events to understand the richness of this approach to behavioral rehearsal. As the situation is a common one in real life, with the client being a member of an audience, treatment effects are presumably more likely to generalize. Further, in taking the floor and requesting a change in procedure, the client was practicing the exercise of his or her rights under circumstances which meant interrupting a sizeable number of people. Whereas a person might behave assertively when few people are involved or in less formal circumstances, the prospect of speaking up in a large, formal meeting might just be too daunting. To the nonassertive person, the presence of so many people would be particularly disconcerting.

To resume the scenario, the speaker continues her talk similar to a classroom lecture, in that she is immediately receptive to questions about any points she is making. Early in the presentation, the client raises his or her hand, receives recognition from the speaker, and stands. Instead of asking one question, the client says, "I have two questions. The first is . . . and the second one is . . ." The client has occupied the floor for sufficient duration to ask two questions rather than one. In addition, the script calls for the client to gesture in a self-confident, expressive manner that should substantially enhance his or her communication. The simulated speaker answers the questions, and the client is seated. As before, the audience has been turning around and some were craning their necks to see the client. A few members of the audience even appeared to disapprove of the client's questions, as expressed in slight frowns or other signs of impatience. On the whole, the reaction was one of casual interest. Variations of this pattern were continued for the duration of the five minute scenario: the speaker would continue for a brief period, another member of the audience might ask a question, and then the client would either follow up the preceding question, possibly by simply contributing a pertinent observation, or initiate another topic. Upon completion of the scenario, the client will have thoroughly practiced an active role in the context of attending a lecture.

Another scenario involved initiating and maintaining a conversation in the context of a party. As this simulation begins, the people are animated; there is loud music, and the usual drinking and eating of snack foods. The client, assumed to be male in this instance, stands during this scenario. The screen array simulates his approach to a group of three people; this is accomplished principally by sighting the camera at eye level and dollying in (moving the camera towards the three people he is to be joining). The people being approached seem quite interested in the topic being discussed and somewhat closed to the idea of having others join them. The client nonetheless persists, introducing himself and remarking on the topic being considered in a manner that injects him into the stream of the discussion. This prompts one of the three original individuals to provide introductions. The client then tells an amusing story appropriate to the context. A moment later he is relating a second anecdote while maintaining eye contact with the simulated figures who are intermittently sipping drinks, eating, and otherwise behaving naturally for this situation. Subsequently, another person approaches the group and greets the client, who then introduces the newcomer to the other three individuals. The scenario continues similarly for a total of five minutes.

This scenario in particular enabled the client to practice entering a group that tended to be closed to new members. The self-denying individual would have felt uncomfortable attempting to enter such a group. By holding the group's attention and relating anecdotes, the client has made a transition from outsider to accepted group member. Making introductions, as the client did for his new acquaintances, is a particularly important assertive response to practice, since it is frequently called for in day-to-day social contacts.

Another scenario focused on refusing requests. The situation simulated a group of people planning a picnic. The camera perspective is that of a person sitting at a table. The client, assumed to be a male again, views the expanse of table on the screen as he would see if actually seated at it. Surrounding the table are four casually dressed people.

The group members begin indicating what they will contribute to the picnic while one person keeps a record of who will bring the beer, the soft drinks, and so forth. The script for the scenario calls for the client to refrain from making any contribution. On his turn to say what he will bring, the client states, "I have too many obligations right now to feel good about taking on new ones. I hope you don't mind if I pass this time." The group does not accept this as the final word, however. They persist by saying they need the client's contribution and point out that everyone else has other obligations as well. The client's response is as follows, "I really would like to help, but I know my limits."

As the scenario proceeds, attention turns to another person who agrees to bring what the client had refused to supply in addition to what he would normally contribute. Seemingly prompted by this demonstration of generous support, a member of the group addresses the client in a confrontive style: "We need some ice cubes. You could at least bring them." The client answers, "You have to hold the line somewhere. There is always one more thing you can do. I am just not taking on anything else right now—no matter how small." The group seems to give grudging assent. With the planning portion of the meeting at an end, the scenario calls for the client to extemporize in talking to the group for approximately one minute. Rather than verbalizing scripted lines, the client is asked to provide the spoken material in this situation. The scenario ends shortly thereafter.

This scenario afforded behavioral rehearsal in refusing requests, but also in a context where such a response might have been especially difficult. Rather than interacting with just one person, the client was receiving demands from a *group*. In addition, the members of the group had each actually made contributions comparable to what they were requesting from the client. This scenario seems to offer the opportunity for rehearsal under particularly troublesome conditions; in fact, each element has been added meticulously to provide the scope of variables likely to be encountered in real life.

Another important element of this scenario was the particular agitation on the part of the person who confronted the client in saying that he could at least bring some ice cubes. Typically self-negating persons would prefer to forego their interests or goals rather than provoke others. In this instance, the client rehearses assertiveness despite fairly strong censure from another person. As this is the third request for the client's assistance, and each has grown more intolerant, the scenario offers the opportunity to practice maintaining an assertive posture against renewed and intensified assaults. This would seem to be a skill truly integral to assertive behavior.

The period of extemporaneous talking was designed for a particular purpose as well. At this point, the client was able to rehearse relating *comfortably* to the people toward whom he had just been assertive under fairly difficult circumstances. Although the authors are unaware of any research on this issue, nonassertive individuals might well feel awkward or even chagrined and exhibit either hostile or withdrawal behavior towards people with whose requests they refused to comply.

The phraseology provided in the scenarios is carefully selected as well. In this latter scenario, the first time the group focused on the client, he said, "I have too many obligations right now to feel good about taking on new ones. I hope you don't mind if I pass this time." These lines are considered to be *reasonable* responses; they serve the speaker's purpose and avoid alienating the persons being addressed. In addition, the lines are generalizeable. The phraseology in this case refers to excessive current obligations, indicates the speaker's negative feeling towards assuming additional responsibilities, and ends on a conversational note in saying, "I hope you don't mind if I pass this time." The client's verbal responses are likely to be applicable almost verbatim to a wide variety of circumstances in which people are making requests he would prefer to decline. Whether confronted with a work supervisor, a spouse, or a friend, the wording would seem as appropriate in achieving the client's purpose while maintaining healthy relations with the requester.

Let us illustrate more fully the characteristic of generalizeability. When being pressed after his first response, the client remains firm in saying, "I really would like to help but I know my limits." The line could have been, "I really would like to help with the picnic by bringing the hot dogs and beer, but I know that with the chairmanship of the volleyball league and with the new baby coming, my hands are already full." The latter statement would have been conversational and seemingly effective at gaining the speaker's end without alienating the requester. On the other hand, though, it would have been so narrow as to be useless for the trainee in other circumstances without substantial modification. When asked sarcastically to "at least bring ice cubes," the responses were: "There is always one more thing you can do. I am just not taking on anything else right now—no matter how small." These statements are likewise seemingly utilizable in a number of contexts. The first statement provides a somewhat persuasive rationale for virtually any refusal by saying, in effect, one cannot wait for demand to slacken—one must stop acceding to requests oneself. Having stated a position for which the requester is likely to feel an affinity, the client follows with a second statement that emphatically declines the request, as shown in the phraseology,—"no matter how small."

When the simulation is adequately prepared, SIT can provide realistic situations offering unusually rich opportunities to practice generalizeable assertive responses. Because the simulation is part of a largely automated system, the trainer or therapist can conveniently provide repetitions of behavioral rehearsals.

The SIT Study

This study utilized simulated interaction training (SIT) with clients rehearsing assertive responses to figures presented on a 40-by-30 inch screen. A total of nine color scenarios with a mean length of approximately five minutes were utilized in the training.

The sample was comprised of 13 college students who responded to advertisements for participants in an assertiveness training program. The group consisted of 11 females and 2 males with the ages ranging from 24 to 53 years with a mean of 34 years. Generally, the group was comprised of "returning" female students who had earlier interrupted their education, often to devote themselves to their families, and were now returning to continue a career.

A within-subjects design was used with pre and post measures from the Conflict Resolution Inventory (McFall 1971), Rathus Assertiveness Scale (Rathus 1973), Semantic Differential (Osgood, Suci, and Tannenbaum 1957) and Personality Dominance Inventory (Doyle and Shafritz 1977).

Training was divided into three one-hour sessions per week for each trainee. The first two of the hour-long sessions were comprised of simulated interaction training (that is, interacting with video-tape scenarios); the third session of each week consisted of group discussion and live role play. The training program extended six weeks for a total of 18 sessions for each trainee.

During the simulated interaction training sessions, a peer counseling procedure was utilized. Since only one person at a time could effectively interact with the screen, it was first assumed that each SIT session would include a trainee and a rater. Since there were 13 trainees, this would have required 13 hours of rating twice weekly to provide two hours of SIT to each trainee per week. This seemed an inordinate demand on trainer resources, in view of the previously prepared videotapes and scripts which would account for the greater share of training during the session.

Inasmuch as the sessions were so highly structured, it was decided to pair the trainees for each session. During the first half hour, one trainee interacted with the screen presentation while the other observed and provided feedback. After a half hour they exchanged roles, so each received equal practice in SIT. In order to monitor this system, an experimenter regularly visited the sessions. Additional feedback on this peer-based mutual training technique was obtained at the weekly group session. According to reports of the trainees and observations of the experimenters, this system functioned quite satisfactorily. In fact, the knowledge that the rater would need a similar function performed for him-/herself by the ratee seemed to lead particularly to conscientious rating and feedback.

Feedback was provided on the following dimensions: fluency, voice volume, emotional tone, eye contact, expressiveness, postural stance, and overall assertiveness. Typically, five scenarios were presented during the trainee's half hour of interaction. These scenarios had been recorded on the video tape so that a minute of silence existed between each. Thus, the trainee or ratee would work through each scenario without being interrupted and receive feedback during the minute of blank video tape.

In accordance with the successive approximations principle, initial scripts were highly structured and provided all the trainee's verbal responses. One consequence of this procedure was that in the early phase of the training fluency tended to be rated quite high, as the trainee could simply read the prepared material. There was also emphasis on eye contact with the screen figures, though. As a result, most trainees felt pressure to memorize the written material in order to deliver the verbal responses while maintaining eye contact. This memorization of the scripted lines, in conjunction with the active practice of delivering them in the context of the large screen simulations, seemed particularly propitious for generalization of the responses. One would predict significant gain scores on the CRI, RAS, and PDI measures of assertiveness since these instruments ask the trainee to assess his or her behavior in real-life situations.

Subsequent scripts faded the prompts by deleting more of the trainee's written lines until in later scripts the responses were almost completely extemporaneous. In one later scenario, the trainee is introduced as a presidential candidate of an organization. The screen view is one of a person looking over a podium and down a long table with people seated on each side. The script then calls for a speech of approximately three minutes followed by questions from the audience. The trainee is only given the time limitations and must provide the content of the speech.

Table 9.1 Pre- to Post-test Differences for the four Assertiveness Measures

Measure	Pretest Mean	Post-test Mean	Mean Gain	t-Statistic
Conflict resolution inventory	145.2	154.7	9.5	3.522*
Rathus assertiveness scale	6.4	15.4	9.0	4.279*
Semantic differential	60.1	65.5	5.4	3.3340*
Personality dominance inventory	57.2	63.6	6.4	5.501*

*$p < .005$ ($df = 12$)

As shown in table 9.1, pretest to posttest differences in assertiveness were significant at least at the .005 level for the CRI, RAS, and PDI as well as the Semantic Differential. These results strongly suggest the treatment was effective. The question could be asked, however, whether the change in these self-report measures was accompanied by an actual change in behavior. In other words did the sought-after generalization occur? In this regard, it is important to note the selection of the Conflict Resolution Inventory was in part determined by Loo's (1971) finding that the CRI and behavioral ratings correlated .82. Given the significant change on this measure in particular, there is basis for considering generalization to have occurred.

The implications of these findings seem far reaching. One could envision SIT materials being prepared for use in a wide variety of circumstances. In fact, during a two-year period Doyle has worked with the Houston Police Department to develop a battery of scenarios for use in the training of police cadets. The police scenarios expose cadets to irate motorists, family quarrels, homicides, and a number of other pressurized situations. In total there are twelve scenarios which were selected as a result of input from veteran police officers. Each relates to an especially difficult situation likely to be encountered in police work. The key goal of this application of SIT is to provide rehearsal for new officers in emotional self-control and non-violent confrontation-management skills when facing annoying and belligerent figures in the realistic context of large screen simulations. It was hoped that the new officers would be less likely to use brutality or excessive force in performing their duty in the real situation. Thus far, the data obtained in follow-up measures involving role playing by officers indicate that trained officers are less likely to use excessive force.

In addition to SIT for police cadets, another project is underway which will develop scenarios for individuals preparing to become classroom teachers. There seems to be an exceptional demand for more training in handling the realities of classroom teaching than is currently given. Aside from police officers and teachers, other occupational groups which could seemingly benefit from SIT might include medical nurses, lawyers, business executives, and front-line work supervisors.

With respect to psychotherapy applications, SIT presents some unique advantages. As an example, it would be conceivable to devise a "parent" video tape that would permit clients to rehearse constructive responses to parent figures. The script for the parent figures might call for precisely the behavior patterns that presumably contributed to the destructive or maladaptive responses of the client during childhood. The client would perform in circumstances that were formerly cues for problem behavior.

In terms of the mechanics of individual psychotherapy, SIT may offer important strengths also. The video-tape simulations permit successive behavioral rehearsals to be accomplished through a largely automatic process. Instead of the therapist enacting a role for each instance of behavioral rehearsal, he or she selects the appropriate videotape scenarios. Meanwhile, the therapist is free to observe and to rate the client's performance. This largely automated system is likely to counteract significantly, the normal human tendencies on the part of the therapists to be preoccupied, to be subject to mood swings, and even to be fatigued, all of which lower performance. Providing the proper video-tape scenario is available and selected, SIT would largely assure high quality and thorough presentation of the appropriate practice situations.

Of course, researchers have long relied on mechanized presentations to achieve standardization. Perhaps as important as the standardization is the content validity of various treatments. During the preparation of a video tape, operationalization of a concept can be accomplished with considerable precision. A scene can be taped and viewed with an eye to improvement and then taped again until the desired version is obtained. This process would insure high content validity of the independent variables.

With regard to standardization, reliance on video simulations to provide a major portion of therapy through behavioral rehearsal would achieve a highly uniform presentation of therapy to each subject. This would permit an unusual opportunity for fairly clean research on therapy per se. One could neatly investigate order effects of a variable, as an example, simply by changing the order in which the simulations incorporating this variable are presented. As a technique, it must be said SIT seems particularly to lend itself to empirical testing.

Conclusion

The coalescence of behavioral techniques in the form of behavioral rehearsal and the emergence of large-screen video projection systems have provided the basis for a unique therapeutic approach. Clients are able to rehearse desirable responses under highly realistic circumstances in SIT, on a regular basis, without a prohibitive drain on therapist resources. SIT has been applied to assertive training and to the development of conflict management skills thus far with significant results. Finally, this technique appears particularly amenable to empirical investigation. In the view of the authors, SIT offers sufficient advantages to warrant widening use and further investigation; it seems appropriate for libraries of video-tape simulations to be made available for use in both clinical practice and research.

References

Doyle, P. and Shafritz, J. 1977. Personality Dominance Inventory. Unpublished Manuscript, University of Houston.

Galassi, M. D., and Galassi, J. P. 1978. Assertion: A critical review. *Psychotherapy: Theory, Research and Practice, 15,* 16-29.

Loo, R. M. Y. 1971. *The effects of projected consequences and overt behavioral rehearsal on assertive behavior.* Unpublished doctoral dissertation, University of Illinois.

McFall, R. M., and Lillesand, D. B. 1971. Behavior rehearsal with modeling and coaching in assertion training. *Journal of Abnormal Psychology, 77,* 313-23.

Osgood, C. E., Suci, G., and Tannenbaum, P. 1957. *The measurement of meaning.* Urbana: University of Illinois Press.

Rathus, S.A. 1973. A 30-item schedule for assessing assertive behavior. *Behavior Therapy, 4,* 398-406.

10
Self-Reliance Training in Depression

Gary Emery

Self-reliance training (SRT) teaches people to overcome excessive dependency and social isolation. SRT is one of the interventions used in cognitive therapy. Before describing self-reliance training for depressed patients, I'll briefly discuss cognitive therapy and its application to depression.

Depression accounts for 75 percent of all psychiatric hospitalizations, and during any given year 15 percent of all adults between 18 and 74 suffer from depression (Secunda, Katz, and Friedman 1978). At the Mood Clinic, University of Pennsylvania, we have developed a new treatment for depression, cognitive therapy (Beck et al. 1979).

Cognitive therapy is based on the cognitive model of emotional disorders (Beck 1976). The model holds that a person's cognitions (verbal and pictorial events in a stream of consciousness) determine how the person feels and acts. In depression, the person reacts to stress or a series of stresses by activating a set of dysfunctional beliefs. The person develops a negative view of himself, the world, and his future.

Depressed persons then systematically distort experiences to agree with their negative conclusions. They mishear, misperceive and misconstrue events to fit this prevailing negative line.

In cognitive therapy, therapists and patients work together to identify and correct distortions. The approach is active and time limited. Patients learn to master problems they consider insurmountable by re-evaluating their thinking. Patients first obtain symptom relief. Later, therapy focuses on uncovering beliefs that lead to the depression and subjecting these beliefs to reality testing.

Researchers have found cognitive therapy to be a promising treatment for depression. Analogue and controlled studies have found cognitive therapy to be more effective than other treatments for depression, including chemotherapy (Shaw 1975, 1977; Rush et al. 1977).

Self-Reliance Training

Self-reliance training is part of cognitive therapy. Patient-therapist interaction and techniques are essentially the same in both. The difference is in the behavior that is targeted for change. Cognitive therapy is more global: a wide variety of patient problems are addressed. Self-reliance training is more specific: dependency and self-absorption are targeted for change.

Self-reliance makes up part of a more general construct: *a person's belief in his or her ability to perform adequately in a given situation*. As shown in table 10.1, part of this construct refers to the person's confidence in his or her ability to carry out the activity with others.

People acting dependently believe they can carry out the activity *only* with others. Self-absorbed persons believe they can adequately perform on their own—but not with others. People acting self-reliantly have confidence they can carry out the activity alone *or* with others.

As an illustration, one patient wanted to see more movies, but because there was no one to go with, she didn't go. She was dependent on others to see movies. She had a number of reasons for not going alone: "I can't decide on what movie to see," "I won't know what to do if someone bothers me at the movie," and, "if I see someone, I'll be so ashamed about being there alone I don't know what I'd do."

Another patient went to the movies alone five or six times a week—sometimes twice in the same day. Although he complained of loneliness, he wouldn't ask others to go with him. He lacked self-reliance to go with others. His reasons: "Other people won't like the same movies I do—they might ruin it for me," "I'd be uncomfortable watching the movie with somebody," and, "I won't be able to discuss the movie intellectually afterwards with the person."

Table 10.1 Confidence in Ability To Carry Out Activities

	Alone	With Others
Dependent	No	Yes
Self-absorbed	Yes	No
Self-reliant	Yes	Yes

Self-reliant people have the choice to go to movies alone or with someone. They're confident they can go and enjoy themselves in either situation.

In a sense, self-reliance is a model for mental health. Deane Shapiro (1978) describes a similar model:

> Initially we need to turn from an other-directed search for approval to an inner-directed search. Yet there may be disadvantages to self-reinforcement. First, if we focus too much on ourselves, we may become narcissistic, self-aggrandizing, without a willingness to share or give to others. Second, we may believe that we have all the answers, and thus close ourselves off from the advice of others. We may become unreceptive, pompous, unfeeling of others. There are several writers in both the Eastern and Western tradition who believe it is to our advantage to go *beyond* self-reinforcement, and to no longer need either the reinforcement of others or ourselves. (P. 184)

Table 10.2 outlines the differences among dependency, self-absorption, and self-reliance behavior.

People can be self-reliant to work and dependent at home. However, people are generally consistent: they are dependent, self-reliant, or self-absorbed across a variety of situations. Underlying beliefs account for this consistency, such as: "I'm basically inadequate, so I have to depend on others," and, "Because others can't be counted on, I have to count on myself."

Depression accentuates a person's dysfunctional beliefs about his or her self-reliance. These beliefs in turn help maintain the depression. This leads to two different subgroups of depressed patients. One group becomes excessively dependent; the other becomes excessively self-absorbed. Some depressed patients present neither of these symptom clusters, and others both. Self-reliance training is geared to help depressed patients that are overly dependent or overly self-absorbed.

Dependency and Depression

On dependency and depression, Beck (1967) writes:

> The accentuated wishes for dependency have only occasionally been included in the clinical descriptions of depression; they have, however, been recognized and assigned a major etiological role in several psychodynamic explanations of depression (Abraham 1911; Rado 1928). The accentuated orality attributed to the depressed patients by those authors includes the kind of wishes that are generally regarded as "dependent"—frank and undisguised intensified desires for help, support and encouragement are very prominent elements in the advanced stage of depression and belong in any clinical description of this syndrome. And other conditions of intensified dependency may be variable and transient characteristics. Desire for help seems to transcend the realistic need for help, i.e., the patient can often reach his objectives without assistance. Receiving help, however, appears to carry emotional meaning for the patient beyond its practical importance and often satisfies, at least temporarily. (P. 32)

Table 10.2. Comparison of Dependency, Self-Absorbed, and Self-Reliance Behavior

	Dependency	Self-Absorbed	Self-Reliance
Interpersonal behavior	Leans on others Other-directed Overly focused on others	Avoids others Social isolation Overly focused on self	Interacts with others True relationship based on sense of independence
Perceived by others	Helpless "Needy" Clinging	Aloof Narcissistic Closed	Mature Capable Open
Self-disclosure	Over-disclosure	Under-disclosure	Discloses appropriate to situation
Choices	Constricted behavioral choices	Constricted behavioral choices	Wide range of choices
Affect	Typically labile Feels helpless	Typically flat Feels alienated	Appropriate to situation
Fears	Fears being alone becoming social isolate	Fears being with others becoming dependent	Minimal interpersonal fears
Self-evaluation	Indirect self-acceptance based on others' opinions	Indirect self-acceptance based on one's achievements	Direct self-acceptance Minimal self-evaluation
Assumptions	I need others. I can't work alone.	I don't need anybody. Others let me down.	I don't need others but I enjoy them.

In mild depression, patients feel an urge to have more and more done for them. They crave help even though they understand they don't need it. In moderate depression, the wish for help is elevated to a need for help. It is considered a necessity. Patients seek help from others before they attempt to do anything.

In severe depression, patients want someone to do everything for them. Patients don't want advice on solving problems, they want the other person to solve the problem. In one case, the patient wanted the psychiatrist to adopt her children and raise them for her.

Depression and Self-Absorption

Another group of patients act the opposite of the dependent patients. They avoid others and become withdrawn. They have no use for others and want to be by themselves. As they become more depressed, the desire for withdrawal increases. Beck (1967) describes the self-absorbed depressed patient:

> The patient thinks continually of ways of diversion or escape. He would like to indulge in passive recreation such as going to the movies, watching television or getting drunk. He daydreams of going to a desert island or of becoming a hobo. At this stage, he may withdraw from most social contact since interpersonal relations seem to be too demanding....In severe cases the wish to avoid or escape is manifested in marked seclusiveness. Not infrequently the patient stays in bed, and when people approach, he may hide under the covers. A patient said, "I just feel like getting away from everybody and everything. I don't want to see anybody or do anything. All I want to do is sleep." (P.30)

Procedures in Self-Reliance Training

The goal of SRT is to increase or reactivate patients' self-reliance skills: they learn to act less dependent and less self-absorbed in more situations. Therapists use an assortment of techniques to help patients reach this goal.

Therapists use these techniques in collaboration with the patient. The therapist and patient form an alliance to define and solve problems. Both play an active role in deciding what goes on in therapy. A team approach, however, isn't always easy to establish.

Many dependent patients want the therapist to solve all their problems, and the self-absorbed patients won't let the therapist help. To transcend this and establish a working alliance, the therapist has to be clinically skillful.

It is helpful for the therapist to explain the difference between *constructive* and *regressive* dependency. Going for therapy can represent constructive dependency: patients have problems they're unable to solve so they seek outside help. On the other hand, in regressive dependency, patients want help for problems they can handle on their own.

Therapists should stress that without safeguards, constructive dependency can deteriorate into regressive dependency. One patient, for example, learned how to control her depression, but she insisted that the therapist continue to help her solve her problems.

Some patients worry about becoming too dependent on the therapist. The therapist can point out that self-reliance training gives the person tools to become more independent. By learning new ways of thinking and acting, the person will eventually become freer and have more choices.

Introduction of Model

Patients frequently confuse self-reliance, dependency, and self-absorption. Dependent patients fear becoming social isolates if they are more self-reliant. Similarly, self-absorbed patients believe steps toward self-reliance lead to dependency. Therapists have to spell out the differences among these three classes of behavior clearly.

Therapists can give patients handouts (such as table 10.3 and fig. 10.1) and other reading material (Beecher and Beecher 1966; Shapiro 1970) to clarify the differences further. The therapist should have a backlog of examples (from other patients, friends, and the therapist's own life) to illustrate the model. Therapists also can ask patients for examples of dependent, self-reliant, and self-absorbed behaviors.

Therapists should review the rationale for being self-reliant periodically. Here's one way this was done.

Therapist:	How did you feel about going to the city by yourself?
Patient:	I felt real good about it.
Therapist:	Why do you think you felt that way?
Patient:	Well, I did something I didn't think I could do.
Therapist:	And what does that mean to you?
Patient:	I guess I'm more capable than I thought.
Therapist:	What people think and feel about themselves depends largely on what they do. People watch how they act and then evaluate themselves accordingly.
Patient:	I've found now that I've started to do more on my own, I no longer feel I'm such a loser.

Most patients respond as this patient did. The more they move from helplessness to resourcefulness, the better they think of themselves.

Homework

Patients play an active role in SRT and carry out homework assignments between sessions. Self-reliance habits are ingrained and difficult to change. The person has to practice new behaviors daily to replace the old habits. It usually takes the patient 6 to 12 months of practice before the new habits become automatic.

Therapists give patients the following general assignments: Try to increase the number of times you act self-reliantly. Each day you'll run into situations where you can choose to be self-reliant—or choose not to be. I suggest you try to act purposefully self-reliant at least once every day. This should be something that's difficult for you. It can range from making a tough phone call to making your own coffee instead of having someone else do it for you.

Self-Monitoring

Therapists try to keep SRT data based. The therapist needs accurate information to make the right interventions and patients need accurate information to correct distortions and to see improvement. The patient's role in the therapeutic alliance is to provide this data through homework.

Patients keep written self-reliance records. They can simply record the situations when they're self-reliant, or they can keep more detailed records. Patients, for example, can rate the degree of self-reliance from 0 to 100; they can record the amount of associated anxiety; and they can write down predictions of what they think will happen. Because they need to reinstate basic self-reliance skills, most depressed patients keep an hourly record of their behavior.

The written record is the starting point for each session. Many patients find self-monitoring has a reactive effect: merely keeping track of self-reliance behavior increases it.

Graded Tasks

The written records will reveal activities the patient is avoiding. Most of the patient's self-reliance problems center around avoidance. The therapist and patient work together to translate the avoidance into solvable problems.

Patients begin by reinstating basic self-reliance skills—ones that were previously in their repertoire but were lost during the depression. Tasks are broken down into manageable steps. Patients first attempt activities that aren't too difficult and have a good chance of success. Each step is a discrete task and can be completed in a short period of time: fixing a meal, cleaning the bedroom, sorting bills, grocery shopping.

Success usually causes a cognitive switch: the depressed person becomes motivated to try more. The patient gradually increases the range and degree of difficulty of the targeted activity.

Behavioral Experiments

Depressed patients typically don't believe they're capable of carrying out even simple activities. Therapists use the strategy of behavioral experiment

1. Start where you're at. You have to work continually at being self-reliant. Don't expect to become self-reliant in every area.
2. Become aware of activities you're reluctant to do yourself—service your car, do your own cooking, go to dinner alone.
3. Become aware of activities you're reluctant to do with others—go to lunch, take a trip, go shopping.
4. Rank these activities from easiest to hardest. Start by doing the easiest and move up to harder ones.
5. Try to do one difficult self-reliant activity every day. What's difficult varies from person to person and how the person is feeling at the time.
6. Become aware of your excuses for not acting self-reliantly. "It's too much for me," "It's too cold to go out," or "I'll do it tomorrow when I feel better."
7. Answer these thoughts, preferably in writing, with more balanced and adaptive thoughts. Example: "That's just an excuse. I'll be better off if I look at my long-term aims rather than avoiding a little discomfort."
8. Develop tolerance for the initial discomfort of acting self-reliantly. You can do this by directing your mind away from what's bothering you to something more neutral and by telling yourself to stay in the situation.
9. Put yourself into situations where you have to act self-reliantly. Example. Accept an invitation to a party where you'll have to talk to others.
10. Determine what beliefs you have to change to become more self-reliant. Example: "I have to do something perfectly or I won't do it," "I'm the only person I can trust," or "I don't measure up to others."
11. Develop initiative. Volunteer to start projects. Make the first move towards another.
12. Tell others that have done activities for you in the past, "I appreciate your help, but I'd like to try to do this on my own." Don't change your mind in the middle.

Fig. 10.1. Self-reliance guidelines

to overcome this resistance. But first, therapists have to elicit the patient's specific thoughts about doing the task. This is done by having the patient, while in the office, imagine going through the activity, in other words, a cognitive rehearsal. During the rehearsal, patients give the reason they can't do the activity.

After the patient discloses the negative predictions, the therapist suggests the patient run an experiment to see if the thoughts are true or not. For example, the patient might say, "It's too hard. I don't think I can do it." The therapist can then say, "You could be right, but I've a hunch you can do it. Would you be willing to test out these two hypotheses to see which is right?" Through a variety of such leads the therapist sparks the patient's interest in trying.

Therapists restructure the patient's negative predictions into hypotheses that can be tested out. The experiments are set up as no-lose situations. If patients follow through, they've had a success experience, and if they don't complete the task, they have still learned something: the reason they didn't

Table 10.3. Examples of Dependency, Self-Absorption, and Self-Reliance Behavior

	Dependency	Self-Absorbed	Self-Reliance
Patient in Therapy			
Number of problems	Overwhelms therapist. Therapist has to distill problems down to manageable number.	Underwhelms therapist. Therapist has to draw problems out.	Brings in enough problems to work on in session and no more.
Problem solving	Wants therapist to solve problems; believes it's therapist's job.	Won't let therapist help; believes should be able to solve problem on own.	Forms alliance with therapist to solve problems.
Mechanics of Therapy	Tries to extend length of session.	Misses sessions. Doesn't return phone calls.	Follows appropriate limits in therapy.
Termination	Doesn't want to end therapy. Returns for treatment even when can handle problems on own.	Premature termination. Doesn't return for treatment until problem is severe.	Terminates when ready and returns when appropriate.
Marriage			
Trust	Overtrusts spouse's ability and undertrusts own.	Undertrusts spouse's ability and overtrusts own.	Trusts self and spouse's ability.
Decision Making	Asks spouse to make nearly all decisions.	Makes decisions unilaterally without spouse.	Can make own decisions based on all available information. Shares decision making.

Table 10.3 *(continued)*

	Dependency	Self-Absorbed	Self-Reliance
Marriage (cont'd)			
Control	Gives up control easily to spouse.	Doesn't give up control to spouse.	Can lead or follow.
Crisis	Overreacts. Wants to share all aspects with spouse.	Underreacts. Won't let spouse in on thinking.	Works with spouse to solve problem.
Patient and Employment			
Job-Finding Strategy	Expects agencies and others to find job. Takes another along on interview.	Doesn't tell of looking for work, thus misses opportunities.	Doesn't hide unemployment and seeks job on own.
Level of Employment	Often underemployed due to lack of confidence.	Often underemployed due to lack of confidence in interpersonal skills.	Employed to potential.
On the Job	Has work excessively checked.	Doesn't ask for help for work not sure of.	Asks for help in work can't do on own.
Perceived by Supervisor	Lacks initiative, easy to manage but lacks self-management.	Not team player, goes off "half-cocked."	Responsible, can be counted on.

do it. This information is crucial in learning to be self-reliant.

Patients usually view their lives in a no-win fashion. The therapist structures the experience as a no-lose situation to provoke discussions of the advantages of trying versus the advantages of not trying. Patients change their self-defeating beliefs largely through disconfirming experiences, and behavioral experiments provide this experience. One patient, for example, believed she was basically helpless, but as she started to do more on her own (fill out her own income tax, return unwanted merchandise), her beliefs began to change. She saw herself as more capable. The major purpose of behavioral experiments is to undermine the patient's dysfunctional beliefs.

Fixed-Role Assignment

Patients can rapidly increase self-reliance by placing themselves in a situation where they have to be self-reliant. One person decided to go on a camping trip alone. To survive the trip, he had to be self-reliant. This is the lazy man's SRT. The person made a big decision that insured smaller ones would be carried out.

Therapists help the patients plan ways to cope with any problems that might arise in this situation. One patient, for example, after she was over her depression wanted to increase her self-reliance. She decided to spend a weekend in New York City by herself. She and the therapist worked out the following script for use while in the city: "I'll tell people I'm going so it'll be harder to back out. I'll make hotel arrangements. That will increase the chance I'll go. I will go out to museums and other sights and not just hide in my room. I'll stick out two days and not come home earlier. If I have any trouble with people approaching me, I'll act like Janet (her roommate) and not be intimidated. Even if I'm anxious, I can force myself to go."

She was able to follow this plan. She not only proved that she could be on her own in a strange city, but she also found she could enjoy herself.

Correcting Cognitive Distortions

Some procedures teach patients to change their thinking directly. These are verbal techniques in contrast to the behavioral techniques discussed earlier. Therapists use the behavioral approaches for the severe symptoms. When the patient improves, the therapist uses more cognitive techniques. Cognitive techniques explore the logic behind the specific cognitions that lead to dependency and self-absorption.

Patients learn to (1) monitor dependency and self-absorption producing thoughts, (2) recognize the connection between these thoughts and how they feel and act, (3) examine the evidence for and against these thoughts, (4) substitute more reality-oriented interpretations, and (5) identify and alter dysfunctional assumptions that predispose them to dependency or self-absorption.

Patients learn to tune into their thinking. When they begin to feel helpless or isolated, they write down their thoughts. One patient had trouble going to work in the morning, so he had his wife drive him there. The following are the types of thoughts he had when this occurred: "I need someone to go with me. I need someone to talk to. I don't want to go alone."

Next, patients learn to answer their thoughts. This patient wrote out: "I don't need help. I just *want* it. I'm capable of driving to work on my own. I've done it plenty of times. I can force myself to go by myself. And if I want to get better, I'll get better." Therapists first help patients answer their thoughts in the office. Later, patients answer on their own, first in writing, then mentally.

Imagery

Often an image rather than a verbal thought precedes the dependency and self-absorbed behavior. In SRT, patients learn to control these images. (For a more detailed discussion of imagery techniques, see Beck and Emery 1979).

One woman, for example, had difficulty in going out to make sales calls. She saw herself as a small, helpless child and the potential customers as big, imposing figures. She overcame this by changing the imagery. She was able to picture herself as a grown person and reduce the size of the customer's image.

Modifying Assumptions

After patients have some experience in correcting thinking errors, therapy focuses on discovering and changing the patient's underlying beliefs. These beliefs or attitudes predispose the person to dependency and self-absorption. After the assumptions are identified, the same general techniques are used to modify them.

Common assumptions of the dependent patient are: (1) I don't measure up to others, (2) bad things happen when I stand up for myself, (3) the world is a dangerous place, (4) I have to do something perfectly before I can do it at all. Beliefs that lead to self-absorbed behavior are: (1) Other people let me down, (2) every time I get involved with others they hurt me, (3) if I do something for others I'm in debt to them, (4) if people find out too much about me, they'll use it against me, (5) if people get to know me, they'll find out I don't measure up.

Patient's beliefs are often difficult to change. For this reason patients are encouraged to continue chipping away at this dysfunctional belief after therapy has ended.

Auxiliary Techniques

Because patients are frequently anxious in carrying out self-reliance behaviors, the therapist teaches them ways to cope with anxiety by distracting themselves away from the anxiety. For example, one patient became anxious in social situations. He learned to concentrate on various details that had no relation to his anxiety. He studied fabric patterns, furniture styles, and random superficial facts about other persons in the group.

Often the person's dependency is made worse by others. One patient's wife took over responsibility for most of his duties. Once in therapy, she even wanted to fill out his activity schedule for. him. In these cases, it's crucial that the significant other is included in therapy. Bedrosian (1979) has written on the role of significant others in cognitive therapy.

Sex Roles and Self-Reliance

Patients in SRT attempt to do as much as they can themselves of everyday activities. This often transcends sexual stereotypes. Many males, for example, have trouble with basic housekeeping jobs: cooking, laundry, cleaning. Men are encouraged to do these activities on their own.

Often patients have social anxiety in trying these activities. Patients are told the best ways to overcome this anxiety is to do more of the activity. One depressed patient, prior to his divorce, was dependent on his wife to take care of his basic needs. When he went to other homes for dinner, he started offering to help with the cooking and the cleanup. Even though initially anxious, he gradually became self-reliant in these basic skills.

Many men rely on others to handle basic tasks on their jobs. To develop a sense of independence and mastery, the individual is encouraged to learn how to perform these activities: this may be making airline reservations, going for coffee, and typing.

The same strategy is used with women. Therapists suggest the patient try new activities even though the patient may believe it's inappropriate for women. One 52-year-old woman, for instance, felt helpless when her husband died. Before he died, they frequently went to dinner together. She stopped doing this after his death because she didn't believe women could go out to dinner alone. There were also many maintenance jobs that she didn't know how to do, such as servicing the car.

After a shaky start, she learned she could go out to dinner by herself. She began to make a production of it; rather than accepting a side table, she would ask the waiter for a better table. Similarly, she became more confident in handling maintenance problems. She began by pumping her own gas at self-service gas stations, then she began checking the car's oil and air. Eventually, she took a course for women on car maintenance.

Self-Reliance and the Elderly

People face unique challenges to self-reliance at each developmental stage. Older individuals, for example, encounter a range of challenges. One of the major ones is social influences. Many believe all old people are dependent or self-absorbed. This places the aged in a chronic conflict; they're caught between stereotypes of the old as weak, incompetent, and egocentric, and their own concepts of themselves as active and competent (Thomae 1970).

As people grow older, they're more inclined to adopt age-related norms: these norms are more restrictive for the elderly. The *depressed* older patient exaggerates this tendency to adopt self-defeating attitudes towards aging and more restrictive behavioral norms.

Older patients often have misconceptions about therapy. They may believe the therapist's job is to solve basic problems such as getting them food stamps. In addition to discussing this issue, the therapist can help by not providing too much help. For instance, one 73-year-old patient wanted to do volunteer work with children. The therapist knew a contact person, but instead of making the call for the patient, he suggested the patient carry through on her own. There is evidence that doing too much for the older patient is counterproductive and can shorten the older person's life span (Bloom and Blenker 1970). For more detailed discussion of cognitive therapy with the elderly, see Emery (1979).

Self-Reliance and Alcoholism

While people with alcohol problems often act dependent, they are more likely to be self-absorbed. Their confidence in their ability to interact with others is low. One example was a 38-year-old woman who sought treatment for depression and alcohol dependency. Her history included three inpatient admissions for alcoholism. Her alcohol abuse began after she ended an affair with a married man 5 years earlier. She believed, "If I become too close to others, they'll find out about my terrible past." Because of this belief, she led a relatively isolated life. Her social experiences were limited to her work.

A treatment goal was for her to expand her social life. She began by taking a night course and gradually increased her social life. She discovered she could control the information she wanted others to know. She also found out when she disclosed about her past others didn't automatically condemn her. At the three-year follow-up, she reported she had been dating regularly and that she had no futher problems with depression or alcohol.

People with substance dependency (alcohol, drugs, and food) often rely on the substance to help them perform—to see them through a party or through a task. The general strategy is for the patient to increase what he or she can do on his own without the help of the substance. For further discussion of alcohol dependency, see Emery and Fox (1977) and Emery and Beck (1979).

Summary

Many attribute dependency to a person's desire to control others and self-absorption to a person's desire to distance oneself from others. I believe, based on experience, this is a low probability—an example of confusing function of behavior with cause.

People *do* manipulate others into helping them, *but* because they *believe* they're incapable of acting on their own. This, not the desire to manipulate others, is the basic motivation. Similarly, people distance themselves because they believe they can't perform with others.

The basic premise of SRT is that people have restrictive beliefs they can learn to change. The overall aim of SRT is to help people increase their options by changing these beliefs. From Emerson's essay, "Self-Reliance" through *Zen and the Art of Motorcycle Maintenance,* self-reliance has been a highly valued goal in our society. Self-reliance training is a way of systematically helping people reach this goal.

References

Beck, A. T. 1967. *Depression: Clinical, experimental, and theoretical aspects.* New York: Harper and Row.

Beck, A. T. 1976. *Cognitive therapy and the emotional disorders.* New York: International Universities Press.

Beck, A. T., Rush, A. J., Shaw, B. F., and Emery, G. 1979. *Cognitive therapy of depression.* New York: Guilford Press.

Beck, A. T. and Emery, G. 1978. *Cognitive therapy of anxiety: A treatment manual* (manuscript). Center for Cognitive Therapy, University of Pennsylvania.

Bedrosian, R. 1979. The use of significant others in cognitive therapy. In *New directions in cognitive therapy,* ed. G. Emery, S. Hollon, and R. Bedrosian, New York: Guilford Press.

Beecher, W., and Beecher, M. 1966. *Beyond success and failure: Ways to self-reliance and maturity.* New York: Pocket Book.

Bloom, M., and Blenker, M. 1970. Assessing functioning of older persons living in the community. *Gerontologist, 10,* 31-37.

Emery, G. 1979. Cognitive therapy with the elderly. In *New directions in cognitive therapy,* ed. G. Emery, S. Hollon, and R. Bedrosian. New York: Guilford Press.

Emery G., and Beck, A. T. 1978. *Cognitive therapy of alcohol and drug dependency* (manuscript). Center for Cognitive Therapy, University of Pennsylvania.

Emery, G., and Fox, S. 1977. Treating alcoholism with broad spectrum behavioral psychotherapy. Paper presented at NATO International Conference on Behavioral Approach to Alcoholism, Bergen, Norway, August, 1977.

Rush, A. J., Beck, A. T., Kovacs, M., and Hollon, S. 1977. Comparative efficiency of cognitive therapy and imipramine in the treatment of depressed outpatients. *Cognitive Therapy and Research, 1,* 19-37.

Secunda, S. K., Katz, M. M., Friedman, R. J., and Schuyler, D. 1973. *Special report 1973: The depressive disorders.* Washington: U.S. Government Printing Office.

Shapiro, D. H. 1978. *Precision nirvana.* Englewood Cliffs, N.J.: Prentice Hall.

Shaw, B. F. 1977. Comparison of cognitive therapy and behavior therapy in the treatment of depression. *Journal of Consulting and Clinical Psychology, 45,* 543-51.

Shaw, B. F. 1975. A systematic investigation of three treatments of depression. Unpublished dissertation, University of Western Ontario, Canada.

Thomae, H. 1970. Theory of aging and cognitive theory of personality. *Human Development, 13,* 1-16.

11

Social Skills Training and Psychosomatic Disorders*

Francisco X. Barrios

The concept of social skills or social competence has achieved considerable popularity among behavior therapists in a remarkably brief period of time. The last few years have seen the publication of a number of books intended for mental health professionals (Gambrill and Richey 1976; Liberman et al. 1975) that have focused on providing methods for teaching a number of social skills, notably assertion.

Despite this recent popularity, there has been no general consensus as to what constitutes social skills or social competence. As noted in the introduction to this book, this concept has been examined by a number of investigators and has been operationalized in several different ways. Argyle (1967) considered the behavior taking place in social interactions to be analogous to motor skills and, accordingly, postulated social competence to be a function of goals of performance, selective perception of cues, central processes, motor responses, feedback, and timing of responses. Goldfried and D'Zurilla (1969) have provided a behavioral definition of social competence that is operationalized as the effectiveness or adequacy with which an individual is capable of responding to the various problematic situations which confront him. Thus, according to this definition, the ability to problem solve is closely tied to the concept of social competence. Lewinsohn and his coworkers (Lewinsohn, Weinstein and Shaw, 1969) have hypothesized that the lack of social skills is an important anticedent in the occurrence of depression. Accordingly, they have defined social skills as the

*This study is based on a dissertation submitted to the Division of Graduate Studies of the University of Cincinnati in partial fulfillment of the requirements for the Ph.D. degree. The author would like to acknowledge the contributions of the members of the dissertation committee, Paul Karoly (Chairman), William Seeman, and William Whitehead, as well as the assistance of Al Fedoravicius and his staff on 2-West, Cincinnati General Hospital.

complex ability both to emit behaviors that are positively or negatively reinforced and not to emit behaviors that are punished or extinguished by others (Libet and Lewinsohn 1973). More recently, Eisler (1976) has defined the concept of social skill as including the abilities to (1) express contrary opinions to those of peers and instructors, (2) ask favors of someone, (3) initiate conversation with peers and strangers, (4) refuse unreasonable requests from strangers and friends, (5) request appointments and dates with others, (6) compliment others, (7) negotiate in "give and take" with family, friends, and spouse, (8) apply successfully for a job, (9) ask for help in solving problems and, (10) resist pressure from others to behave in a manner contrary to one's beliefs (p. 381).

Regardless of which of this bewildering array of definitions one chooses to adopt, the idea that deficits in social and interpersonal functioning play a significant role in the etiology and maintenance of behavioral disorders is not a new one. The relationship between social skill deficits and psychopathology has been proposed for over a decade by Zigler and Phillips and their co-workers (Phillips and Zigler 1961; Zigler and Phillips 1961). Using a measure of social competence derived from demographic variables, such as marital status, employment history, and educational level, and applying it retrospectively to existing case-history material, Zigler and Phillips concluded that, whereas patients with relatively greater social competence manifested complaints that could be traditionally labeled neurotic, patients with less social competence tended to manifest more acting-out behavior (such as suicide attempts or violent behavior). Moreover, Zigler and Phillips found that premorbid levels of social competence tended to be good predictors of length of hospitalization and posthospitalization adjustment.

Despite this relatively well established connection, a similar link between social skill deficits and the presence of specifically psychosomatic or psychophysiological disorders has not been well established until relatively recently. The present paper will provide a brief review of the current status of the concept of psychosomatic disorders, describe the hypothesized connection between social skill deficits and the onset of such disorders, and provide an illustration of the use of social skills training in the treatment of psychosomatic disorders.

Psychosomatic Disorders: Current Status of the Concept

The Diagnostic and Statistical Manual of the American Psychiatric Association (1968) defines psychosomatic or psychophysiological disorders as being characterized by: (1) psychological stress or emotional arousal as causative agents, (2) the presence of actual tissue damage in the organism, and (3) autonomic, rather than central, nervous system innervation of the affected areas. Additionally, a differentiation has been made between these disorders, which include hypertension, ulcers, asthma, and headaches, and hysterical conversion reactions and hypochondriasis, which are respectively noted for somatic dysfunction and excessive preoccupation with bodily symptoms (Buss 1966; Maher 1966).

Despite this general agreement as to what constitutes a psychophysiological disorder, there has been no corresponding consensus regarding relevant etiological variables. Most of the theories of the origins of these disorders have developed from two viewpoints, relatively isolated from each other, and emphasize either biological or psychological variables respectively. Regardless of their emphasis, these theories have usually shared one common feature, their tendency to identify a single variable as the most important determinant of most, if not all, psychophysiological disorders.

On the one hand, biological theories of psychosomatic disorders have tended to rely heavily on the concepts of stress (Selye 1956) and pre-existing somatic weakness (Wolff 1953). According to the former, prolonged exposure to threatening environmental stimuli is the cause of continuous arousal of the sympathetic nervous system which, over time, will lead to exhaustion and failure of the physiological mechanisms maintaining this prolonged arousal. According to the latter, such factors as genetic predisposition and prior illnesses result in the weakening of certain organ systems in the body, which leads to a high degree of vulnerability when the organism is subjected to subsequent stress. A relatively sophisticated variant of the somatic weakness theory is that of inherited autonomic patterns (Lacey, Bateman, and Van Lehn 1953), which states that each individual reacts to a variety of environmental stressors in a consistent, hierarchical, physiological response pattern. Thus, over a period of time, that physiological response system that is maximally reactive in an individual could conceivably develop into a psychophysiological disorder, assuming that the individual concerned was exposed to an inordinate amount of stress.

On the other hand, theories that emphasize the psychological origins of psychological disorders have traditionally originated within a psychodynamic or trait orientation. Like biological theories of psychosomatic disorders, these theories place a great deal of importance on one variable as the principal cause of disorders, to the exclusion of all other factors. For example, Dunbar (1943) postulated that different personality traits were responsible for the eventual appearance of different psychosomatic disorders. Thus, patients suffering from cardiac arrhythmia were seen as being sensitive, insecure, and fearful of manifesting hostility, whereas hypertensive patients were hypothesized to be ambitious, perfectionistic, and ambivalent. In contrast, Alexander (1950; Alexander and

Flagg 1965) emphasized the effects of certain basic personality conflicts that were specific to each psychosomatic disorder. Reflecting the psychoanalytic orientation of this approach, a typical specific conflict would be Alexander's conceptualization of asthma patients as suffering from excessive, unresolved dependence upon the mother, a conflict expressed by a symptom that represents a suppressed cry for the mother. Yet another psychologically based approach to the origin of psychosomatic disorders is that of Graham (Grace and Graham 1952). This approach stresses that, rather than specific personality traits or specific intrapsychic conflicts, the critical variable in producing psychosomatic disorders is an individual's attitude to a stressful situation. The basic similarity of this approach to those previously described would appear to lie in the fact that, although each espouses a different etiological variable, all assume that a degree of one-to-one specificity exists between the various precipitating variables and different psychosomatic disorders.

Despite the proliferation of theories concerned with the etiology of psychophysiological disorders, there has been no corresponding trend in this literature suggesting that any of these theories have any unique or specific implications for the treatment of these disorders. Rather, there appears to have developed a consensus to the effect that, regardless of etiological variables, treatment of psychophysiological disorders should focus most immediately upon somatic treatment of the physiological symptoms (such as drug treatment, rest, diet or surgery) in order to stabilize the individual's physical condition (Lachman 1972). Once this is accomplished, however, Alexander and Flagg (1965) state that, "Psychotherapy is the only treatment which can alter the patient's psychic conflict, which constitutes the primary disturbance in the chain of events" (p. 874). In this context, psychotherapy usually refers to psychodynamically oriented therapy, which has typically had as its goal either the establishment of an anxiety-reducing therapeutic relationship or the achievement of insight into the nature of the anxiety producing unconscious conflicts.

As may be readily seen, the heretofore prevailing approach of searching for the specific single causes of a relatively circumscribed group of disorders has been in existence for a considerable period of time. Nevertheless, this approach has encountered considerable criticism, on the grounds that it possesses limited scientific value and has not tended to be supported by empirical data (Lader 1972; Weiss 1974). In addition, it has been further suggested that, in order to be relevant, the psychosomatic approach should pay less attention to intrapsychic variables and more to the socioecological variables (Schwab, McGinnis, Morris, and Schwab, 1970).

The current state of the psychosomatic approach has perhaps best been summarized by Lipowski (1968). Among the principal characteristics of the revised psychosomatic model, Lipowski lists: (1) a trend away from the search for psychogenesis of a limited number of disorders, (2) a focus on the relationship between specific psychological variables and physiological processes, rather than specific diseases, (3) a stress on psychological description, rather than interpretation, (4) an emphasis on the effects of environmental influences, mediated through symbolic activity, on the maintenance of health and development of illness, (5) a concern with the psychosocial conditions that determine the timing of onset of many diseases and their course, and (6) greater awareness of the complex factors that maintain health and precipitate and determine the course of all diseases, along with the greater emphasis on controlled clinical and experimental studies (p. 417). Therefore, the revised conceptualization of problems usually labeled as psychosomatic has been expanded to include far more than the disorders originally studied by Alexander and French (1948), that is, hyperthyroidism, neurodermatitis, peptic ulcer, rheumatoid arthritis, essential hypertension, bronchial asthma, and ulcerative colitis. In addition, it has become generally agreed that behavioral and environmental factors play a role in the predisposition, development, and outcome of all physical disorders, although the degree of importance of these factors may vary considerably from one disorder to another. There is, nevertheless, yet another kind of dysfunction that has recently been added to those disorders labeled psychosomatic. This consists of those patients who present physical complaints for which no organic cause can be adequately determined and who have traditionally been labeled as suffering from hysterical conversion reactions, hypochondriasis, psychogenic pain, or somatization reactions.

Pilowsky (1969) has taken a look at these patients and has concluded that the traditional diagnostic practice of differentiating between these patients and those labeled as psychophysiological reactions is not very useful; the practice has, in fact, led to a considerable amount of confusion. Pilowsky further maintains that, despite clearly delineated theoretical differences, it is exceptionally difficult in practice to distinguish successfully among these conditions. Therefore, it is Pilowsky's contention that perpetuating the distinctions only maintains a system with very little heuristic value and few, if any, implications for treatment. The solution proposed by Pilowsky to this dilemma is the replacement of these overlapping diagnostic categories by a concept known as abnormal illness behavior. This concept, which has been independently proposed by other investigators and labeled "pain behavior" (Fordyce 1976; Fordyce, Fowler, Lehman, and DeLateur, 1968; Sternbach 1968, 1974), represents a departure from the conventional psychiatric approaches, in that it de-emphasizes traditional nosological labels and focuses instead on a cluster of functionally related behaviors as its area of interest.

The concept of pain behavior can thus be best understood by referring to the sociological concepts of the sick role (Parsons 1951) and of illness behavior (Mechanic 1962, 1972). According to Parsons, the sick role refers to a social role granted by society to a person when he or she suffers an illness that is legitimized by medical sanction. An individual in the sick role is thus permitted to engage in certain behaviors, such as visiting physicians and taking medications, and to avoid other normally required behaviors, such as work or physical activity. This, however, is contingent upon the individual's cooperation in his treatment in order to become well again. Mechanic (1962, 1972) proposed the concept of illness behavior to refer to "the ways in which given symptoms may be differentially perceived, evaluated, and acted (or not acted) upon by different kinds of persons" (p. 189). This, then, refers to the way in which all individuals react to pain or illness, with some persons ignoring pain and avoiding treatment at one end of a continuum and others responding to the slightest physical symptom at the other end. Viewed from this perspective, the concept of abnormal illness behavior proposed by Pilowsky describes a situation in which an individual exhibits behaviors characteristic of the sick role, but lacks the objective pathology required for social sanctioning.

Despite minor discrepancies, there appears to be fairly general agreement among investigators as to the components of abnormal illness behavior. Pilowsky (1969) identifies a presence of physical complaints, usually involving pain, anxiety, depression, and frequent hospitalizations and surgical interventions. Fordyce (1976; Fordyce et al. 1968) describes verbal complaints, nonverbal pain behaviors, such as moaning or grimacing, decreased physical activity level, special postures, and frequent requests for help or pain-relieving medication from others. Sternbach (1974) has included depression, using physical illness as coping style, and anxiety. Blackwell, Wooley, and Whitehead (1974) have identified pain or disability disproportionate to disease or tissue damage, a lifestyle arranged around the sick role, a constant search for diagnosis and treatment that never succeeds, interpersonal behaviors that elicit caretaking responses from physicians and relatives, and successful avoidance of social or occupational activities, for which the individual may lack the skills or have experienced failure in the past.

If the reconceptualization of the psychomatic approach is understood to include all of the disorders discussed above, it is obvious not only that it encompasses a far wider range of phenomena than it did originally, but also that such a model has implications for defining its events of interest, their assessment, and their treatment different from the original concept of psychosomatic disorders. In the first place, the current model of psychosomatic disorders encompasses not only individuals with psychophysiological disorders, but also those traditionally labeled hysterical, hypochondriacal, and somatopsychological disorders, i.e., individuals whose behavior has changed as the result of a purely physical event, such as trauma or infectious disease. Another traditional distinction that is ignored by this revised approach is that of physical or "real" pain, as opposed to "psychogenic" pain. As Sternbach (1968) has pointed out, pain is not a unitary phenomenon, but a construct which can refer to neurological, physiological, cognitive-affective, or behavioral events, any one of which can occur independently of the others. Thus, one implication of the revised psychosomatic approach is that, as long as the behavioral topography of various individuals is similar, there would appear to be little need for diagnostic labels.

In the view of the recent developments described above in the area of psychosomatic medicine, it is apparent that a need for new therapeutic strategies in this area has been created. The techniques of behavior therapy or behavior modification would appear to be especially well-suited for dealing with the problems presented by the revised psychosomatic approach, given the emphasis on socio-environmental variables and lack of interest in diagnostic labels. The speed and magnitude of the impact of behavior therapy on this area can best be appreciated by a brief review of the relevant literature. Yates (1970) and Kanfer and Phillips (1970) do not mention either psychosomatic disorders or possible applications of behavioral principles to these disorders in their classic behavior therapy texts. Bandura (1969) limits his discussion to references to two case studies. The first of these, by Walton (1960), deals with a case of neurodermatitis treated by means of withholding social attention for scratching behavior. The second, by Ayllon and Haughton (1962), describes the extinction of frequent somatic complaints, also accomplished by the removal of social reinforcement. In addition, Bandura mentions Miller's (1969) work on the operant conditioning of autonomic functioning and notes its potential in treatment of psychosomatic disorders. Since that time, there has been an exponential increase of both clinical applications and publications on this topic, including review chapters in behavior therapy texts (Knapp and Peterson 1976; Shapiro and Surwit 1976) and entire books (Birk 1973; Katz and Zlutnick 1975; Williams and Gentry 1977).

The expansion of the principles of behavior therapy into the area of physical health care has even resulted in the recent popularization of a new term. In an effort to avoid the controversial and often misleading label of "psychosomatic," this area has recently come to be known as behavioral medicine (Williams and Gentry 1977). Blanchard (1977) has described the domain of behavioral medicine as encompassing four distinct areas: (1) the application of behavioral principles as an adjunct to surgical and chemical means of intervention in the treatment of disorders that have been traditionally considered medical (such as headaches, hypertension, and obesity); (2) the use of these principles in the provision of standard medical treatment, that is, as a means of enchancing adherence to medical prescriptions; (3) direct conditioning of physiological responses by means of biofeedback procedures; and (4) as a tool in the establishment of behaviors designed to enhance health, thus serving a primary prevention function.

Social Competence and Psychosomatic Disorders

As might be expected, given the degree of recent interest in applying behavioral principles to the management of physical disorders, a wide variety of behavioral intervention techniques has been employed within the last few years. For example, Fordyce and his co-workers (Fordyce 1976; Fordyce et al. 1971) have employed a rather straightforward application of operant principles in the modification of operant pain behavior, that is, verbalized complaints, grimaces, abusing medication, inappropriate help-seeking behavior, and unwillingness to walk. Levendusky and Pankratz (1975) have described the use of behavioral self-control techniques (Kanfer and Karoly 1972) as an alternative to pain medication with a client in an inpatient setting. Relaxation training (Bernstein and Borkovec 1973) has been a frequently used technique in the treatment of physical disorders because of its ability to reduce the level of autonomic arousal. Thus, relaxation training has been utilized in the treatment of asthma (Alexander 1972; Sirota and Mahoney 1974), neurodermatitis (Bar and Kuypers 1973), and has been proposed as a treatment for essential hypertension (Schwartz and Shapiro 1973). In addition there appears to be some evidence that relaxation training may be an effective treatment modality in the management of sleep disturbance (Borkovec and Fowles 1973; Nicassio and Bootzin 1974). Perhaps the greatest amount of work to date, however, has taken place in the realm of biofeedback training. Reviews of the clinical biofeedback literature (Blanchard and Young 1974; Shapiro and Surwit 1976) indicate that the bulk of the clinical biofeedback research has been conducted in the areas of blood pressure feedback for hypertension (Schwartz and Shapiro 1973), heart rate feedback for cardiac arrhythmias (Weiss and Engel 1971) and electromyograph (EMG) feedback for a variety of purposes, most notably muscle retaining (Johnson and Garton, 1973), elimination of sub-vocal speech during reading (Hardyck, Petrinovich, and Ellsworth 1966), relaxation training (Raskin, Johnson, and Rondestvedt 1973), and the reduction of headaches (Budzynski, Stoyva, Adler, and Mullaney 1973).

Compared with the abundance of literature describing the application of these behavioral techniques to physical problems, social skills training is a relative newcomer. Nevertheless, it does seem reasonable to hypothesize that social skills training would be an appropriate intervention strategy for these disorders. Wolpe (1973) maintains that assertion training is helpful in numerous situations, including those in which "the suppression of action that would give outward expression to feeling results in continuing inner turmoil, which may produce psychosomatic symptoms and even pathological changes in predisposed organs'' (p. 81). Birk (1973) has urged the incorporation of several related behavioral strategies, such as biofeedback, relaxation training, and assertion training into a broad-based program designed to focus on the various sources of arousal and anxiety responsible for psychosomatic symptoms. In his discussion of Mitchell's work, which will be described in more detail below, Price (1974) refers to the work by Hokanson (Hokanson and Burgess 1962; Stone and Hokanson 1969) to suggest that the inhibition of emotional behavior or the inability to cope successfully with stress, which is observed in temporary cardiovascular arousal in the laboratory, may lead to migraine attacks or hypertension in some genetically predisposed individuals. On the basis of this evidence, Price suggests that assertion training may be an important treatment modality in the management of physical disorders.

Despite the intuitive appeal of this position, there has been to date a scarcity of empirical data. A notable exception to this is the work of Mitchell (1969; Mitchell and Mitchell 1971; Mitchell and White 1976, 1977). This research, which has concentrated on the application of behavioral techniques to migraine headaches, represents one of the few attempts to date of applying social skills training procedures to a population usually considered to be suffering from a medical disorder. In an initial study, Mitchell (1969) treated ten migraine subjects with a combination of applied relaxation training, desensitization, and assertion training, and found that migraine attacks decreased by 67 percent after treatment, while three control subjects reported no change in frequency. Later, a pair of studies reported by Mitchell and Mitchell (1971) compared subjects undergoing the ''combined desensitization'' procedure (relaxation plus desensitization plus assertion training) to subjects receiving relaxation training alone, desensitization alone, and no treatment. The results of these studies revealed that, in both instances, the combined treatment package (which included assertion training) was significantly more effective than single treatments or the no treatment control group in reducing both the frequency of migraine episodes and the hours of duration of attack. More recently, Mitchell and White (1976) published a case study in which a female migraine patient was treated by a variety of behavioral techniques collectively labeled as ''behavioral self-management.'' In addition to training in such areas as defining problems behaviorally, goal setting, self-monitoring and self-recording, and relaxation training, training was provided in assertive skills via modeling and behavioral rehearsal. The results indicated that the patient reported a mean migraine reduction of 7 percent after baseline, 72 percent after treatment, and 81 percent after booster training. In an even more recent study, Mitchell and White (1977) compared subjects who underwent self-recording and self-monitoring procedures over a 60-week period with subjects who were given training similar to that described in the preceding case study.

Results of this study tended to indicate that, although self-monitoring and self-recording did not affect the frequency of migraine headaches, the self-management training did succeed in at least a 50 percent decrease in migraine frequency.

The Present Study

As Mitchell's data indicate, the application of a social skills training program to patients suffering from a "psychosomatic" disorder appears to have great potential benefit. However, the evidence to date for this is indirect, insofar as the application of such a program has always been in conjunction with other behavioral techniques, such as relaxation training or desensitization. The purpose of the present study, then, was to (1) isolate and test the efficacy of a behavioral-social skills training approach treatment of migraine headaches, (2) compare the effectiveness of this social skills training approach with that of temperature biofeedback (Sargent, Green, and Walters 1973), and (3) compare the effectiveness of social skills training to that of relaxation training alone, which was found to be relatively ineffective by Mitchell and Mitchell (1971). In addition, a test was made of Mitchell and White's (1976) hypothesis that a skills-training approach should be the most effective treatment modality, by virtue of its modification of responses occurring earlier in the response chain than those of either relaxation or biofeedback training.

The study was conducted in an inpatient facility at a university-affiliated medical center, specializing in the behavioral treatment of patients manifesting chronic pain and/or disability (for a more detailed description of this program, see Blackwell, Wooley, and Whitehead 1974; Fedoravicius, et al. 1977; Wooley and Blackwell 1975; Wooley, Blackwell, Fedoravicius, Terry, Bird, and Pudlish, 1976). Although relaxation training, biofeedback, and social skills training constituted an integral part of the regular inpatient program, these treatments were usually administered concurrently, thus rendering it impossible to separate the effects of each type of training from the others. In addition, aside from the fact that all of the inpatients in the program manifested chronic pain and disability disproportionate to tissue damage, they tended to be a heterogeneous group of patients, manifesting many different types of somatic complaints. For that reason, it was decided to recruit volunteer outpatients for the present study, all of whom would manifest the same presenting complaint. In view of the fact that Mitchell's work had been conducted exclusively with migraine headache patients, it was decided to conduct the present study using patients with that complaint.

Method

Subjects. Subjects were 24 female outpatient volunteers, 18 years of age and older, having been diagnosed by a physician as suffering from migraine headaches. Whenever possible, an attempt was made to include subjects who had: (1) a history of headaches dating back at least two years, (2) an average headache frequency of at least one or two times a week, (3) unilateral head pain, (4) a history of similar headaches in at least one family member, (5) responsiveness of headache to treatment by ergotamine tartrate, (6) prevalence of some sensory-perceptual disturbance prior to onset of most headaches, (7) occurrence of nausea, vomiting, or photophobia during the headache phase at least part of the time, and (8) gradual (at least 10 to 15 minutes), rather than sudden onset of headache. However, due to the difficulty involved in obtaining large numbers of subjects, it was decided to include in the study individuals who met at least 50 percent of the criteria. Subjects were recruited from the general community by means of advertisement in the university and city newspapers. At the time of initial contact, subjects signed a consent form for release of information, which was sent to their personal physicians requesting relevant information from their medical records.

Subjects were randomly assigned to one of three groups. These groups were: (1) the social competence or social skills training, (2) temperature biofeedback training, and (3) relaxation training. In the absence of a no treatment control group, each subject served as her own control during the one-month baseline period prior to the experimental intervention. Data were also collected during a one-month intervention period and a one-month follow-up period.

Procedure. During an introductory group meeting, prospective subjects were given a brief explanation of the purpose of this study and were informed of what they would expect to take place if they agreed to participate in this study. After a general discussion of the different treatment modalities to be used in the present study, subjects were asked to fill out a treatment contract, a release of information form, and a battery of self-report inventories, including Gambrill and Richey's (1975) Assertion Inventory (AI). In addition, prospective subjects were asked to provide a refundable deposit. They were asked to write out four checks for five dollars apiece, payable to a charity of their choice, and informed that this money would be completely refunded, but would only be available to them at the end of the one-month baseline period, after two weeks of training, at the end of the four-week training phase, and at the end of a one-month follow-up.

All prospective subjects were informed at this time that contacting physicians to obtain information, scoring the self-report inventories, and assigning subjects to groups would take about four weeks. Therefore, they were asked to begin collecting baseline headache data in the meantime. They were further informed that any prospective subjects whose personal physician disapproved of her participation in the study would have her money completely refunded at the end of the four-week baseline period. All persons attending these introductory meetings agreed to participate under these conditions.

During the next four weeks, subjects kept daily records of the frequency and intensity of their headaches, as well as of their medication intake, by means of data sheets based upon those developed by Sargent, Walters, and Green (1973). These sheets required the subjects to monitor on a daily basis the presence or absence of headache, the type of headache, intensity of pain, duration of headache, degree of disability from the headache, the presence or absence of associated symptoms, and the type and amount of medication used.

Although self-monitoring of some behaviors has been found to have reactive effects on their frequency (Kazdin 1974a; McFall 1970), it does not appear that these reactive effects are the same across all behaviors (Sieck and McFall 1976). Thus, based on some preliminary observations by Mitchell and White (1976), it was tentatively concluded that self-monitoring procedures would have minimally reactive effects on the target behaviors relative to this study.

During the last week of the four-week baseline period, subjects were recontacted and informed of which treatment group they had been assigned to. For the next four weeks, the experimental procedures differed for each of the three treatment groups. Subjects in the relaxation-training group attended group sessions, composed of five subjects each, twice a week. In these sessions, they were provided with instructions for achieving muscle relaxation based on Bernstein and Borkovec's (1973) progressive relaxation training. These sessions were administered by one of two graduate students in clinical psychology, including the present author. The twice-weekly sessions, which lasted approximately 45-60 minutes each, continued for four weeks, a total of eight sessions. In addition to the relaxation-training sessions, subjects were instructed to practice the relaxation techniques at home twice each day for a total of approximately one hour, as well as whenever they felt a headache starting, and to record the total amount of time practiced each day on their daily headache charts. Subjects in this group were provided with a treatment rationale that focused on the importance of reducing the amount of physiological arousal in order to prevent migraine headache.

Subjects in the temperature biofeedback training group received instructions in learning to control blood flow to the hands in a manner based upon the procedures described by Sargent, Walters, and Green (1973). That is, they were first provided with a list of "autogenic phrases" (Schultz and

Luthe 1969), designed to help them achieve a state of passive relaxation throughout the body and also to achieve warmth in the hands. The principal difference in the present study and Sargent et al.'s procedure is that, instead of using a "temperature trainer" that indicates the difference in temperature between the forehead and the index finger, subjects in the present study used a thermobiofeedback unit that measures the temperature in the index finger only. In addition, the emphasis in the present study was more on the actual hand warming training than on having the subjects repeat the autogenic phrases to themselves during each session. Rather, subjects were encouraged to generate their own cognitive statements and images that facilitated hand warming.

As with the relaxation-training group, subjects were run in small groups (two subjects instead of five). Since they had to share the available thermobiofeedback unit, each subject spent about one-half of each 30-minute session actually obtaining direct feedback and the rest of the time trying to achieve a relaxed, "hand warming" state either by means of practicing the autogenic phrases or by generating their own cognitive images. An experimenter, who was also a graduate student in clinical psychology, was present in the room at all times to facilitate transfer of the biofeedback unit from one subject to another, by means of a junction box. However, the experimenter remained silent throughout the session except whenever it was necessary to provide the subject with any instructions.

This group also received twice-weekly sessions for a total of four weeks, each session lasting approximately one-half hour. In addition each subject was instructed to practice at home twice a day using a fever thermometer for a total of about an hour, as well as whenever they felt the onset of a headache. The treatment rationale given to subjects in this group was that, whereas migraine episodes appear to be the result of too much blood in the head (vasodilation), hand warming is thought to reduce this blood volume by diverting it to the hands. No mention was made of Sargent et al.'s sympathetic control hypothesis, which states that patients learning hand warming are, in effect, learning to "turn off" excessive sympathetic outflow.

The purpose of the social skills training group, on the other hand, was to attempt to provide subjects with new interpersonal coping skill for situations that usually lead to anxiety, anger, or frustration in their daily lives. Theoretically, this should prove helpful in reducing migraine attacks, given the observation that migraine attacks often have significant psychological precipitants (Bakal 1975). The present study attempted to use this group to isolate the therapeutic effectiveness of Mitchell and Mitchell's (1971) combined desensitization procedure minus the relaxation and desensitization components.

Subjects in this group, as in the other two groups, met twice a week for a total of four weeks. Sessions for this group, however, lasted 45-60 minutes, a period comparable to that of the relaxation-training group. Subjects met in groups of five. The therapist in this experimental condition was either a clinical psychology graduate student or a psychiatric nurse with experience conducting social skill training groups. The procedure for this group was similar to Mitchell and White's (1976) case study using behavioral self-management for treatment of migraines. Subjects were given a brief introduction of such behavioral concepts as conditioning, reinforcement, and self-monitoring and how these concepts might apply to the onset, maintenance, and possible change of their migraine episodes. Subjects were taught to self-monitor their behavior, identify interpersonal situations that contribute to the onset or worsening of their headaches, and identify certain of their own behavioral excesses or deficits that prevented them from being maximally effective, as well as aspects of other persons' behavior that contributed to their headaches.

In addition, subjects in this group were taught social competence skills by means of a procedure based on that described by Liberman et al. (1976), which relies heavily upon: (1) behavioral rehearsal of selected relevant situations, with each subject having a chance to role play these situations; (2) feedback from therapist and other subjects, both of a positive and of a corrective nature; (3) modeling by therapist or other subjects of appropriate behaviors; and (4) individualized assignments, to be completed between sessions and recorded on subject's daily charts, along with their headache data. Treatment rationale for these subjects focused on the prophylactic effect of social competence training in preventing daily stress from accumulating and resulting in sufficient tension levels to trigger migraine attacks.

In addition, all three treatment groups continued daily monitoring of headache activity and medication intake throughout the intervention period. At the end of the one-month training phase, subjects were post-tested on the same self-report inventories given to them at the time of initial contact.

Immediately after the conclusion of the intervention phase, there was a follow-up period identical to the baseline period. Subjects were asked to continue their daily record keeping for another four weeks and a follow-up contact was scheduled for all subjects one month after the end of treatment. The last of the subject's deposit money was refunded to them at this time.

Results

Pre-existing Group Differences. Due to the nature of this study, it was impossible to follow strictly a procedure of random assignment to treatment groups. Some of the reasons for this were: (1) availability of facilities, (2) therapist availability, and (3) subjects' personal schedules. Therefore, subjects were assigned to treatment groups as follows: prior to the study, subjects were provided with a schedule of times and asked to check those hours during which they would be available for training. Then, subjects were organized into groups by the investigator on the basis of their responses to this schedule. The next step was to contact the therapists and ask them to list their availability. Finally, after the subjects were arranged into groups and had been assigned a therapist, the groups were randomly assigned to the three training conditions.

Due to this procedural variation, it was decided to compare subjects in the three training conditions with each other on certain relevant variables (age, time since migraine onset, estimated frequency, intensity, and duration of migraine episodes) in order to ensure that no pretreatment group differences existed (table 11.1). Statistical analysis of these variables indicated that subjects assigned to social skills training, relaxation training, and biofeedback training did not differ significantly from each other prior to training in age ($F = 0.20$), number of years since the onset of migraines ($F = 2.80$), monthly frequency of migraines ($F = 1.63$), rate of migraine intensity ($F = 0.29$), or duration of migraines ($F = 1.67$). Data for these comparisons were taken from subjects' responses to a preexperimental questionnaire.

Table 11.1. Demographic Characteristics of Experimental Subjects

		Social Skills Training	Relaxation Training	Biofeedback Training
Age (Yrs.)	$\overline{X}$	34.78	36.44	38.71[1]
	S.D.	10.78	14.08	13.30
Time since migraine onset (Yrs.)	$\overline{X}$	16.22	15.22	19.29[2]
	S.D.	12.76	5.59	16.23
Migraine frequency (X/Mo.)	$\overline{X}$	9.14	6.67	5.08[3]
	S.D.	10.33	9.72	5.57
Migraine intensity (0-10)	$\overline{X}$	8.22	8.43	8.71[4]
	S.D.	2.33	1.27	1.38
Migraine duration (Hrs.)	$\overline{X}$	16.56	29.22	41.57[5]
	S.D.	21.86	27.70	62.60

1) F= 0.20, N.S.
2) F= 2.18, N.S.
3) F= 1.63, N.S.
4) F= 0.29, N.S.
5) F= 1.67, N.S.

Table 11.2. Means and Standard Deviations of Daily Self-Monitored Headache Variables

		Social-Skills Training (n = 9)		Relaxation Training (n = 8)		Biofeedback Training (n = 7)	
		$\overline{X}$	S.D.	$\overline{X}$	S.D.	$\overline{X}$	S.D.
Number of Migraines (days)	Pre:	6.89	4.81	4.00	2.39	6.57	7.41
	Post:	5.22	3.23	2.50	1.41	4.43	4.58
	Follow-up:	3.56	2.79	3.75	1.83	4.00	5.10
Number of Total headaches (days)	Pre:	14.78	3.90	10.00	7.31	11.57	8.20
	Post:	12.56	6.48	7.75	7.13	7.00	4.16
	Follow-up:	8.11	3.98	6.50	4.69	5.43	5.47
Total self-reported headache intensity (1-4/day)	Pre:	26.67	9.33	20.25	12.68	23.86	19.39
	Post:	19.11	10.80	15.25	13.88	12.29	7.02
	Follow-up:	12.44	5.03	15.50	10.62	9.86	7.99
Number of days with associated symptoms (days)	Pre:	5.33	4.42	5.50	4.31	4.86	7.29
	Post:	3.00	1.58	5.63	5.93	3.29	3.45
	Follow-up:	2.78	2.39	3.13	2.75	3.86	5.18
Total self-reported degree of disability (0-4/day)	Pre:	7.56	3.43	8.88	6.77	9.57	8.46
	Post:	5.56	3.36	7.63	7.99	3.71	2.21
	Follow-up:	3.44	2.13	6.50	5.07	3.14	2.73
Total migraine duration (hrs.)	Pre:	55.33	39.82	42.38	38.98	56.43	69.56
	Post:	42.89	38.47	31.50	26.92	41.00	48.77
	Follow-up:	20.00	17.08	47.75	33.03	35.00	52.21
Total number of medication taken	Pre:	49.89	43.58	25.75	24.61	74.43	90.65
	Post:	25.22	25.16	17.13	19.51	41.29	43.37
	Follow-up:	18.44	14.66	18.63	20.44	29.86	36.52

Daily Self-Reported Headache Data. The principal variables of clinical interest in the present study consisted of the observations recorded daily by subjects on their daily headache sheets. As mentioned above, subjects were requested to record on these sheets the frequency of migraine episodes, the frequency of all types of headaches, the degree of headache intensity, the frequency of associated symptoms, the degree of headache-produced disability, the duration of migraine episodes, and the number of medications taken.

Based on Mitchell and Mitchell's (1971) findings, there was a precedent for assuming that relaxation training alone would not be a very effective therapeutic technique. Moreover, in Mitchell and White's (1976) opinion, the social skills training group might have been expected to show greater change in these variables than the biofeedback training group, insofar as the former group placed greater emphasis on training subjects to cope with environmental stressors prior to headache onset, whereas the latter focused primarily on the last link in the behavioral chain preceding the onset of migraine headache attacks.

Nevertheless, the results failed to bear out these hypotheses. A series of one-between/one-within analyses of variance indicated that there were no differential rates of change among the three training groups on any of the daily self-reported headache variables. In fact, the results for each of these variables were quite uniform (tablc 11.2), revealing a significant pretreatment-posttreatment main effect for frequency of migraine episodes ($F=5.98$, $p < .01$), frequency of all types of headaches ($F=19.12$, $p < .001$), headache intensity ($F=14.53$, $p < .001$), frequency of associated symptoms ($F=4.05$, $p < .025$), degree of headache-produced disability ($F=9.68$, $p < .001$), duration of migraine episodes ($F=3.23$, $p < .05$), and number of medications taken ($F=7.68$, $p < .005$). In all cases, main effects for treatment groups and interaction effects were not statistically significant.

Furthermore, a correlation matrix computed for these variables (table 11.3) reveals that, prior to treatment, there existed significant intercorrelations among all of the listed variables. Of these 21 significant correlation coefficients, eight were significant at the $p < .05$ level, ranging from $r=.41$ to $r=.48$. The remaining 13 coefficients were significant at the $p < .01$ level and ranged from $r=0.51$ to $r=.84$. A similar correlation matrix for these variables computed after the start of the training phase, however, reveals a different pattern (table 11.4). Out of the 21 correlation coefficients, only ten reached significance. If these ten coefficients, two were significant at the $p < .05$ level and the remaining eight were significant at the $p < .01$ level. Similarly, a correlation matrix for these variables during the follow-up period (table 11.5) shows a slight increase in overall intercorrelation (14 significant correlations out of 21; three at the $p < .05$ level and 11 at the $p < .01$ level) which, nevertheless, does not match that of the pretreatment levels.

Thus, an examination of these results reveals that the various self-monitored aspects of migraine episodes, such as frequency, intensity, duration, and number of medications taken, tended to correlate very highly with each other prior to treatment. A noteworthy phenomenon to be found in these data would appear to be the fact that the amount of medication intake, which was significantly correlated with all other variables prior to treatment, became consistently nonsignificantly correlated once treatment began and remained so during the follow-up period, thus accounting for most of the difference in degree of intercorrelation at these times compared to the pretreatment period.

Table 11.3. Intercorrelations Among Daily Self-Monitored Headache Variables Prior to Treatment

	Migraine Frequency	Total Headache Frequency	Total Headache Intensity	Assoc. Symptom Frequency	Total Degree of Disability	Total Migraine Duration	Total number of Medications
Migraine frequency	1.00	.43*	.62**	.46*	.48*	.84**	.48*
Total headache frequency		1.00	.84**	.58**	.66**	.41*	.58**
Total headache intensity			1.00	.61**	.79**	.59**	.68**
Assoc. symptom frequency				1.00	.69**	.51**	.41*
Total degree of disability					1.00	.42*	.51**
Total migraine duration						1.00	.43*
Total number of medications							1.00

*p < .05 **p < .01

Table 11.4. Intercorrelations Among Daily Self-Monitored Headache Variables After Treatment

	Migraine Frequency	Total Headache Frequency	Total Headache Intensity	Assoc. Symptom Frequency	Total Degree of Disability	Total Migraine Duration	Total number of Medications
Migraine frequency	1.00	.47*	.26	.27	.18	.82**	.33
Total headache frequency		1.00	.89**	.46**	.66**	.50**	.36
Total headache intensity			1.00	.60**	.73**	.33	.22
Assoc. symptom frequency				1.00	.80**	.49**	.04
Total degree of disability					1.00	.39	.05
Total migraine duration						1.00	.33
Total numberof medications							1.00

*$p < .05$ **$p < .01$

Table 11.5. Intercorrelations Among Daily Self-Monitored Headache Variables at One-Month Follow-up

	Migraine Frequency	Total Headache Frequency	Total Headache Intensity	Assoc. Symptom Frequency	Total Degree of Disability	Total Migraine Duration	Total number of Medications
Migraine frequency	1.00	.59**	.51**	.78**	.32	.83**	.03
Total headache frequency		1.00	.85**	.62**	.42*	.62**	.08
Total headache intensity			1.00	.59**	.76**	.66**	.20
Assoc. symptom frequency				1.00	.41*	.81**	−.10
Total degree of disability					1.00	.48*	.20
Total migraine duration						1.00	−.06
Total number of medications							1.00

$^*p < .05$ $^{**}p < .01$

In summary, it may be stated that all three of the training procedures employed in the present study appear to be effective in reducing the frequency, intensity, duration, and medication intake associated with migraine headaches, at least at a statistically significant level. Contrary to Mitchell and Mitchell's findings, it was not found that relaxation training alone was a less effective technique for reducing migraine headaches than other behavioral techniques. In addition, it was found that social skills training by itself possessed some degree of effectiveness, at least comparable to that of biofeedback, in reducing these episodes of migraine headaches.

Assertion Inventory Scores. The results of the Gambrill and Richey Assertion Inventory Scale proved to be quite similar to those of the daily self-reported headache variables. Once again, the results indicated that there were significant decreases over time in the discomfort scores, as well as significant increases over time on response probability (or assertion) scores. Group x time interaction effects failed to reach significance in both instances. Thus, there was no reason to believe that any of the groups changed at significantly different rates over time. However, subjects did manifest statistically higher levels of assertiveness and lower levels of interpersonal anxiety after training.

Discussion

On the basis of the results obtained in the present study, it may be tentatively concluded that social skills training appears to be therapeutically effective in the management of migraine headaches. However, contrary to Mitchell and White's (1976) assertion, it cannot be concluded that biofeedback and relaxation training are less effective than social skills training by virtue of being more "symptom oriented" and thus failing to provide patients with coping mechanisms for stress in general. In fact, the data fail to support the hypothesis that there was any differential effectiveness among the three treatment modalities employed in the present study.

In view of the above results, several questions readily arise. Among these are: (1) Were the observed changes in target behaviors real, or were they artifacts of the methodology employed in this study? (2) If the observed changes reflect actual decreases in the target behaviors, what were the specific mechanisms operating to produce the treatment? (3) What is the present status of social skills training as a viable therapeutic technique for physical disorders? (4) In what direction does future research in this area need to move?

The finding that it made no essential difference which treatment subjects were assigned to, insofar as the effect on the principal clinical target variables was concerned, raises immediate questions of whether any actual change in these measures took place, or whether the observed results occurred as a function of some artifact operating on all the treatment groups. More specifically, it may be asked whether these data were affected by reactivity or poor accuracy in self-recording (Kazdin 1974a; McFall 1970).

In order to answer this question, a brief review of the parameters of reactivity in self-monitoring may be helpful. This phenomenon has been reported in case studies (Maletsky 1974), within-subject experiments (Lipinski and Nelson 1974), and between-subject experiments (Johnson and White 1971). However, as Sieck and McFall (1976) have pointed out, this reactive effect is not uniform across all behaviors, but is largely dependent on factors such as the perceived value of the target behavior. Ciminero, Nelson, and Lipinski (1977) have reviewed the literature on variables that influence the degree of reactivity in self-monitoring and have concluded that variables which are relevant include: (1) valence of the target, with undesirable behaviors likely to decrease (Nelson, Lipinski, and Black 1976) and positive target behaviors likely to increase (Broden, Hall, and Mitts 1971); (2) motivation of subjects, with degree of motivation directly related to amount of reactivity (McFall and Hammen 1971); (3) presence of feedback (Kazdin 1974b) or reinforcement (Nelson et al., 1976), tending to increase reactivity; and (4) number of behaviors monitored, with reactivity greatest when only one behavior is monitored (Hayes and Cavior 1977). In addition, Ciminero et al. suggested that the longevity of these effects may be decreased when self-monitoring takes place on a continuous, rather than intermittent, basis and when the behavior being monitored has a relatively long history.

With respect to the accuracy of self-monitoring, it appears that it is improved when the self-monitored response is nonverbal (Cavior and Marabotto 1976), when subjects are not engaging in competing responses (Epstein, Miller, and Webster 1976), and when subjects are adults rather than children (Kazdin, 1974b).

Keeping the above literature in mind, the self-monitored headache data used in the present study may tentatively be evaluated. Insofar as it can be ascertained, the subjects in the present study were well-motivated to decrease the frequency of their symptoms. It may also be reasonably assumed that the variables self-monitored possessed a negative valence. On the basis of these observations, it might be expected that the obtained results were not free of a reactive effect. However, when it is taken into account that subjects received no feedback or reinforcement for their self-monitoring, that they monitored a number of different variables, and that the self-monitoring occurred on the continuous basis and focused on events of relatively long-standing duration, it may be tentatively concluded that the presence of a reactive effect was not sufficient to account for all of the observed changes in these variables.

A similar conclusion may be reached when judging the accuracy of self-monitoring by the criteria described above. One possible threat to the accuracy in the present study might arise from the failure to observe Jeffrey's (1974) suggestion that an independently assessed baseline be obtained before the start of self-monitoring. However, as Ciminero et al. point out, such a baseline is impossible to implement when the target behaviors of interest are covert, as they were in the present study. In any event, assuming that the baseline period in the present study consisted of data that were artificially low due to reactivity, it could be argued that the results provide a conservative estimate of the effects of the intervention. That is to say, if it had been possible to obtain a baseline prior to the beginning of self-monitoring, there would appear to be data to indicate that the frequency, intensity, and duration of the migraine episodes would have been even higher than they were in the observed baseline period.

Having ascertained that (a) no differential rate of therapeutic change existed among treatment groups and (b) not all of the observed change was due to factors such as reactivity or inaccuracy of self-monitoring, the next question that arises is what was this observed change due to? In other words, it must be asked whether any specific treatment effects took place, or whether this change could be accounted for by nonspecific factors, such as expectancy of improvement.

Before this question can be answered, a more detailed definition of nonspecific factors should be introduced. Bernstein and Nietzel (1977) have suggested that Orne's (1962) concept of demand characteristics is best able to subsume all of the nonspecific influences present in behavior modification. Chief among these are the concepts of placebo effects (Shapiro 1971) and expectancy effects (Lick and Bootzin 1970), which may be seen as equivalent for all practical purposes.

Since the first studies employing attention placebo control groups appeared (Lang, Lazovik, and Reynolds 1965; Paul 1966), the influence of demand characteristics has been acknowledged in diverse areas of psychology, particularly outcome research in psychotherapy, where almost every study presently includes such a control group (Bernstein and Nietzel 1977). The topic has generated considerable debate from both those who argue that nonspecific variables are responsible for most therapeutic change (Frank 1973) and those who are not convinced that the power of these variables has been adequately demonstrated (Wilkins 1973).

In any event, the present study attempted to evaluate the relative contribution of nonspecific effects by means of what Kazdin and Wilcoxon (1976) referred to as the empirically derived control strategy. In practice, this entails asking subjects to rate on a seven-point scale the plausibility of treatment rationale, its potential effectiveness, and subjects' willingness to participate in the treatment used in this study. This was done prior to assignment to treatments and again at the end of treatment. Despite the potential hazard of using self-report ratings (Kazdin and Wilcoxon 1976), it was felt that this method would provide at least a rough indication of subjects' expectancy.

The results of these ratings, reported elsewhere (Barrios 1977), indicated that none of the three treatments employed in the present differed significantly at pretest from each other or from insight-oriented psychotherapy or pharmacotherapy in terms of rated plausibility or effectiveness. Thus, there is some evidence to indicate that, prior to assignments to treatment group, there were no differential expectancies regarding the likelihood of deriving benefit from any of these techniques. On the basis of these results, it may be tentatively concluded that demand characteristics did not account for all of the observed changes in the headache variables.

If this is correct, it does remain to be explained precisely by what means the observed changes took place. Most recent formulations of the efficacy of behavior therapy, at least with migraine patients, tend to focus on a generalized lowering of physiological arousal as the key therapeutic ingredient. Sargent et al. (1973), for example, attribute the success of temperature biofeedback to the lowering of sympathetic arousal via limbic and hypothalamic mechanisms. Mitchell and Mitchell (1971) postulated that their "combined desensitization" treatment was successful because it treated both the constricted emotional expression of their subjects via assertion training, as well as excessive sympathetic nervous system arousal, by means of relaxation and desensitization. Finally, Blanchard and Epstein (1977) have concluded that "relaxation, broadly conceived, may account for many of the clinical effects" in behavioral treatment of migraines (p. 239). That is to say, regardless of whether this lowering of physiological arousal is part of an active coping skill (such as relaxation training), or whether it is conceived of as a "passive" phenomenon (such as biofeedback), the end results appear to be much the same. The social skills training subjects, by virtue of repeated behavioral rehearsal in a nonthreatening environment, and positive social reinforcement from peers and therapist, as well as possible success experiences in the natural environment during the training phase, may well have experienced a level of lowered physiological arousal comparable to that of the other two groups. Evidence for this may be found in the results of the assertion inventory, which indicate that subjects in the social skills training group reported lower levels of social anxiety after training, comparable to those of the two groups of subjects that were more directly trained in anxiety-reduction techniques.

In light of the above discussion, several general conclusions may be enumerated at this point. They are as follows: (1) social skills training would seem to be a viable and effective treatment strategy in the management of at least some "psychosomatic" disorders, (2) on the basis of the available evidence, there is no reason at present to conclude that any one behavioral intervention strategy is clearly superior to others, at least in the treatment of migraine headaches, (3) the nature of the specific change mechanism responsible for the therapeutic effect of behavioral techniques, including social skills training, on migraines remains unclear. However, some of the results obtained in the present study provide at least indirect evidence that lowered physiological arousal may be primarily responsible for the therapeutic effects, and (4) in view of the fact that at present there appears to be no one behavioral treatment of choice, the decision of which behavioral strategy to employ in the treatment of migraines should be dictated by other considerations, such as the cost-effectiveness of the strategy. In general, if similar clinical results can be obtained by using relatively inexpensive techniques, such as relaxation training, then it would seem to make sense to use these simpler methods.

In addition to the above conclusions, several suggestions for future research deserved to be mentioned. The first of these concerns the role and effect of drugs on the treatment of psychosomatic disorders. In a sense, the present study examined the effects of behavior therapy plus drugs on migraines, due to the fact that it was unfeasible, as well as ethically questionable, to deprive subjects of their medications. Future research would do well to consider this factor and attempt to gain some degree of control over it, perhaps by standardizing the kind and/or dosage of drug used, or perhaps by using medication as an independent variable. With a few exceptions (Liberman and Davis 1975), behavior therapists have tended to ignore the effects of this potentially powerful variable, an oversight which cannot be continued if behavioral medicine is to continue to be conceptualized within the framework of a "biopsycho-social model" of man (Engel 1977).

Further research also needs to be conducted to determine whether social skills training appears to be an effective therapeutic procedure with other biologically based disorders, besides migraine headaches. To date, the work of Mitchell and his co-workers, as well as the present study, has tended to focus on migraine headache patients, perhaps as a result of the fact that migraine patients are usually characterized as having difficulty in expressing anger or other emotions (Henryk-Gutt and Rees 1973). At present, however, the general applicability of social skills training as an effective therapeutic technique for "psychosomatic" disorders remains an open question.

Another area that certainly would appear to deserve attention would be an assessment of the results of the implementation of behavioral techniques, such as social skills training, on different response systems, such as physiological, subjective-cognitive, and overt-motoric (Lang 1968). Given the widely assumed relative independence of these three response systems (Hersen 1976), it should stand to reason that an intervention such as social skills training would have differential impact.

When additional research in these areas is conducted, it may become possible to assess more clearly the parameters within which behavioral intervention methods, such as social skills training, are effective in the treatment of psychophysiological disorders. For the present, however, in the absence of more conclusive data, all conclusions about this area must be regarded as tentative and awaiting adequate empirical verification and replication.

References

Alexander, A. B. 1972. Systematic relaxation and flow rates in asthmatic children: relationship to emotional precipitants and anxiety. *Journal of Psychosomatic Research, 16,* 405-10.

Alexander, F. 1950. *Psychosomatic medicine.* New York: Norton.

Alexander, F., and Flagg, G.W. 1965. The psychosomatic approach. In *Handbook of clinical psychology,* ed. B. Wolman. New York: McGraw-Hill.

Alexander, F., and French, T. 1948. *Studies in psychosomatic medicine.* New York: Ronald.

American Psychiatric Association. 1968. *Diagnostic and statistical manual of mental disorders,* 2nd ed. Washington, D.C.: American Psychiatric Association.

Argyle, M. 1967. *The psychology of interpersonal behavior.* Baltimore, MD.: Penguin.

Ayllon, T., and Haughton, E. 1962. Control of the behavior of schizophrenic patients by food. *Journal of the Experimental Analysis of Behavior, 5,* 343-52.

Bakal, D.A. 1975. Headache: A biopsychological perspective. *Psychological Bulletin, 82,* 369-82.

Bandura, A. 1969. *Principles of behavior modification.* New York: Holt, Rinehart and Winston.

Bar, L. H. J., and Kuypers, B. R. M. 1973. Behavior therapy in dermatological practice. *British Journal of Dermatology, 88,* 591-98.

Barrios, F. X. 1977. The behavioral assessment and modification of the physiological, subjective, and socio-behavioral correlates of migraine headaches. Unpublished Ph.D. dissertation, University of Cincinnati.

Bernstein, D. A., and Borkovec, T. D. 1973. *Progressive relaxation training: A manual for the helping professions.* Champaign, Ill.: Research Press.

Bernstein, D. A., and Nietzel, M. T. 1977. Demand characteristics in behavior modification: The natural history of a "nuisance." In *Progress in behavior modification,* ed. M. Hersen, R.M. Eisler, and P. M. Miller. Vol. 4. New York: Academic Press.

Birk, L., ed. 1973. *Biofeedback: Behavioral medicine.* New York: Grune and Stratton. 1973.

Blackwell, B., Wooley, S., and Whitehead, W. 1974. Psychosomatic illness: A new treatment approach. *Cincinnati Journal of Medicine, 55,* 95-98.

Blanchard, E. B. 1977. Behavioral medicine: A perspective. In *Behavioral approaches to medical treatment,* ed. R. B. Williams and W. D. Gentry. Cambridge, Mass.: Ballinger.

Blanchard, E. B., and Epstein, L. H. 1977. The clinical usefulness of biofeedback. In *Progress in behavior modification,* ed. M. Hersen, R. M. Eisler, and P. M. Miller. Vol. 4. New York: Academic Press.

Blanchard, E. B., and Young, L. D. 1974. Clinical applications of biofeedback training: A review of the evidence. *Archives of General Psychiatry, 30,* 573-89.

Borkovec, T. D., and Fowles, D. C. 1973. Controlled investigation of the effects of the progressive and hypnotic relaxation on insomnia. *Journal of Abnormal Psychology, 82,* 153-58.

Broden, M., Hall, R. V., and Mitts, B. 1971. The effect of self-recording on the classroom behavior of two eighth-grade students. *Journal of Applied Behavior Analysis, 4,* 191-99.

Budzynski, T. H., Stoyva, J. M., Adler, C. S., and Mullaney, D. J. 1973. EMG biofeedback and tension headache: A controlled outcome study. *Psychosomatic Medicine, 35,* 484-96.

Buss, A. H. *Psychopathology.* 1966. New York: Wiley.

Cavior, N., and Marabotto, C. 1976. Monitoring verbal behaviors in dyadic interaction. *Journal of Consulting and Clinical Psychology, 44,* 68-76.

Ciminero, A. R., Nelson, R. O., and Lipinski, D. P. 1977. Self-monitoring procedures. In *Handbook of behavioral assessment.* ed. A. R. Ciminero, K. S. Calhoun, and H. E. Adams. New York: Wiley.

Dunbar, F. *Psychosomatic diagnosis.* 1943. New York: Hoeber-Harper.

Eisler, R. M. 1976. The behavioral assessment of social skills. In *Behavioral assessment: a practical handbook,* ed. M. Hersen and A. S. Bellack. Elmsford, N.Y.: Pergamon Press.

Engel, B. T. 1973. Comment on self-control of cardiac functioning: A promise as yet unfulfilled. *Psychological Bulletin, 81,* 43.

Engel, G. L. 1977. The need for a new medical model: A challenge for biomedicine. *Science, 196,* 129-36.

Epstein, L. H., Miller, P.M., and Webster, J. S. 1976. The effects of reinforcing concurrent behavior on self-monitoring. *Behavior Therapy, 7,* 89-95.

Fedoravicius, A. S., Barrios, F. X., Franchi, A. A., and Fine, A. 1977. The effects of social skills training on levels of assertiveness and social anxiety in a chronically ill population. Presented at the 11th Annual Meeting of the Association for the Advancement of Behavior Therapy, December, 1977.

Fensterheim, H., and Baer, J. 1975. *Don't say yes when you want to say no.* New York: D. McKay.

Fordyce, W. E. 1976. *Behavioral methods for chronic pain and illness.* St. Louis: Mosby.

Fordyce, W. E., Fowler, R. S., Lehman, J. F., and De Lateur, B. J. 1968. Some implications of learning in problems of chronic pain. *Journal of Chronic Diseases, 21,* 179-90.

Frank, J. D. 1973. *Persuasion and healing,* rev. ed. Baltimore: Johns Hopkins Press. 1973.

Gambrill, E. D., and Richey, C. A. 1975. An Assertion Inventory for use in assessment and research. *Behavior Therapy, 6,* 550-61.

Gambrill, E. D., and Richey, C. A. 1976. *It's up to you: Developing effective social skills.* Millbrae: Les Femmes.

Goldfried, M. R., and D'Zurilla, T. J. 1969. A behavioral-analytic model for assessing competence. In *Current topics in clinical and community psychology.* ed. C. D. Spielberger. Vol. 1. New York: Academic Press.

Grace, W. J., and Graham, D. T. 1952. Relationship of specific attitudes and emotions to certain bodily diseases. *Psychosomatic Medicine, 14,* 243-51.

Hardyck, C. D., Petrinovich, L. F., and Ellsworth, D. W. 1966. Feedback of speech muscle activity during silent reading: Rapid extinction. *Science, 154,* 1467-68.

Hayes, S. C., and Cavior, N. 1977. Multiple tracking and the reactivity of self-monitoring: I. Negative behaviors. *Behavior Therapy, 9,* 819-31.

Henryk-Gutt, R., and Rees, W. L. 1973. Psychological aspects of migraine. *Journal of Psychosomatic Research, 17,* 141-53.

Hersen, M. Historical perspectives in behavioral assessment. 1976. In *Behavioral assessment: A practical handbook,* ed. M. Hersen and A. Bellack. Elmsford, N.Y.: Pergamon Press.

Hokanson, J. E., and Burgess, M. 1962. The effects of three types of aggression on vascular processes. *Journal of Abnormal and Social Psychology, 64,* 446-49.

Jeffrey, D. B. 1974. Self-control: Methodological issues and research trends. In *Self-control: Power to the person,* ed. M. J. Mahoney and C. E. Thoresen. Monterey, Calif.: Brooks-Cole.

Johnson, H. E., and Garton, W. H. 1973. Muscle re-education in hemiplegia by use of electromyographic device. *Archives of Physical Medicine and Rehabilitation, 54,* 320-25.

Johnson, S. M., and White, G. 1971. Self-observation as an agent of behavioral change. *Behavior Therapy, 2,* 488-97.

Kanfer, F. H., and Karoly, P. 1972. Self-control: A behavioristic excursion into the lion's den. *Behavior Therapy, 3,* 398-416.

Kanfer, F. H., and Phillips, J. S. 1970. *Learning foundations of behavior therapy.* New York: Wiley.

Katz, R. C., and Zlutnick, S. 1974. *Behavior therapy and health care: Principles and applications.* Elmsford, N.Y.: Pergamon Press.

Kazdin, A. E. 1974a. Self-monitoring and behavior change. In *Self-control: Power to the person,* ed. M. J. Mahoney and C. E. Thoresen. Monterey, Calif.: Brooks/Cole.

Kazdin, A. E. 1974b. Reactive self-monitoring: The effects of response desirability, goal setting, and feedback. *Journal of Consulting and Clinical Psychology, 42,* 704-16.

Kazdin, A. E., and Wilcoxon, L. A. 1976. Systematic desensitization and non-specific treatment effects: A methodological evaluation. *Psychological bulletin, 83,* 729-58.

Knapp, T. J., and Peterson, L. W. 1976. Behavior management in medical and nursing practice. In *Behavior modification: Principles, issues, and applications,* ed. W. E. Craighead, A. E. Kazdin, and M. J. Mahoney. Boston: Houghton Mifflin.

Lacey, J. I., Bateman, D. E., and Van Lehn, R. 1953. Autonomic response specificity: An experimental study. *Psychosomatic Medicine, 15,* 18-21.

Lachman, S. J. 1972. *Psychosomatic disorders: A behavioristic interpretation.* New York: Wiley.

Lader, M. 1972. Psychophysiological research and psychosomatic medicine. In *Physiology, emotion, and psychosomatic illness,* ed. R. Porter and J. Knight. Ciba Foundation Symposium 8. New York: Elsevier.

Lang, P. J. 1968. Fear reduction and fear behavior: Problems in treating a construct. In *Research in psychotherapy,* (Vol. 3) ed. J. M. Shlien. Washington, D.C.: American Psychological Association.

Lang, P. J. 1971. The application of psychophysiological methods to the study of psychotherapy and behavior modification. In *Handbook of psychotherapy and behavior change,* ed. A. E. Bergin and S. L. Garfield. New York: Wiley.

Lang, P. J., Lazovik, A. D., and Reynolds, D. J. 1965. Desensitization, suggestibility, and pseudotherapy. *Journal of Abnormal Psychology, 70,* 395-402.

Levendusky, P., and Pankratz, L. 1975. Self-control techniques as an alternative to pain medication. *Journal of Abnormal Psychology, 84,* 165-68.

Lewinsohn, P. M., Weinstein, M. S., and Shaw, D. A. 1969. Depression: A clinical-research approach. In *Advances in behavior therapy, 1968.* ed. R. D. Rubin and C. M. Franks. New York: Academic Press.

Liberman, R. P., and Davis, J. 1975. Drugs and behavior analysis. In *Progress in behavior modification,* ed. M. Hersen, R. M. Eisler, P. M. Miller. Vol. 1. New York: Academic Press.

Liberman, R. P., King, L. W., De Risi, W. J., and McCann, M. 1975. *Personal effectiveness: Guiding people to assert themselves and improve their social skills.* Champaign, Ill.: Research Press.

Libet, J. M., and Lewinsohn, P. M. 1973. Concept of social skill with special reference to the behavior of depressed persons. *Journal of Consulting and Clinical Psychology, 40,* 304-12.

Lick, J., and Bootzin, R. 1970. Expectancy, demand characteristics, and contact desensitization in behavior change. *Behavior Therapy, 1,* 176-83.

Lipinski, D. P., and Nelson, R. D. 1974. The reactivity and unreliability of self-recording. *Journal of Consulting and Clinical Psychology, 42,* 118-23.

Lipowski, Z. J. 1968. Review of consultation psychiatry and psychosomatic medicine: III. Theoretical issues. *Psychosomatic Medicine, 30,* 395-422.

Maher, B. A. 1966. *Principles of Psychopathology: An experimental approach.* New York: McGraw-Hill.

Maletzky, B. M. 1974. Behavior recording as treatment: A brief note. *Behavior Therapy, 5,* 107-11.

McFall, R. M. 1970. Effects of self-monitoring on normal smoking behavior. *Journal of Consulting and Clinical Psychology, 35,* 135-42.

McFall, R. M., and Hammen, C. L. 1971. Motivation, structure, and self-monitoring: Role of non-specific factors in smoking reduction. *Journal of Consulting and Clinical Psychology, 37,* 80-86.

Mechanic, D. 1962. The concept of illness behavior. *Journal of Chronic Diseases, 15,* 189-94.

Mechanic, D. 1972. Social psychologic factors affecting the presentation of bodily complaints. *New England Journal of Medicine, 286,* 1132-39.

Miller, N. E. 1969. Learning of visceral and glandular responses. *Science, 163,* 434-45.

Mitchell, K. R. 1969. The treatment of migraine: An exploratory application of time limited behavior therapy. *Technology, 14,* 50.

Mitchell, K. R., and Mitchell, D. M. 1971. Migraine: An exploratory treatment application of programmed behavior therapy techniques. *Journal of Psychosomatic Research, 15,* 137-57.

Mitchell, K. R., and White, R. G. 1976. Control of migraine headache by behavioral self-management: A controlled case study. *Headache, 16,* 178-84.
Mitchell, K. R., and White, R. G. 1977. Behavioral self-management: An application of the problem of migraine headaches. *Behavior Therapy, 8,* 213-21.
Nelson, R. O., Lipinski, D. P., and Black, J. L. 1976. The reactivity of adult retardates' self-monitoring: A comparison among behaviors of different valences, and a comparison with token reinforcement. *The Psychological Record, 26,* 189-201.
Nicasso, P., and Bootzin, R.A. 1974. A comparison of progressive relaxation and autogenic training as treatments for insomnia. *Journal of Abnormal Psychology, 83,* 253-60.
Orne, M. T. 1962. On the social psychology of the psychological experiment: With particular reference to demand characteristics and their implications. *American Psychologist, 17,* 776-83.
Parsons, T. 1951. *The social system.* New York: Free Press of Glencoe.
Paul, G. L. 1966. *Insight vs. desensitization in psychotherapy: An experiment in anxiety reduction.* Stanford: Stanford University Press.
Phillips, L., and Zigler, E. 1961. Social competence: The action-thought parameter and vicariousness in normal and pathological behaviors. *Journal of Abnormal and Social Psychology, 63,* 137-46.
Pilowsky, I. 1969. Abnormal illness behavior. *British Journal of Medical Psychology, 42,* 347-51.
Price, K. P. 1974. The application of behavior therapy to the treatment of psychosomatic disorders: Retrospect and prospect. *Psychotherapy: Theory, research, and practice, 11,* 138-55.
Raskin, M., Johnson, G., and Rondestvedt, J. W. 1973. Chronic anxiety treated by feedback-induced muscle relaxation. *Archives of General Psychiatry, 28,* 263-67.
Sargent, J. S., Green, E. E., and Walters, E. D. 1973. Preliminary report on the use of autogenic feedback training in the treatment of migraine and tension headaches. *Psychosomatic Medicine, 35,* 129-35.
Sargent, J. S., Walters, E. D., and Green, E. E. 1973. Psychosomatic self-regulation of migraine headaches. *Seminars in Psychiatry, 5,* 415-28.
Schultz, J. H., and Luthe, W. 1969. *Autogenic therapy,* vol. 1. New York: Grune and Stratton.
Schwab, J. J., McGinnis, N. H., Morris, L. B., and Schwab, R. B. 1970. Psychosomatic medicine and the contemporary social scene. *American Journal of Psychiatry, 126,* 1632-42.
Schwartz, G. E., and Shapiro, D. 1973. Biofeedback and essential hypertension: Current findings and theoretical concerns. *Seminars in Psychiatry, 5,* 493-503.
Selye, H. 1956. *The stress of life.* New York: McGraw-Hill.
Shapiro, A. K. 1971. Placebo effects in medicine, psychotherapy, and psychoanalysis. In *Handbook of psychotherapy and behavior change,* ed. A. E. Bergin and S. L. Garfield. New York: Wiley.
Shapiro, D., and Surwit, R. S. 1976. Learned control of physiological function and disease. In *Handbook of behavior modification and behavior therapy,* ed. H. Leitenberg. Englewood Cliffs, N.J.: Prentice-Hall.

Sieck, W. A., and McFall, R. M. 1976. Some determinants of self-monitoring effects. *Journal of Consulting and Clinical Psychology, 44,* 958-65.

Sirota, A. D., and Mahoney, M. J. 1974. Relaxing on cue: The self-regulation of asthma. *Journal of Behavior Therapy and Experimental Psychiatry, 5,* 65-66.

Smith, M. J. 1975. *When I say no, I feel guilty.* New York: The Dial Press.

Sternbach, R. A. 1966. *Principles of psychophysiology.* New York: Academic Press.

Sternbach, R. A. 1968. *Pain: A psychophysiological analysis.* New York: Academic Press.

Sternbach, R. A. 1974. *Pain patients: Traits and treatment.* New York: Academic Press.

Stone, L. J., and Hokanson, J. E. 1969. Arousal reduction via self-punitive behavior. *Journal of Personality and Social Psychology, 12,* 72-79.

Walton, D. 1960. The application of learning theory to the treatment of a case of neurodermatitis. In *Behavior therapy and the neuroses,* ed. H. J. Eysenck. Elmsford, New York: Pergamon Press.

Weiss, J. H. 1974. The current state of the concept of a psychosomatic disorder. *International Journal of Psychiatry in Medicine, 5,* 473-82.

Weiss, T., and Engel, B. T. 1971. Operant conditioning of heart rate in patients with premature ventricular contractions. *Psychophysiology, 8,* 263-64.

Wilkins, W. 1973. Expectancy of therapeutic gain: An empirical and conceptual critique. *Journal of Consulting and Clinical Psychology, 40,* 69-77.

Williams, R. B., and Gentry, W. D., eds. 1977. *Behavioral approaches to medical treatment.* Cambridge, Mass.: Ballinger.

Wolff, H. G. 1953. *Stress and disease.* Springfield, Ill.: Thomas.

Wolpe, J. 1973. *The practice of behavior therapy.* 2nd ed. Elmsford, New York: Pergamon Press.

Wooley, S., Blackwell, B., Fedoravicius, A., Terry, A., Bird, B. and Pudlish, C. 1976. Illness behavior: A learning theory model for psychosomatic disorders. Presented at the 10th Annual Meeting of the Association for the Advancement of Behavior Therapy, December, 1976.

Wooley, S. C., and Blackwell, B. 1975. A behavioral probe into social contingencies on a psychosomatic ward. *Journal of Applied Behavior Analysis, 8,* 337-39.

Yates, A. J. 1970. *Behavior therapy.* New York: Wiley.

Zigler, E., and Phillips, L. 1961. Social competence and outcome in psychiatric disorders. *Journal of Abnormal and Social Psychology, 63,* 264-71.

12
Social Power and the Elderly

Mary Jane Rotheram and
Nan Corby

Introduction

This chapter focuses on training social skills as a means of alleviating stress and increasing personal happiness among the elderly. Many of the problems encountered as we grow older are related to changes in personal relationships, age-linked cultural norms, and the amount of power exercised by elderly in society. Short-term interventions aimed at increasing social competence can be useful in helping the elderly deal with these problems more effectively. This chapter will review special issues that arise when applying social skills training with the elderly.

No adequate definition of good social skills exists to date. Perhaps O'Malley (1978) has the best description. He states that social skills are the thoughts, feelings, and behaviors which help a person reach personal goals in a manner benefiting both the person and others in the environment. In trying to operationalize this definition, there are certainly some behaviors, thoughts, or feelings that would be clearly labeled socially competent or assertive. For example, establishing eye contact is generally viewed as assertive. Whispering or talking in a very low voice is considered passive. It is also true, however, that thc label of social competence will also vary depending on the person performing the behavior, biases on the part of the evaluator of the actions, and the situational context. In evaluating social competence in the elderly, cohort differences in the definitions of assertive behavior exist. In addition, the culture responds differently as a function of age, and there is a change in a person's skill level and the types of problems encountered with increasing age. These processes create special problems for the elderly and for trainers of social skills.

Social Problems and Aging

The problems clearly emerge as we attempt to clarify the components of social skills. In approaching social skills training, Argyle and Kendon (1967) have specified five types of skills necessary for socially competent responses. A person must: (1) accurately assess social cues, (2) set a goal in the interaction, (3) problem solve the situation, (4) implement an effective social behavior, and (5) evaluate his or her performance and coordinate it with other people. At each stage of this model the elderly experience special vulnerabilities. For example, at step one—assessing social cues—the elderly are often influenced by outdated definitions of appropriate social behavior. The elderly person's cohort group holds different norms for appropriate behavior and when interacting in cross-age groups, the elderly person may misperceive social signals. In addition, the perceptions of younger cohort groups, which are also age-linked, result in negative reactions to elderly. For example, a more negative social label is applied to an elderly person swearing or engaging in extramarital sexual behavior than is associated with younger people (Kahana 1976). Steps two and three in the Argyle and Kendon (1967) model stress the ability to set clear goals and to apply problem-solving strategies. As a cohort group, the elderly often hold a strong value for independence, and it is not socially acceptable to make requests of others. Younger cohorts clearly label this value as passivity. These cohort values also enter into the elderly's ability to solve problems. Since the social rules do not allow them to make requests of other people, the elderly person's resources in attempting to reach a goal are exhausted with a first request. Perceiving fewer options limits the elderly's ability to innovatively solve problems. This demands that an essential component of social skills training should facilitate interpersonal problem solving. Again, at step four, as the elderly attempt to implement socially assertive strategies, they often experience anxiety. Their social role has shifted, and they are working in new social settings such as the welfare or Medicare system. The elderly must adjust their response style. Lifelong habits and a loss of quickness make this adaption more difficult. The high anxiety further reduces coping.

Social skills training provides specific methods of increasing competency at each step of the social interaction process. Kuypers and Bengston (1973) have hypothesized that increased social competence will help the elderly person by: (1) reducing susceptibility to loss and increasing self-confidence, (2) reducing dependence and increasing self-reliance, (3) leading the elderly to perceive themselves as able, and (4) maintaining coping skills. Changes towards increased social assertiveness will be particularly useful to the elderly in three areas: (1) it assists the elderly in forming new relationships, (2) negative social stereotypes of old age held by society and the elderly person can be broken, and (3) personal power, the ability to exert control over one's life, is increased. Let us briefly examine each of these problems areas.

Friends

Close interpersonal relationships provide intimacy, social integration, and a reliable alliance (Weiss 1969, 1974). Human beings function most effectively and with the greatest satisfaction when they feel confident that they have trusted friends to rely upon to interact with. Old people have the same social and interpersonal needs as the young, including the need and desire for intimate confidants (Dean 1966; Kahana 1976). With increasing age, it becomes increasingly difficult to satisfy these needs.

For many elderly people, relationships with friends and family often hinge on the joint participation of a spouse (Blau 1961). The death of a spouse is not only a significant loss of a loved one, but also the loss of a link to the rest of the social world. (Cumming and Henry 1961). Social isolation results. This isolation leads to poor physical health, increased depression, loneliness, and increased rates of psychiatric disturbances, particularly suicides (Henderson 1977; Bernardo 1967, 1968, 1970; Bock and Webber 1972; Maddison and Walker 1967; Brown, Brolchain, and Harris 1975).

Changes in housing patterns also increase social isolation (Lowenthal 1968; Rosow, 1967). Widowhood brings shifts in housing, often to living as a member of a group of unattached women. This relocation process leads to what has been called the "unexpected community." (Hochschild 1973; Jacobs 1969). For many, it provides an opportunity for new supportive friendships with people who are likely to have had similar experiences. For others, it may be another push toward social isolation (Jacobs 1969; Stephens 1974).

Friends can compensate for the loss of a spouse (Moriwaki 1973; Miller and Ingham 1976). For example, the health of widows in the year following their bereavement is significantly dependent upon the degree to which they perceive their social environment to be supportive (Maddison and Walker 1967; Maddison and Viola 1968). Again, supportive friends have been found to be the distinguishing factor between adequate coping and poor health, and serve as a buffer against future social losses and the more traumatic losses accompanying widowhood and retirement (Lowenthal and Haven 1968). In institutional settings, Gottesman (1970) has found that adjustment is facilitated by new social relationships. This research indicates friendship networks are critical among the elderly and that frequent contact with many people is more important than having a few highly intimate relationships.

While relationships are critical to survival of the elderly, older people have greater difficulty in initiating new relationships than do younger people who have jobs and children which tend to facilitate social interaction. The problem is intensified because relationship networks among the elderly have often been stable for many years and initiation skills have not been practiced. When meeting new people, the elderly find that the social rules have changed, particularly in romantic relationships. For example, while many young women now call men for dates, few elderly women see themselves in the role of the initiator in romantic relationships. The elderly are likely to have a firmly established set of rules for acceptable social interactions, and they are initially hesitant to change in order to gain social rewards. However, research using operant conditioning procedures effectively increased social interaction in geriatric patients (Sachs 1975) and demonstrated that social behaviors among the elderly are modifiable.

Social skills training is directly aimed at acquiring new relationships. In a short-term intervention, the elderly generate ways and places to meet new people as well as rehearse skills required to initiate contact. The training group itself serves to facilitate friendships and social interactions.

Power

The powerlessness of old age is an often repeated theme. The theme emerges because it accurately reflects reality. The elderly suffer from a lack of personal power, i.e., an ability to control their own lives. This lack of personal influence affects not only the personal lives of individual elderly and their physical and emotional health, but also the social, economic, and political impact of the elderly as a group. While linked to economic and social problems associated with aging, the lack of power also comes from two social sources, negative stereotypes of elderly and the role of patient or "sickie" that is assigned to the elderly. A long list of consistently derogatory adjectives appears in the studies of the old-age stereotypes: weak, helpless, dependent, less powerful and less able to effect societal changes, ineffective, and less competent (Rubin and Brown 1975; Martin 1971; Berezin 1972; Cameron 1973).

These problems point to a need for increased social coping skills and problem-solving abilities among the elderly. Instead of coping, the elderly have frequently responded to challenges by withdrawing or accepting the stereotypes (Gottesman and Brody 1975). The acceptance of the stereotypes is encouraged and reinforced in the environment. For example, Berger and Berger (1971) report how nurses reinforce the elderly for being quiet and passive. The frequency of the elderly person's passive behavior rises. This results in a drop not only in social functioning, but also in cognitive processing. It is evident that accepting negative stereotypes will result in negative effects on the elderly including a loss of self-esteem. These stereotypes will also lead to unproductive communications between young and old people.

Martin and Martin (1971) have demonstrated how such a system may be established. They point out how complaining and loss of recall may be operantly conditioned in the elderly. When an older person has been institutionalized, complaining may prolong a relative's visit and establish obligations for future visits. This results in short-term reinforcement for the complainer, but has the long-term consequence of the visitor avoiding contact. Guilt will eventually lead the visitor to return. The complaint cycle will, however, recur. An intermittent-reinforcement schedule has become established and the complaining behaviors of the older person persist. While this is not productive for either party, it is likely to be maintained indefinitely.

Instead of complying with and resigning to role stereotypes, the elderly need to challenge the norm of passivity. By increasing personal power, the elderly can effect increases in social power. As evidence, agressiveness or assertiveness is the only variable that has been found to predict adaptive and "in-tact" functioning one year after a person has been admitted to an institution (Turner, Tobin, and Lieberman 1972). According to the investigators, "In a setting in which many residents are physically and/or mentally incapacitated to some degree, an aggressive resident is best able to meet his needs because he is able to assertively reach out for himself" (Turner, Tobin, and Lieberman 1972). For the elderly, many of whom face nursing home or other short- or long-term institutionalization at some time or another, a lack of assertiveness can have far-reaching consequences. Breaking out of unproductive but firmly established nonassertive communication patterns can be facilitated by short-term social skills training (Lange and Jakubowski 1976).

The intervention that is described below was developed from previous research and from clinical experience in assertiveness training with the elderly and with other groups. The model is being presented here to assist, modify, and further investigate its function and usefulness with the elderly.

Social Skills Training

Entry Strategies

The method of initiating the intervention varies depending on whether it is used with an institutionalized or an noninstitutionalized population.

Institutional Strategy. Behavior-change techniques often fail when used in institutional settings because trainers fail to consider the influence the social environment exerts on maintaining current behaviors. For example, Pollock and Lieberman (1974) have reported instances of incontinence in elderly patients being maintained by reinforcement from an institutional staff. Training clients in a nursing home to be more assertive is likely to produce a negative outcome, unless the staff is prepared to assist and to cooperate in facilitating increased assertiveness. It is predictable that staff prefer to manage unassertive patients. Passive residents do not make as many requests; their needs are more easily ignored, and it takes less staff to meet their demands. Trainers could be engineering battles between staff and residents by eliciting negative feedback for their clients.

In an institution, staff members must participate in the training. This will accomplish a number of goals:

1. The staff will have clear information on the goals and techniques of assertiveness training and realistic expectations about changes that will take place in residents who receive this training.
2. Their cooperation and assistance will be gained.
3. They will learn methods of encouraging assertiveness among the residents.
4. They will increase in appropriate assertive behavior themselves and be able to discriminate aggression and assertiveness.
5. Some of the staff will be able to function as trainers of patients in the project.

Training representatives from each group in a system (nurses, staff, and patients in a nursing home, for example) is the ideal prerequisite for instituting a successful intervention. In this method, the trainers train the staff. The staff trains the first groups of residents. These residents in turn become paraprofessional trainers of the next group of residents. The process continues until all members of the interpersonal network are trained. This chaining, or "therapeutic pyramid," has been described by Whalen and Henker (1973).

If it is not possible to begin by training the staff, staff should at least receive an introduction to the program. The first three goals described above will be accomplished. In particular, staff should also be warned of potential "overkill" situations where the newly assertive residents may become temporarily aggressive. The staff should also be given specific instructions on methods of encouraging assertiveness. Their assistance is important and necessary to the success of the project.

Noninstitutionalized Settings. Social effectiveness training can be used in two ways:

1. As an adjunct to an already organized service program for the elderly, such as a lunch care program. The training facilitates cohesiveness among the participants and increases the personal effectiveness of the member.

2. As an organizing activity to draw members together in an age-graded community, such as an apartment house for the elderly.

A variety of community intervention programs have been successful in organizing the elderly into groups, such as lunch care programs and craft guilds. Critical to the success of these programs is the ability of the coordinators to facilitate social interaction. Zarit, Corby, Rotheram and Armstrong (1976) employed effectiveness training as an adjunct service to a lunch service program. Employing a pyramid design similar to that suggested for institutionalized populations, a training group was initially organized for a small group of elderly members and the administration staff of the program. Combining the two populations in the training groups led to both sides airing their views on a number of problems the lunch program was experiencing. The result was an increased understanding of the central issues and resolution of a number of problems. During the second stage of training, the elderly participants—with minimal supervision by the original assertion training leaders—organized and conducted training sessions for the rest of the elderly paraprofessional leaders. This procedure took longer than most assertiveness training programs, six months compared to a typical three-month program. The newly trained leaders began conducting their own groups during the fourth month of training. This assured the elderly that there would be a forum for dealing with problems that arose in the groups the elderly trainers were conducting. Rather than abruptly ending contact at the end of six months, the leaders established a procedure for gradual withdrawal of supervision and support. Meetings were held every two weeks, then shifted to once a month. In the final stage, the leader maintained a relationship as a consultant for problem situations. Such a design increases the elderly participants' feelings of power and control over their own services. It also facilitates and reinforces the notion that this will be an ongoing program that will not be discontinued as soon as the intervention agents withdraw.

Social effectiveness training is one strategy that can be used by community workers to organize a community network for elderly (Kaswan and Schwebel: personal communication, 1978). Again a pyramid network is established. In organizing such groups, selection of a problem situation facing the entire community may facilitate initial participation. For example, the elderly in the Silverlake District of Los Angeles are frequently robbed the day their checks arrive from Social Security. People are initially brought together around a problem of mutual concern, e.g., how to guard themselves from thieves. Effectiveness training is a useful technique to assist the elderly in attaining their goals and maintaining cohesiveness in the community group. In one consultation setting, the elderly convinced the banks to deposit Social Security checks directly into their accounts. The assertion training aided the elderly in dealing with bank personnel and also in gathering community support for the program. In addition, the training facilitated the establishment and growth of close interpersonal relationships among community members.

Cross-Age Groups in the Community. As a therapeutic intervention, increased assertiveness leads to greater communication, clearer problem resolution, and increased intimacy in relationships (Alberti and Emmons 1971). This is particularly true in a family setting. All members of a family are simultaneously taught to behave more assertively with each other. The family is taught: (1) to make clear requests, (2) to set limits and say no, (3) to express themselves emotionally across a broad range of feelings, and (4) methods of breaking cycles of escalating negative interactions among family members.

Two strategies have been suggested for conducting assertiveness training for families. One technique is to draw together *all* members of one family. This includes grandparents, aunts, or uncles. While we typically fantasize a nuclear family of a mother, father, and young children, the extended family remains a reality for many Americans. Speck and Attneave (1972) have advocated network therapy in which all members of a family system join together to help each other or solve a common problem. This would certainly include elderly family members. If the problem has been defined as belonging to the elderly client, employing assertion training to treat the family unit will increase the family's skills in dealing with future problems that arise, and will help break family member's stereotypes about the elderly person.

A second strategy is to form cross-age groups composed of members from a number of different families. Again, elderly participants are central to success of this therapy group. Besides the social skills obtained by the clients, the following benefits are available: (1) group members gain insight into age related problems, (2) members can practice being assertive with people who closely resemble their own family in age-life experiences, but with whom they do not have destructive and habitual communication patterns, and (3) negative stereotypes of elderly are challenged. Cross-age assertion groups can be beneficial to all participants.

Initial Assessment

The importance of an initial assessment of specific assertion problems among the elderly has been demonstrated by Edinberg, Karoly, and Geeser (1977) and by Berger and Rose (1977). Results of assessment studies have indicated that assertiveness in the elderly is situationally specific.

A comprehensive intervention program requires that the researcher and/or clinician develop an individually tailored assessment package employing Goldfried and D'Zurilla's (1969) model of behavior analysis. An outline of the step-by-step process follows.

Elicit problematic social situations from target population.
Compose extensive list representative of problems experienced by the population.
Collect reliability and validity data from significant others to target population as to alternative responses to situations and appropriateness of responses.
Use data to construct training program format, behavioral role-play test, and rating manual for behavioral test.

An example of how this procedure has been used to design an intervention program can be found in Berger and Rose (1977). Problem situations are elicited from the target population of elderly. The trainers can then clearly address issues representative of the concerns of the elderly people involved in the program. A checklist of problem situations is created. Descriptions of the elderly person's typical behavioral responses in these situations are collected from a number of people in the elderly person's environment. The trainer gains consensus among the older person and others in his setting on the definition of the problem. Using data from both sources, a final form of an assertion problem checklist is constructed and administered. This completed assessment program can be used to provide direction in designing the intervention program.

When this model cannot be used to design and implement an intervention program, a behavioral role-play test similar to those constructed by Eisler, Miller, and Hersen (1973) has been found to be an effective assessment tool. Edinberg et al. (1977) developed eight role-playing situations appropriate for use with the aged. These role plays provide an acceptable range of situational variability for the assessment of assertiveness. These role-play descriptions involve the following situations:

1. Interacting with a physician regarding a just-completed medical examination.
2. Disagreeing with one's children about the necessity for a move to a nursing home.
3. A fraud scheme such as selling roofing for a nondamaged roof.
4. Dealing with red tape in a Social Security Office.
5. Receiving the wrong change in a transaction in the grocery store.
6. Refusing a request for money.
7. Accepting an offer of assistance from family members.
8. Responding to an expression of concern by a staff member at a citizen's center.

A stimulus person role plays the eight situations with the elderly client. The responses of the confederate are predetermined and constant to insure reliability across subjects. Trained observers rate the appropriateness of verbal and nonverbal responses. From these baseline assessments, behavioral goals which are tailored for each individual can be set (Edinberg et al. 1977).

Group Leader

The leader of an assertiveness intervention is often younger than the elderly participants. A leader is most effective when he or she personally models assertive behavior, clearly acts as a facilitator of group interaction, and serves as an information resource person. The elderly are better able to identify effective methods of dealing with assertion issues faced by other elderly people than are younger professionals. A professional may have more formal knowledge of social service benefits and agencies, but the elderly group members may have superior practical information and suggestions about dealing with the local agencies and their representatives. The leader functions as a facilitator of client-to-client interactions and attends closely to the problems and solutions brought up by the clients. In the role as a facilitator, the leader encourages group members to provide solutions for each other rather than relying on the group leader for solutions.

Balance in the degree of influence the leader exercises is crucial. While avoiding the role of a controlling, all-knowing savior, the group leader must demonstrate himself as useful to the group. Generally, this trust can be established in the first session by the leader dealing successfully with an external problem, such as how to get Social Security checks. While a young leader can challenge values, crossing the elderly's preconceptions of acceptable behavior too radically can be disastrous. For example, a leader who comes wearing dirty jeans, beads, and who curses is unlikely to gain the group's trust. Such behavior is at the opposite end of the continuum from the elderly's definition of what is acceptable.

In the pyramid training model discussed earlier, the leader begins to fade out as facilitator after three months. First, the leader attends every other session, then moves to every third session, and then attends intermittently. The leader also begins to switch his or her role in the group by disclosing personal assertion problems.

The young leader can be particularly useful to the group by providing data on cohort differences in cultural norms. Social behavior is guided by a person's conception of acceptable behavior. These norms change over time. For example, opening a car door for a woman is not now seen as an essential part of gentlemanly conduct. The younger leader can inform the elderly person concerning changing norms and can facilitate the acquisition of behavior considered assertive in cross-generational settings.

Social Skills Training Format

Group, not individual, training is important, and cohesiveness among that group is equally important. Edinberg (1976) compared discussion groups to social skills training intervention and a no-treatment control. He found that the discussion groups were as effective as the social skills training. In the dicussion group, the elderly participants were socially active and formed cohesive social units. This social function is a primary goal of social skills training. If groups do not become cohesive, the intervention is of little value.

The word "therapy" does not have positive valence among the elderly. "Assertiveness" is often seen as synonymous to "aggressiveness" (and not only among the elderly, cf. Turner, Tobin, and Lieberman 1972). The term "effectiveness training" has been found to be a good alternative.

The length of each session needs to be short, not more than an hour, followed by time for socializing. This is recommended both for clients who have short attention spans and for those who have physical disabilities and might find a longer session physically uncomfortable.

Cognitive factors need to be addressed in obtaining socially assertive behavior in this age group. To behave assertively, persons need to believe they have the right to be assertive and must covertly reinforce themselves for behaving assertively. Cohort differences exist in the definitions of acceptable behavior. This accounts for a significant amount of the passivity found among the elderly. For example, in one assertiveness training group, a 70-year-old woman wanted to tell her 37-year-old son to take a bath more often. He had been living with her for a month, and his mother found his personal hygiene habits offensive. Telling him so, no matter how kindly, "just wasn't done," according to her social value system. While this value has changed significantly in younger cohort groups, making direct requests remains a taboo among the elderly. The elderly participants agreed among themselves that asking her son to take a bath may be too pushy. Instead of asking directly, the elderly hint and nag. The elderly perceive their behavior as following acceptable social conventions. Values and definitions of appropriate behavior have changed for today's youth, and to facilitate mutually by satisfying cross-age interactions, the elderly need to be informed of the differences.

Elderly people, like anyone else, have the right to request or refuse, and this choice is fundamental to the decision to adopt assertive behaviors in a given situation. Because of the conflicting social values that are especially prevalent among the elderly, the importance of these personal rights to request and refuse must be emphasized. Alberti and Emmons (1971) have developed a list of rights or values that facilitate the development of assertiveness. We have modified this list slightly to deal with elderly participants. The five major beliefs are presented below:

1. You have the right to feel good about yourself. You are wonderful. Rewarding yourself for the good things you do and feel is not conceited. Punishing yourself is not being humble. Self-punishment does not show respect for others or for yourself.

This challenges a value of self-depreciation held by the elderly. In addition, this belief is critical for facilitating generalization following training. Generalization of newly acquired assertive behaviors is a central problem when working with the elderly.

2. You have the right to ask for what you want directly. When you do not ask directly, you are manipulating others. The other person does not get a chance to refuse. Hinting is a demand, not a request. Asking directly shows that you have confidence in the other person's assertiveness. Also, your needs are as important as the other person's and you have the right to attempt to satisfy your needs.

3. You have the right to say "no" clearly, without making excuses. You are not obligated to fulfill other people's needs. Making excuses makes you sound weak and apologetic.

4. Reciprocity is basic to all good relationships. As with children, there is often an imbalance in relationships with the elderly due to social customs.

When talking to an older person, many persons have the implicit expectation that the older person will talk and the younger person listen. The young person will dutifully listen or report on how he is succeeding in life. People at all ages find their greatest satisfaction in relationships that are reciprocal The level of disclosure, areas of disclosure, and frequency of social rewards and punishers needs to be fairly even in order for relationships to be mutually beneficial for both parties. This demands that elderly break the passive role of old age, especially in cross-generational relationships. Changing this belief demands change on the part of the young and old members of the relationship. This is most successfully accomplished in cross-generational groups. Role plays are conducted with younger people where disclosures are made in areas not generally discussed with the elderly. The elderly also practice asking questions to elicit information across many topics.

5. You do not have to act old. Maladaptive habits may develop as a function of the elderly's conception of his or her role as an old person. Believing old people are hunched and complaining, an elderly person might adjust to this expectation, changing posture and voice in a negative direction. The negative stereotypes of aging do not have to be accepted. This right has been effectively demonstrated by the leader engineering a session where the elderly are asked to walk and dress as they did at 40 years of age. Major changes in posture and nonverbal behavior are found. Most elderly find the experience so reinforcing that postural changes persist. Video-tape feedback has proved very important in delivering information to elderly on their nonverbal behavior. While no research data are available, the video tape appeared to increase attraction to the group and was most effective in the elderly accepting the feedback on nonverbal behavior. The video tape also

provided incentive for elderly members to dress up and participate in community activities, especially in institutional settings. Video tapes of past social skills groups are especially useful when used as an initial orientation session and recruitment for elderly clients in a nursing home. Edinberg et al. (1977) report that elderly people can discriminate between their socially acceptable, but passive, responses and appropriately assertive responses on paper-and-pencil tests. Behavioral implemention of assertiveness calls upon an entirely different set of beliefs and values. For example, in a recent group in a VA hospital, the elderly group liked the staff and felt they received good treatment. The group agreed that this would end if they made too many requests. The staff might be displeased and not be so nice. This indicates that once the belief and values have been reviewed behavioral practice must be implemented.

After 60-70 years, the verbal and nonverbal skills necessary to be assertive are present in the behavioral repertoire of the elderly person. The major problem is eliciting the behaviors in varying situational contexts where high anxiety is experienced. The elderly know how to establish eye contact, smile, stand assertively, disclose feelings, ask others. Faced with new situations, the elderly are not able to use these skills.

Anxiety control is central to the success of the elderly person's assertiveness. The elderly person is more likely to lose reasoning and memory abilities when experiencing high anxiety. Relaxation techniques involving fantasies have been particularly useful with this age group. Once the belief system and anxiety level are addressed, the practice of assertive behaviors through role play is much easier.

To address the cognitive and behavioral components of social skills, a group setting with eight to ten members and one or two leaders is employed. The group format proceeds as follows:

Discussion of Success in Being Assertive. To develop a cohesive group and encourage self-reinforcement, successes are discussed each session. The members are asked to recount instances during the week where they have behaved assertively. The leader and group members reward all attempts to be assertive. The leader needs to emphasize the importance of reinforcing the person for behaving assertively, not for getting what was wanted. Being assertive increases the chances the person will achieve his or her goals. It does not guarantee success. Group reinforcement helps the person to continue to be assertive in future encounters. Reasons for failure are discussed. This may well take a majority of the group meeting. Irrational beliefs about rights to be assertive are frequently raised during this period. Ellis' (1975) techniques for disputing irrational thoughts and emphasizing personal rights are effective in dealing with the elderly clients. The unassertive person is asked to project the consequences of his assertiveness. For example, the leader asks, "What could happen if you told your daughter you would like her to visit twice a month?" At the worst the daughter will say no. Catastrophic fantasies on the consequences of assertive behavior are challenged. The fantasies can be exaggerated to a ridiculous point until the group laughs at the exaggerated consequences. For a complete discussion of these techniques, see Ellis (1975).

Problem Presentation and Rehearsal. In contrast to a number of assertion programs with younger populations, social skills programs for the elderly do not have a preset weekly agenda. The agenda is tailored to match the problems reported by elderly clients during the assessment phase. At each session, the leader prepares a problem area and a canned role play scene for group members to rehearse. The area may be dealing with doctors or welfare workers, making new friends. After presenting the problem, the group discusses several ways to handle each situation. The solutions are rank ordered as to escalating assertiveness. For example, if you are in pain in a nursing home, you may try any of a number of strategies. Seven possible strategies are listed below in order of the need of escalating assertiveness. After trying each alternative, the person chooses whether he wants to escalate the intensity of the request. Sample options in the nursing home are:

1. ask the nurse for a pain reliever
2. ask to see the head nurse
3. call the doctor yourself and request medication
4. call a different doctor and request a physical examination to determine what is wrong and some relief
5. call a relative to intercede for you
6. call the board of examiners of nursing homes
7. call a local news station and report inefficiency in the home

The importance of being able to generate alternatives has been demonstrated with younger populations (Spivack, Platt, and Shure 1976). It is especially important that the elderly person realize and perceive that options are available. A strong belief among the elderly is that receiving a refusal once means the issue is settled. This is especially true when the elderly are dealing with any type of authority, e.g., a doctor, a nurse, or a Social Security worker. The generation of options focuses on how to plan back-up strategies if one method of goal seeking is unsuccessful. Having confidence that there are other ways of reaching a goal facilitates the acquisition of assertive behavior.

Each group member needs a resource person she or he can meet with outside of the group. When a problem arises between sessions, the resource person functions to generate problem-solving alternatives, to serve as a role play partner, and to provide support. The leader facilitates the development of such relationships by assigning group members to dyads. Homework assignments are given that require the pair to meet outside the group. This buddy system has been used in other self-help programs such as Alcoholics Anonymous and Weight Watchers.

Behavioral Rehearsal. The elderly person must become skilled and confident in his social behaviors. This is accomplished by role playing problem situations. A triad is established with a protagonist, antagonist, and coach. Modeling and coaching are central factors in successful assertiveness training programs (Lange and Jakubowski 1976). Discrimination learning of assertive behaviors is generally facilitated in younger groups through the use of color-coded tokens as cues (Flowers and Booraem 1975). Some groups of elderly people find this tool more awkward, however, than do the younger group members. The use of tokens should be evaluated on the basis of the general cognitive functioning of the group in question, and its ability to attend to the group process. The coach's role is also more flexible with an aged population. The steps for giving feedback should be less rigid and allow more flexible expressiveness for the elderly person's individual style. In role playing the situation, positive feedback from the group is given for assertive verbal and nonverbal behaviors. Shaping procedures using a model of successive approximations are used to establish assertive responses. For example, the following requests reflect increasing levels of assertiveness in asking for a change of a doctor's appointment:

1. Saying in an apologetic voice and downcast eyes, "If it is not too much trouble and you're not busy, well, I apologize for being so lax, but can I change my appointment."
2. Saying same words with a nonapologetic voice.
3. With an assertive voice, asking, "I'm sorry, I know you're busy, but could I change my appointment from Wednesday to Monday?"
4. Looking at the person in an assertive voice saying, "If you're not busy, I would like an appointment on Monday at 3:00. I already have an appointment for Wednesday, at 2:00."
5. Looking at the person and assertively saying, "I have an appointment for Wednesday at 2:00. I would like that appointment switched to Monday at 3:00.
   Thanks."

   At each rehearsal, the person is reinforced for his improvements and informed of one verbal or nonverbal characteristic to try to change in the next role play. The scenes are rehearsed until the elderly group member feels comfortable in his or her performance and the group agrees it is well done. If the rehearsal is taking a long time, the leader requests the triad to rehearse outside of the group setting and return when the rehearsal is perfected.

Group Goal-setting. The elderly group members commit themselves to practice new assertive behaviors at home during the week. Arrangements are made to contact each other during the week to ensure that homework is performed. The primary goal of homework is often social contact with another group member.

Social-interaction Time. This gives participants a chance to practice newly acquired skills in a non-task-oriented setting and is crucial to the development of group cohesion. This is true whether the group be of elderly persons themselves or of peer counselors or other paraprofessionals who intend to work with the elderly. In a group of elderly, the intervention may continue indefinitely with no leaders. The forced group interaction provides supportive relationship contact that can mitigate negative emotional and physical consequences of isolation.

Research

Very little research has been reported on the effects of these kinds of interventions with the elderly. Two studies have evaluated specific social skills training with the elderly without finding positive effects. Edinberg (1976) compared assertiveness training to a discussion group and a no-treatment control group, all of elderly people. No significant differences were found on a behavioral role-play measure.

In contrast, Berger and Rose (1977) found a significant increase in assertiveness due to social skills training in a behavioral role-play task that was maintained for two months. This positive impact, however, was found only in situations which had been rehearsed during the training. The effects did not generalize to new situations, nor were they evident on self-report measures or in a real-life situation with a social worker. The short training period (three one-hour sessions), the failure to employ methods to enhance generalization, the use of individual instead of group intervention, and "attitudinal lag" (Goldsmith 1973) were used to explain the results. Further research is needed to evaluate the effectiveness of this intervention with the elderly, especially when it specifically incorporates techniques related to generalization and group cohesiveness.

Summary

The indications for using assertiveness training as an intervention in assisting the elderly in dealing with some of the psychosocial aspects of aging have been reviewed. Specific issues discussed have included social and personal power and effectiveness, especially in institutional settings, shifts in relationships due to widowhood and retirement, and the function and effects of "power" and "friends" in old age.

The importance of tailoring individual programs to deal with specific target problems was emphasized, with such assessment occurring in the initial intervention sessions. Cognitive-behavioral approaches were suggested as being potentially very valuable with this population, which appears to have social values that tend to reduce their assertive responses. Group assertiveness training with its opportunity for social interaction and cohesiveness was recommended as a preferred modality.

References

Alberti, R., and Emmons, M. 1970. *Your perfect right.* San Luis Obispo: Impact.

Argyle, M., and Kendon, A. 1967. The experimental analysis of social performances. In *Advances in experimental social psychology,* ed. L. Berkowitz, vol. 3. New York: Academic Press.

Balint, M. 1957. *The doctor, his patient and the illness.* London: Pitmans Medical.

Berezin, M.A. 1972. Psychodynamic considerations of aging and the aged: An overview. *American Journal of Psychiatry, 128,* 1483-91.

Berger, M. M. and Berger, L. F. 1971. An innovative program for a private psychogeriatric day center. *Journal of the American Geriatrics Society, 19,* 332-36.

Berger, R. M. and Rose, S. D. 1977. Interpersonal skill training with institutionalized elderly patients. *Journal of Gerontology, 32,* 346-53.

Bernardo, F. M. 1967. Social adaptation to widowhood among a rural-urban aged population. *Washington agricultural experiment station bulletin 689.* Pullman, Washington: College of Agriculture, Washington State University.

Bernardo, F. 1970. Survivorship and social isolation: The case of the aged widower. *Family Coordinator, 19,* 11-15.

Bernardo, F. 1968. Widowhood status in the United States: Perspective on a neglected aspect of the family life cycle. *Family Coordinator, 17,* 191-203.

Blau, Z. 1961. Structural constraints on friendship in old age. *American Sociological Review, 26,* 429-39.

Bock, E. W. and Webber, I. L. 1972. Suicide among the elderly: Isolating widowhood and mitigating alternatives. *Journal of Marriage and the Family, 34,* 24-31.

Bowlby, J. 1977. The making and breaking of affectional bonds. Aetiology and psychopathology in the light of attachment theory. *British Journal of Psychiatry, 130,* 201-10.

Bowlby, J. 1973. *Attachment and loss: Separation: Anxiety and anger.* Vol. 2. London: Hogarth Press.

Breytspraak, L.M. 1974. Achievement and the self-concept in middle age. In *Normal aging II*, ed. E. Palmore. Durham, NC: Duke University Press.

Brown, G. W., Bhrolchain, M. N., and Harris, T. 1975. Social class and psychiatric disturbance among women in an urban population. *Sociology, 9,* 225-54.

Burnside, I. M. 1969. Group work among the aged. *Nursing Outlook, 17,* 68-71.

Burnside, I. M. 1971. Long-term group work with the hospitalized aged. *The Gerontologist, 1,* 213-18.

Cameron, P. 1973. Which generation is believed to be intellectually superior and which generation believes itself intellectually superior? *International Journal of Aging and Human Development, 4,* 157-70.

Cook, F. L., Skogan, W. G., Cook, T. D., and Antunes, G. F.1978. Criminal victimization of the elderly: The physical and economic consequences. *Gerontologist, 18,* 338-49.

Corby, N. 1975. Assertion training with aged populations. *The Counseling Psychologist, 5,* 69-73.

Corby, N. 1976. *Intervention strategies for the aged: A call for research.* Paper presented at the meeting of the Western Psychological Association, Los Angeles, April, 1976.

Cumming, E. and Henry, W. H. 1961. *Growing old: The process of disengagement.* New York: Basic Books.

Dean, S. R. 1966. Sin and senior citizens. *Journal of the American Geriatric Society, 14,* 935-38.

Edinberg, M. A. 1976. Behavioral assessment and assertion training of the elderly. Unpublished Doctoral dissertation, University of Cincinnati.

Edinberg, M. A., Karoly, P. A., and Geeser, G. C. 1977. Assessing assertion in the elderly: An application of the behavioral analytic model of competence. *Journal of Clinical Psychology, 33,* 869-74.

Eisler, R. M., Miller, P. M., and Hersen, M. 1973. Components of assertive behavior. *Journal of Clinical Psychology, 29,* 295-99.

Ellis, A. 1975. *How to live with a neurotic.* New York: Crown Publishers.

Fensterheim, H. 1972. Behavior therapy: Assertive training in groups. In *Progress in group and family therapy.* ed. C. J. Sager and H. S. Kaplan. New York:Brunner/Mazel.

Flowers, J. V. and Booraem, C. D. 1975. Assertion Training: The training of trainers. *Counseling Psychologist 5,* 29-36.

Flowers, J. V. and Guerra, J. 1974. The use of client-coaching in assertion training with large groups. *Community Mental Health Journal, 10,* 414-17.

Gaitz, C. M., and Scott, J. A. 1975. Analysis of letters to "Dear Abby" concerning old age. *Gerontologist, 15,* 47-50.

Goldfarb, A. 1972. Group therapy with the old and aged. In *Group Treatment of mental illness,* ed. H. I. Kaplan and B. J. Fadock. New York: E. P. Dutton 113-31.

Goldfried, M. R. and D'Zurrila, T. J. 1969. A behavioral-analytic model for assessing competence. In *Current topics in clinical and community psychology,* ed. C. D. Speilberger, vol. 1. New York: Academic Press.

Goldsmith, J. B. 1973. Systematic development and evalution of a behavioral program for training psychiatric inpatients in interpersonal skills. Doctoral dissertation, University of Wisconsin, Madison. *Dissertation Abstracts Int'l.,* 1973, *34,* 2305B.

Gottesman, L. and Brody, E. 1975. Psycho-social intervention programs within the institutional setting. In *Long-term care: A handbook for researchers, planners, and providers,* ed. S. Sherwood. New York: Spectrum.

Henderson, S. 1977. The social network support and neurosis: The function of attachment in adult life. *British Journal of Psychiatry, 131,* 185-91.

Hochschild, A. R. 1973. *The unexpected community.* Englewood Cliffs, N.J.: Prentice-Hall.

Hoyer, W. J. 1973. Application of operant techniques to the modification of elderly behavior. *Gerontologist, 13,* 18-22.

Hoyer, W. J., Mishara, B. L., and Riebel, R. G. 1975. Problem behaviors as operant. Applications with elderly individuals. *Gerontologist, 15,* 452-56.

Jacobs, Ruth H. 1969. The friendship club: A case study of the segregated aged. *Gerontologist, 9,* 276-80.

Kahana, B. 1976. Social and psychological aspects of sexual behavior among the aged. In *Aging and reproductive physiology,* ed. E. S. E. Hafey, vol. 2. Ann Arbor, Mich.: Ann Arbor Science.

Kuypers, J. A. and Bengston, V. L. 1973. Competence and social breakdown : A social-psychological view of aging. *Human Development, 16,* 37-49.

Lange, A. J., and Jakubowski, P. 1976. *Responsible assertive behavior,* Champaign, Ill.: Research Press.

Langer, E. J., and Rodin, J. 1976. The effects of choice and enhanced personal responsibility for the aged: A field experiment in an institutional setting. *Journal of Personality and Social Psychology, 34,* 191-98.

Lewis, C. N. 1970. *Reminiscence and self-concept in old age.* Unpublished doctoral dissertation. Boston: Boston University Graduate School.

Liederman, P. C., Green, R. and Liederman, V. R. 1967. Outpatient group therapy with geriatric patients. *Geriatrics, 22,* 148-53.

Lowenthal, M. F. 1968. Social isolation and mental illness in old age. In *Middle age and aging,* ed. B. L. Newgarten. Chicago: University of Chicago Press.

Lowenthal, M. F. and Haven, C. 1968. Interaction and adaptation: Intimacy as a critical variable. *American Sociological Review, 33,* 20-30.

Maddison, D. C. and Walker, W. L. 1967. Factors affecting the outcome of conjugal bereavement. *British Journal of Psychiatry, 113,* 1057-67.

Maddison, D. C. and Viola, A. 1968. The health of widows in the year following bereavement. *Journal of Psychosomatic Research, 12,* 279-306.

Manaster, A. 1972. Therapy with the "senile" geriatric patient. *International Journal of Group Psychotherapy, 22,* 250-57.

Marlowe, L. 1971. *Social psychology.* Boston: Holbrook Press.

Martin, J. D. 1971. Power, dependence, and the complaints of the elderly: A social exchange perspective. *Aging and Human Development, 2,* 108-12.

McFall, R. M. and Twentyman, C. 1973. Four experiments on the relative contributions of rehearsal, modeling, and coaching to assertion training. *Journal of Abnormal Psychology, 81,* 199-218.

McTavish, D. G. 1971. Perceptions of old people: A review of research methodologies and findings. *Gerontologist, 11,* 90-101.

Miller, P. M., and Ingham, J. G. 1976. Friends, confidants and symptoms. *Social Psychiatry, 11,* 51-58.

Moriwaki, S. Y. 1973. Self-disclosure, significant others and psychological wellbeing in old-age. *Journal of Health and Social Behavior, 14,* 226-32.

Neugarten, B. L. and Datan, N. 1973. Sociological perspectives on the life cycle. In *Life-span developmental psychology,* ed. P. B. Baltes and K. W. Schaie. New York: Academic Press.

Pollock, D. D. and Liberman, R. P. 1974. Behavior therapy of incontinence in demented inpatients. *Gerontologist, 14,* 488-91.

Rechtschaffen, A. 1959. Psychotherapy with geriatric patients. *Journal of Gerontology, 14,* 73-83.

Rodin, J., and Langer, E. J. 1977. Long-term effects of a control-relevant intervention with the institutionalized aged. *Journal of Personality and Social Psychology, 35,* 897-902.

Rosencrantz, H. A., Pihlblad, C. T. and McNevin, R. E. 1971. Social participation of older people in the small town, cited in L. Marlowe, *Social psychology.* Boston: Holbrook Press.

Rosow, I. 1967. *Social integration of the aged.* 1968. New York: Free Press.

Rosow, I. Housing and local ties of the aged. In *Middle age & aging,* ed. B. L. Neugarten. Chicago: University of Chicago Press.

Rubin, K. H. and Brown, I. D. R. 1975. A life-span look at person perception and its relationship to communicative interaction. *Journal of Gerontology, 30,* 461-68.

Sachs, D. A. 1975. Behavioral techniques in a residential nursing home facility. *Journal of Behavior therapy and Experimental Psychiatry, 6,* 123-27.

Schaie, K. W. and Schaie, J. P. 1977. Clinical assessment and aging. In *Handbook of the psychology of aging,* ed. J. F. Birren and K. W. Schaie. New York: Van Nostrand Reinhold Co.

Schulz, R. 1976. Effects of control and predictability on the psychological well-being of the institutionalized aged. *Journal of Personality and Social Psychology 33,* 563-73.

Speck, R. and Attneave, C. 1972. Social Network Intervention. In *Progress in Group and Family Therapy,* ed. C. J. Sager and H. S. Kaplan. New York: Brunner Mazel.

Spivack, G., Platt, J., and Shure, M. 1976. *The problem solving approach to adjustment.* San Francisco: Jossey-Bass Publishers.

Stephens, J. 1974. Romance in the SRO. *Gerontologist, 14,* 279-82.

Turner, B. F., Tobin, S. S. and Lieberman, M. A. 1972. Personality traits as predictors of institutional adoption among the aged. *Journal of Gerontology, 27,* 61-68.

Weiss, R. S. 1969. The fund of sociability. *Trans-Action 6,* 36-43.

Weiss, R. S. 1974. The provisions of social relationships. In *Doing unto others,* ed. Z. Rubin. New York: Prentice Hall. 17-26.

Zarit, S. H., Corby, N., Rotheram, M. J., and Armstrong, M. 1976. *Assertion training with the elderly.* Symposium presented at the annual meeting of the Gerontology Society, New York, Oct. 1976.

Author Index

Subject Index

Test Index

About the Editors

Diana Pickett Rathjen (Ph.D., University of Texas; B.A., University of Chicago) is an assistant professor of psychology at Rice University. Her interest is the application of empirical findings in psychology to interpersonal and organizational problems.

Dr. Rathjen has consulted to organizations and schools and is currently serving as psychologist and Division Director of the Civil Service Department of the City of Houston where her responsibilities include testing, training and directing research. She has published in the area of assessment and development of social competence in personal and work settings and has developed social skills programs which incorporate behavioral and cognitive techniques.

Dr. Rathjen has served as guest editor for several psychological journals and is co-editor of *Cognitive Behavior Therapy: Research and Application* with John Foreyt.

John P. Foreyt (Ph.D., Florida State University) is an associate professor in the Departments of Medicine and Psychiatry at Baylor College of Medicine-The Methodist Hospital, Houston, Texas. In addition to teaching and consulting, Dr. Foreyt serves as principal investigator of the Baylor College of Medicine National Heart and Blood Vessel Research and Demonstration Center's Diet Modification Program.

Dr. Foreyt has published widely in the area of behavioral treatments of dietary disorders, behavioral techniques in institutions, and psychological assessment. Before coming to Baylor College of Medicine, Dr. Foreyt was Director of the Behavior Modification Token Economy Program at Florida State Hospital, Chattahoochee, and a faculty member in the Department of Psychology, Florida State University.

Dr. Foreyt is editor of *Behavioral Treatments of Obesity* and co-editor of *Obesity: Behavioral Approaches to Dietary Management,* and *Mental Examiner's Source Book.*

About the Contributors

Francisco X. Barrios, Ph. D.
Department of Psychiatry
Baylor College of Medicine
Houston, Texas

Mary Ann Bash, Ph. D.
University of Colorado
Medical Center
Denver, Colorado

Peter C. Bishop
Program in Behavioral Sciences
University of Houston
Clear Lake City, Texas

Bonnie Camp, M.D., Ph. D.
University of Colorado
Medical Center
Denver, Colorado

Nancy I. Cook
Department of Psychology
University of Houston
Houston, Texas

Nan Corby, Ph. D.
Department of Psychology
State University of New York
Stony Brook, New York

Roger D. Cox, Ph. D.
Department of Psychology
Indiana State University
Terre Haute, Indiana

Patrick H. Doyle, Ph. D.
Program in Behavioral Sciences
University of Houston
Clear Lake City, Texas

Gary Emery, Ph. D.
Department of Psychology
University of Southern California
Los Angeles, California

John P. Foreyt, Ph. D.
Departments of Medicine
and Psychiatry
Baylor College of Medicine

Arnold Goldstein, Ph. D.
Department of Psychology
Syracuse University
Syracuse, New York

William B. Gunn, Ph. D.
Chesterfield County Schools
Richmond, Virginia

Gerald E. Harris
Department of Psychology
University of Houston
Houston, Texas

Mary A. Miller
Program in Behavioral Sciences
University of Houston
Clear Lake City, Texas

Diana Pickett Rathjen, Ph. D.
Department of Psychology
Rice University
Houston, Texas

Arthur Robin, Ph. D.
Department of Psychology
University of Maryland
Baltimore City, Maryland

Mary Jane Rotheram, Ph. D.
Department of Psychology
Ohio State University
Columbus, Ohio

Myrna Shure, Ph. D.
Department of Mental Health Science
Hahnemann Medical College and Hospital
Philadelphia, Pennsylvania

W. Andrew Smith
Program in Behavioral Sciences
University of Houston
Clear Lake City, Texas

Robert Sprakfin, Ph. D.
V. A. Hospital
Syracuse, New York

John P. Vincent, Ph. D.
Department of Psychology
University of Houston
Houston, Texas

Pergamon General Psychology Series

Editors: Arnold P. Goldstein, Syracuse University
Leonard Krasner, SUNY, Stony Brook

Vol. 1. WOLPE—*The Practice of Behavior Therapy, Second Edition*
Vol. 2. MAGOON *et al*—*Mental Health Conselors at Work*
Vol. 3. McDANIEL—*Physical Disability and Human Behavior, Second Edition*
Vol. 4. KAPLAN *et al*—*The Structural Approach in Psychological Testing*
Vol. 5. LaFAUCI & RICHTER—*Team Teaching at the College Level*
Vol. 6. PEPINSKY *et al*—*People and Information*
Vol. 7. SIEGMAN & POPE—*Studies in Dyadic Communication*
Vol. 8. JOHNSON—*Existential Man: The Challenge of Psychotherapy*
Vol. 9. TAYLOR—*Climate for Creativity*
Vol. 10. RICKARD—*Behavioral Intervention in Human Problems*
Vol. 14. GOLDSTEIN—*Psychotherapeutic Attraction*
Vol. 15. HALPERN—*Survival: Black/White*
Vol. 16. SALZINGER & FELDMAN—*Studies in Verbal Behavior: An Empirical Approach*
Vol. 17. ADAMS & BOARDMAN—*Advances in Experimental Clinical Psychology*
Vol. 18. ZILLER—*The Social Self*
Vol. 19. LIBERMAN—*A Guide to Behavioral Analysis & Therapy*
Vol. 22. PEPINSKY & PATTON—*The Psychological Experiment: A Practical Accomplishment.*
Vol. 23. YOUNG—*New Sources of Self*
Vol. 24. WATSON—*Child Behavior Modification: A Manual for Teachers, Nurses, and Parents*
Vol. 25. NEWBOLD—*The Psychiatric Programming of People: Neo-Behavioral Orthomolecular Psychiatry*
Vol. 26. ROSSI—*Dreams and the Growth of Personality: Expanding Awareness in Psychotherapy*
Vol. 27. O'LEARY & O'LEARY—*Classroom Management: The Successful Use of Behavior Modification, Second Edition*
Vol. 28. FELDMAN—*College and Student: Selected Readings in the Social Psychology of Higher Education*
Vol. 29. ASHEM & POSER—*Adaptive Learning: Behavior Modification with Children*
Vol. 30. BURCK *et al*—*Counseling and Accountability: Methods and Critique*
Vol. 31. FREDERIKSEN *et al*—*Prediction of Organizational Behavior*
Vol. 32. CATTELL—*A New Morality from Science: Beyondism*
Vol. 33. WEINER—*Personality: The Human Potential*
Vol. 34. LIEBERT, NEALE & DAVIDSON—*The Early Window: Effects of Television on Children and Youth*
Vol. 35. COHEN *et al*—*Psych City: A Simulated Community*
Vol. 36. GRAZIANO—*Child Without Tomorrow*
Vol. 37. MORRIS—*Perspectives in Abnormal Behavior*

Vol. 38. BALLER—*Bed Wetting: Origins and Treatment*
Vol. 40. KAHN, CAMERON, & GIFFEN—*Psychological Methods in Evaluation and Counseling*
Vol. 41. SEGALL—*Human Behavior and Public Policy: A Political Psychology*
Vol. 42. FAIRWEATHER *et al*—*Creating Change in Mental Health Organizations*
Vol. 43. KATZ & ZLUTNICK—*Behavior Therapy and Health Care: Principles and Applications*
Vol. 44. EVANS & CLAIBORN—*Mental Health Issues and the Urban Poor*
Vol. 45. HILLNER—*Psychology of Learning: A Conceptual Approach*
Vol. 46. BARBER, SPANOS & CHAVES—*Hypnosis, Imagination and Human Potentialities*
Vol. 47. POPE—*The Mental Health Interview*
Vol. 48. PELTON—*The Psychology of Nonviolence*
Vol. 49. COLBY—*Artificial Paranoia—A Computer Simulation of Paranoid Processes*
Vol. 50. GELFAND & HARTMANN—*Child Behavior Analysis and Therapy*
Vol. 51. WOLPE—*Theme and Variations: A Behavior Therapy Casebook*
Vol. 52. KANFER & GOLDSTEIN—*Helping People Change: A Textbook of Methods, Second Edition*
Vol. 53. DANZIGER—*Interpersonal Communication*
Vol. 54. KATZ—*Towards the Elimination of Racism*
Vol. 55. GOLDSTEIN & STEIN—*Prescriptive Psychotherapies*
Vol. 56. HERSEN & BARLOW—*Single-Case Experimental Designs: Strategies for Studying Behavior Changes*
Vol. 57. MONAHAN—*Community Mental Health and the Criminal Justice System*
Vol. 58. WAHLER, HOUSE & STAMBAUGH—*Ecological Assessment of Child Behavior: A Clinical Package for Home, School, and Institutional Settings*
Vol. 59. MAGARO—*The Construction of Madness—Emerging Conceptions and Interventions into the Psychotic Process*
Vol. 60. MILLER—*Behavioral Treatments of Alcoholism*
Vol. 61. FOREYT—*Behavioral Treatments of Obesity*
Vol. 62. WANDERSMAN, POPPEN & RICKS—*Humanism and Behaviorism: Dialogue and Growth*
Vol. 63. NIETZEL, WINETT, MACDONALD & DAVIDSON—*Behavioral Approaches to Community Psychology*
Vol. 64. FISHER & GOCHROS—*Handbook of Behavior Therapy with Sexual Problems. Vol. I: General Procedures. Vol. II: Approaches to Specific Problems*
Vol. 65. HERSEN & BELLACK—*Behavioral Assessment: A Practical Handbook*
Vol. 66. LEFKOWITZ, ERON, WALDER & HUESMANN—*Growing Up To Be Violent: A Longitudinal Study of the Development of Aggression*
Vol. 67. BARBER—*Pitfalls in Human Research: Ten Pivotal Points*
Vol. 68. SILVERMAN—*The Human Subject in the Psychological Laboratory*

Vol. 69. FAIRWEATHER & TORNATZKY—*Experimental Methods for Social Policy Research*
Vol. 70. GURMAN & RAZIN—*Effective Psychotherapy: A Handbook of Research*
Vol. 71. MOSES & BYHAM—*Applying the Assessment Center Method*
Vol. 72. GOLDSTEIN—*Prescriptions for Child Mental Health and Education*
Vol. 73. KEAT—*Multimodal Therapy with Children*
Vol. 74. SHERMAN—*Personality: Inquiry & Application*
Vol. 75. GATCHEL & PRICE—*Clinical Applications of Biofeedback: Appraisal and Status*
Vol. 76. CATALANO—*Health, Behavior and the Community: An Ecological Perspective*
Vol. 77. NIETZEL—*Crime and Its Modification: A Social Learning Perspective*
Vol. 78. GOLDSTEIN, HOYER & MONTI—*Police and the Elderly*
Vol. 79. MIRON & GOLDSTEIN—*Hostage*
Vol. 80. GOLDSTEIN *et al*—Police Crisis Intervention
Vol. 81. UPPER & CAUTELA—*Covert Conditioning*
Vol. 82. MORELL—*Program Evaluation in Social Research*
Vol. 83. TEGER—*Too Much Invested to Quit*
Vol. 84. MONJAN & GASSNER—*Critical Issues in Competency-Based Education*
Vol. 85. KRASNER—*Environmental Design and Human Behavior: A Psychology of the Individual in Society*
Vol. 86. TAMIR—*Communication and the Aging Process: Interaction Throughout the Life Cycle*
Vol. 87. WEBSTER, KONSTANTAREAS, OXMAN & MACK—*Autism: New Directions in Research and Education*
Vol. 88. TRIESCHMANN—*Spinal Cord Injuries: Psychological, Social and Vocational Adjustment*
Vol. 89. CARTLEDGE & MILBURN—*Teaching Social Skills to Children: Innovative Approaches*
Vol. 90. SARBIN & MANCUSO—*Schizophrenia — Medical Diagnosis or Moral Verdict?*
Vol. 91. RATHJEN & FOREYT—*Social Competence: Interventions for Children and Adults*
Vol. 92. VAN DE RIET, KORB & GORRELL—*Gestalt Therapy: An Introduction*
Vol. 93. MARSELLA & PEDERSEN—*Cross-Cultural Counseling and Psychotherapy*
Vol. 94. BRISLIN—*Cross-Cultural Encounters: Face-to-Face Interaction*
Vol. 95. SCHWARTZ & JOHNSON—*Psychopathology of Childhood: A Clinical-Experimental Approach*